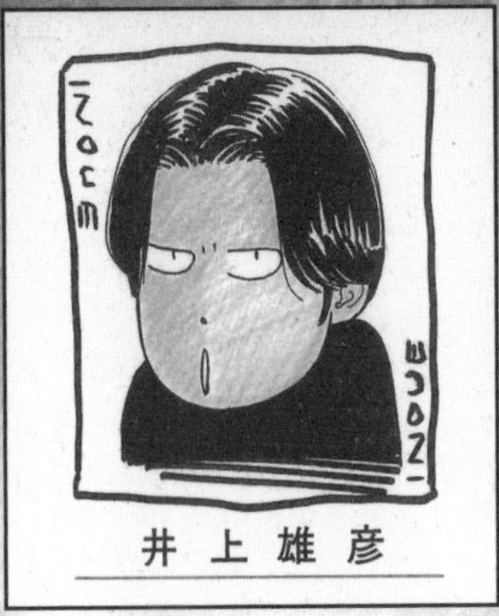
井上雄彦

Takehiko Inoue

OLD CUSTOMS ARE HARD TO BREAK, AND PEOPLE RESIST CHANGE. ARE THESE BEHAVIORS UNIQUE TO JAPAN? I SEE THEM EVERYWHERE I GO.

THE RECENT FUKUOKA UNIVERSIADE TURNED OUT TO BE A HISTORIC TOURNAMENT FOR THE JAPANESE BASKETBALL COMMUNITY. KEEP YOUR EYES ON THE DOMESTIC LEAGUE AND THE NATIONAL TEAM. IF YOU GO TO A GAME, YOU'LL FIND A PLAYER THAT YOU WANT TO ROOT FOR.

Takehiko Inoue's *Slam Dunk* is one of the most popular manga of all time, having sold over 100 million copies worldwide. He followed that series up with two titles lauded by critics and fans alike—*Vagabond*, a fictional account of the life of Miyamoto Musashi, and *Real*, a manga about wheelchair basketball.

SLAM DUNK
Vol. 26: Power Match

SHONEN JUMP Manga Edition

STORY AND ART BY TAKEHIKO INOUE

English Adaptation/Stan!
Translation/Joe Yamazaki
Touch-up Art & Lettering/James Gaubatz
Cover & Graphic Design/Matt Hinrichs
Editor/Mike Montesa

© 1990 - 2013 Takehiko Inoue and I.T. Planning, Inc.
Originally published in Japan in 1995 by Shueisha
Inc., Tokyo. English translation rights arranged with
I.T. Planning, Inc. All rights reserved.

The SLAM DUNK U.S. trademark is used with
permission from NBA Properties, Inc.

Some scenes have been modified from the original
Japanese edition.

The stories, characters and incidents mentioned in this
publication are entirely fictional.

Printed in Canada

Published by VIZ Media, LLC
P.O. Box 77010
San Francisco, CA 94107

10 9 8 7 6 5 4 3 2 1
First printing, February 2013

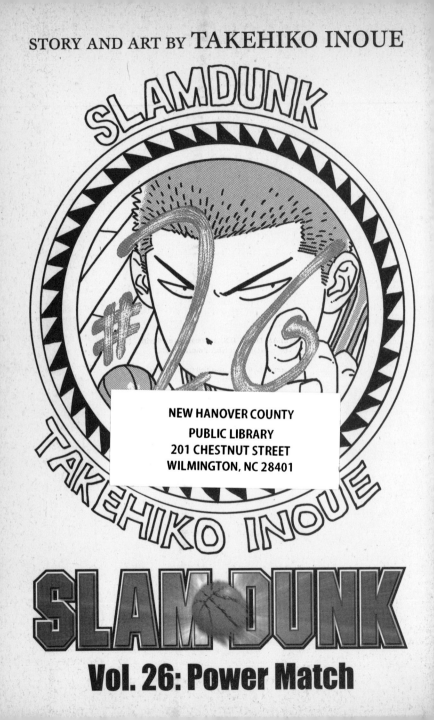

STORY AND ART BY TAKEHIKO INOUE

SLAMDUNK

TAKEHIKO INOUE

SLAM DUNK

Vol. 26: Power Match

Character Introduction

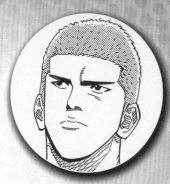

Hanamichi Sakuragi
A first-year at Shohoku High School, Sakuragi is in love with Haruko Akagi.

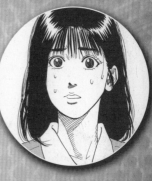

Haruko Akagi
Also a first-year at Shohoku, Takenori Akagi's little sister has a crush on Kaede Rukawa.

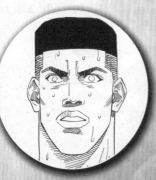

Takenori Akagi
A third-year and the basketball team's captain, Akagi has an intense passion for his sport.

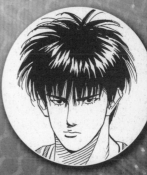

Kaede Rukawa
The object of Haruko's affection (and that of many of Shohoku's female students!), this first-year has been a star player since junior high.

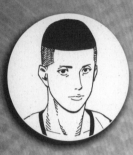

Sawakita

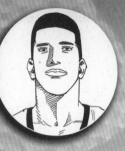

Fukatsu

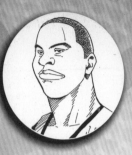

Kawata

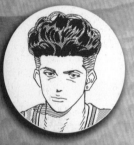

Ryota Miyagi
A problem child with
a thing for Ayako.

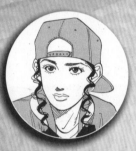

Ayako
Basketball Team
Manager

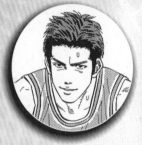

Hisashi Mitsui
An MVP during
junior high.

Our Story Thus Far

Hanamichi Sakuragi is rejected by close to 50 girls during his three years in junior high. He joins the basketball team to be closer to Haruko Akagi, but his frustration mounts when all he does is practice day after day.

Shohoku advances through the Prefectural Tournament and earns a spot in the Nationals.

Shohoku defeats Osaka's Toyotama High in the first round, and now must face Akita's Sannoh Kogyo, last year's national champions and considered by most to be the best team in the country. Shohoku starts the game with Miyagi setting Sakuragi up for an alley-oop, stunning the crowd. Their surprise attack is a success! But Sannoh's going to show everyone why they're Number 1!

Vol. 26:
Power Match

Table of Contents

READ THIS WAY

SHOOTER

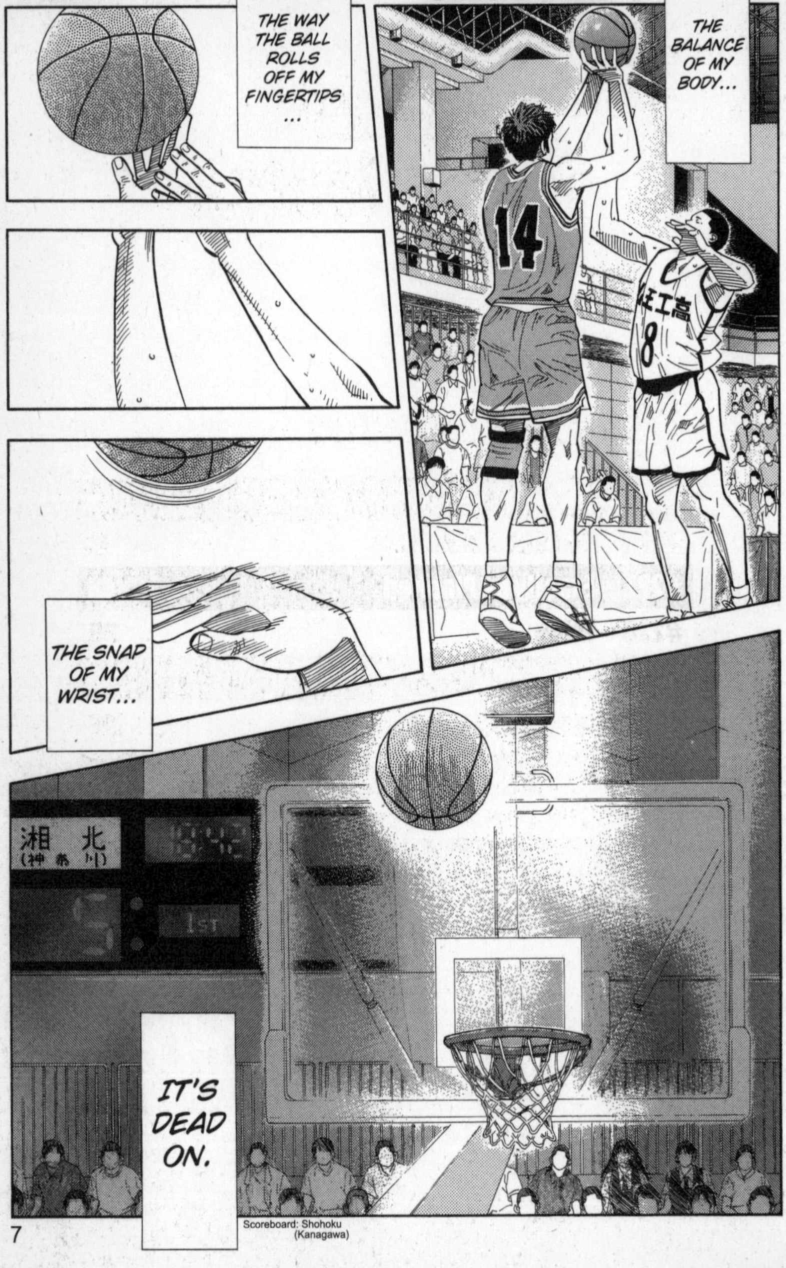
THE BALANCE OF MY BODY...
THE WAY THE BALL ROLLS OFF MY FINGERTIPS ...
THE SNAP OF MY WRIST...
湘北
(神奈川)
1ST
IT'S DEAD ON.

Scoreboard: Shohoku (Kanagawa)

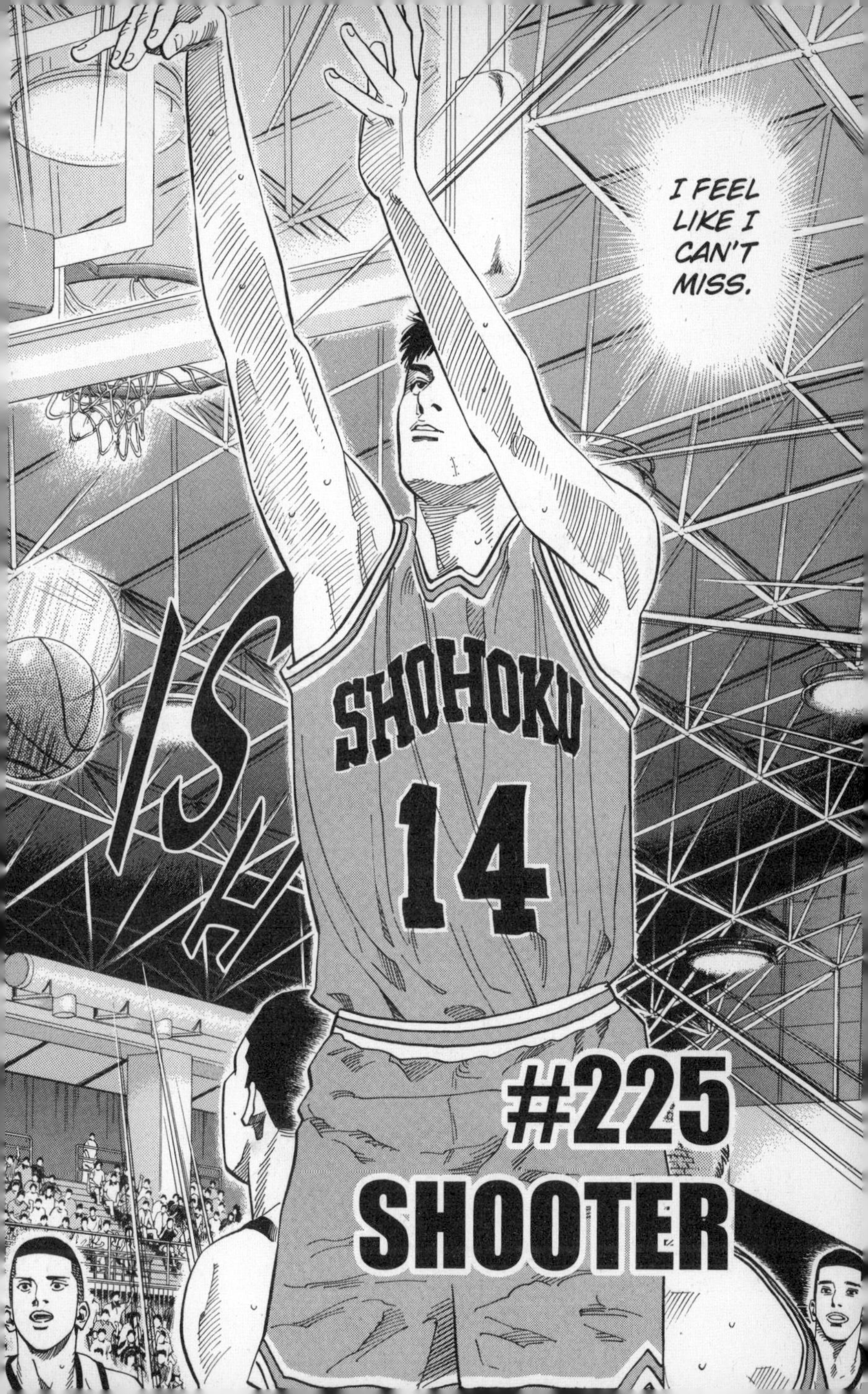
I FEEL LIKE I CAN'T MISS.
SHHH
SHOHOKU
14
#225
SHOOTER

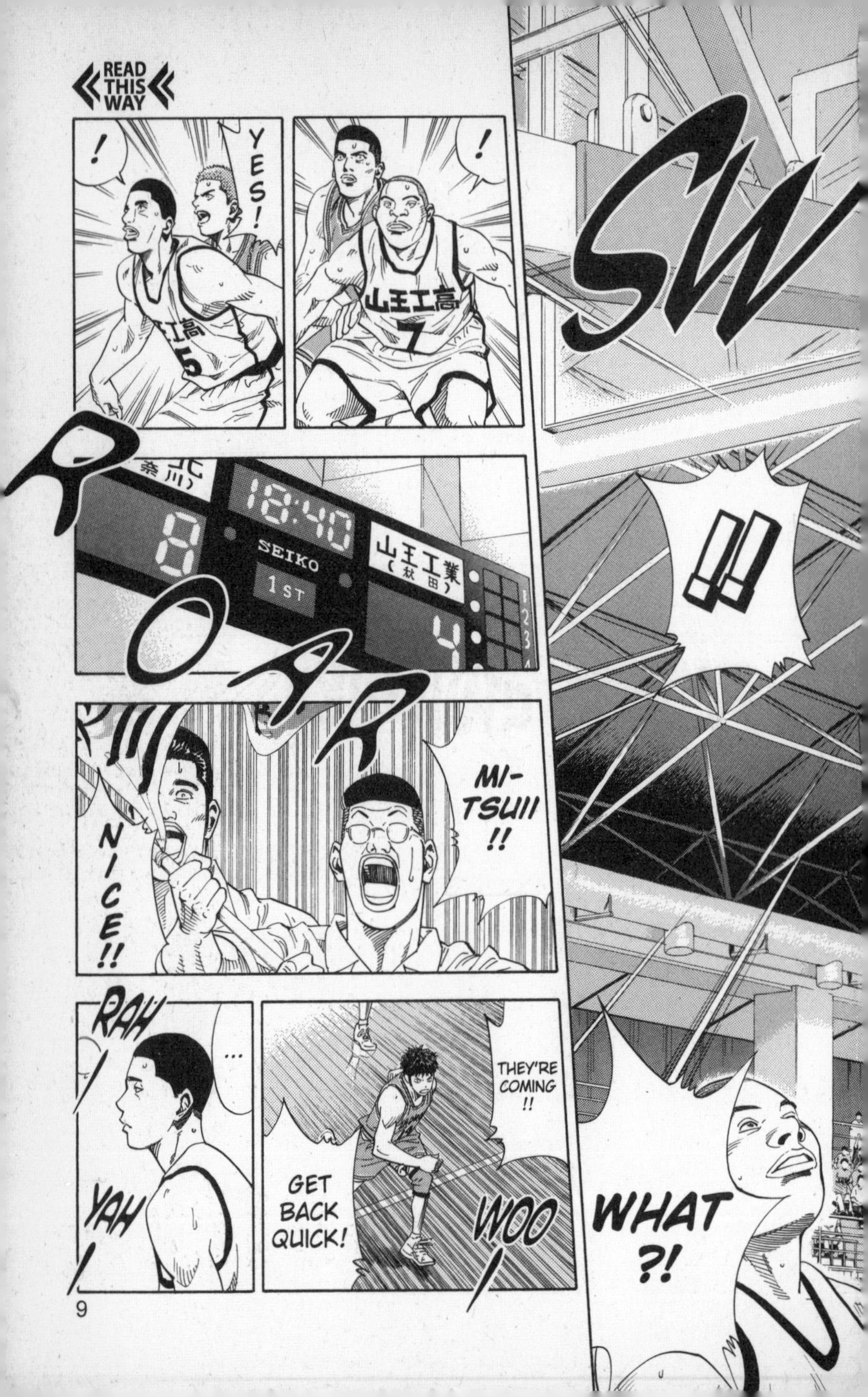
SWI
!!
WHAT ?!
READ THIS WAY
!
山王工高
7
!
YES!
5
ROAR
18:40
SEIKO
1ST
8
山王工業
(秋田)
4
MI-TSUII !!
NICE!!
THEY'RE COMING !!
WOO!
GET BACK QUICK!
...
RAH!
YAH!

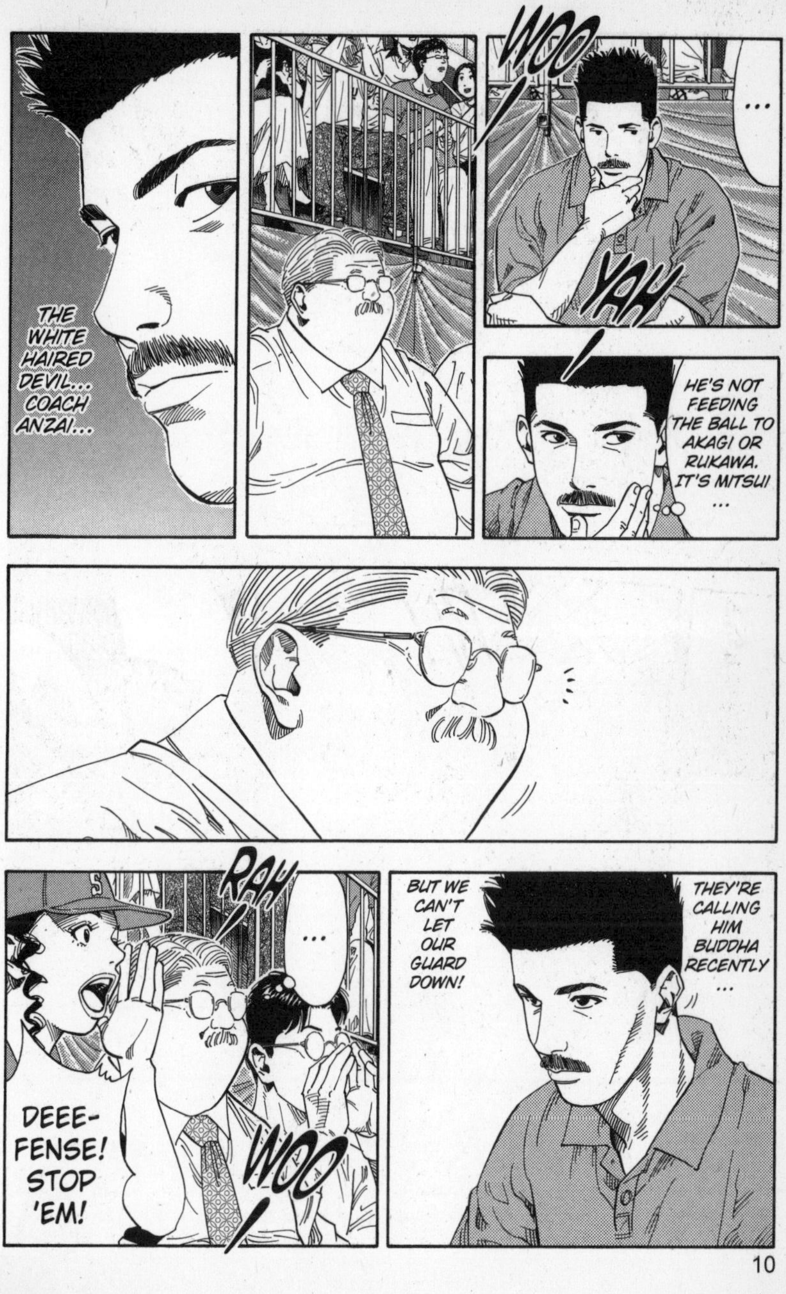
WOO
...
YAH
HE'S NOT FEEDING THE BALL TO AKAGI OR RUKAWA. IT'S MITSUI ...
THE WHITE HAIRED DEVIL... COACH ANZAI...
THEY'RE CALLING HIM BUDDHA RECENTLY ...
BUT WE CAN'T LET OUR GUARD DOWN!
RAH
...
DEEE-FENSE! STOP 'EM!
WOO

READ THIS WAY

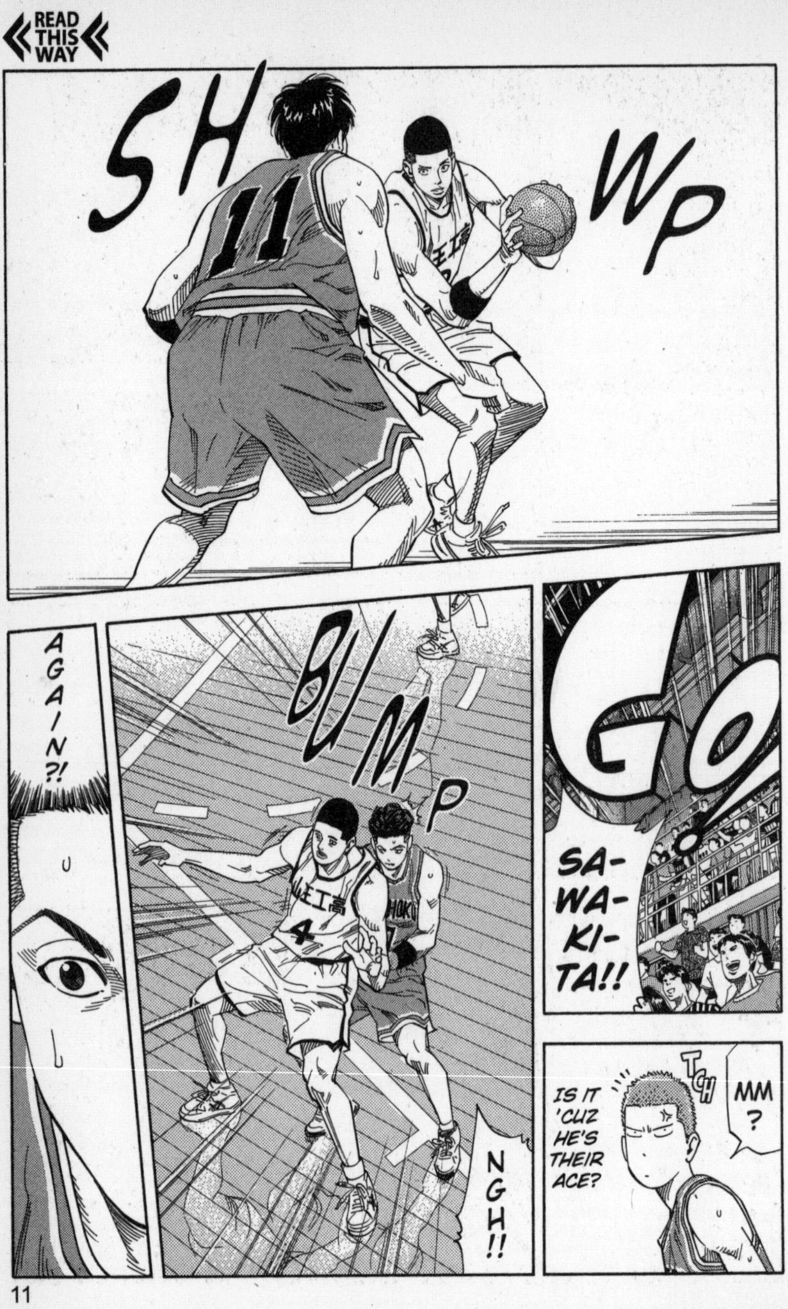
SH
WP
GO!
SA-WA-KI-TA!!
MM?
TCH
IS IT 'CUZ HE'S THEIR ACE?
BUMP
NGH!!
AGAIN?!

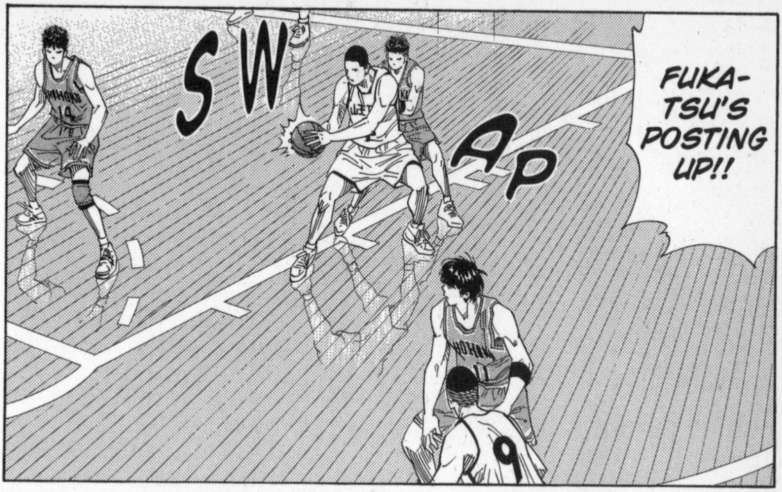
FUKA-TSU'S POSTING UP!!
SWAP
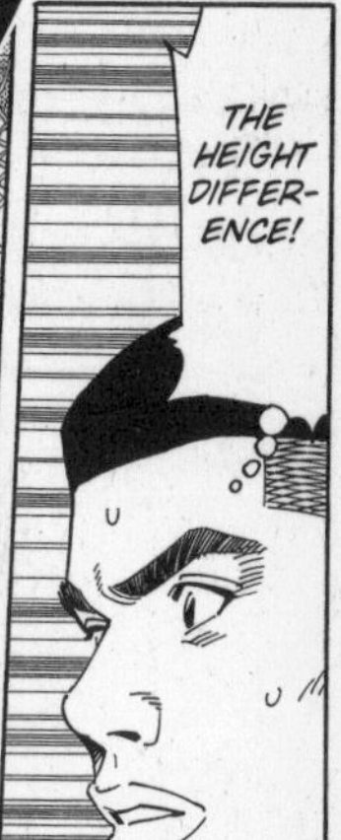
THE HEIGHT DIFFER-ENCE!
I WON'T LET THEM ...!
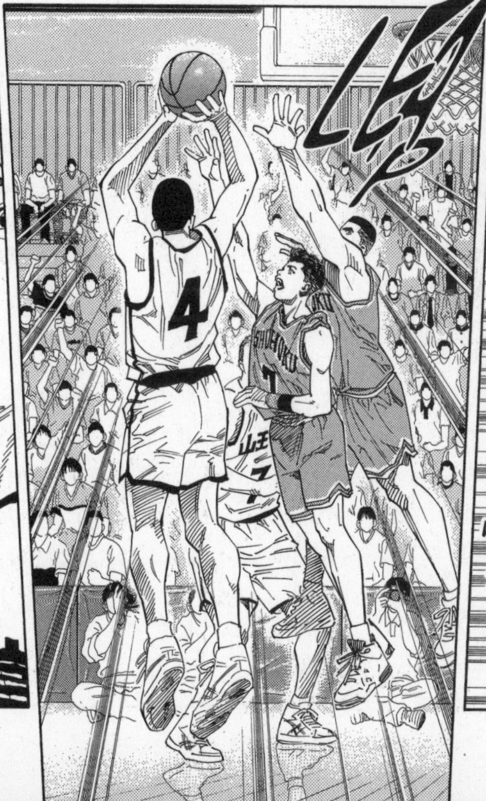
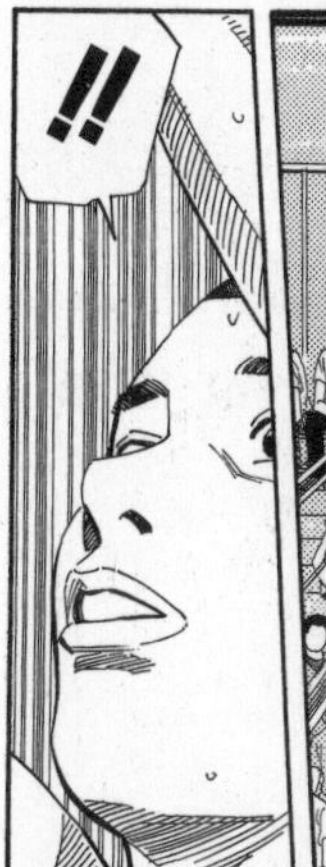
!!

READ THIS WAY

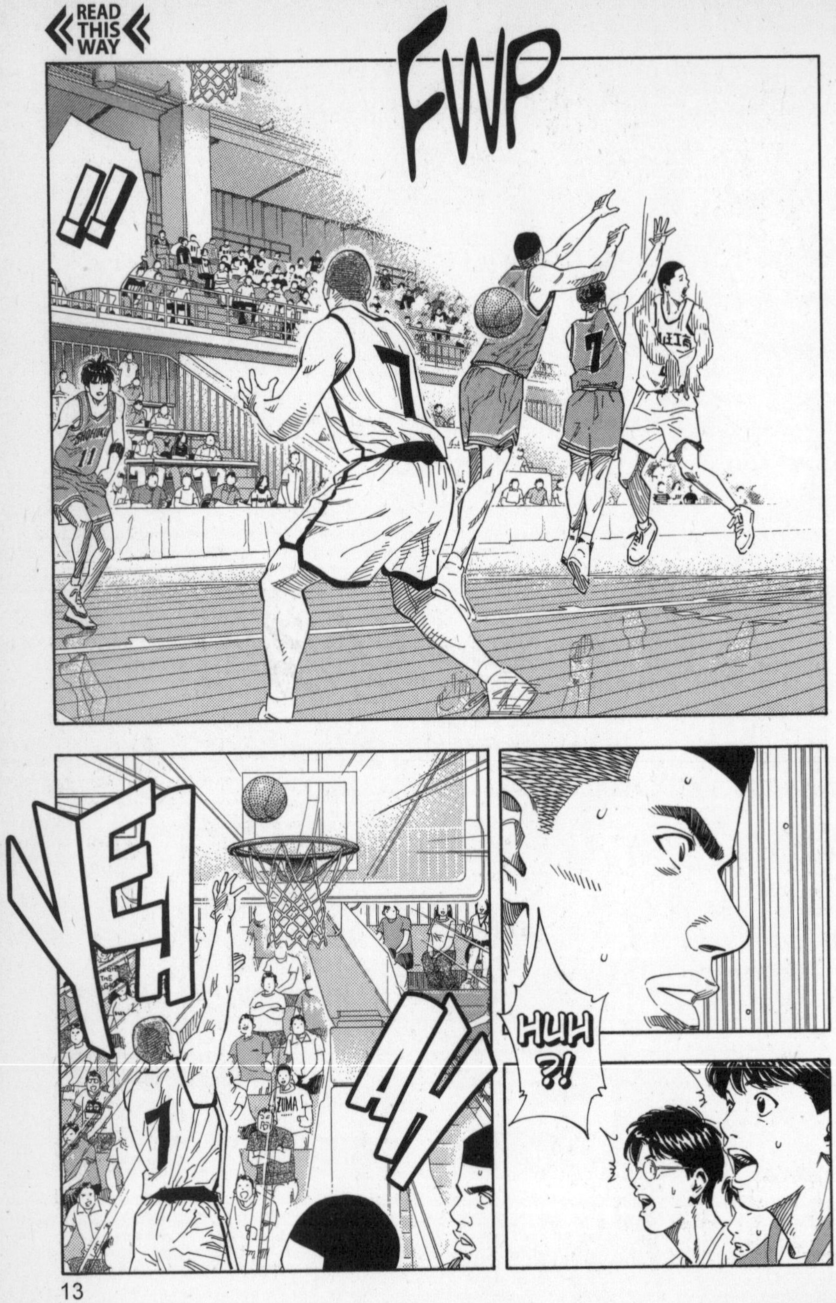
FWP
!!
HUH ?!
YEAH
AH

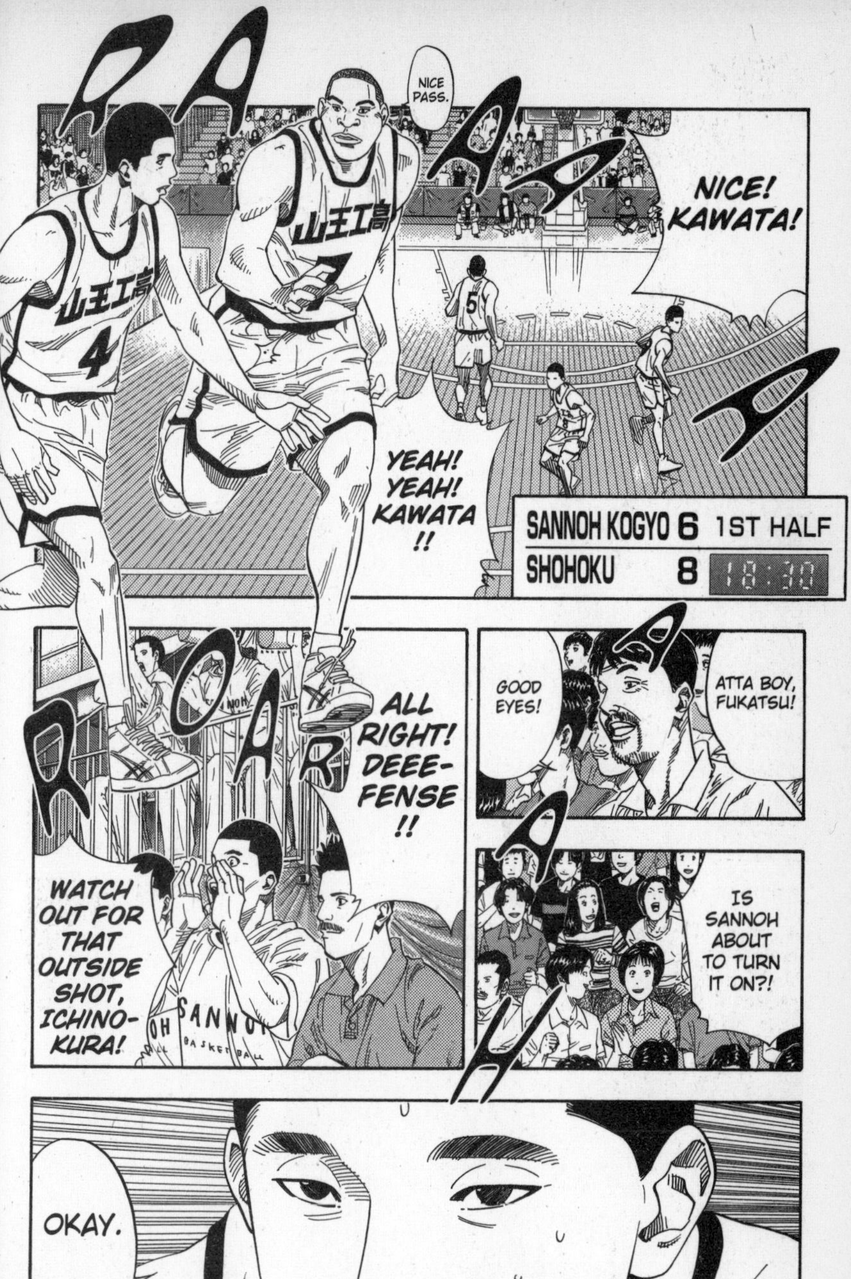
RAAAAAA
NICE! KAWATA!
NICE PASS.
YEAH! YEAH! KAWATA !!
SANNOH KOGYO 6 1ST HALF
SHOHOKU 8 18:30
ATTA BOY, FUKATSU!
GOOD EYES!
IS SANNOH ABOUT TO TURN IT ON?!
AAH
ROAR
ALL RIGHT! DEEEE-FENSE !!
WATCH OUT FOR THAT OUTSIDE SHOT, ICHINO-KURA!
OKAY.

READ THIS WAY

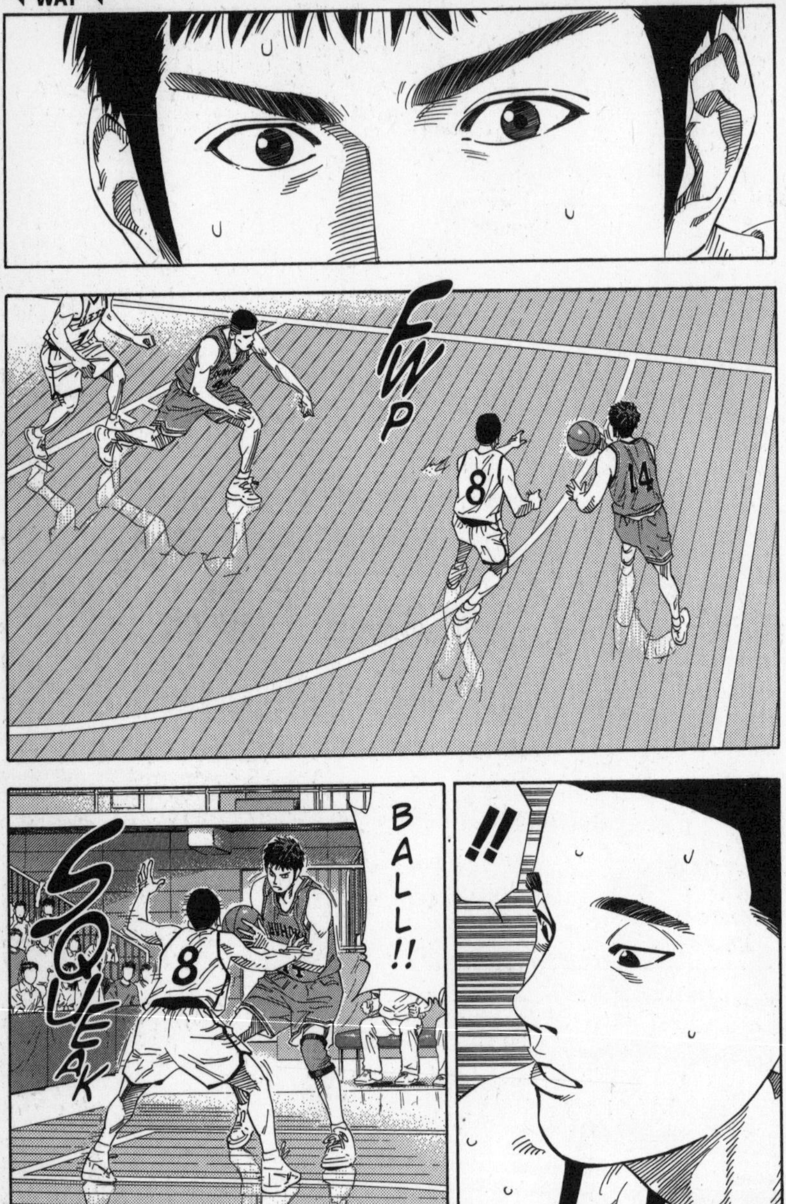
FWP
!!
BALL!!
SQUEAK

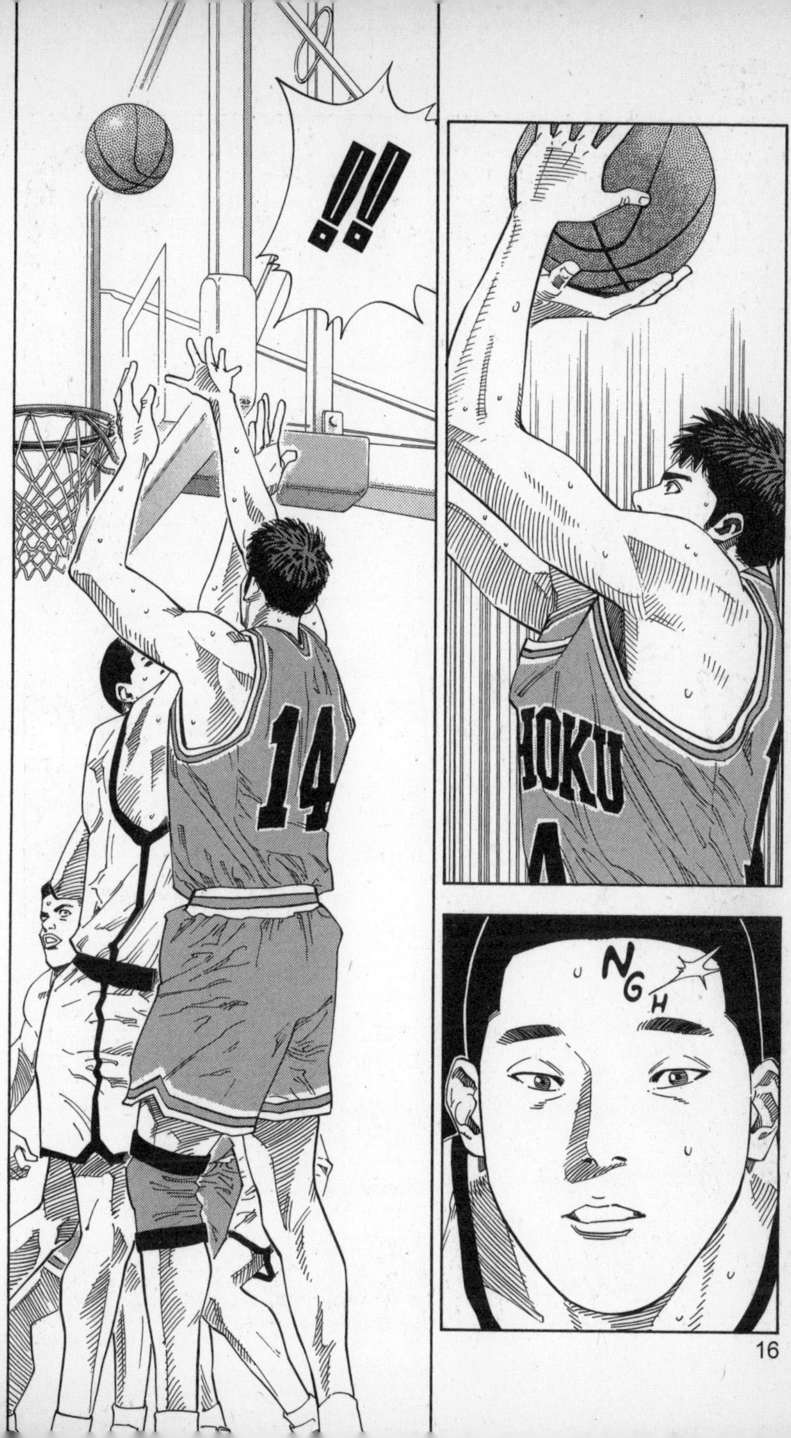
NGH
!!

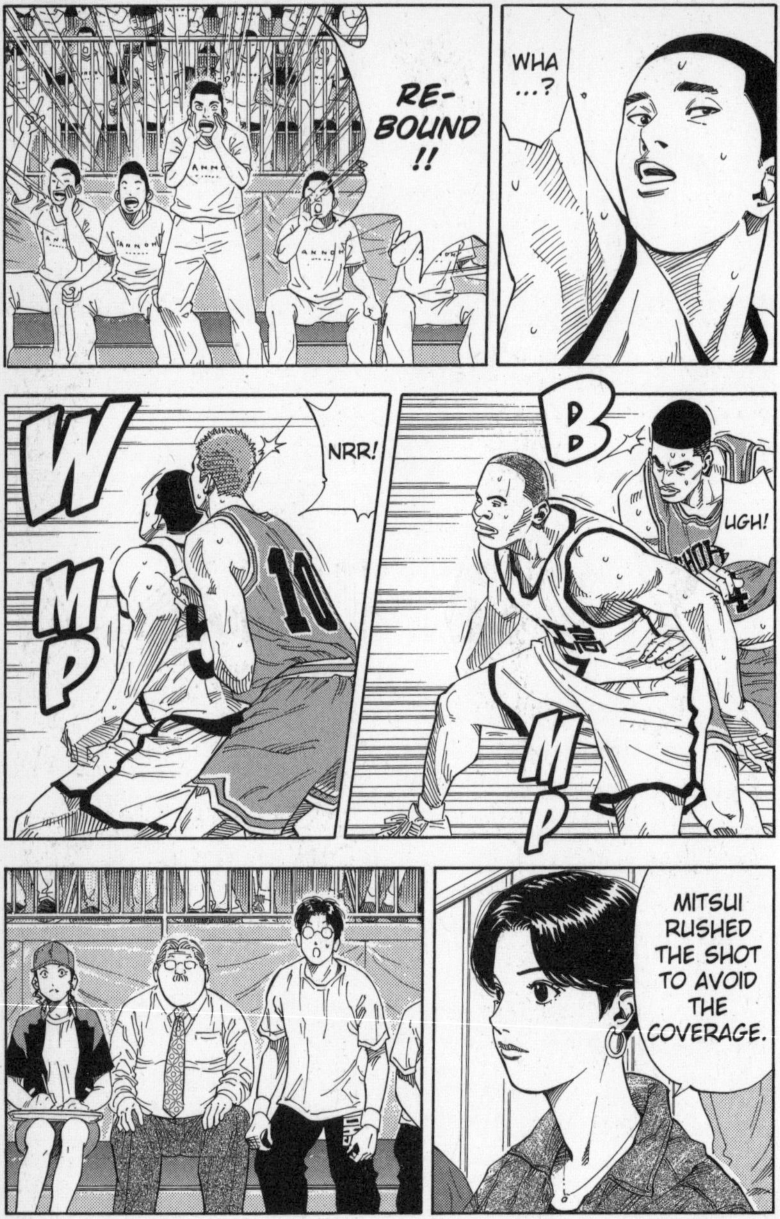
WHA ...?
RE-BOUND !!
B
UGH!
MMP
NRR!
WMMP
MITSUI RUSHED THE SHOT TO AVOID THE COVERAGE.

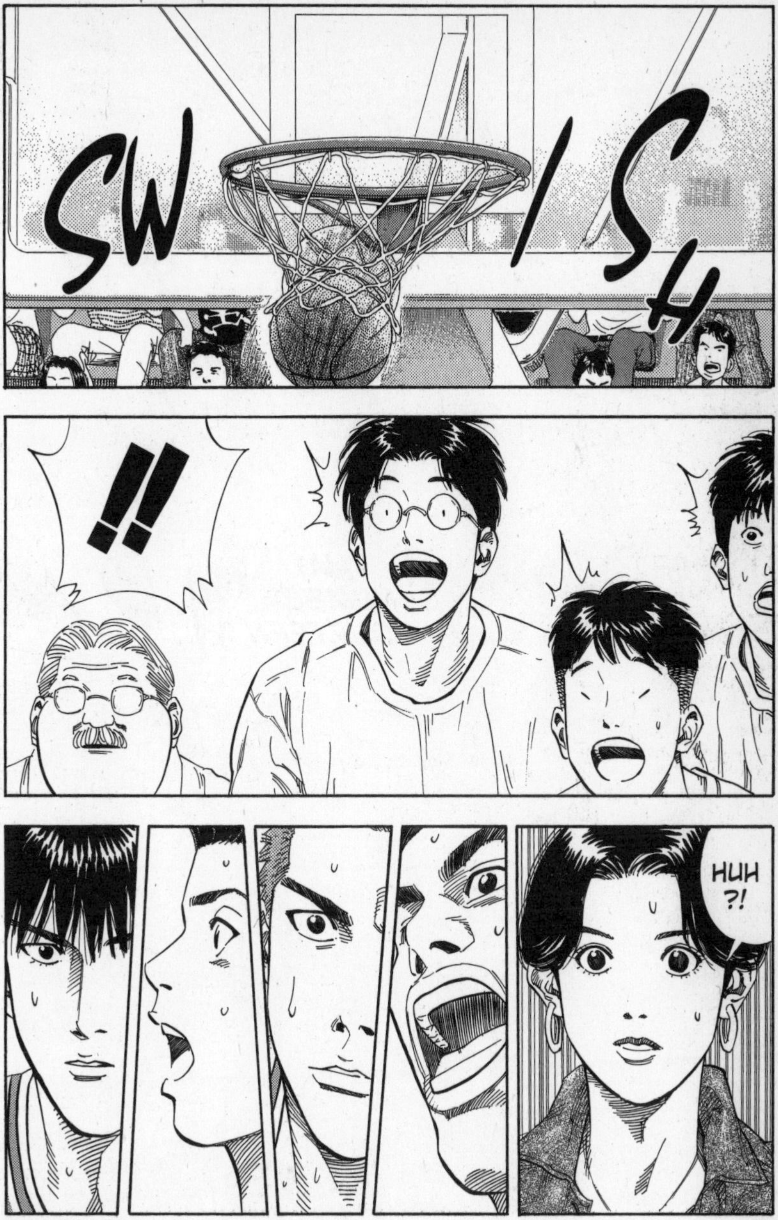
SWISH
!!
HUH ?!

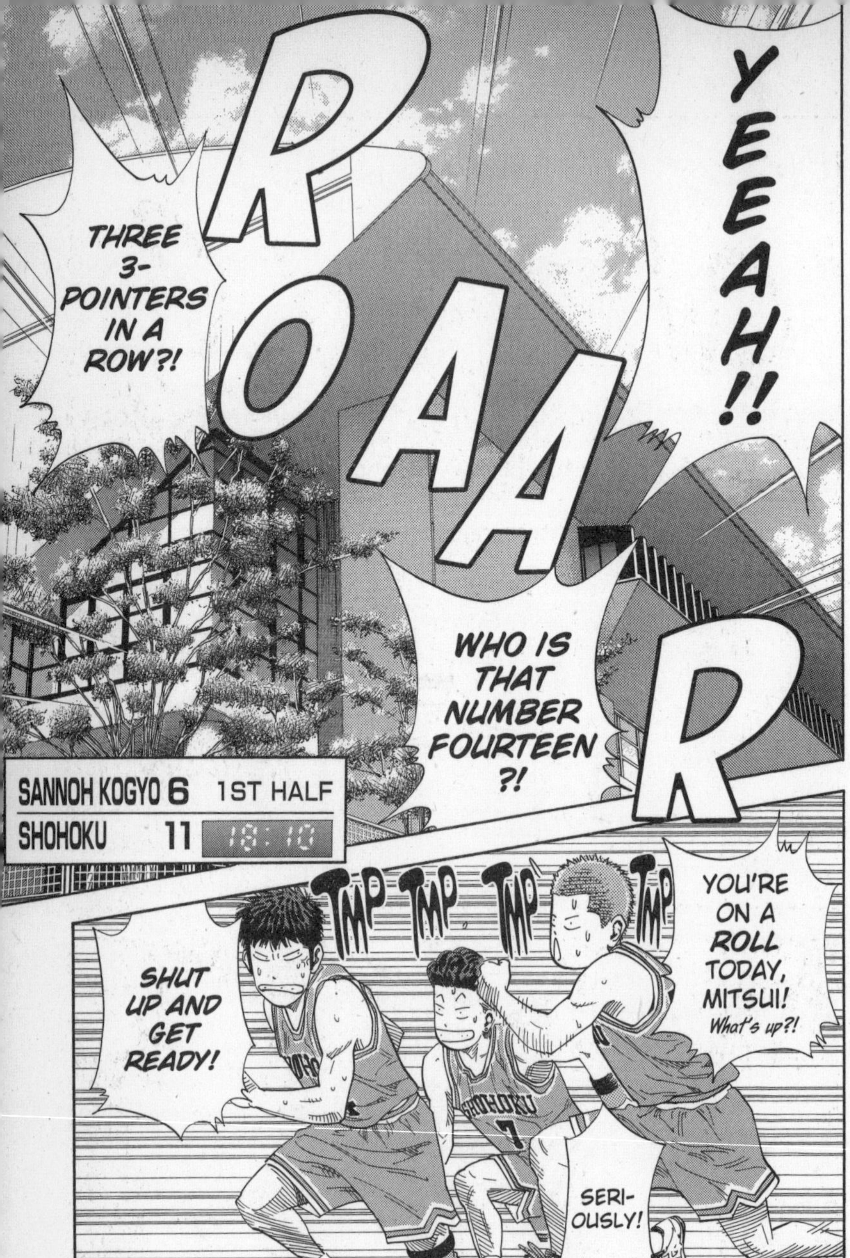
YEEAAH!!
ROAAAR
THREE 3-POINTERS IN A ROW?!
WHO IS THAT NUMBER FOURTEEN?!
SANNOH KOGYO 6
SHOHOKU 11
1ST HALF
18:10
YOU'RE ON A ROLL TODAY, MITSUI!
What's up?!
TMP TMP TMP TMP
SERI-OUSLY!
SHUT UP AND GET READY!

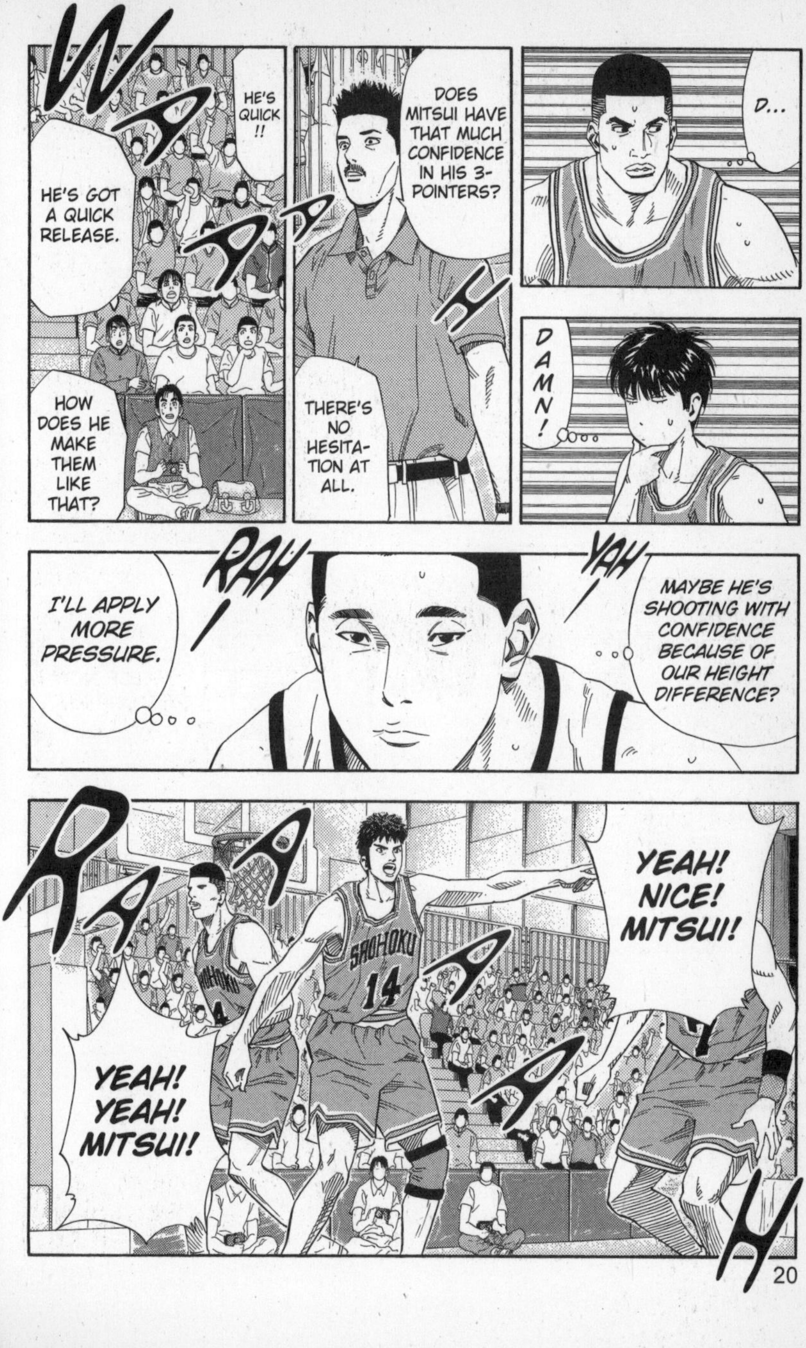
D...
DAMN!
DOES MITSUI HAVE THAT MUCH CONFIDENCE IN HIS 3-POINTERS?
THERE'S NO HESITATION AT ALL.
WAAAAH
HE'S QUICK!!
HE'S GOT A QUICK RELEASE.
HOW DOES HE MAKE THEM LIKE THAT?
MAYBE HE'S SHOOTING WITH CONFIDENCE BECAUSE OF OUR HEIGHT DIFFERENCE?
YAH
RAH
I'LL APPLY MORE PRESSURE.
YEAH! NICE! MITSUI!
RAAAAAH
YEAH! YEAH! MITSUI!

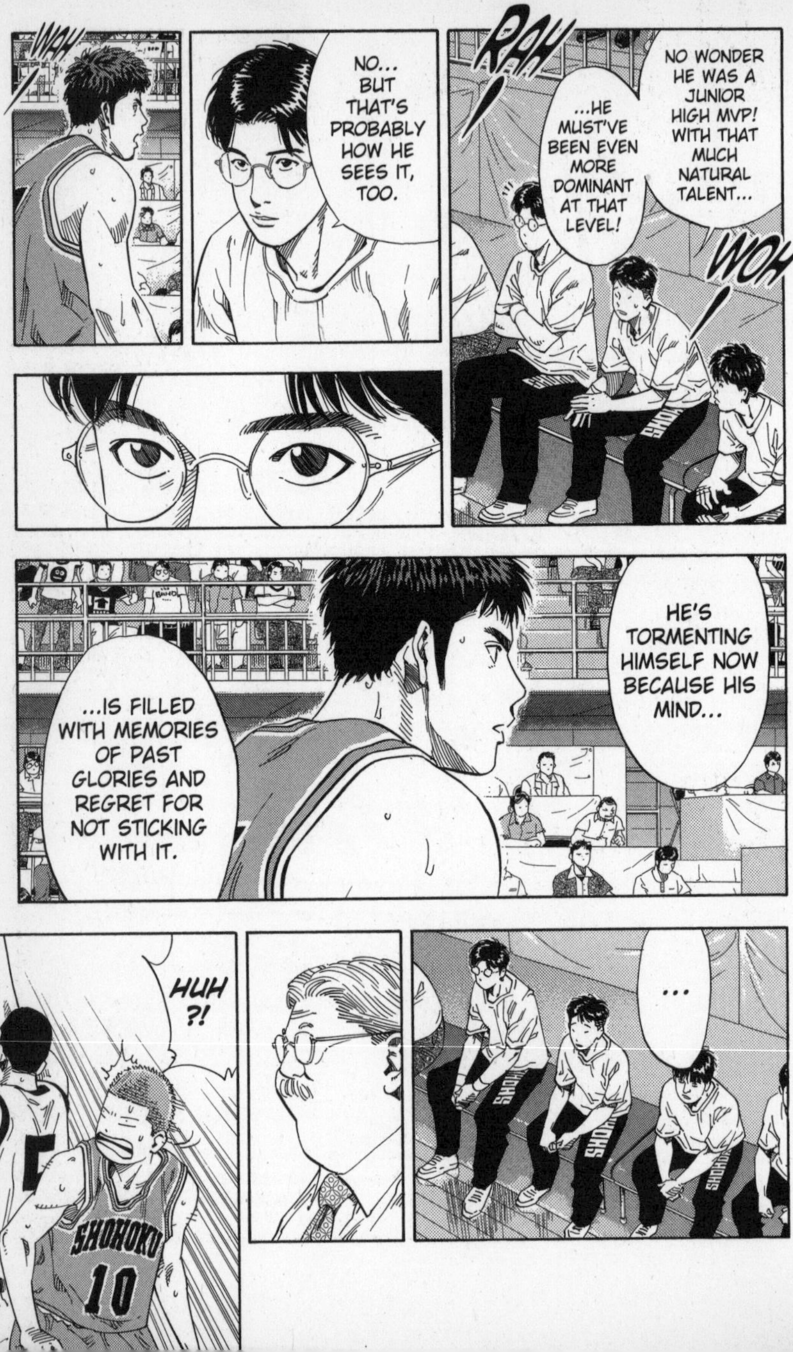
RAH
NO WONDER HE WAS A JUNIOR HIGH MVP! WITH THAT MUCH NATURAL TALENT...
...HE MUST'VE BEEN EVEN MORE DOMINANT AT THAT LEVEL!
WOH
NO... BUT THAT'S PROBABLY HOW HE SEES IT, TOO.
WAH
HE'S TORMENTING HIMSELF NOW BECAUSE HIS MIND...
...IS FILLED WITH MEMORIES OF PAST GLORIES AND REGRET FOR NOT STICKING WITH IT.
...
HUH ?!

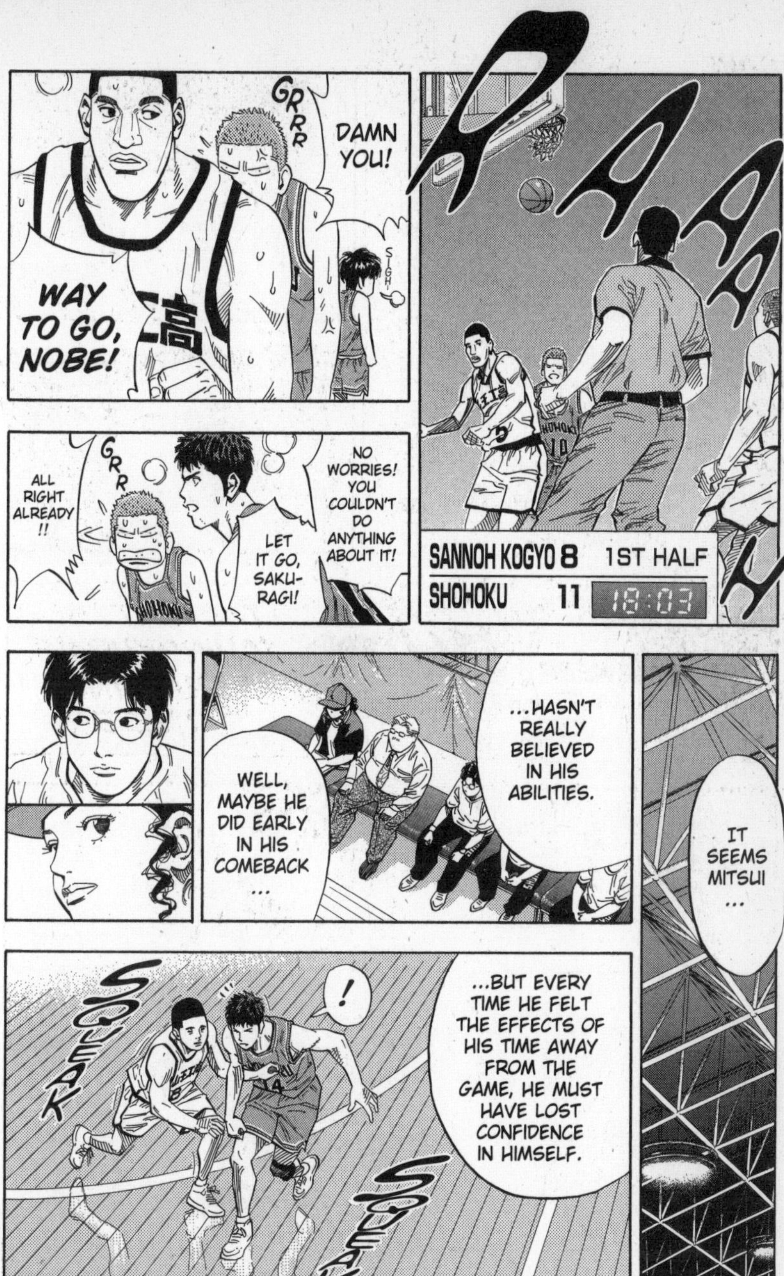
AAAAH
SANNOH KOGYO 8 1ST HALF
SHOHOKU 11 18:03
GRRR
DAMN YOU!
SIGH
WAY TO GO, NOBE!
NO WORRIES! YOU COULDN'T DO ANYTHING ABOUT IT!
LET IT GO, SAKURAGI!
GRR
ALL RIGHT ALREADY!!
IT SEEMS MITSUI...
...HASN'T REALLY BELIEVED IN HIS ABILITIES.
WELL, MAYBE HE DID EARLY IN HIS COMEBACK...
...BUT EVERY TIME HE FELT THE EFFECTS OF HIS TIME AWAY FROM THE GAME, HE MUST HAVE LOST CONFIDENCE IN HIMSELF.
!
SQUEAK
SQUEAK

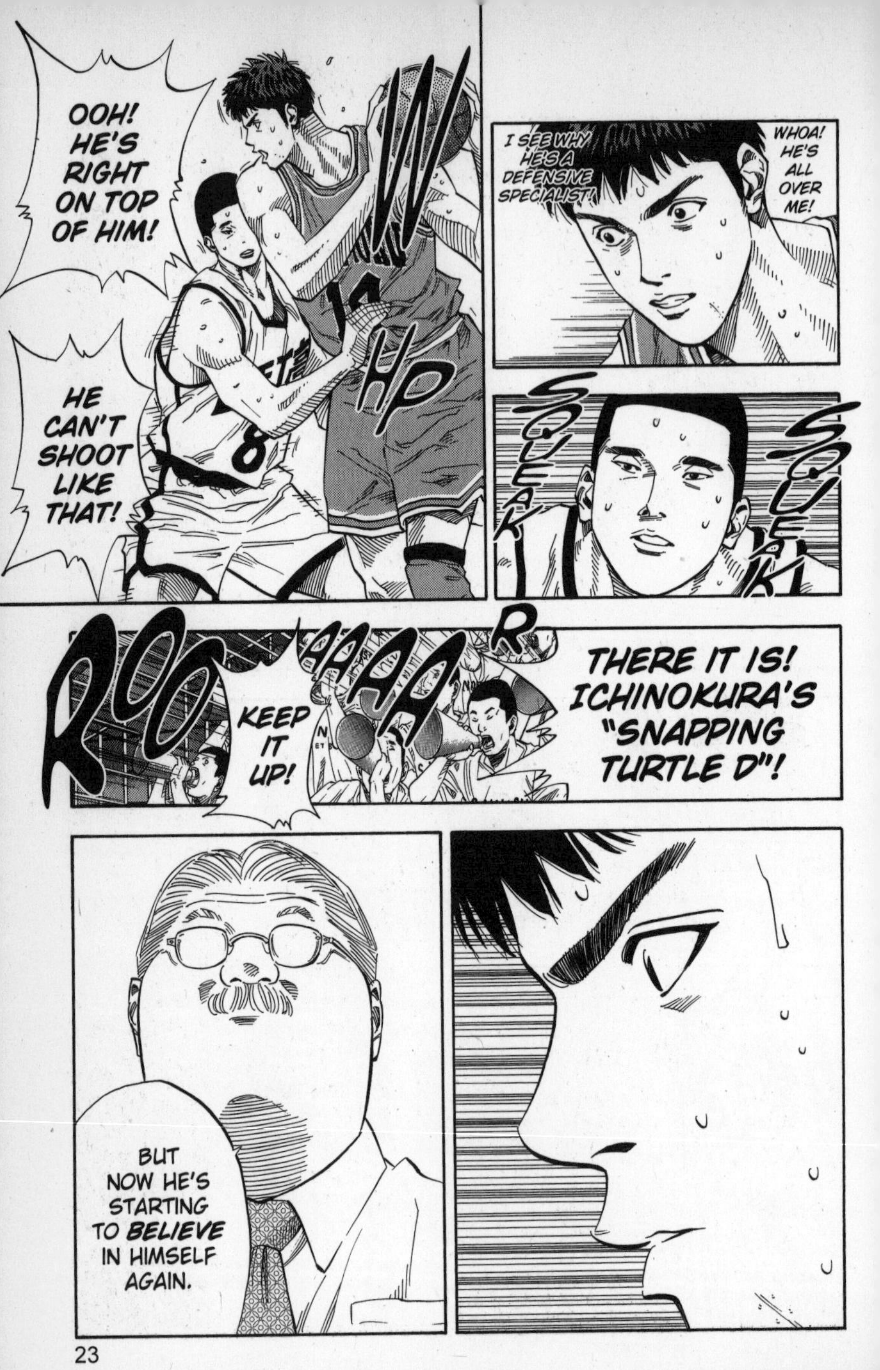
WHOA! HE'S ALL OVER ME!
I SEE WHY HE'S A DEFENSIVE SPECIALIST!
SQUEAK
SQUEAK
HP
OOH! HE'S RIGHT ON TOP OF HIM!
HE CAN'T SHOOT LIKE THAT!
THERE IT IS! ICHINOKURA'S "SNAPPING TURTLE D"!
ROOOAAAAAR
KEEP IT UP!
BUT NOW HE'S STARTING TO *BELIEVE* IN HIMSELF AGAIN.

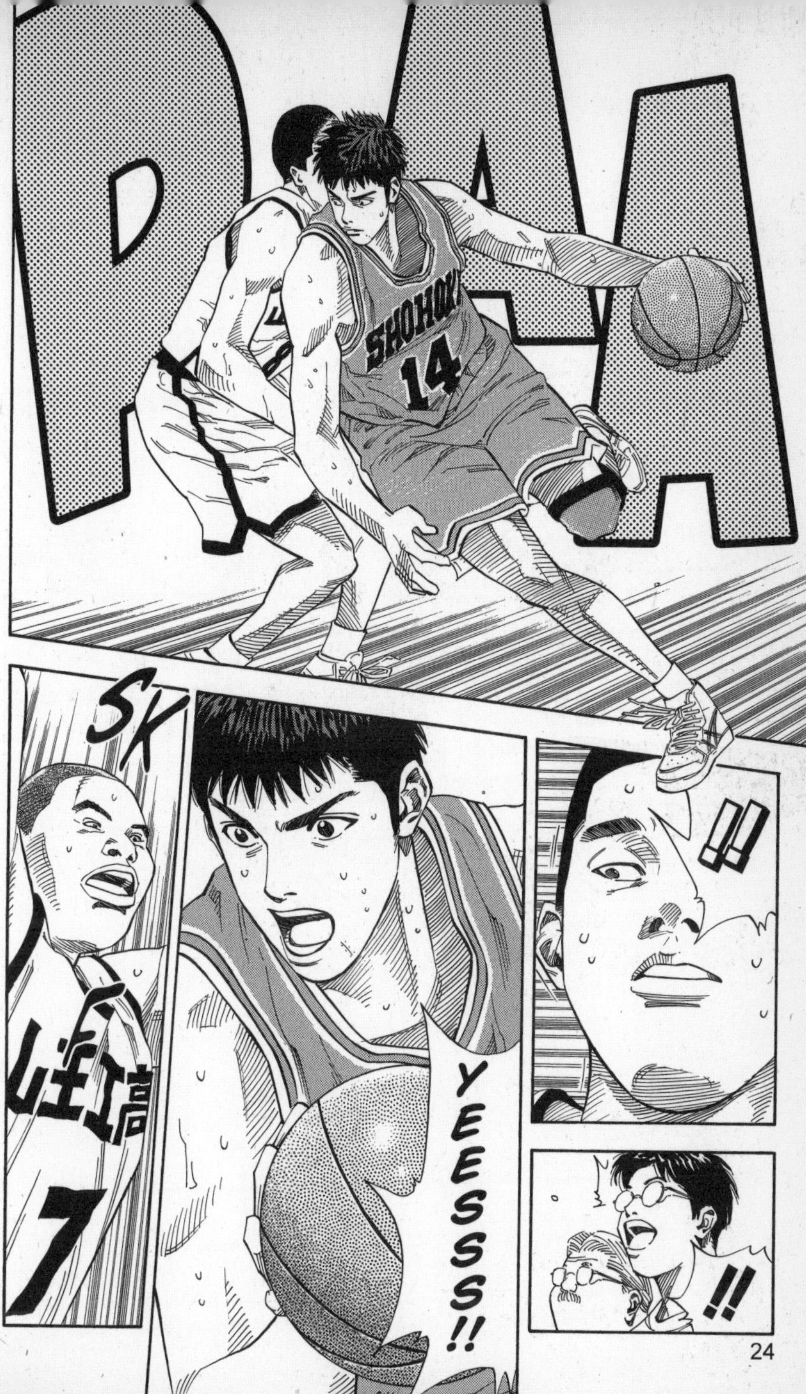
DAA
!!
!!
YEESSS!!
SK

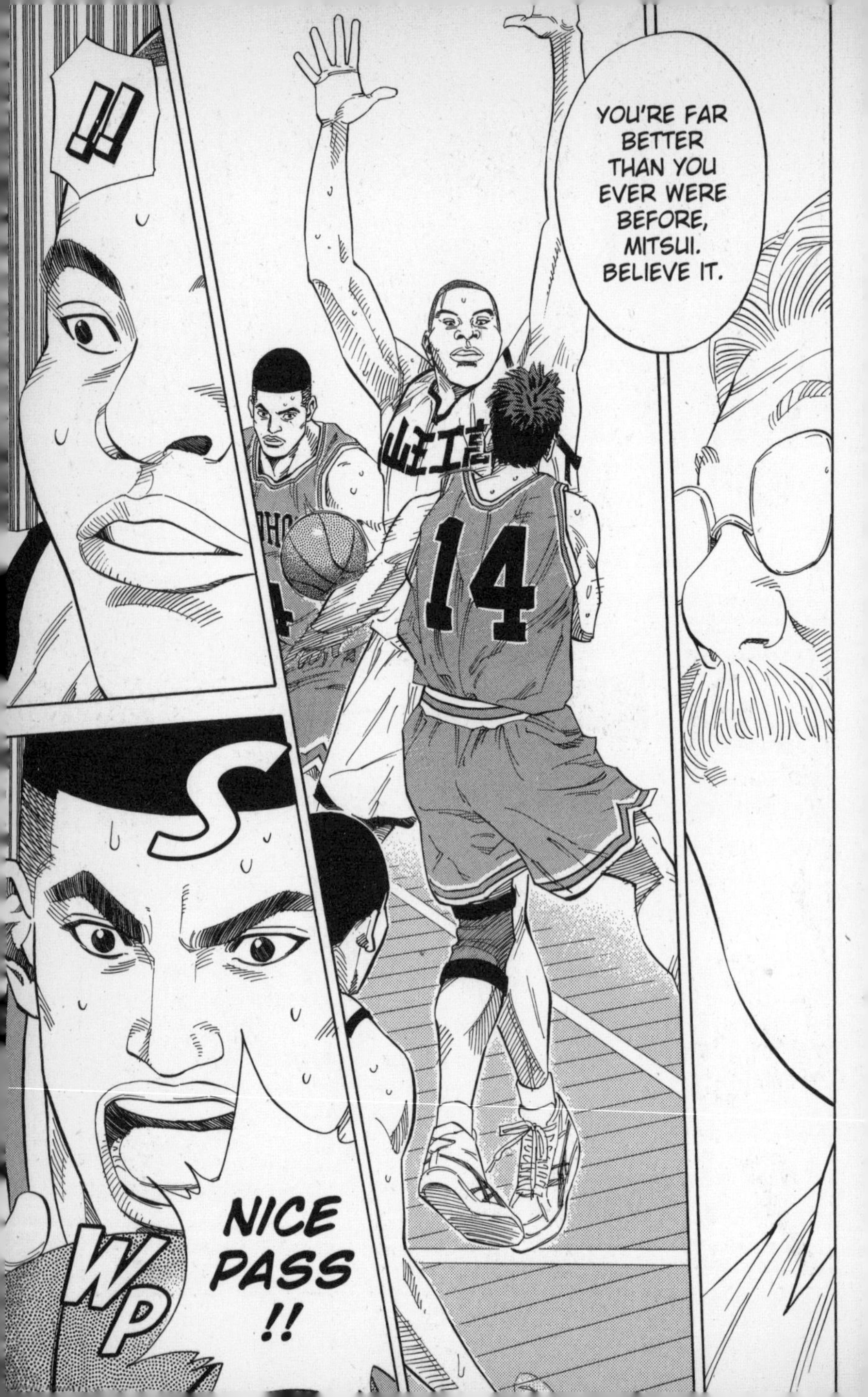
YOU'RE FAR BETTER THAN YOU EVER WERE BEFORE, MITSUI. BELIEVE IT.
!!
S
NICE PASS !!
WP

Live in the present...
Mitsui!

SLAM DUNK

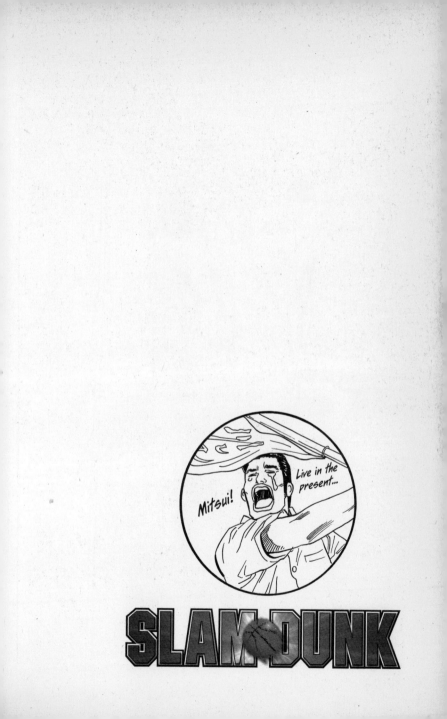

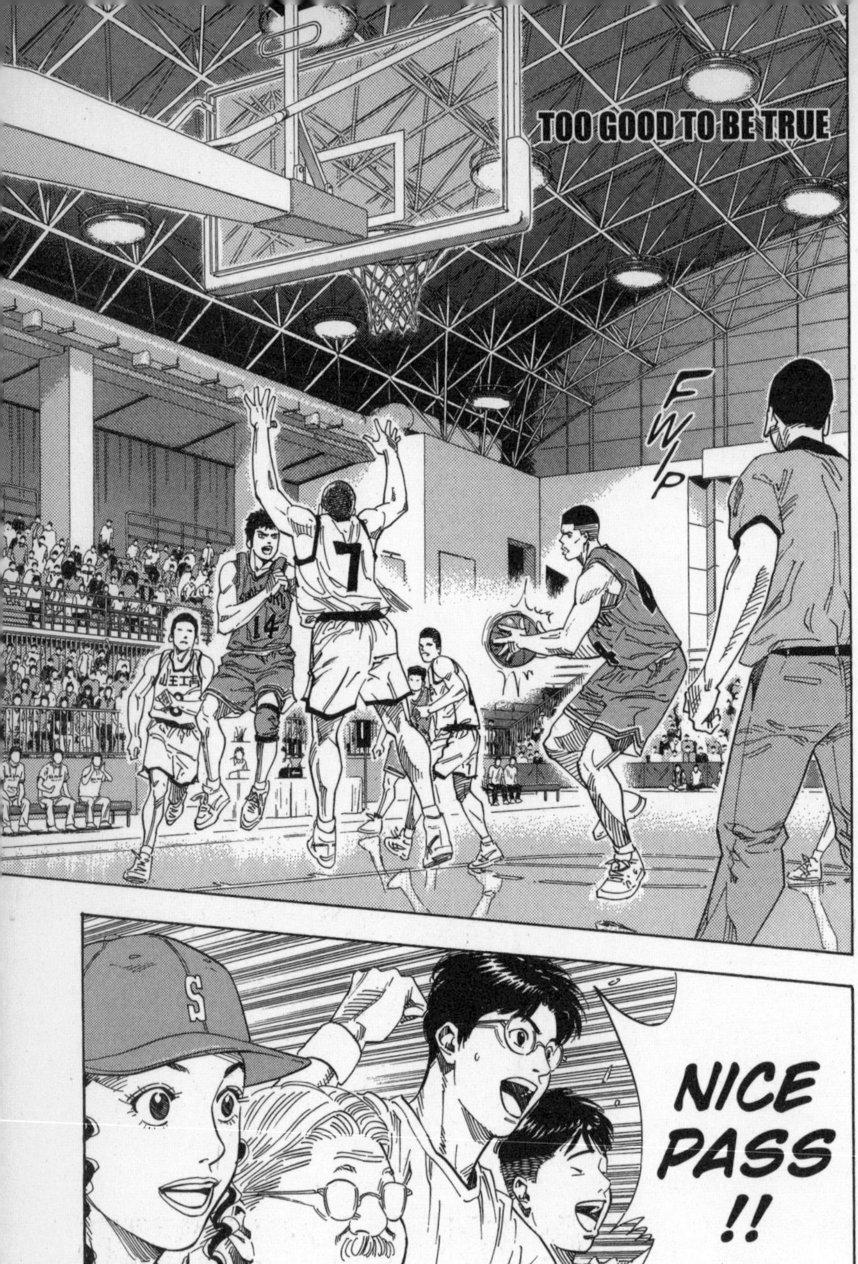
TOO GOOD TO BE TRUE
FWIP
NICE PASS!!

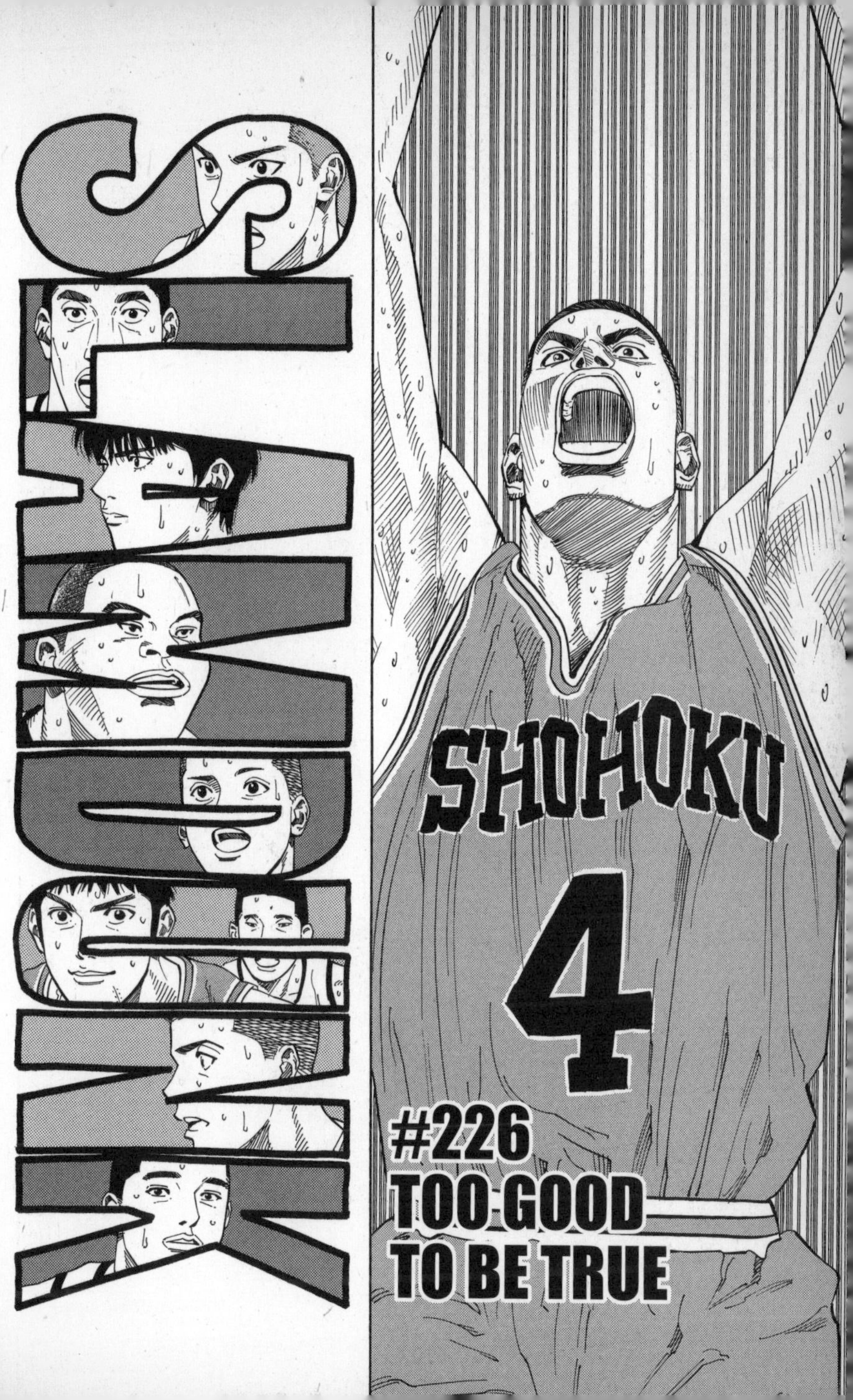
SHOHOKU
4
#226
TOO GOOD
TO BE TRUE
SLAM DUNK

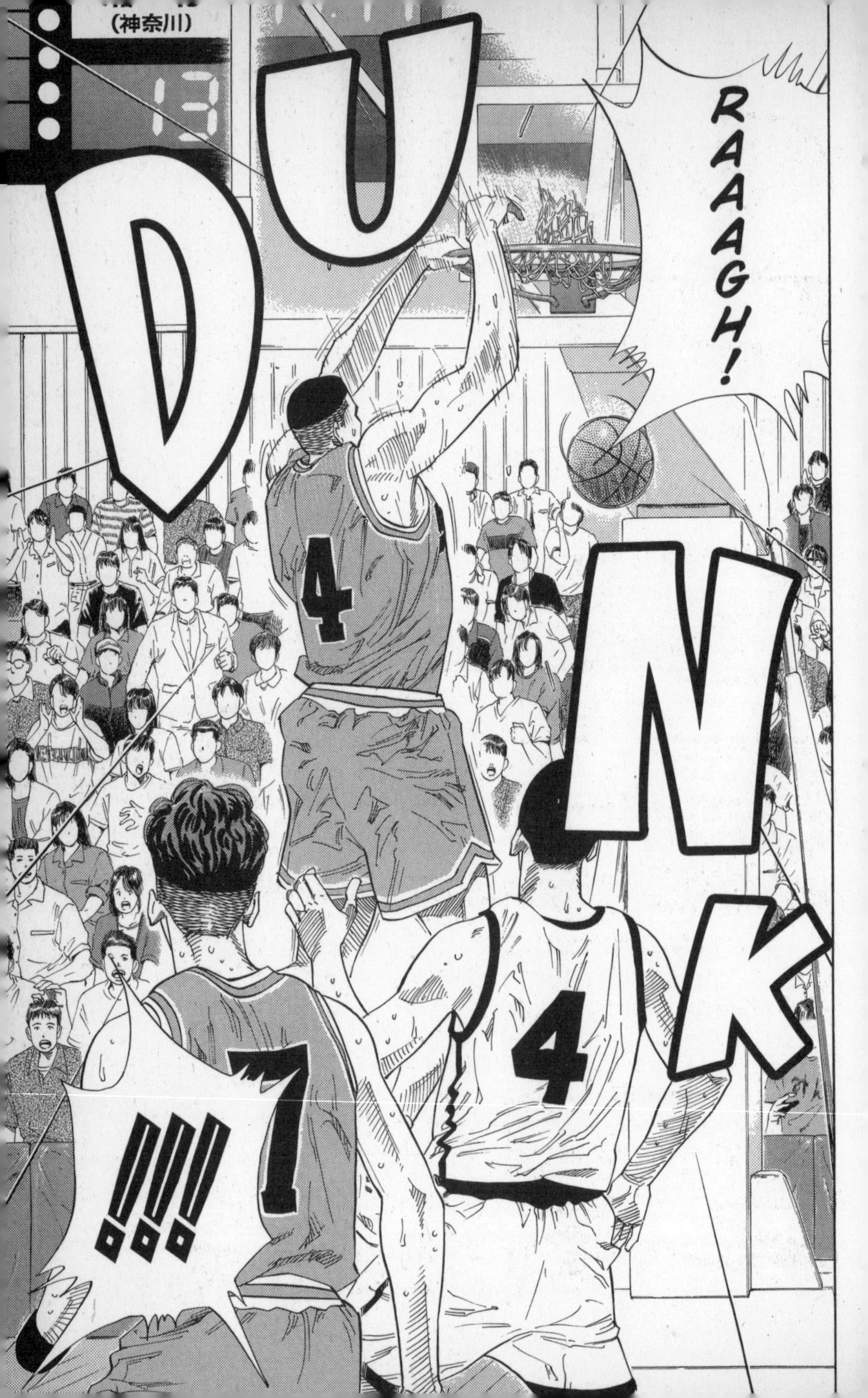
(神奈川)
13
RAAAGH!
DUNK
!!!

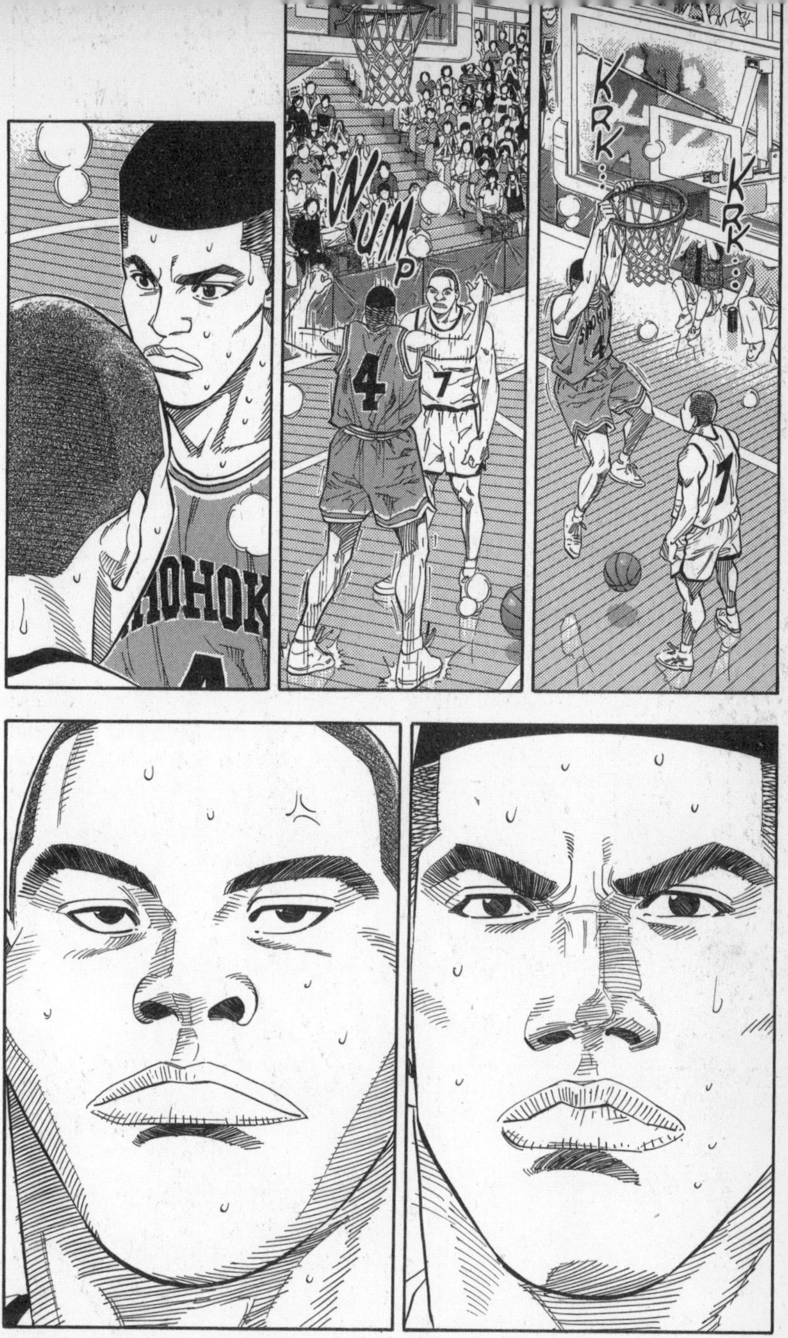
KRK...
KRK...
WUMP

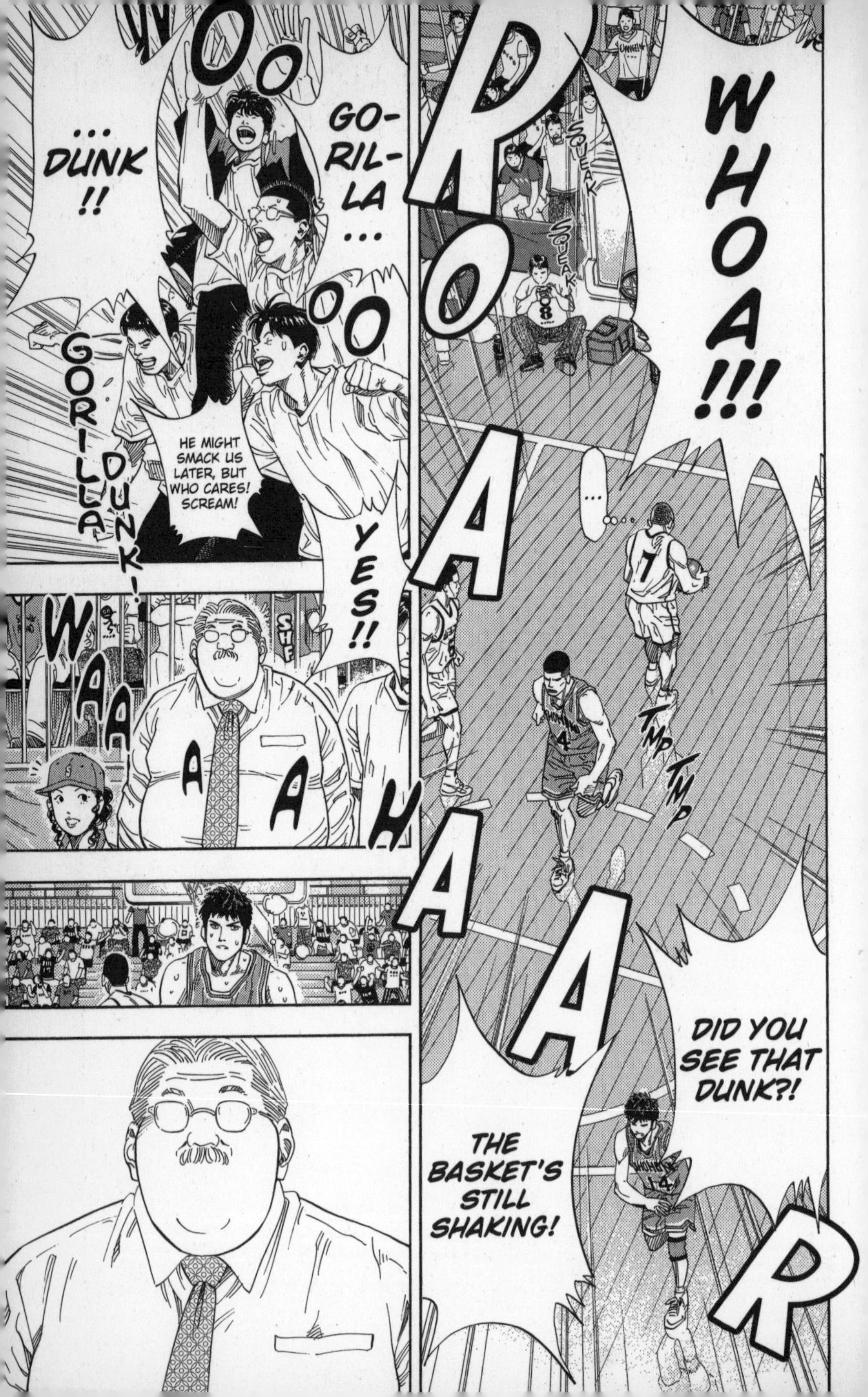
PAOAAAAR
WHOA!!!
SQUEAK
SQUEAK
...
TMP TMP
DID YOU SEE THAT DUNK?!
THE BASKET'S STILL SHAKING!
WOOOO
GO-RIL-LA...
...DUNK!!
GORILLA DUNK!
HE MIGHT SMACK US LATER, BUT WHO CARES! SCREAM!
YES!!
WAAAAAH

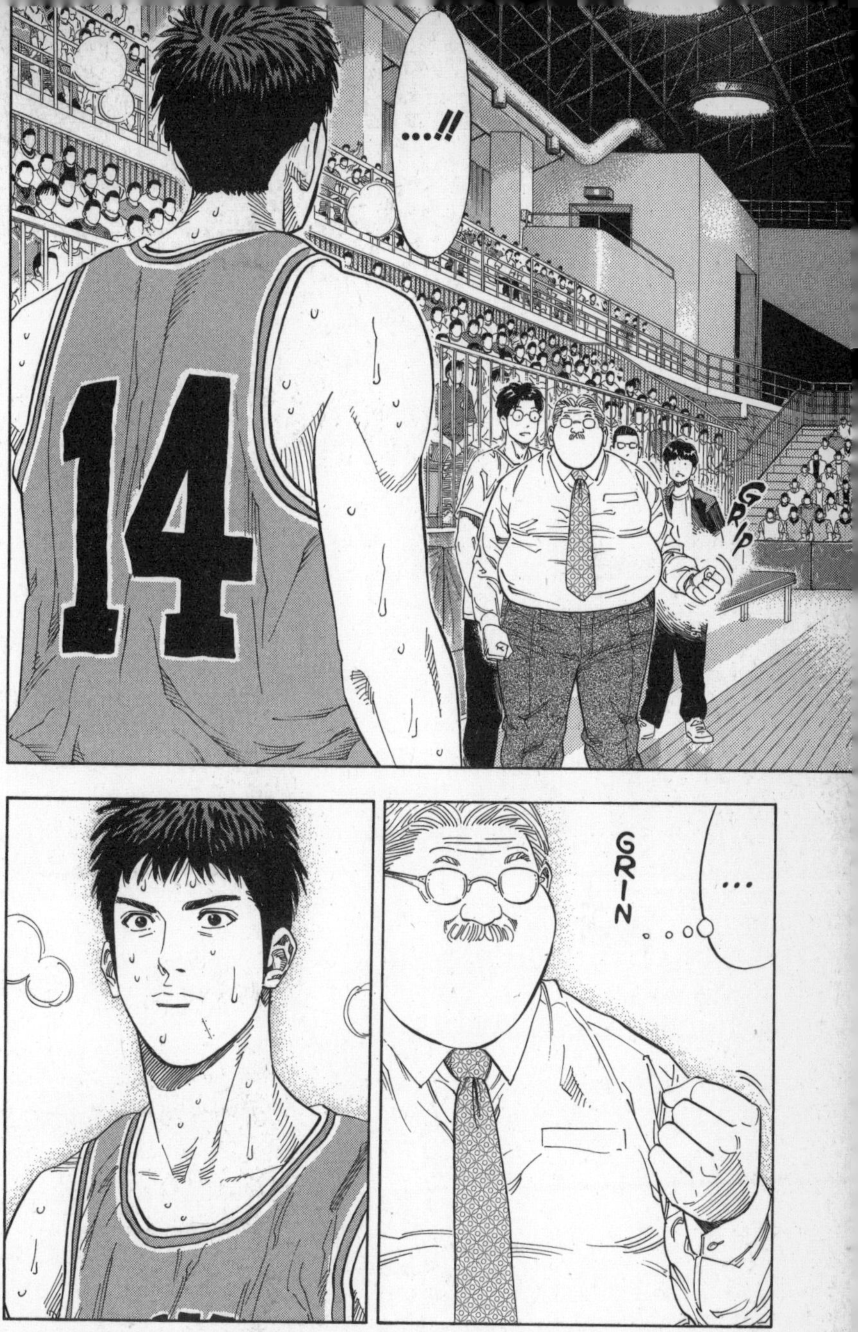
...!!
GRIP
GRIN
...

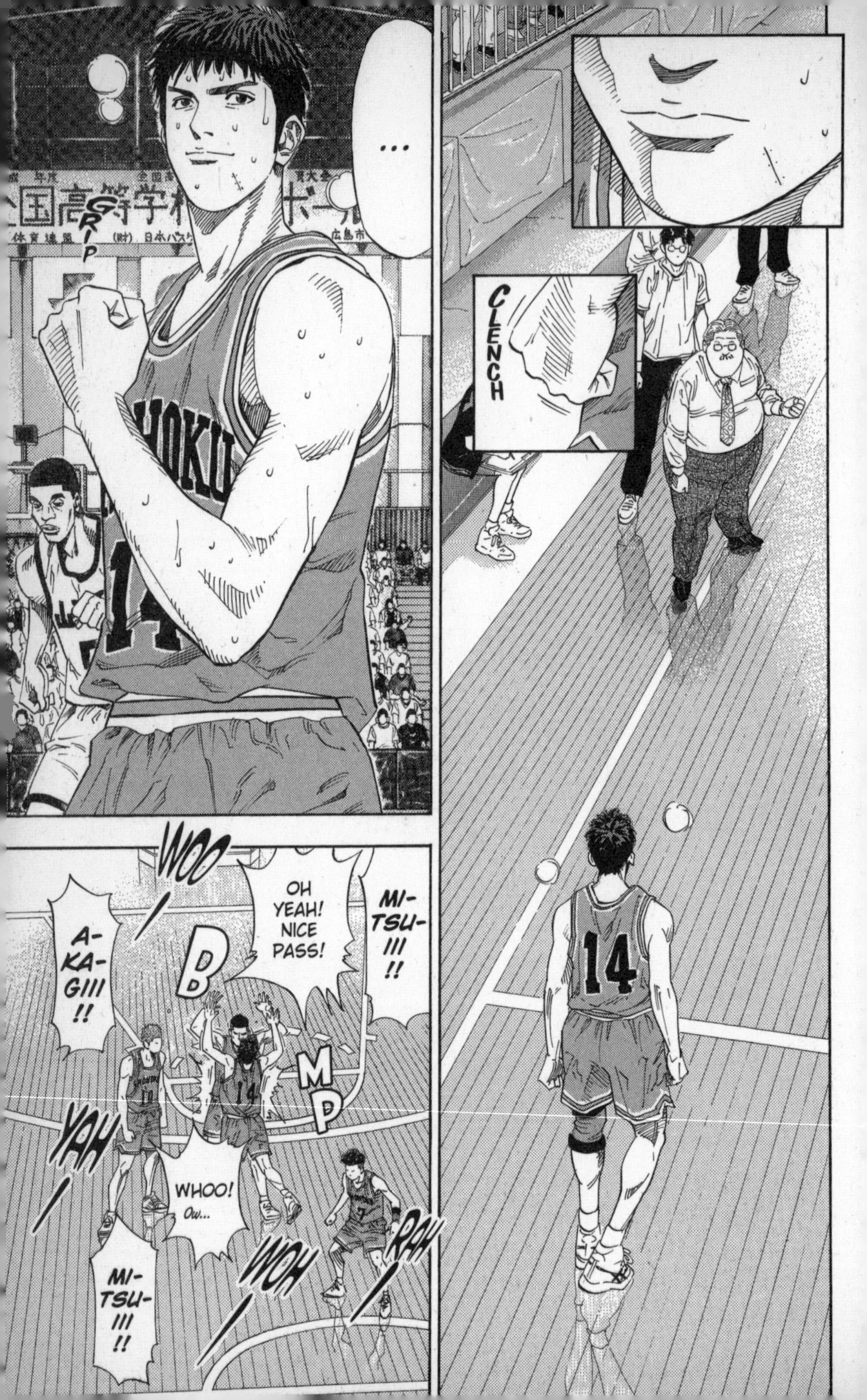
CLENCH
...
GRIP
WOO
MI-TSU-III!!
OH YEAH! NICE PASS!
A-KA-GIII!!
BMP
YAH
WHOO! Ow...
RAH
WOH
MI-TSU-III!!

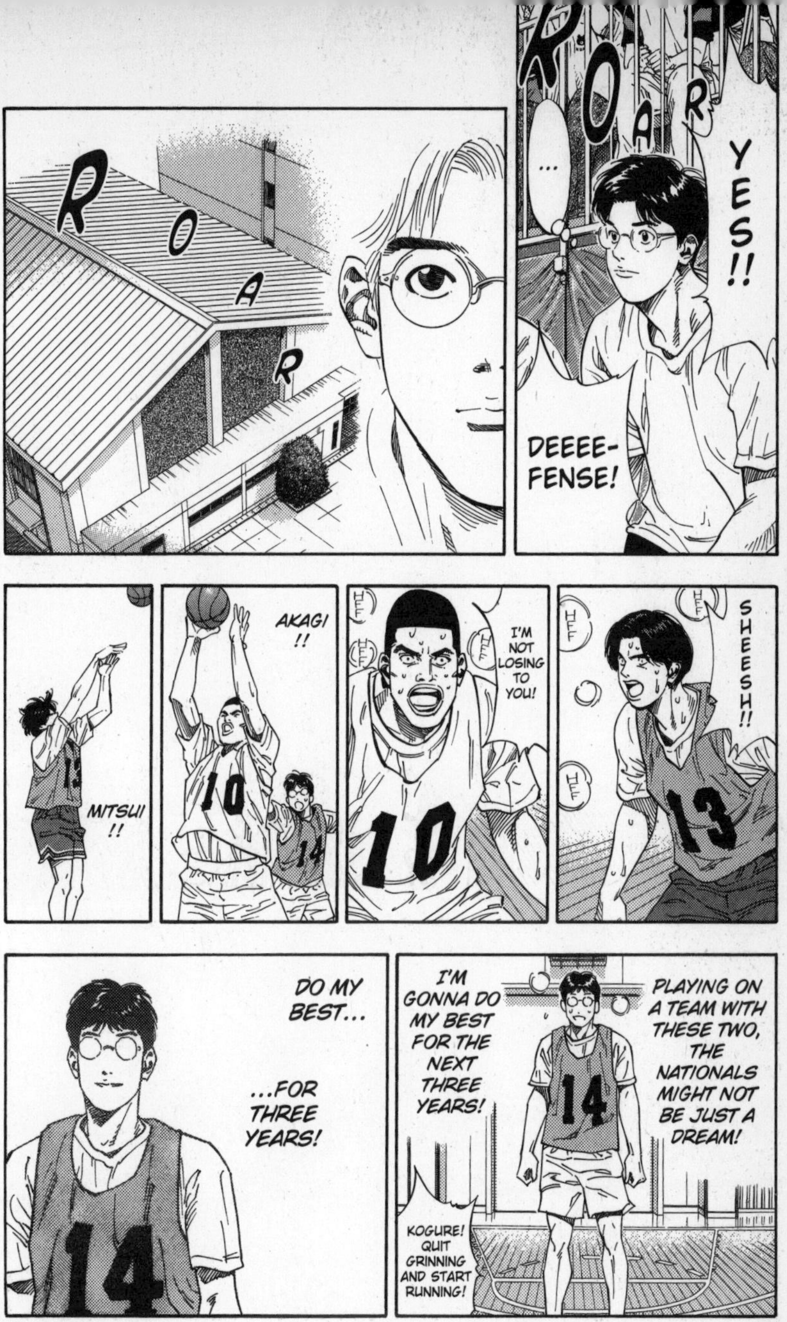
ROAR
YES!!
...
DEEEE-FENSE!
ROAR
HFF
SHEESH!!
HFF
HFF
HFF
HFF
I'M NOT LOSING TO YOU!
AKAGI!!
MITSUI!!
PLAYING ON A TEAM WITH THESE TWO, THE NATIONALS MIGHT NOT BE JUST A DREAM!
I'M GONNA DO MY BEST FOR THE NEXT THREE YEARS!
KOGURE! QUIT GRINNING AND START RUNNING!
DO MY BEST...
...FOR THREE YEARS!

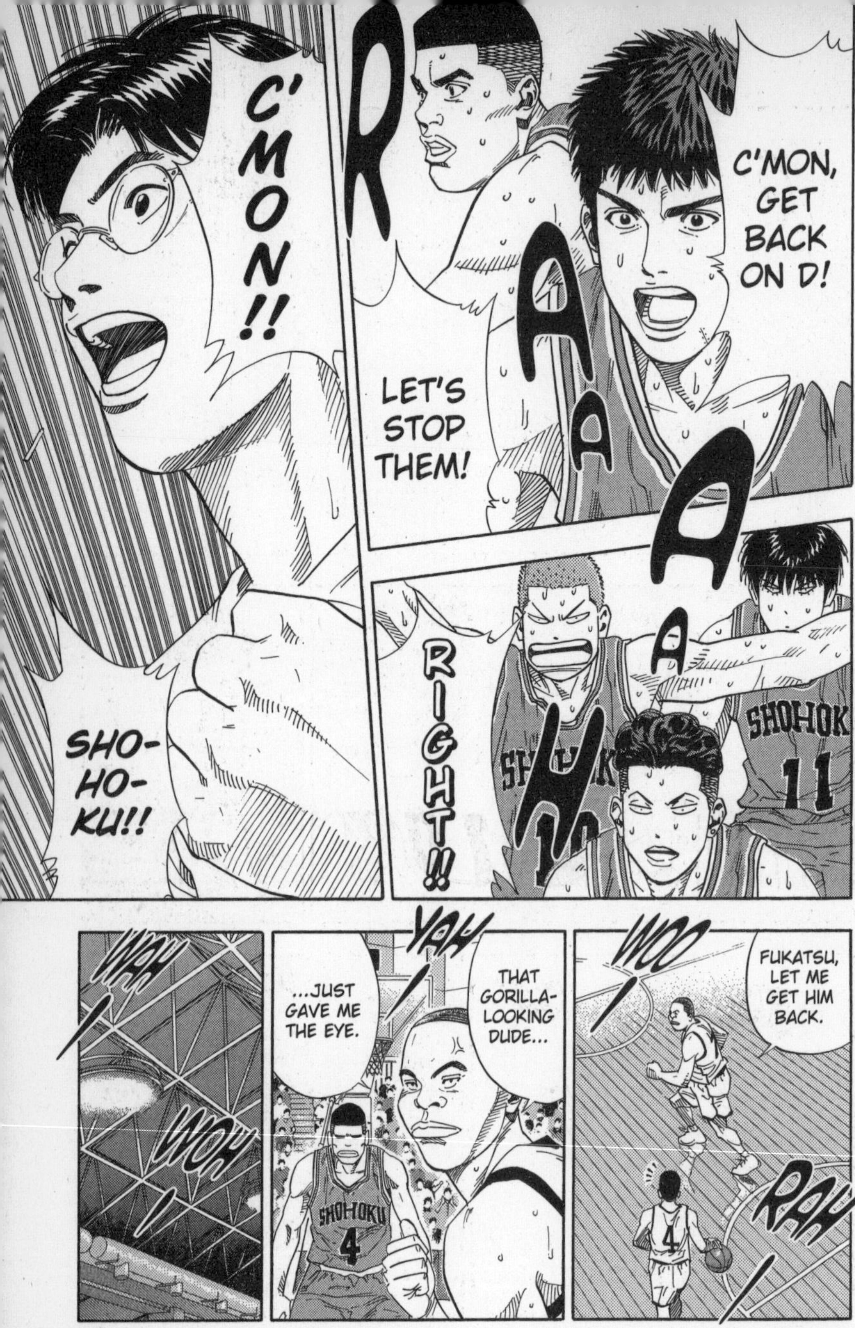
C'MON, GET BACK ON D!
LET'S STOP THEM!
RAAAAAH
RIGHT!!
C'MON!!
SHO-HO-KU!!
WOO
FUKATSU, LET ME GET HIM BACK.
RAH
YAH
THAT GORILLA-LOOKING DUDE...
...JUST GAVE ME THE EYE.
WAH
WOH

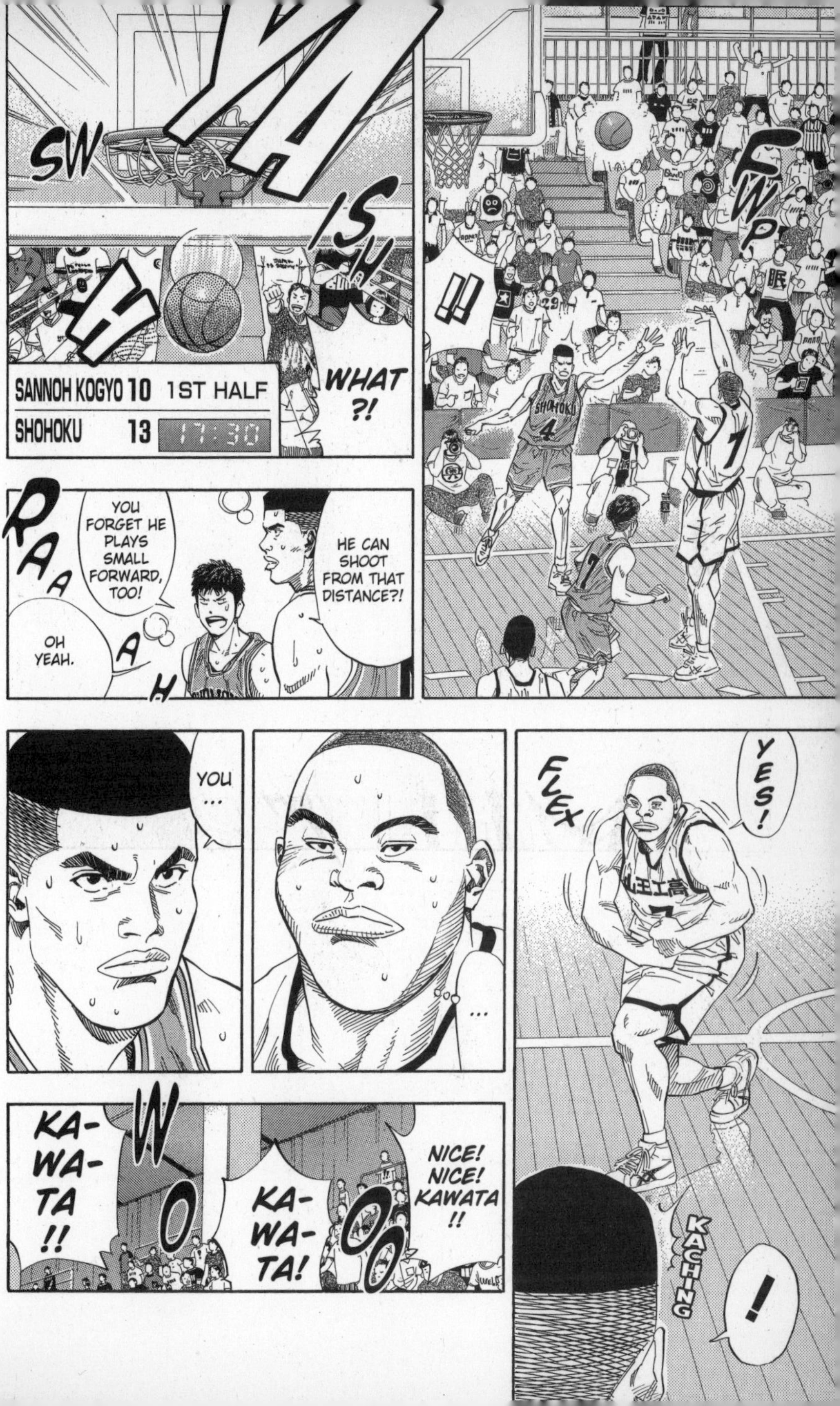
FWP
!!
SWISH
SANNOH KOGYO 10 1ST HALF
SHOHOKU 13 17:30
WHAT ?!
HE CAN SHOOT FROM THAT DISTANCE?!
YOU FORGET HE PLAYS SMALL FORWARD, TOO!
OH YEAH.
RAAAAH
YES!
FLEX
KACHING
!
...
YOU ...
NICE! NICE! KAWATA !!
KA-WA-TA!
WOO
KA-WA-TA !!

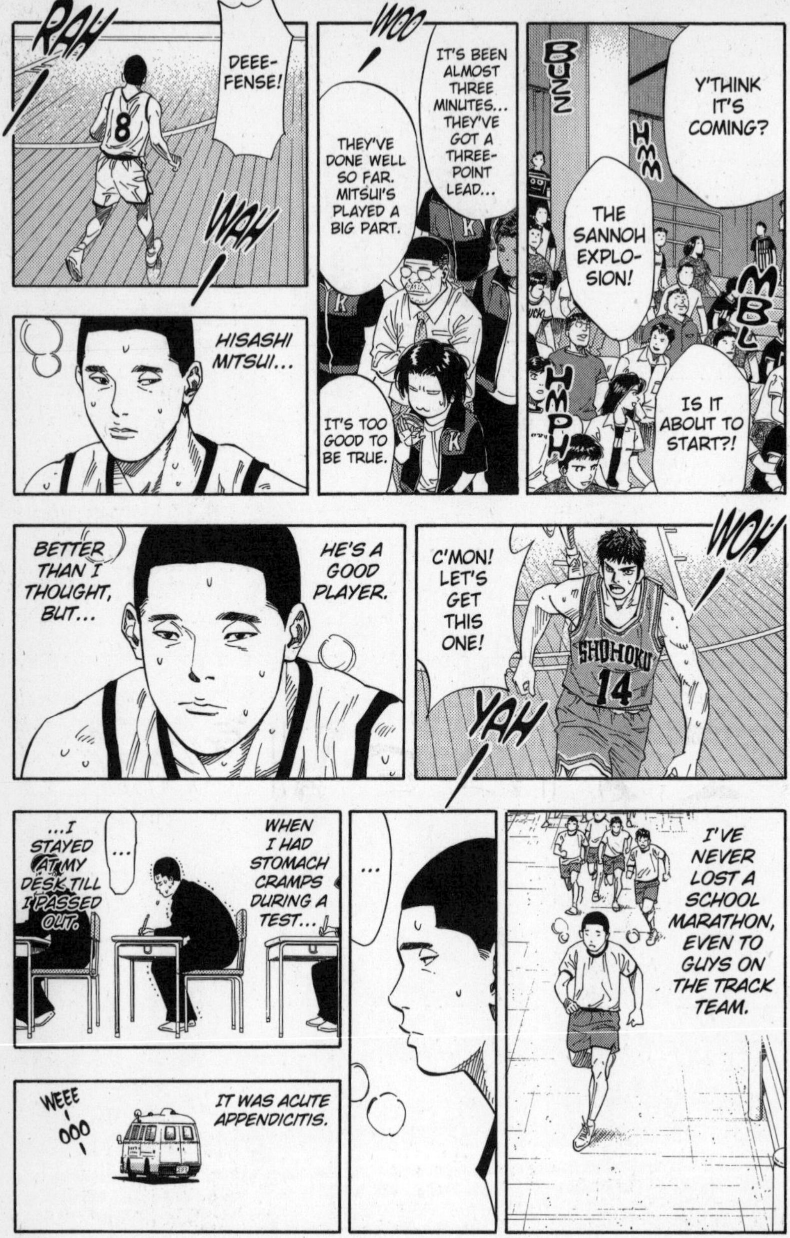

Y'THINK IT'S COMING?
BUZZ
HMM
THE SANNOH EXPLOSION!
MMBL
HMPH
IS IT ABOUT TO START?!
WOO
IT'S BEEN ALMOST THREE MINUTES... THEY'VE GOT A THREE-POINT LEAD...
THEY'VE DONE WELL SO FAR. MITSUI'S PLAYED A BIG PART.
IT'S TOO GOOD TO BE TRUE.
RAH
DEEE-FENSE!
WAH
HISASHI MITSUI...
WOH
C'MON! LET'S GET THIS ONE!
YAH
HE'S A GOOD PLAYER.
BETTER THAN I THOUGHT, BUT...
I'VE NEVER LOST A SCHOOL MARATHON, EVEN TO GUYS ON THE TRACK TEAM.
...
WHEN I HAD STOMACH CRAMPS DURING A TEST...
...
...I STAYED AT MY DESK TILL I PASSED OUT.
WEEE OOO
IT WAS ACUTE APPENDICITIS.

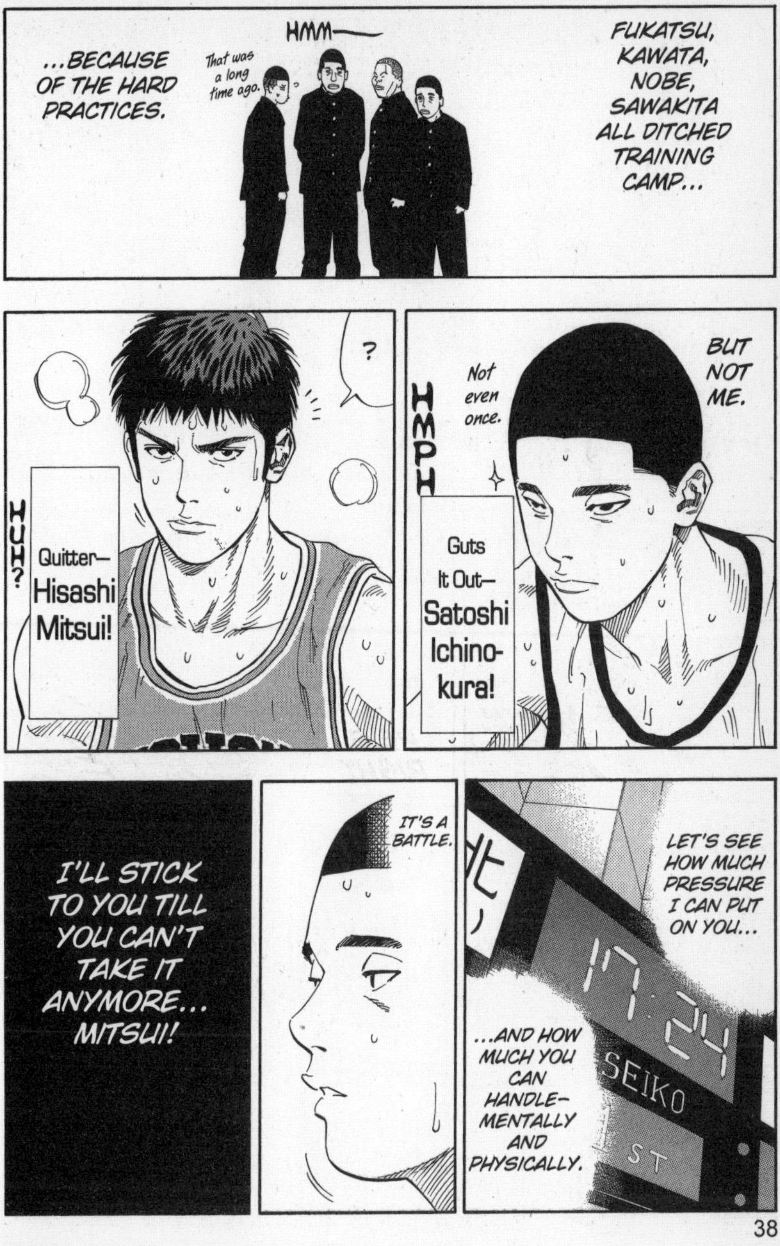
FUKATSU, KAWATA, NOBE, SAWAKITA ALL DITCHED TRAINING CAMP...
HMM—
That was a long time ago.
...BECAUSE OF THE HARD PRACTICES.
BUT NOT ME.
Not even once.
HMPH
Guts It Out— Satoshi Ichinokura!
?
HUH?
Quitter— Hisashi Mitsui!
LET'S SEE HOW MUCH PRESSURE I CAN PUT ON YOU...
...AND HOW MUCH YOU CAN HANDLE—MENTALLY AND PHYSICALLY.
17:24
SEIKO
IT'S A BATTLE.
I'LL STICK TO YOU TILL YOU CAN'T TAKE IT ANYMORE... MITSUI!

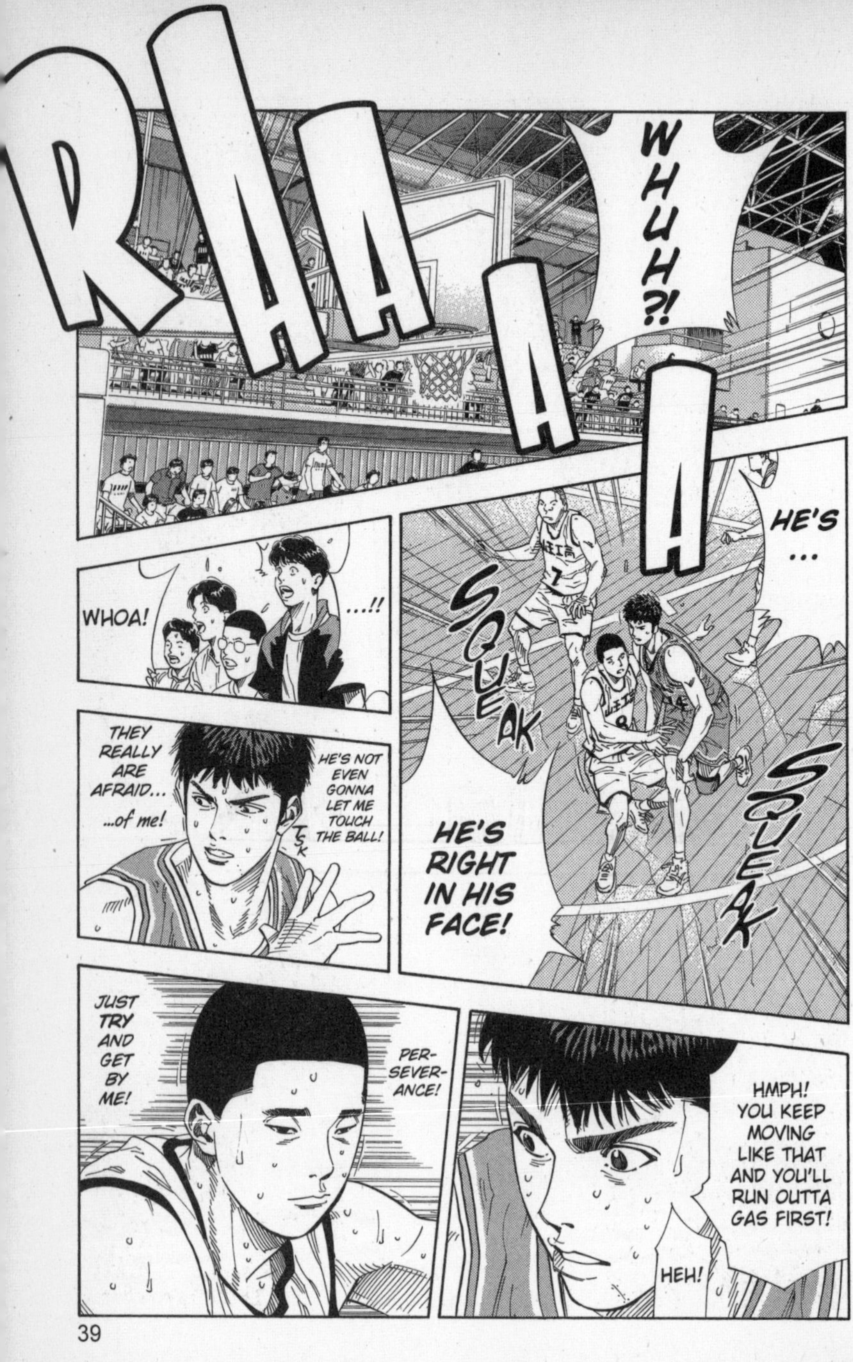
RAAAAA
WHUH?!
HE'S ...
SQUEAK
HE'S RIGHT IN HIS FACE!
SQUEAK
...!!
WHOA!
HE'S NOT EVEN GONNA LET ME TOUCH THE BALL!
TSK
THEY REALLY ARE AFRAID...
...of me!
HMPH! YOU KEEP MOVING LIKE THAT AND YOU'LL RUN OUTTA GAS FIRST!
HEH!
PER-SEVER-ANCE!
JUST TRY AND GET BY ME!

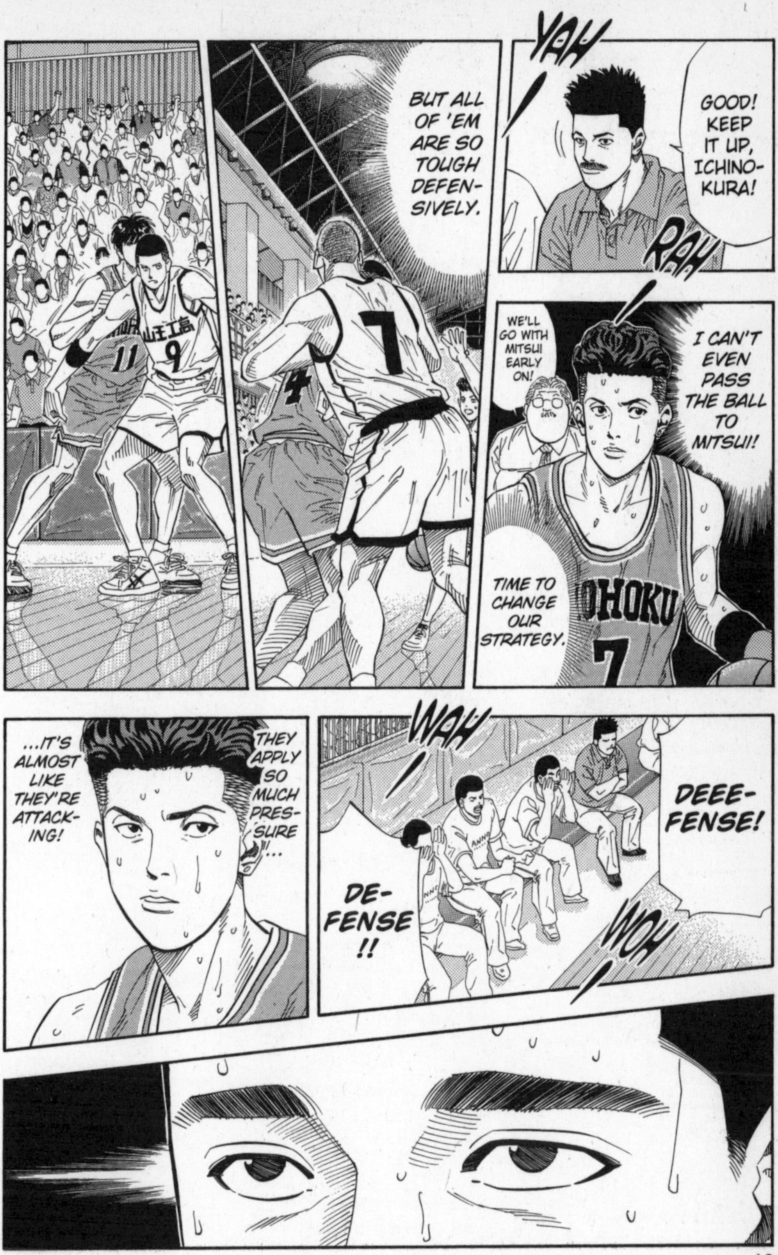
YAH
GOOD! KEEP IT UP, ICHINO-KURA!
RAH
I CAN'T EVEN PASS THE BALL TO MITSUI!
WE'LL GO WITH MITSUI EARLY ON!
TIME TO CHANGE OUR STRATEGY.
BUT ALL OF 'EM ARE SO TOUGH DEFEN-SIVELY.
WAH
DEEE-FENSE!
DE-FENSE !!
WOH
THEY APPLY SO MUCH PRES-SURE !!...
...IT'S ALMOST LIKE THEY'RE ATTACK-ING!

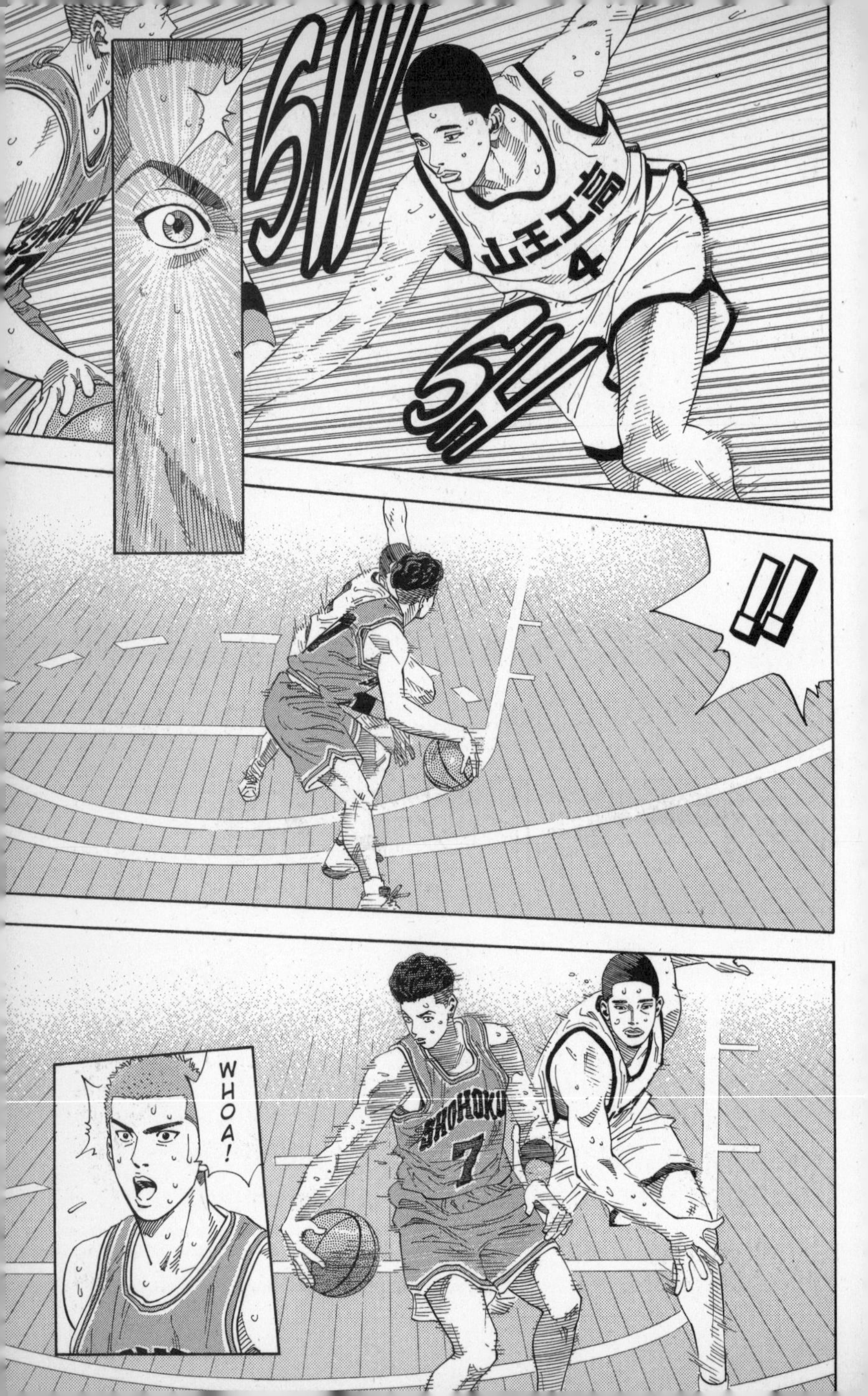
SW
SH
!!
WHOA!

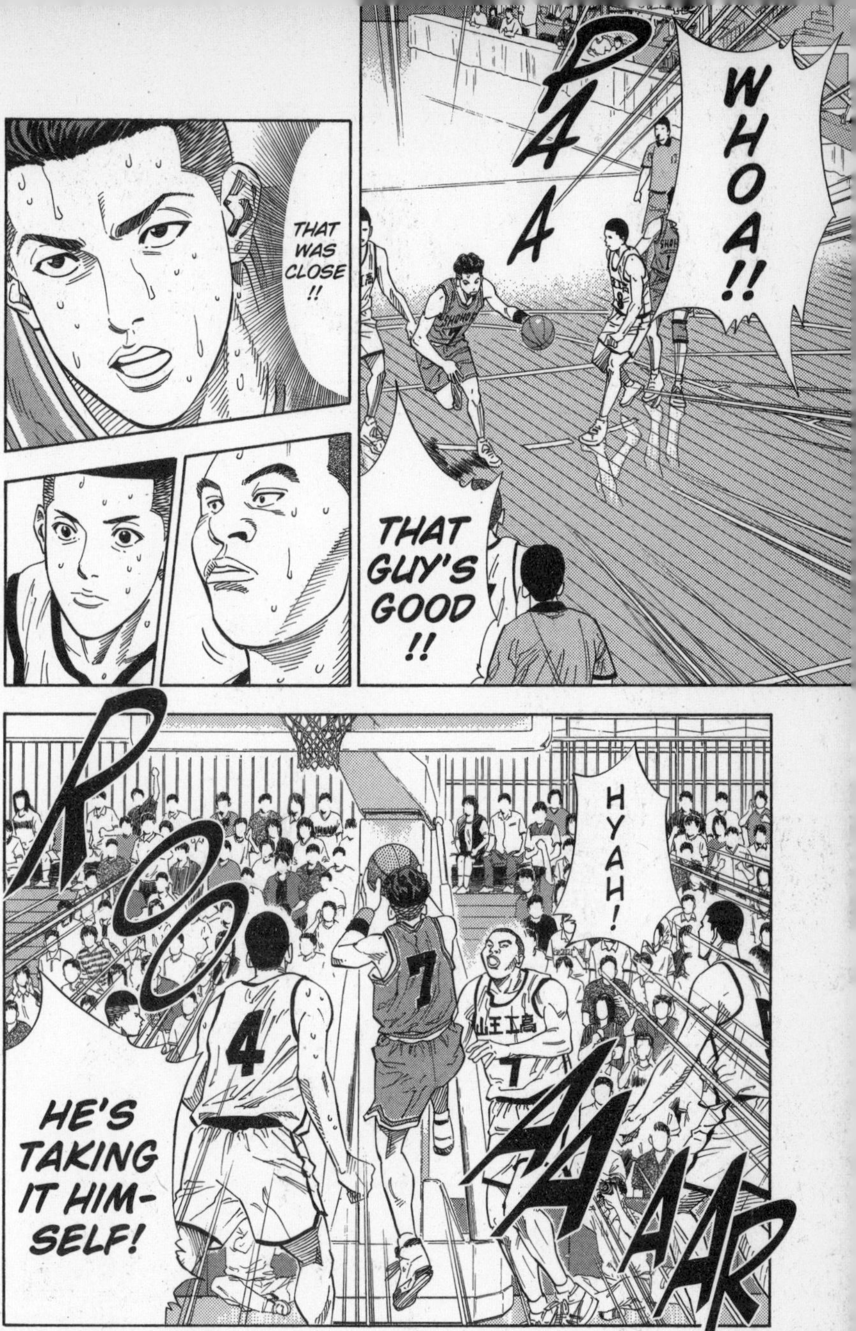
WHOA!!
PAAA
THAT GUY'S GOOD!!
THAT WAS CLOSE!!
HYAH!
ROOAAAAR
HE'S TAKING IT HIM-SELF!

READ THIS WAY

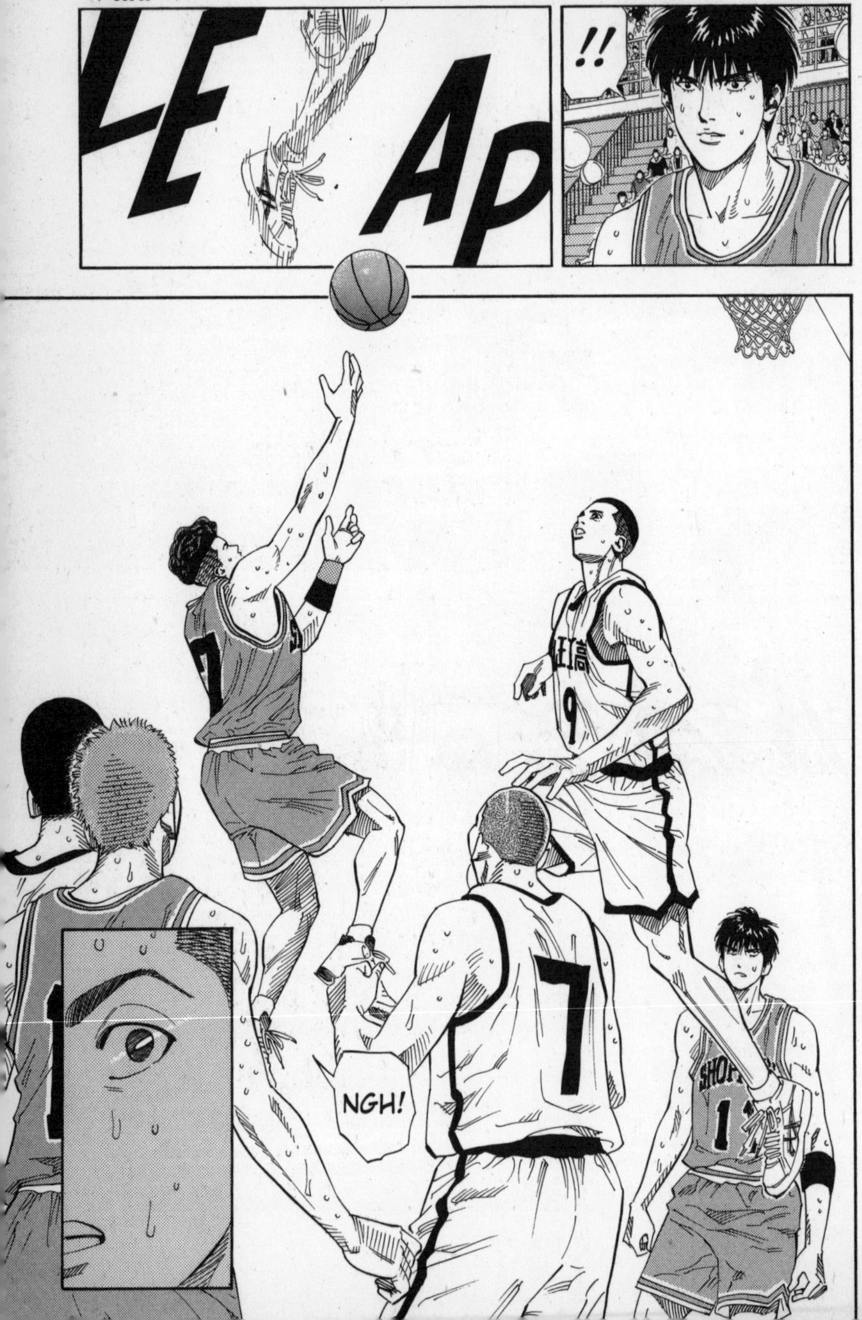
!!
LEAP
NGH!

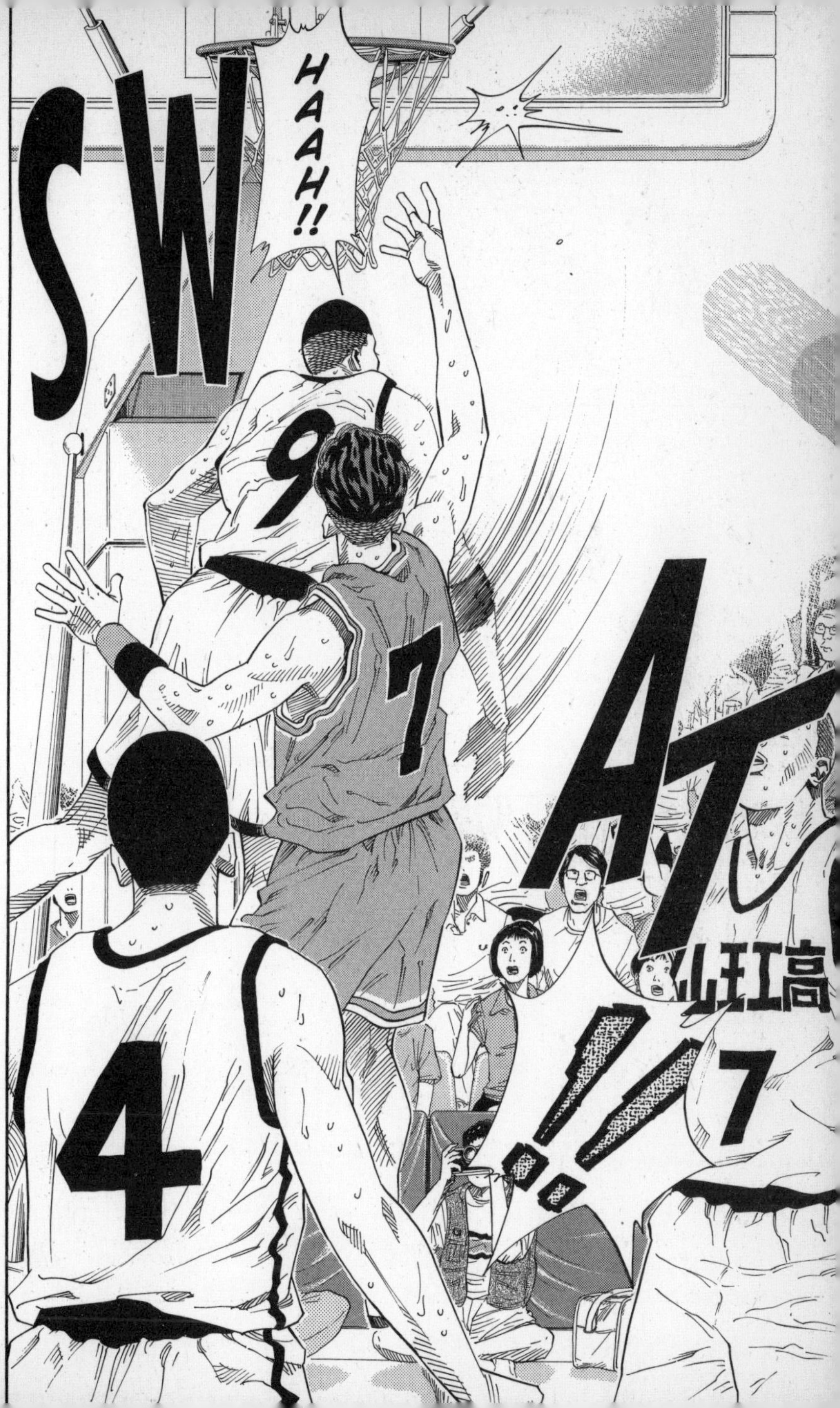
HAAAH!!
SWAT
山王工高
!!

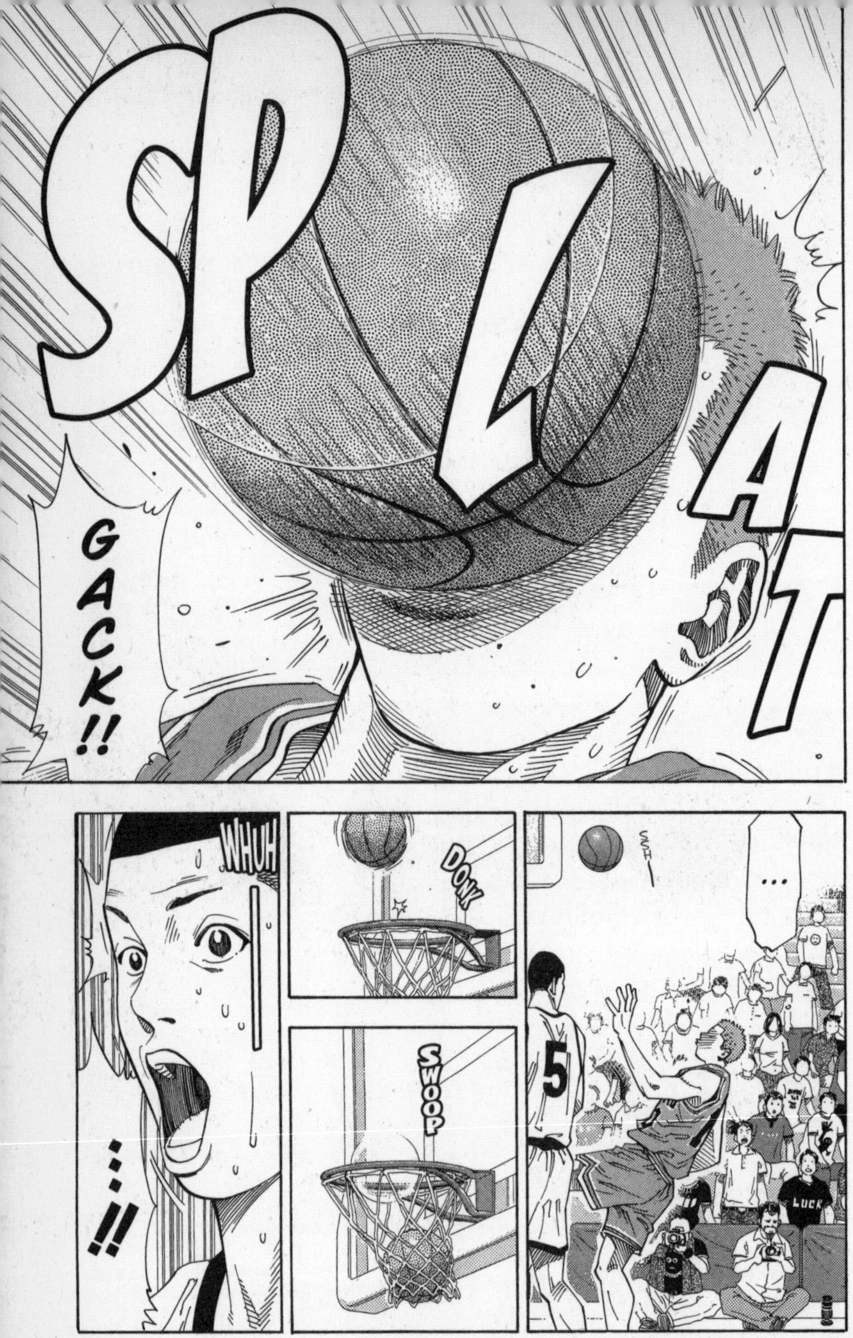
SPLAT
GACK!!
SSH—
...
DONK
SWOOP
WHUH
...!!

EXACTLY AS PLANNED

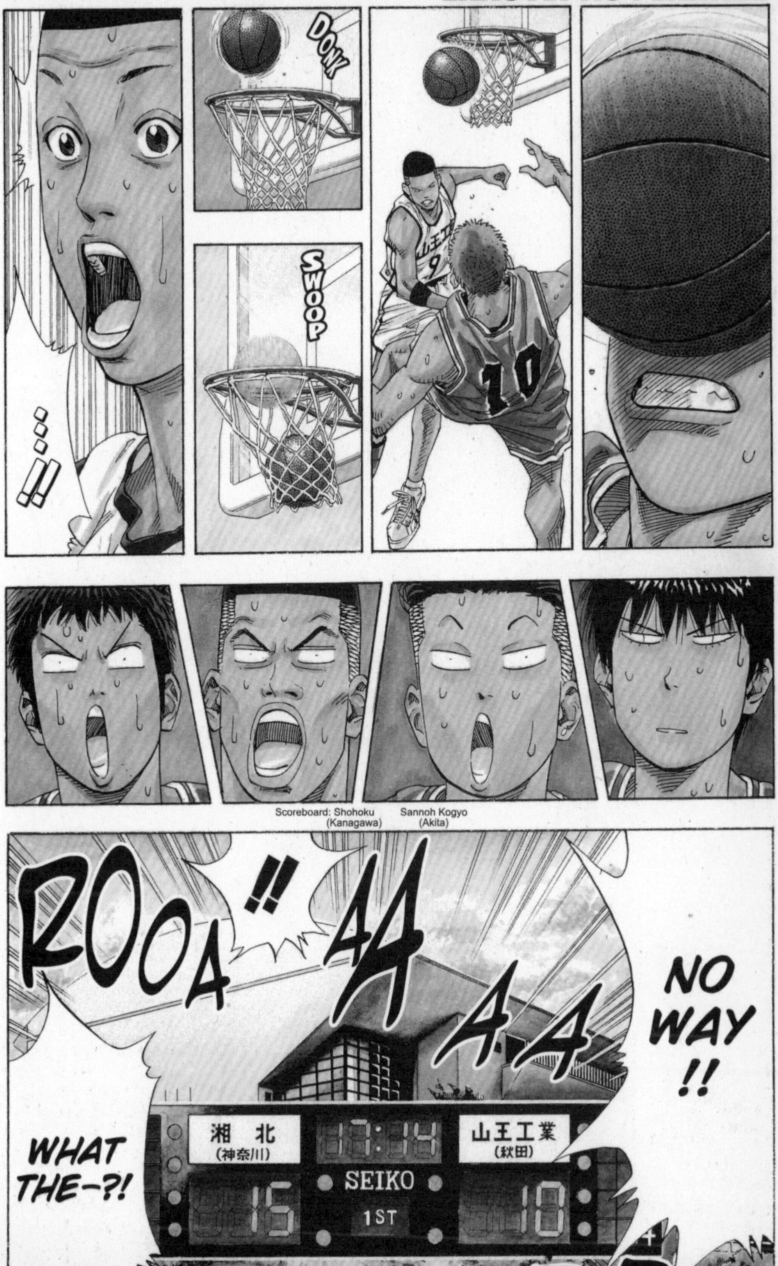
DONK
SWOOP
...!!
Scoreboard: Shohoku (Kanagawa) Sannoh Kogyo (Akita)
NO WAY !!
ROOA!! AA AA
湘北 (神奈川)
山王工業 (秋田)
SEIKO
1ST
15
10
WHAT THE-?!
DRD

READ THIS WAY

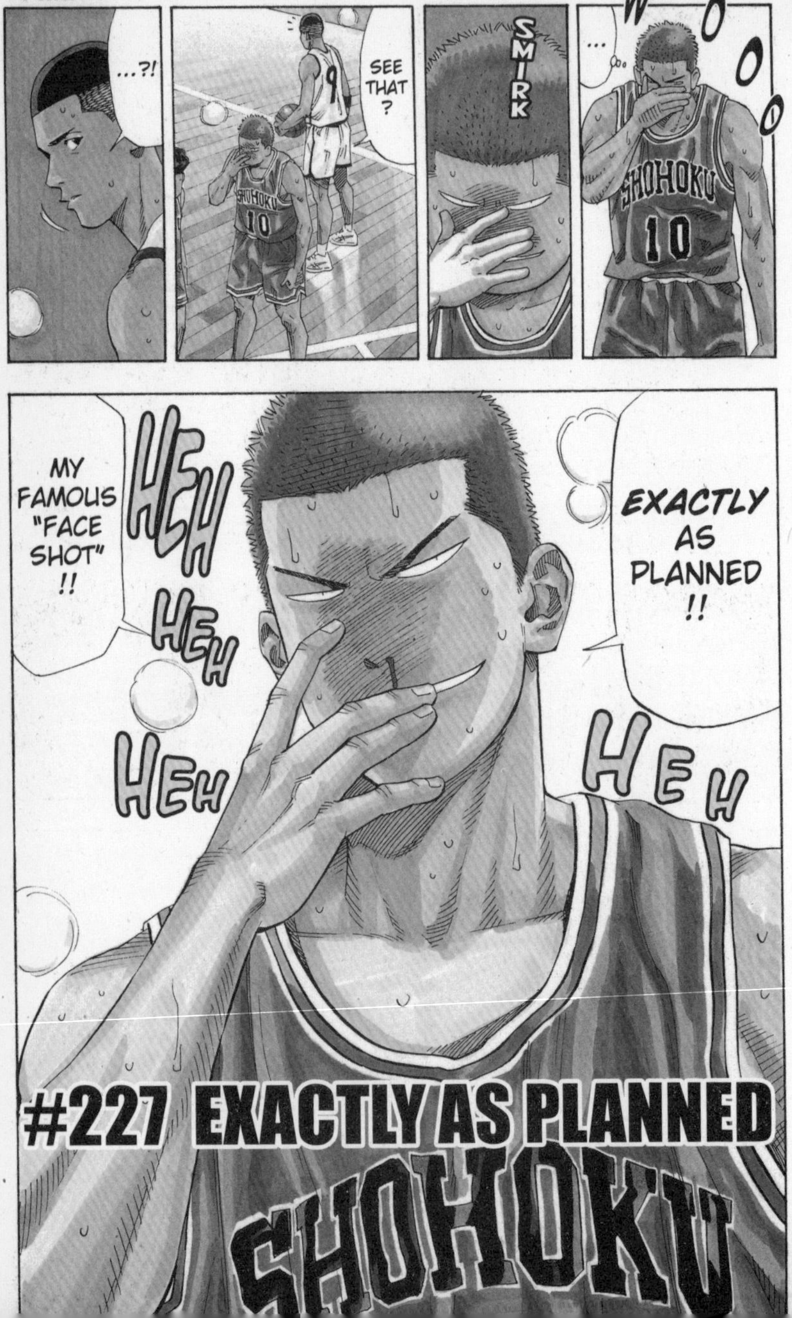
...
WOOO
SMIRK
SEE THAT ?
...?!
EXACTLY AS PLANNED !!
HEH HEH
MY FAMOUS "FACE SHOT" !!
HEH HEH HEH
SHOHOKU

#227 EXACTLY AS PLANNED

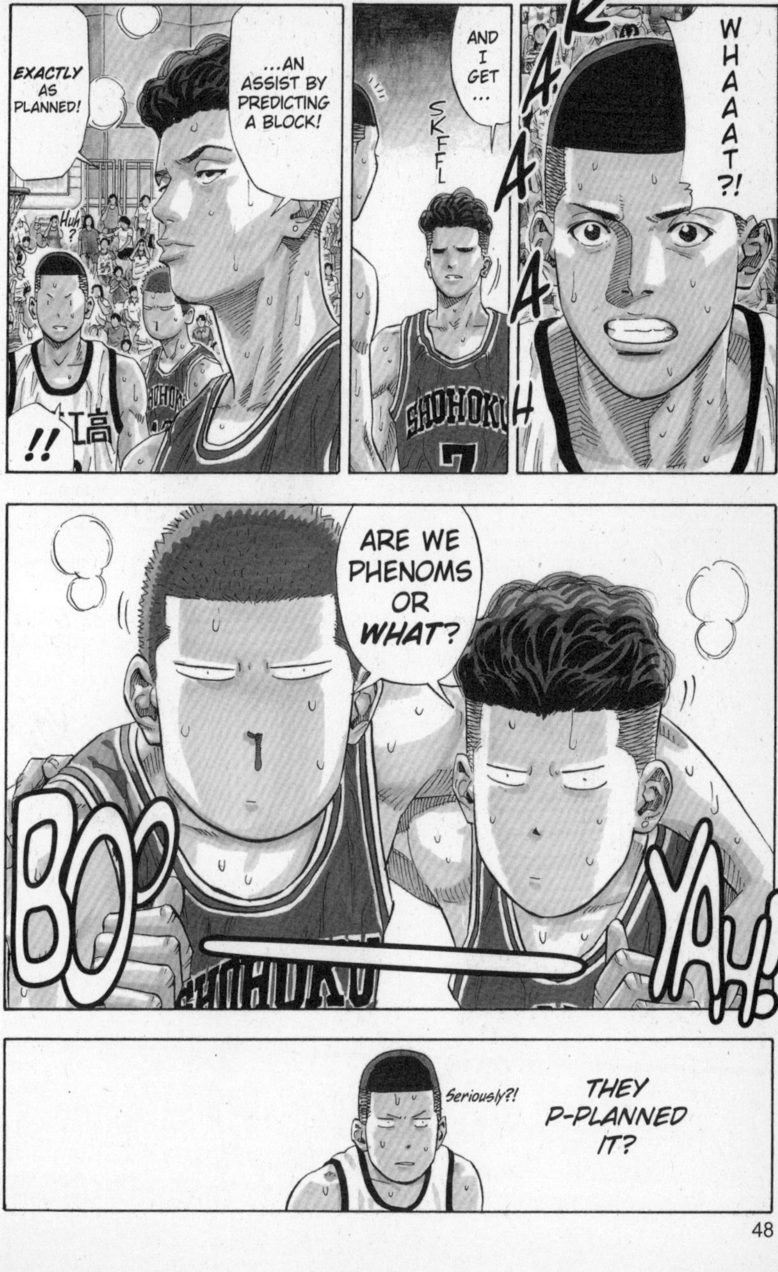
WHAAAAT?!
RAAAAH
AND I GET...
SKFFL
...AN ASSIST BY PREDICTING A BLOCK!
EXACTLY AS PLANNED!
Huh?
!!
ARE WE PHENOMS OR WHAT?
BO—YAH!
THEY P-PLANNED IT?
Seriously?!

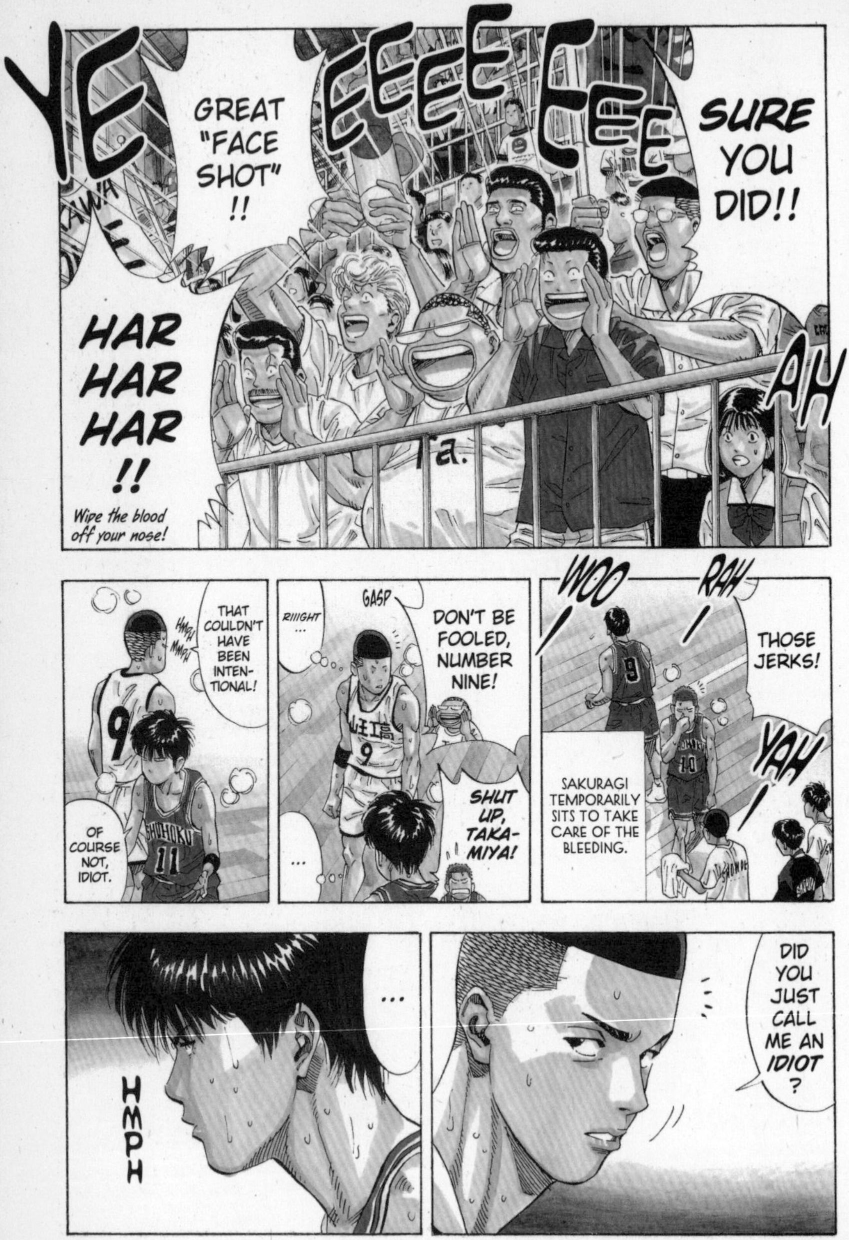
SURE YOU DID!!
YEEEEEEEEEE
GREAT "FACE SHOT" !!
AH
HAR HAR HAR !!
Wipe the blood off your nose!
WOO
RAH
THOSE JERKS!
YAH
SAKURAGI TEMPORARILY SITS TO TAKE CARE OF THE BLEEDING.
GASP
DON'T BE FOOLED, NUMBER NINE!
RIIIGHT ...
SHUT UP, TAKAMIYA!
...
THAT COULDN'T HAVE BEEN INTENTIONAL!
HMPH MMPH
OF COURSE NOT, IDIOT.
DID YOU JUST CALL ME AN IDIOT?
...
HMPH

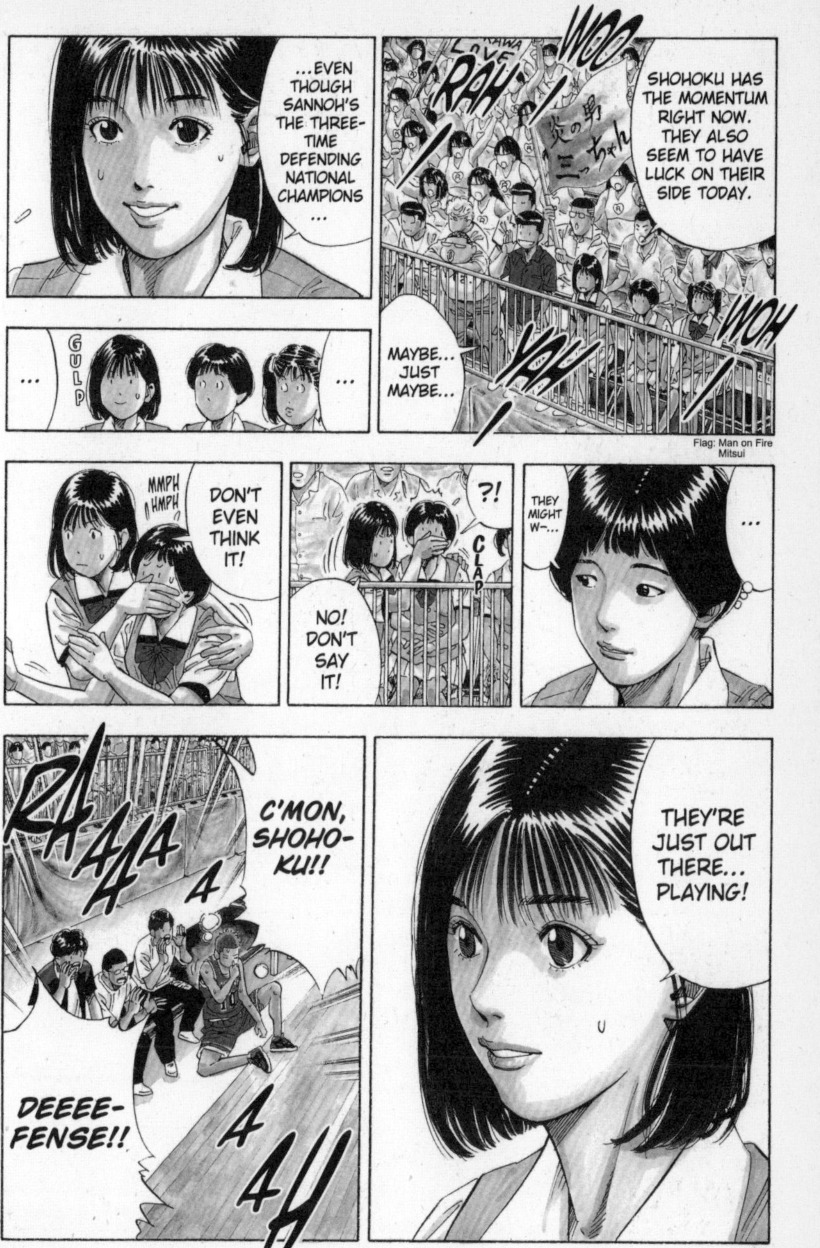
WOO RAH
SHOHOKU HAS THE MOMENTUM RIGHT NOW. THEY ALSO SEEM TO HAVE LUCK ON THEIR SIDE TODAY.
WOH YAH
MAYBE... JUST MAYBE...
...EVEN THOUGH SANNOH'S THE THREE-TIME DEFENDING NATIONAL CHAMPIONS...
...
GULP
...
THEY MIGHT W—...
...
?!
CLAP
NO! DON'T SAY IT!
MMPH HMPH
DON'T EVEN THINK IT!
THEY'RE JUST OUT THERE... PLAYING!
C'MON, SHOHO-KU!!
RAAAAAAAAH
DEEEE-FENSE!!

Flag: Man on Fire Mitsui

READ THIS WAY

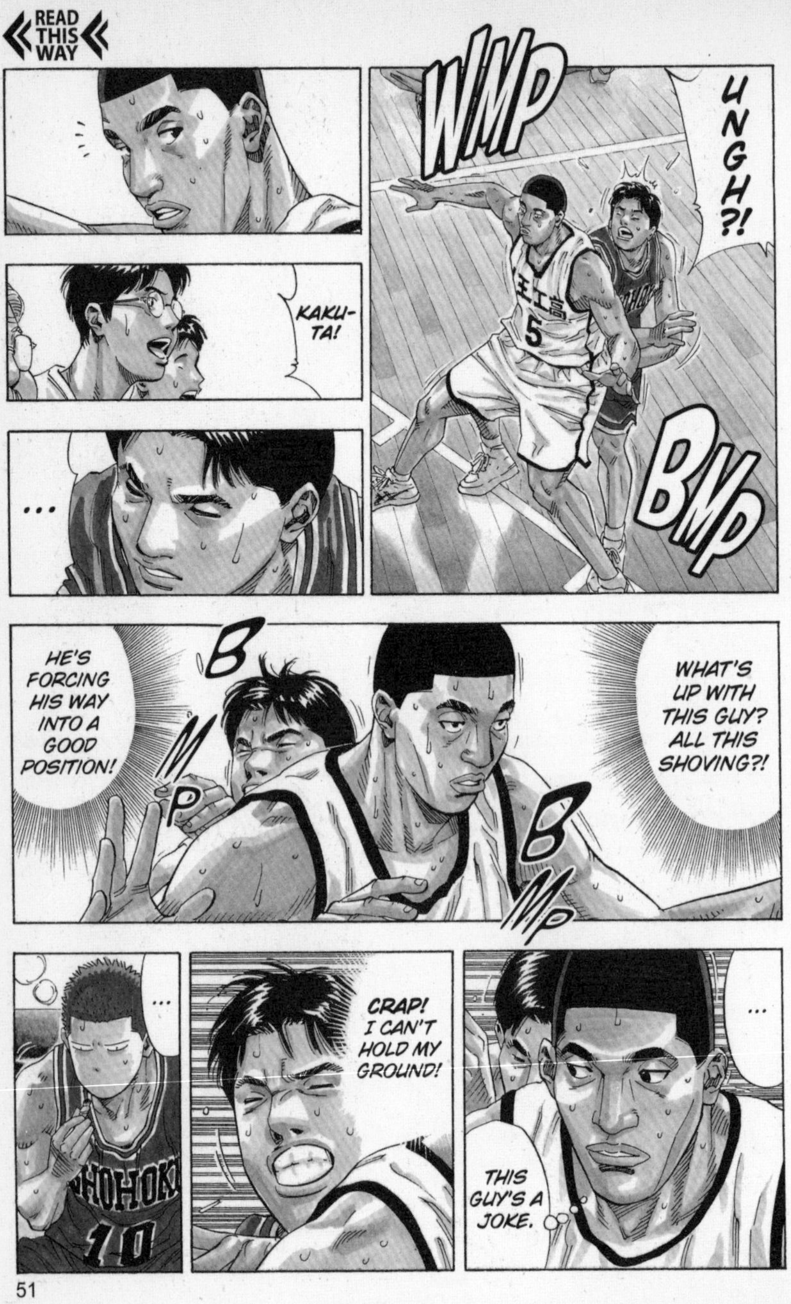
WMP
UNGH?!
BMP
KAKU-TA!
...
WHAT'S UP WITH THIS GUY? ALL THIS SHOVING?!
BMP
BMP
HE'S FORCING HIS WAY INTO A GOOD POSITION!
...
THIS GUY'S A JOKE.
CRAP! I CAN'T HOLD MY GROUND!
...

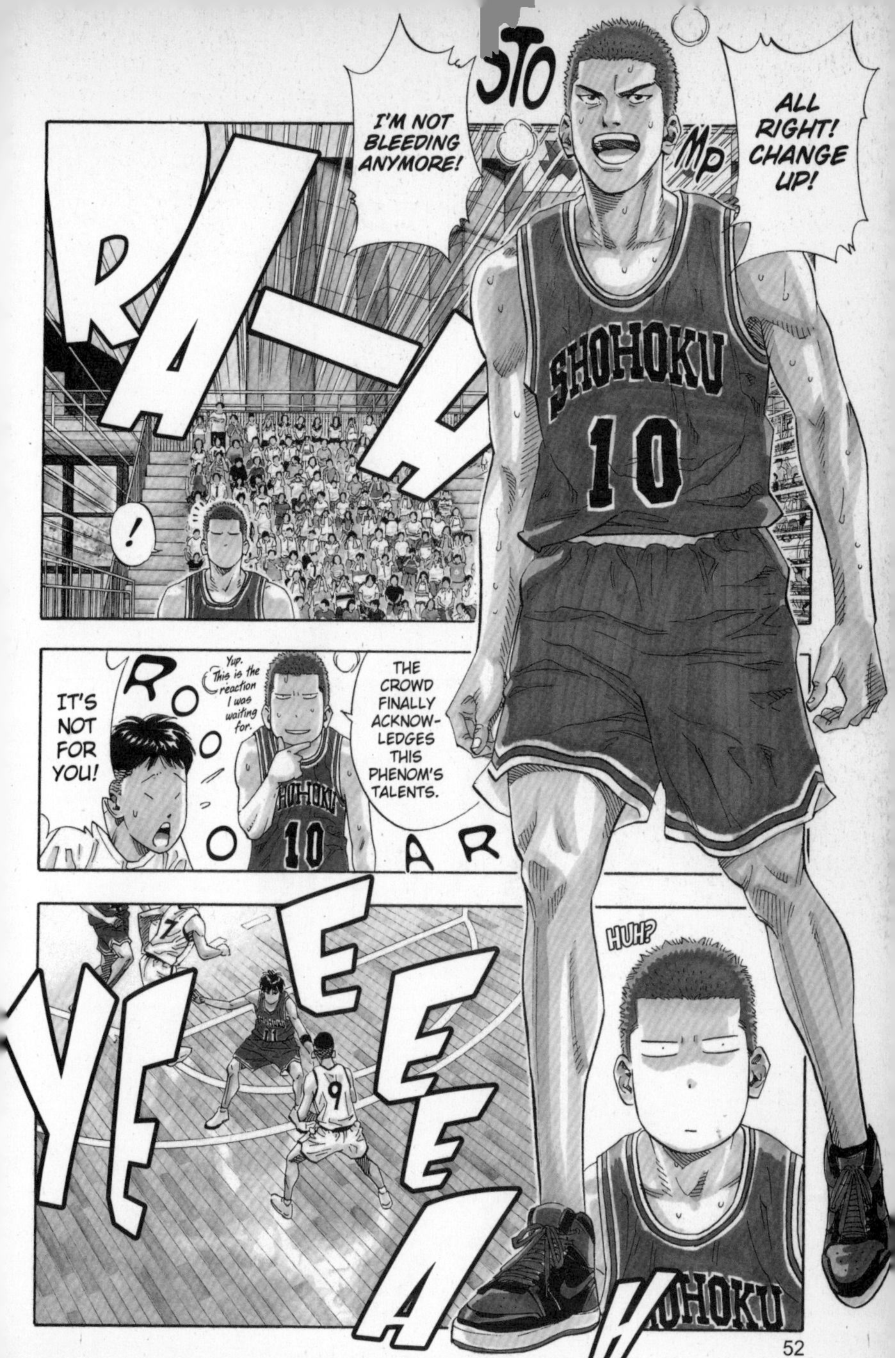
ALL RIGHT! CHANGE UP!
STO
MP
I'M NOT BLEEDING ANYMORE!
RA-A
!
THE CROWD FINALLY ACKNOW-LEDGES THIS PHENOM'S TALENTS.
Yup. This is the reaction I was waiting for.
IT'S NOT FOR YOU!
ROOOOAR
HUH?
YEEEEAH

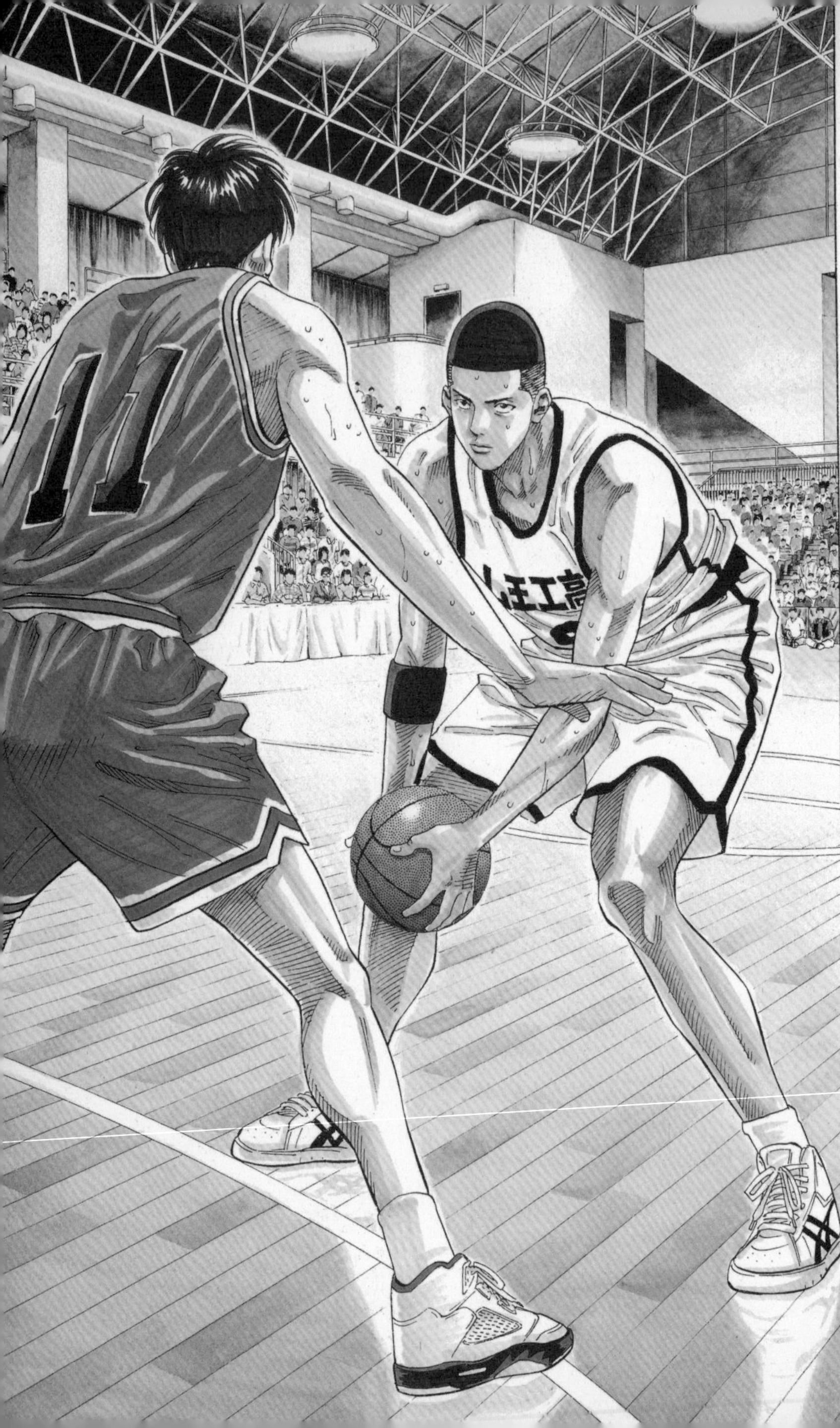

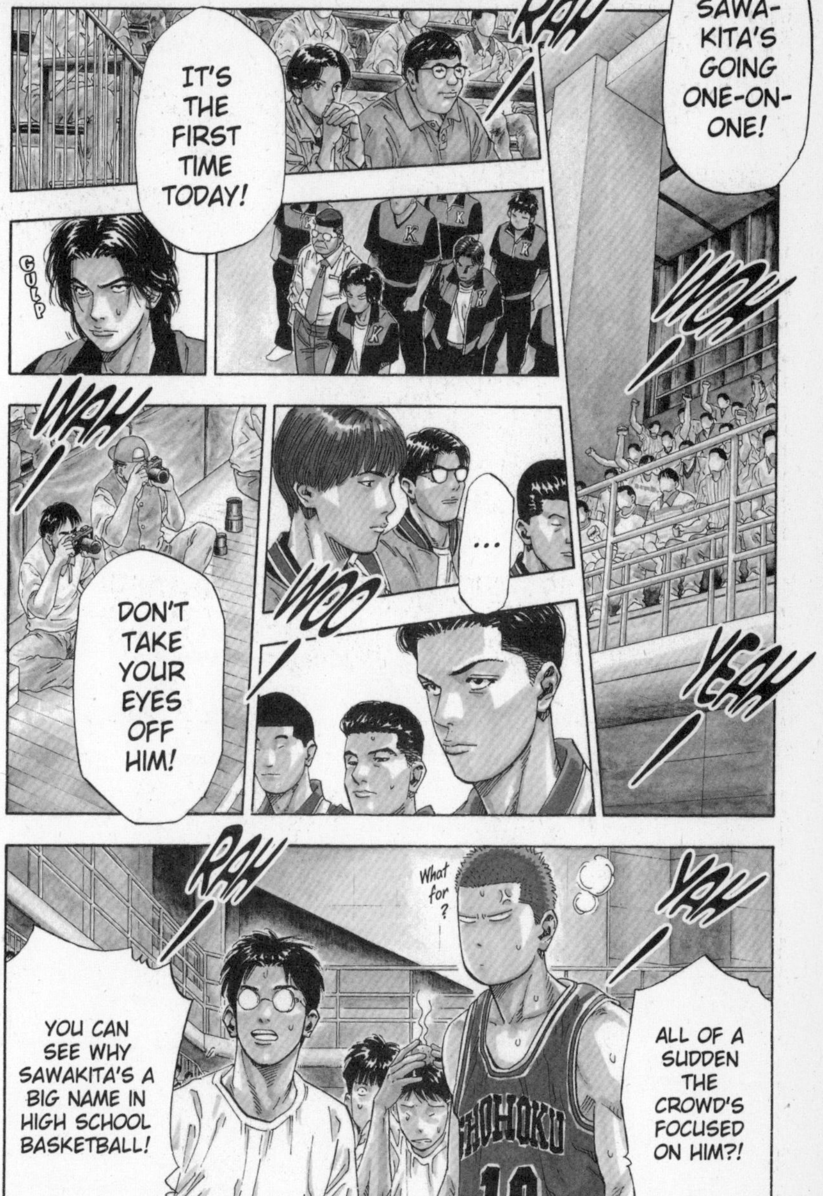
SAWA-KITA'S GOING ONE-ON-ONE!
RAH!
WOW!
YEAH!
IT'S THE FIRST TIME TODAY!
GULP
WAH!
...
WOO!
DON'T TAKE YOUR EYES OFF HIM!
YAH!
ALL OF A SUDDEN THE CROWD'S FOCUSED ON HIM?!
What for?
RAH!
YOU CAN SEE WHY SAWAKITA'S A BIG NAME IN HIGH SCHOOL BASKETBALL!

READ THIS WAY

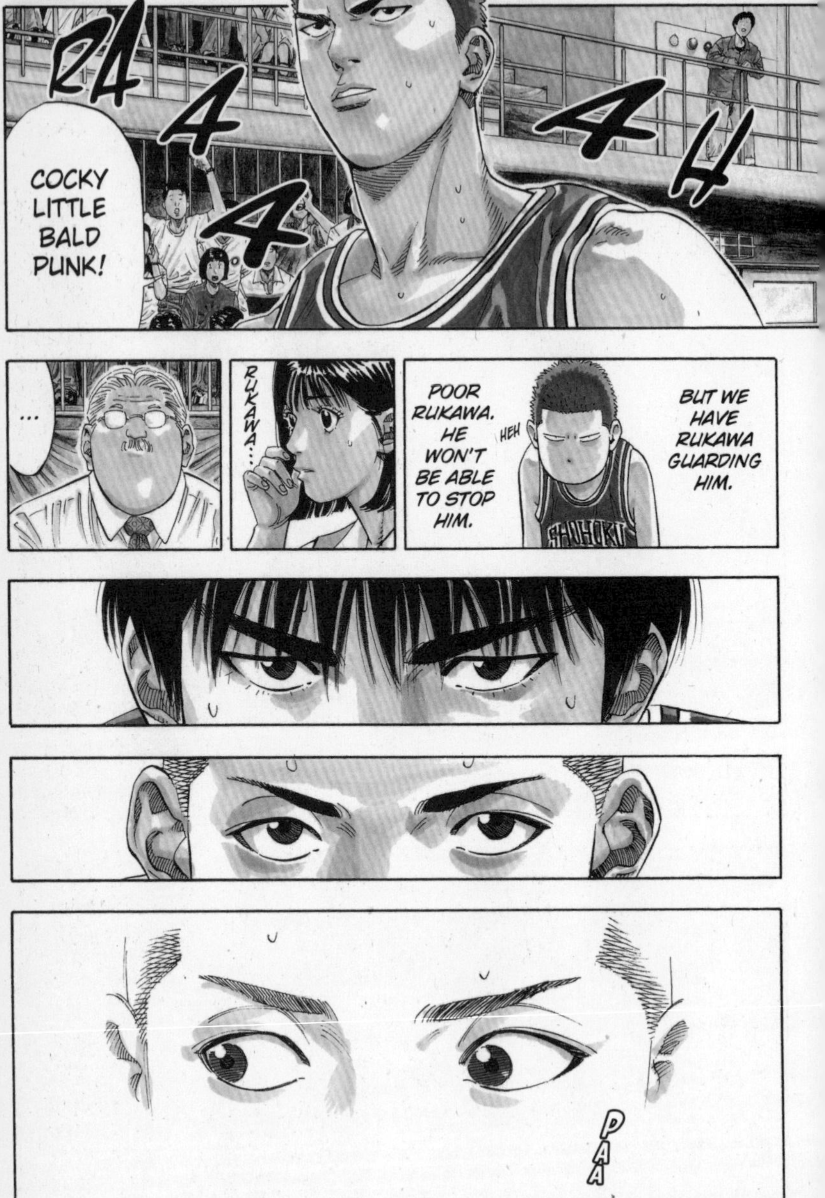
RAAAAH
COCKY LITTLE BALD PUNK!
BUT WE HAVE RUKAWA GUARDING HIM.
HEH
POOR RUKAWA. HE WON'T BE ABLE TO STOP HIM.
SHOHOKU
RUKAWA...
...
PAA

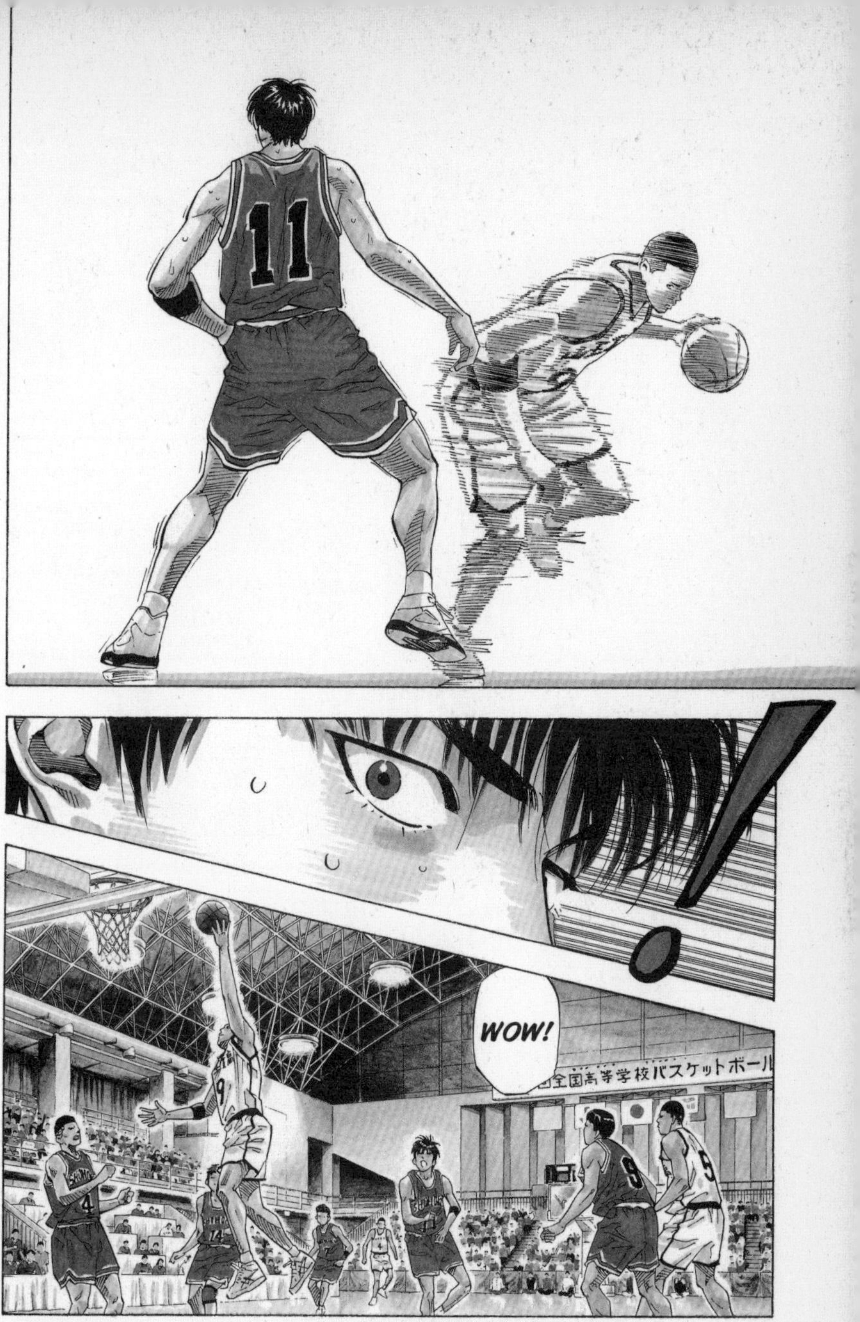
WOW!
全国高等学校バスケットボール
Sign: National High School Basketball Championship

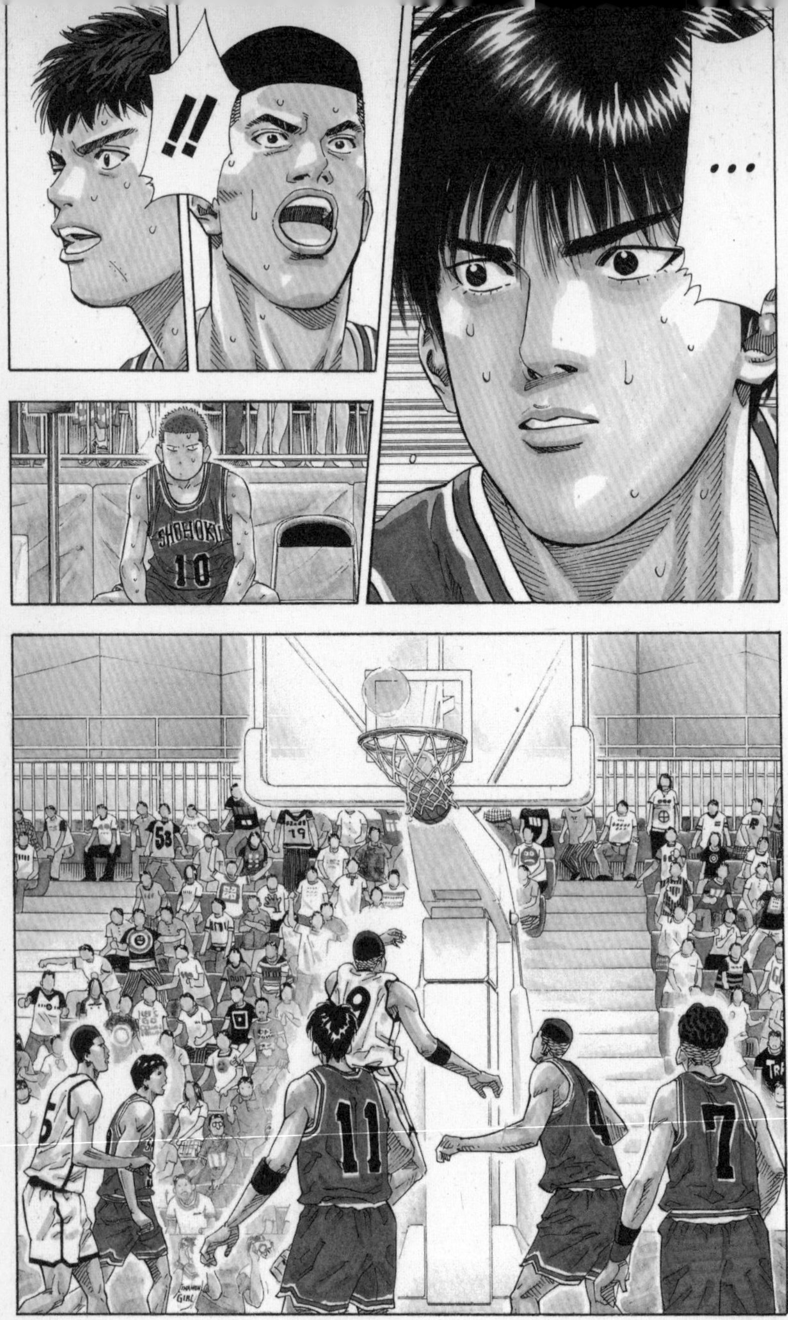
…
!!
SHOHOKU

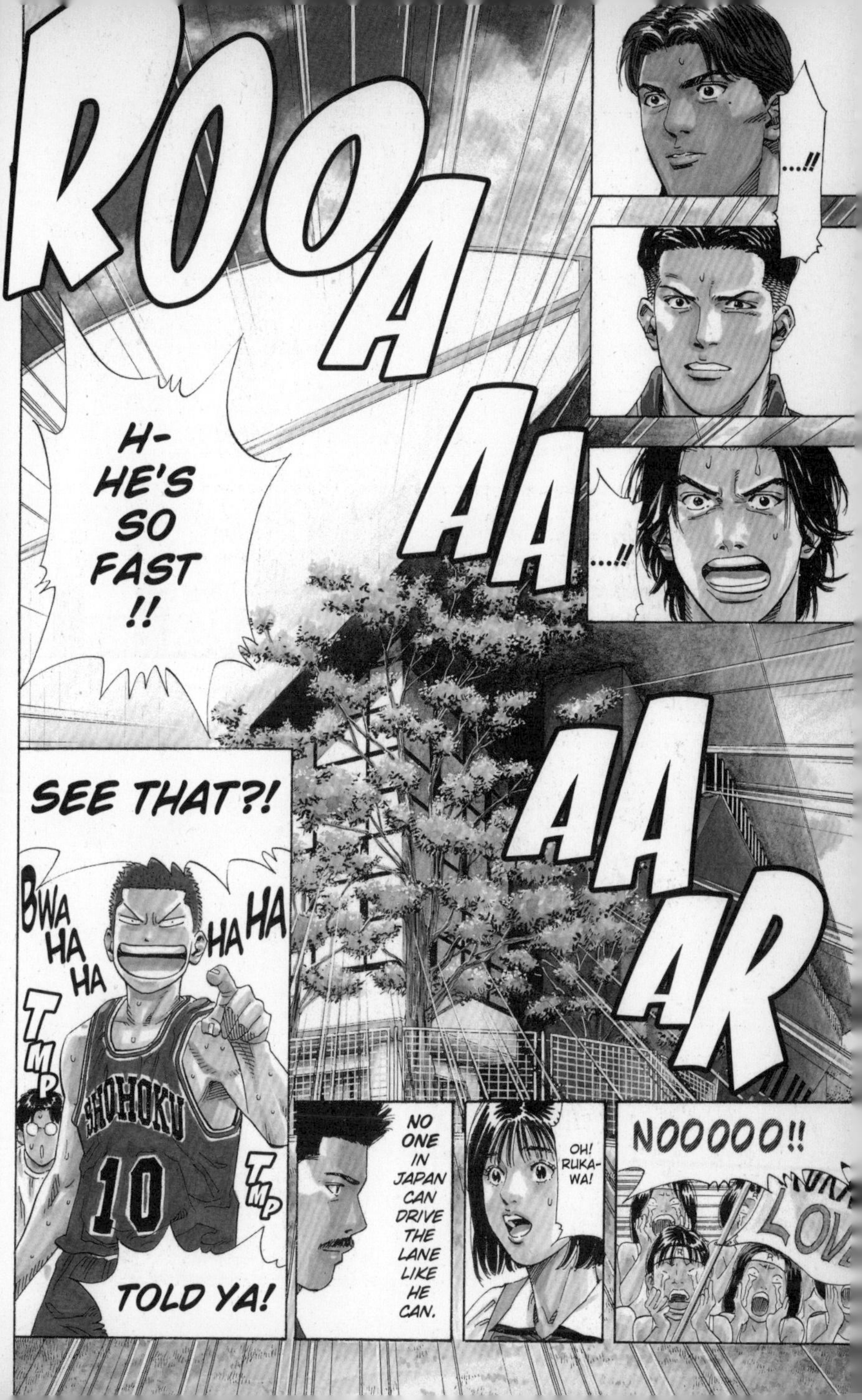
...!!
...!!
KOOAAAAAAAR
H-HE'S SO FAST!!
NOOOOO!!
OH! RUKAWA!
NO ONE IN JAPAN CAN DRIVE THE LANE LIKE HE CAN.
SEE THAT?!
BWA HA HA HA HA
TMP
TMP
TOLD YA!

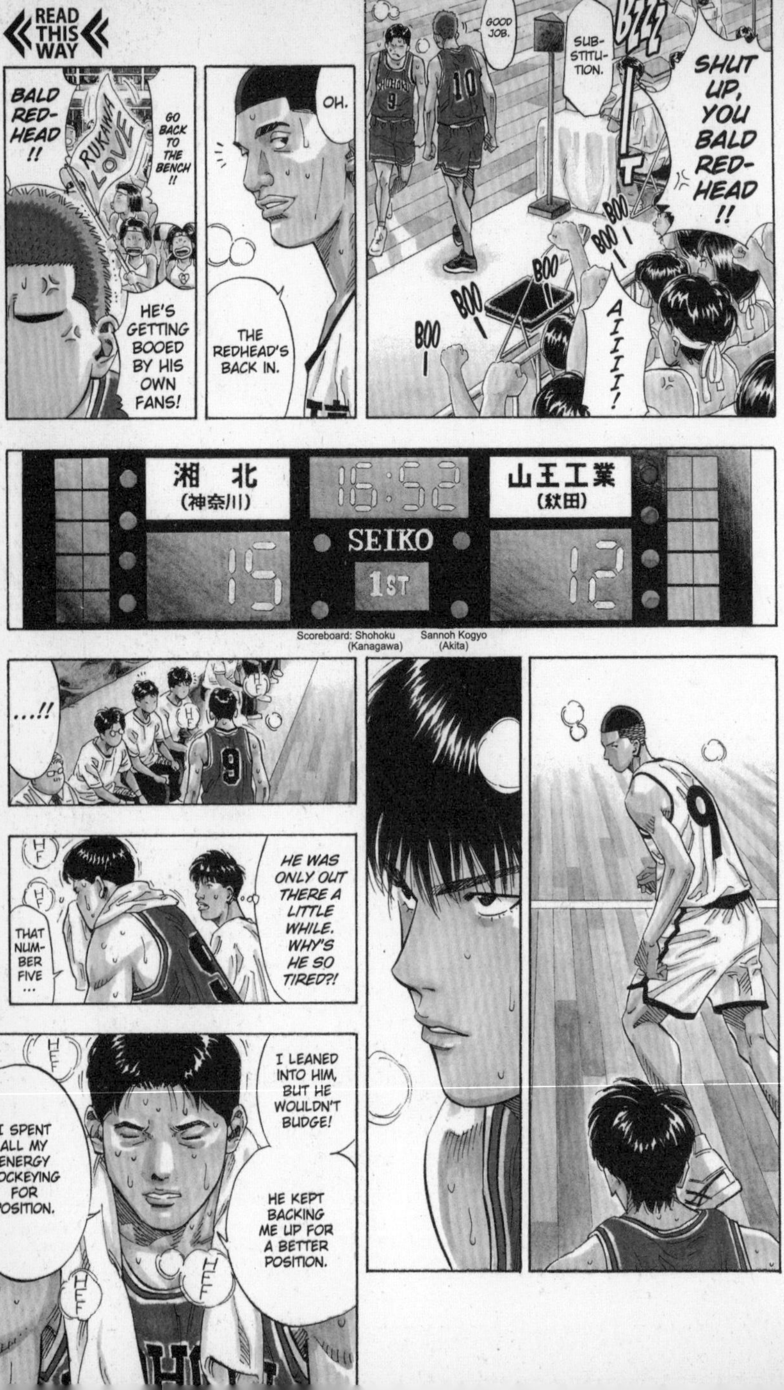
READ THIS WAY
SHUT UP, YOU BALD RED-HEAD!!
BZZZ
SUB-STITU-TION.
GOOD JOB.
BOO BOO BOO BOO BOO
AIIIII!
OH.
THE REDHEAD'S BACK IN.
GO BACK TO THE BENCH!!
BALD RED-HEAD!!
RUKAWA LOVE
HE'S GETTING BOOED BY HIS OWN FANS!
湘北
(神奈川)
16:52
山王工業
(秋田)
SEIKO
15
1ST
12
...!!
HE WAS ONLY OUT THERE A LITTLE WHILE. WHY'S HE SO TIRED?!
THAT NUM-BER FIVE...
I LEANED INTO HIM, BUT HE WOULDN'T BUDGE!
HE KEPT BACKING ME UP FOR A BETTER POSITION.
I SPENT ALL MY ENERGY JOCKEYING FOR POSITION.
Scoreboard: Shohoku (Kanagawa) Sannoh Kogyo (Akita)

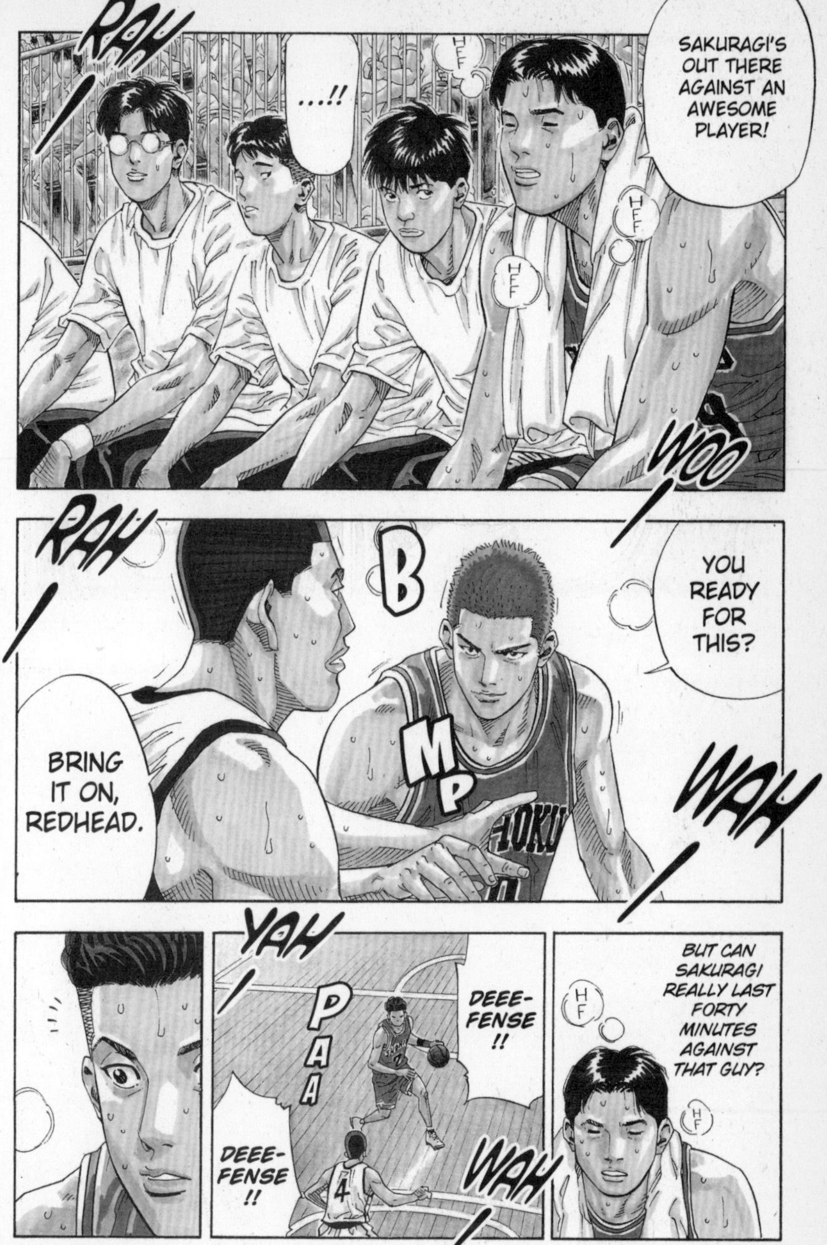
SAKURAGI'S OUT THERE AGAINST AN AWESOME PLAYER!
HFF
HFF
...!!
HFF
RAH
WOO
YOU READY FOR THIS?
B
MP
BRING IT ON, REDHEAD.
RAH
WAH
BUT CAN SAKURAGI REALLY LAST FORTY MINUTES AGAINST THAT GUY?
HF
HF
DEEE-FENSE !!
YAH
PAA
DEEE-FENSE !!
WAH

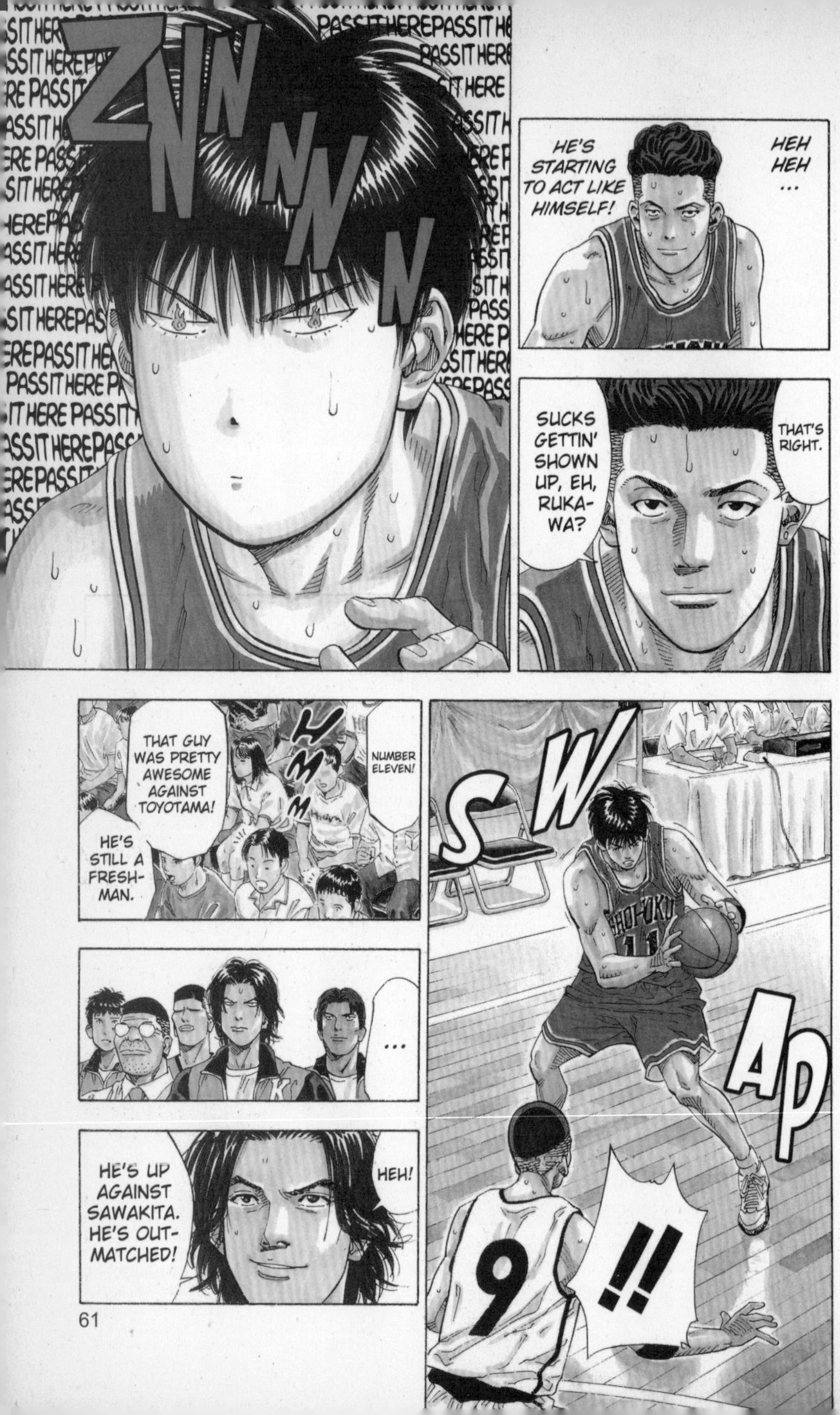
HEH HEH ...
HE'S STARTING TO ACT LIKE HIMSELF!
THAT'S RIGHT.
SUCKS GETTIN' SHOWN UP, EH, RUKAWA?
ZNNNNNNN
PASS IT HERE PASS IT HERE
SW
AP
!!
NUMBER ELEVEN!
THAT GUY WAS PRETTY AWESOME AGAINST TOYOTAMA!
HMMM
HE'S STILL A FRESHMAN.
...
HEH!
HE'S UP AGAINST SAWAKITA. HE'S OUT-MATCHED!

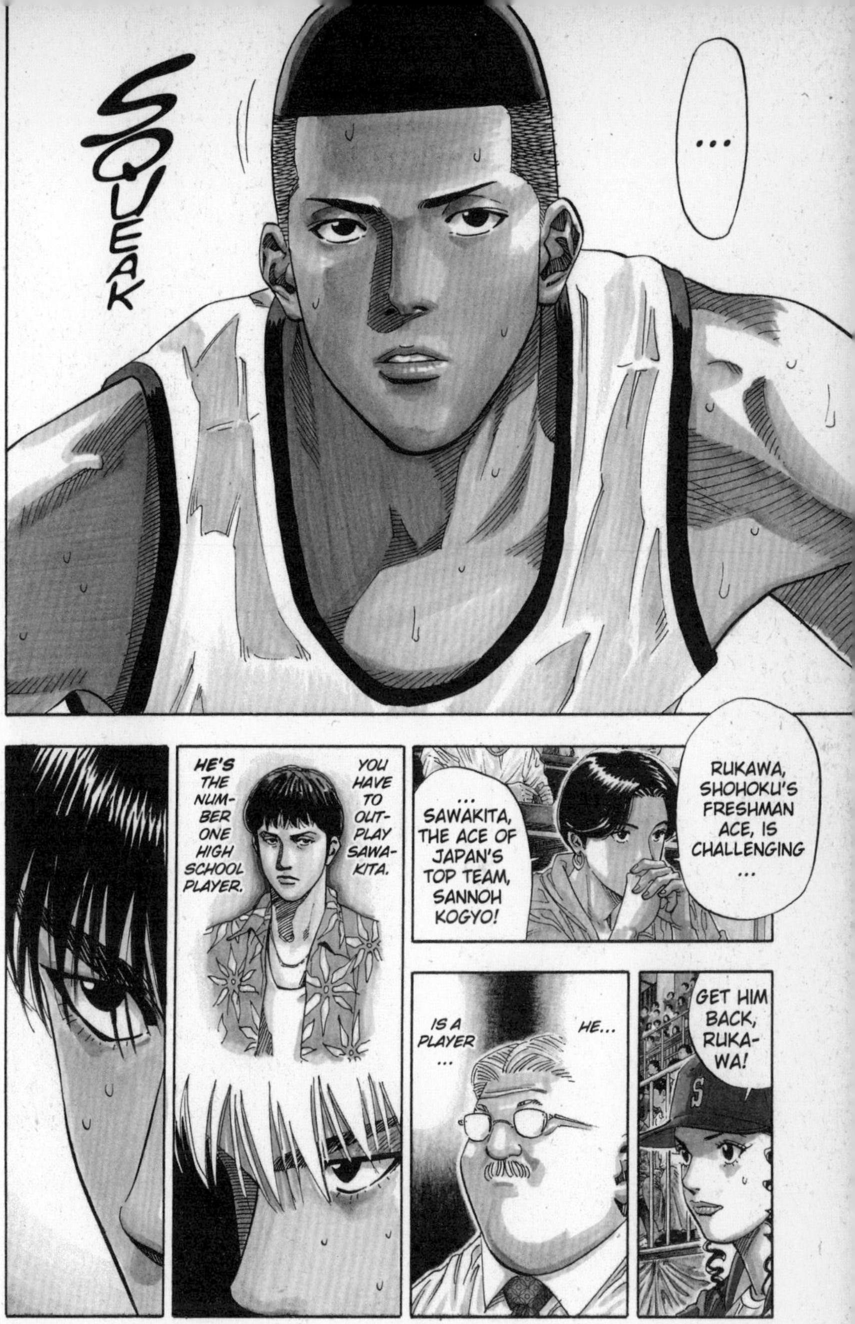
SQUEAK
...
RUKAWA, SHOHOKU'S FRESHMAN ACE, IS CHALLENGING ...
... SAWAKITA, THE ACE OF JAPAN'S TOP TEAM, SANNOH KOGYO!
GET HIM BACK, RUKAWA!
HE...
IS A PLAYER ...
YOU HAVE TO OUTPLAY SAWAKITA.
HE'S THE NUMBER ONE HIGH SCHOOL PLAYER.

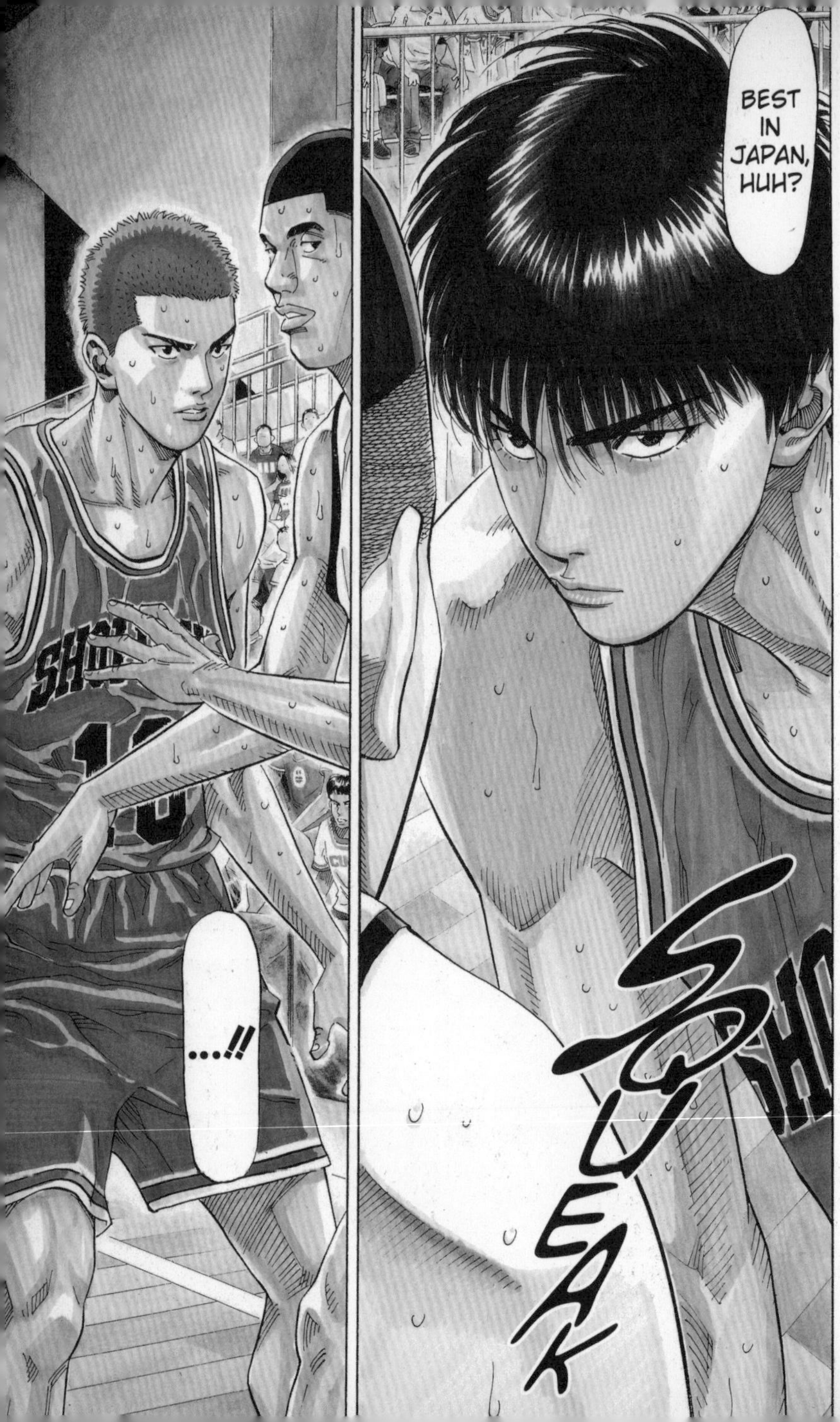
BEST IN JAPAN, HUH?
SQUEAK
...!!

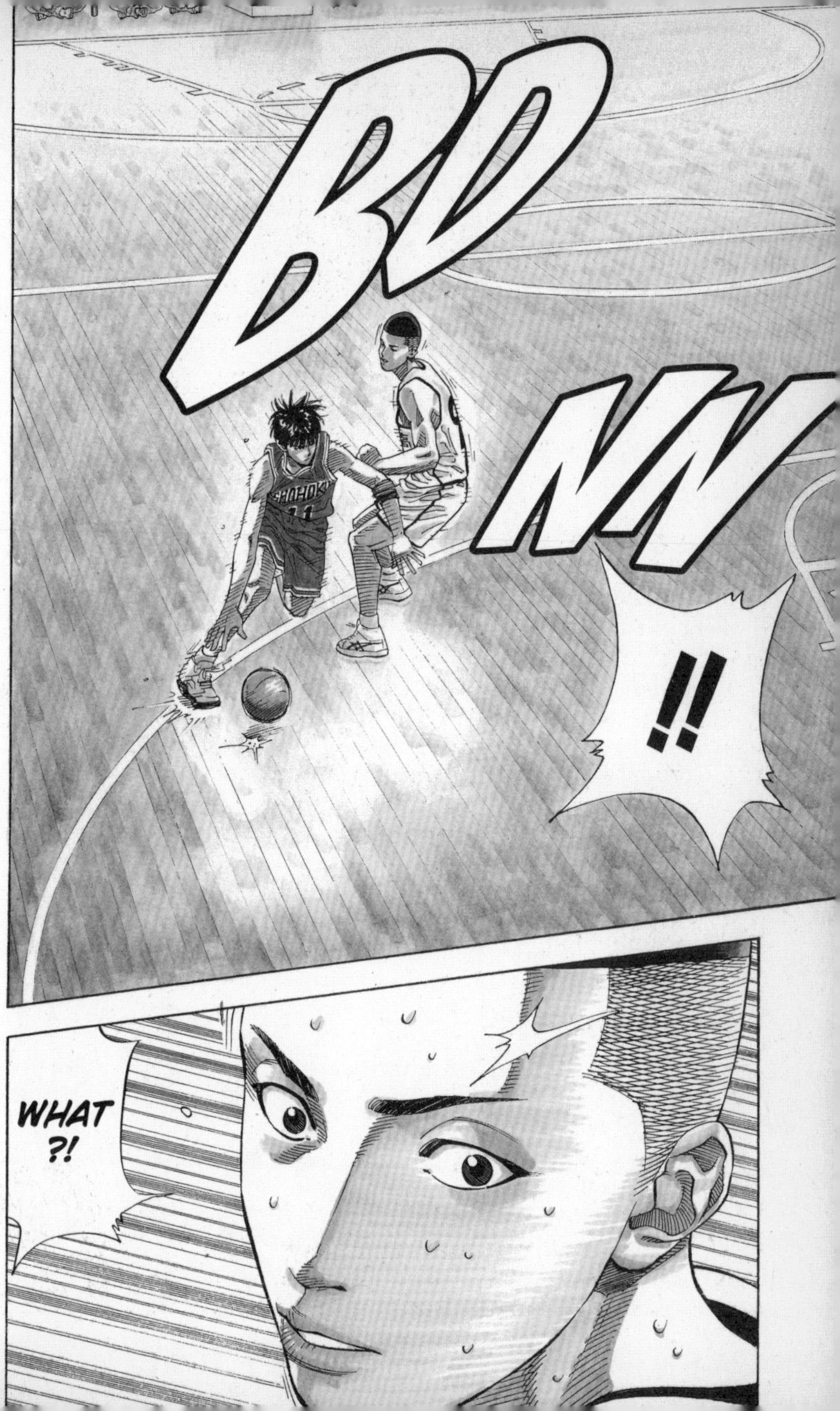
BDMN
!!
WHAT ?!

READ THIS WAY

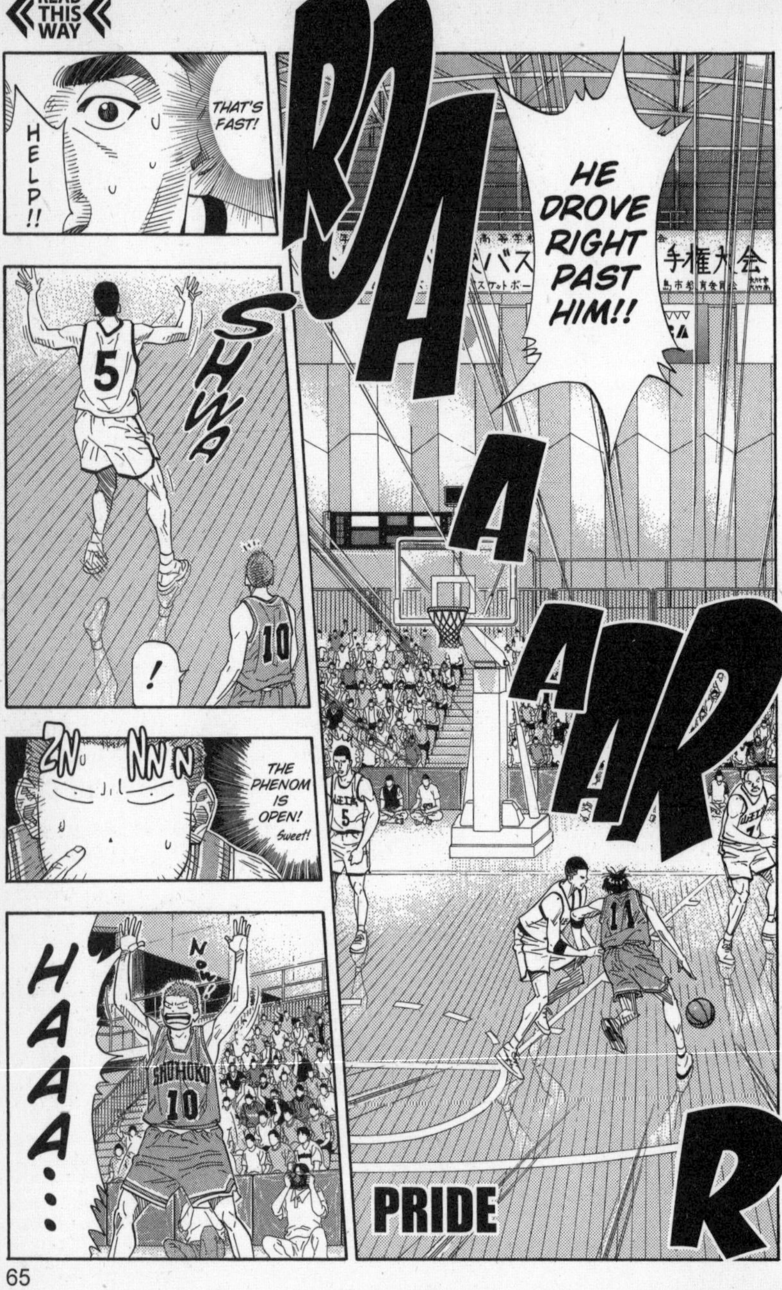

ROAAAARR
HE DROVE RIGHT PAST HIM!!
PRIDE
THAT'S FAST!
HELP!!
SHWA
!
ZNNNN
THE PHENOM IS OPEN!
Sweet!
NOW!
HAAAA...

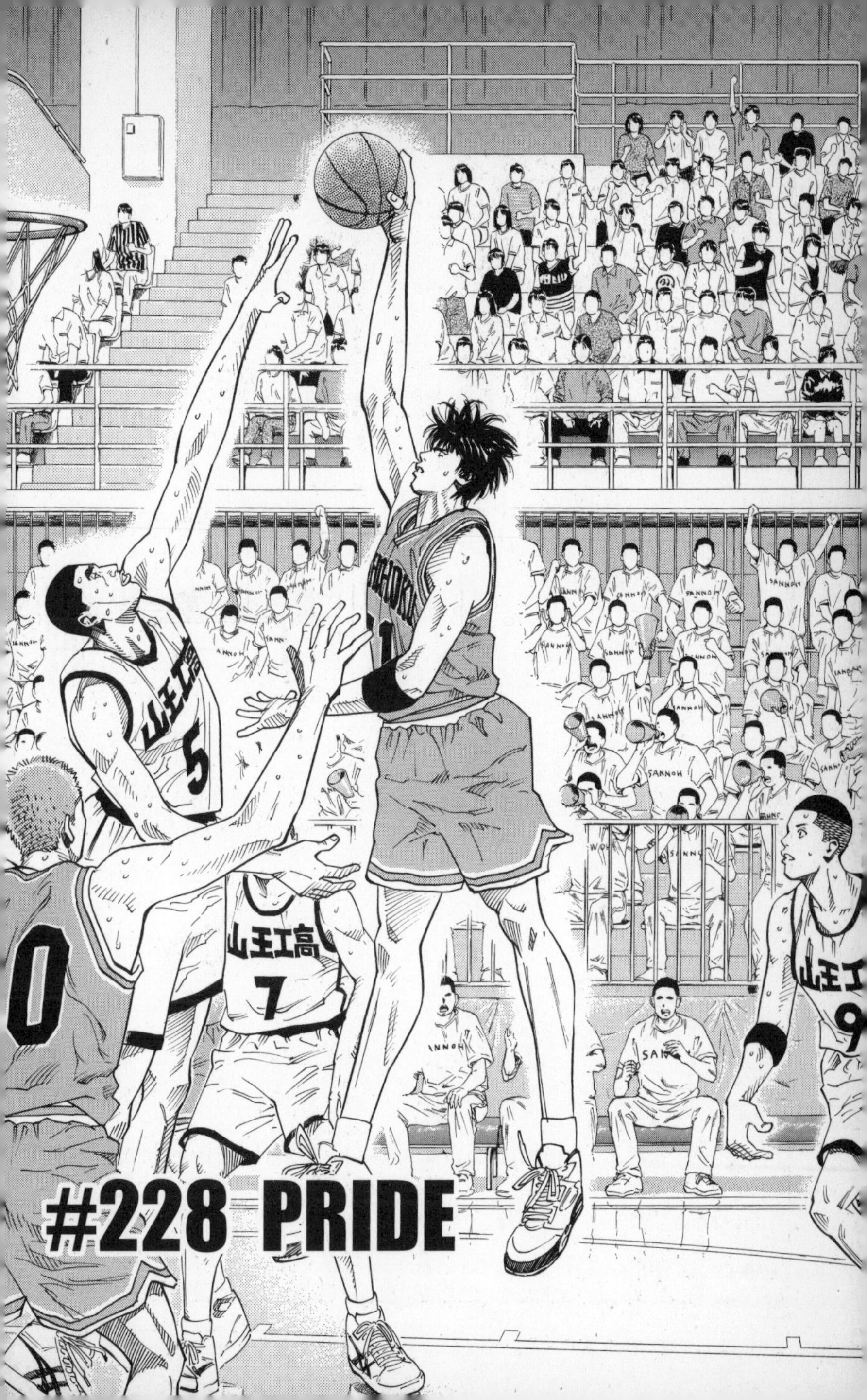
山王工高
#228 PRIDE

READ THIS WAY

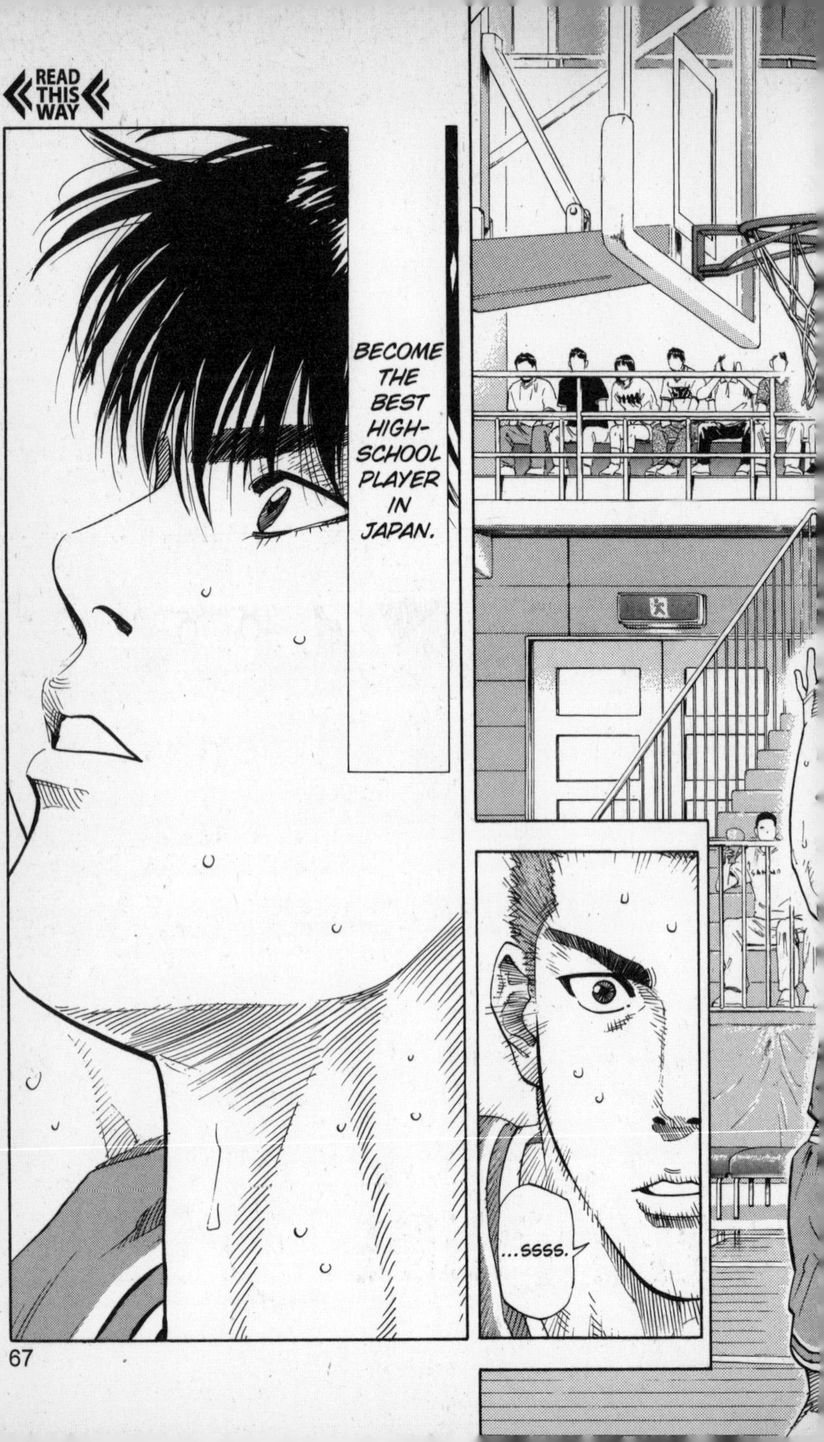
...SSSS.
BECOME THE BEST HIGH-SCHOOL PLAYER IN JAPAN.

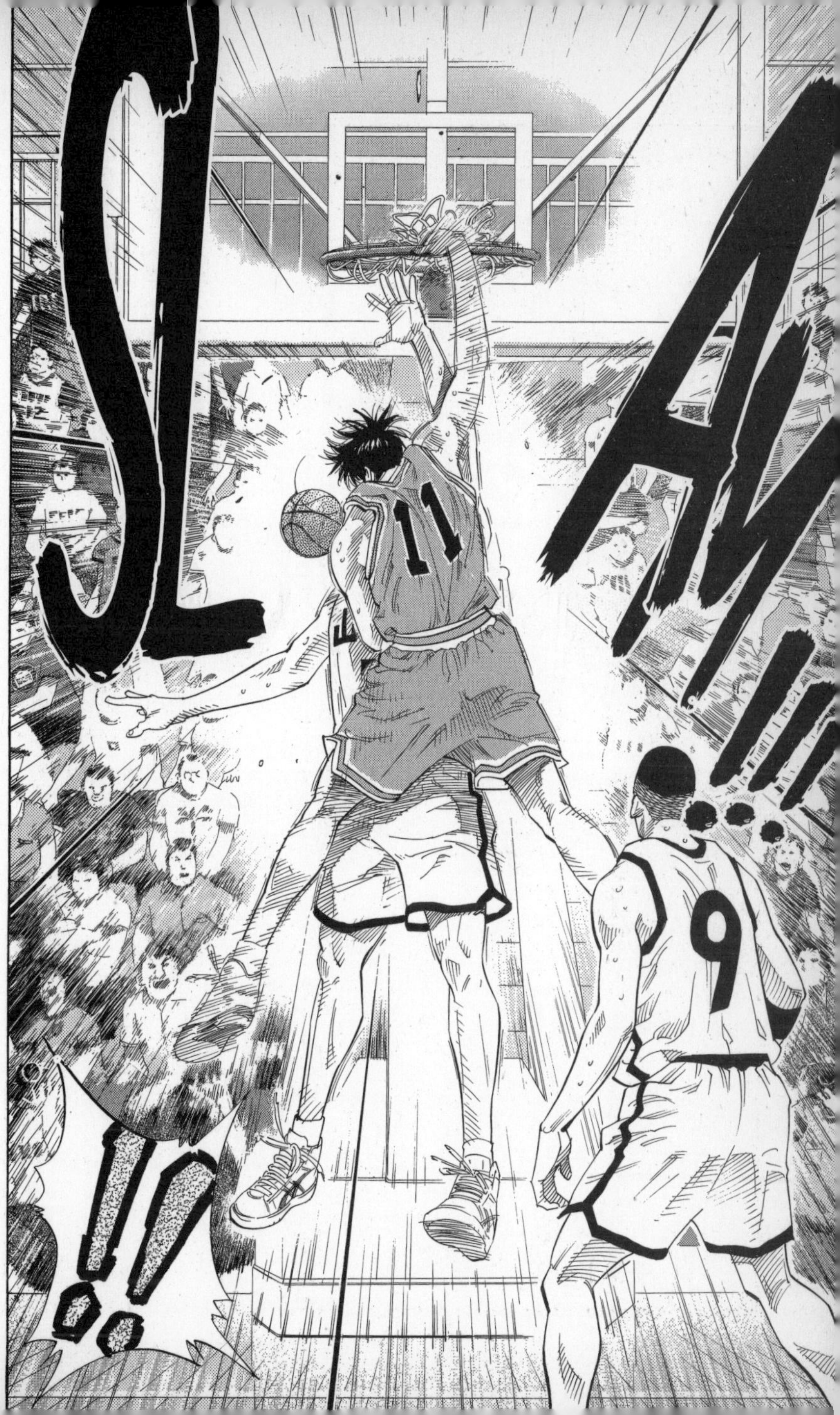
SLAM
!!

READ THIS WAY

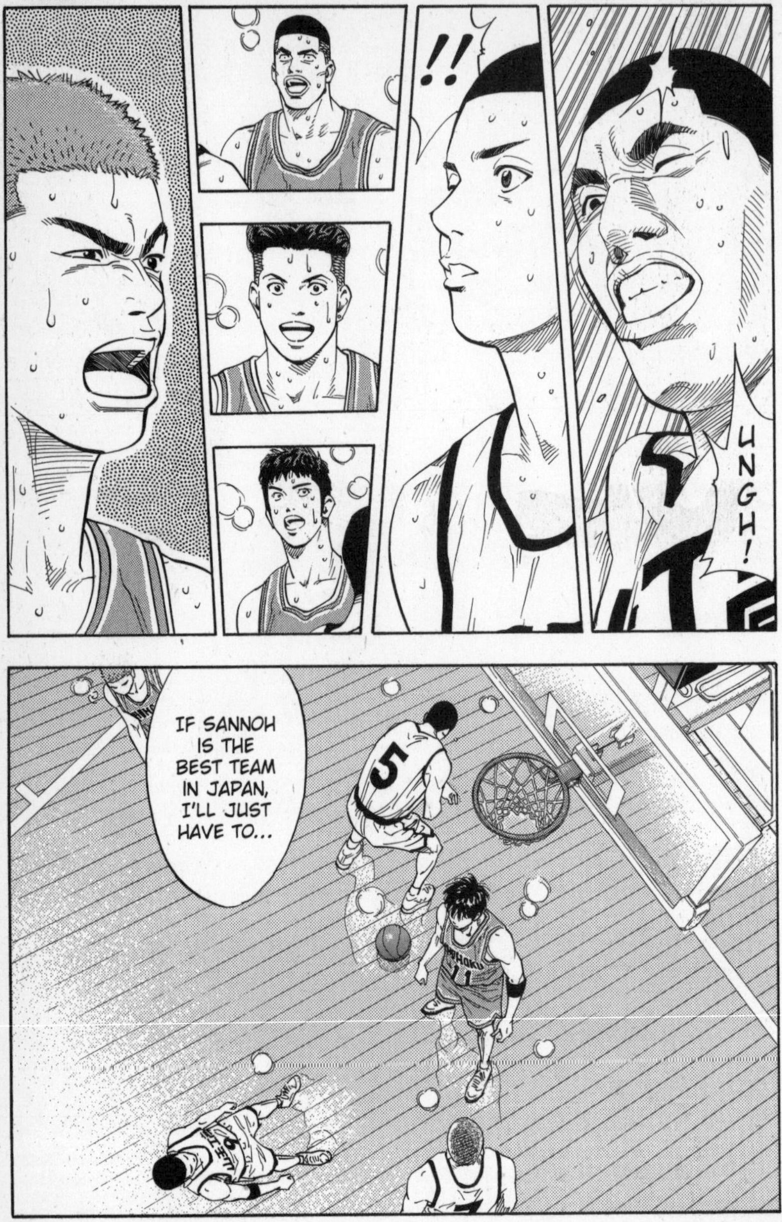
UNGH!
!!
IF SANNOH IS THE BEST TEAM IN JAPAN, I'LL JUST HAVE TO...

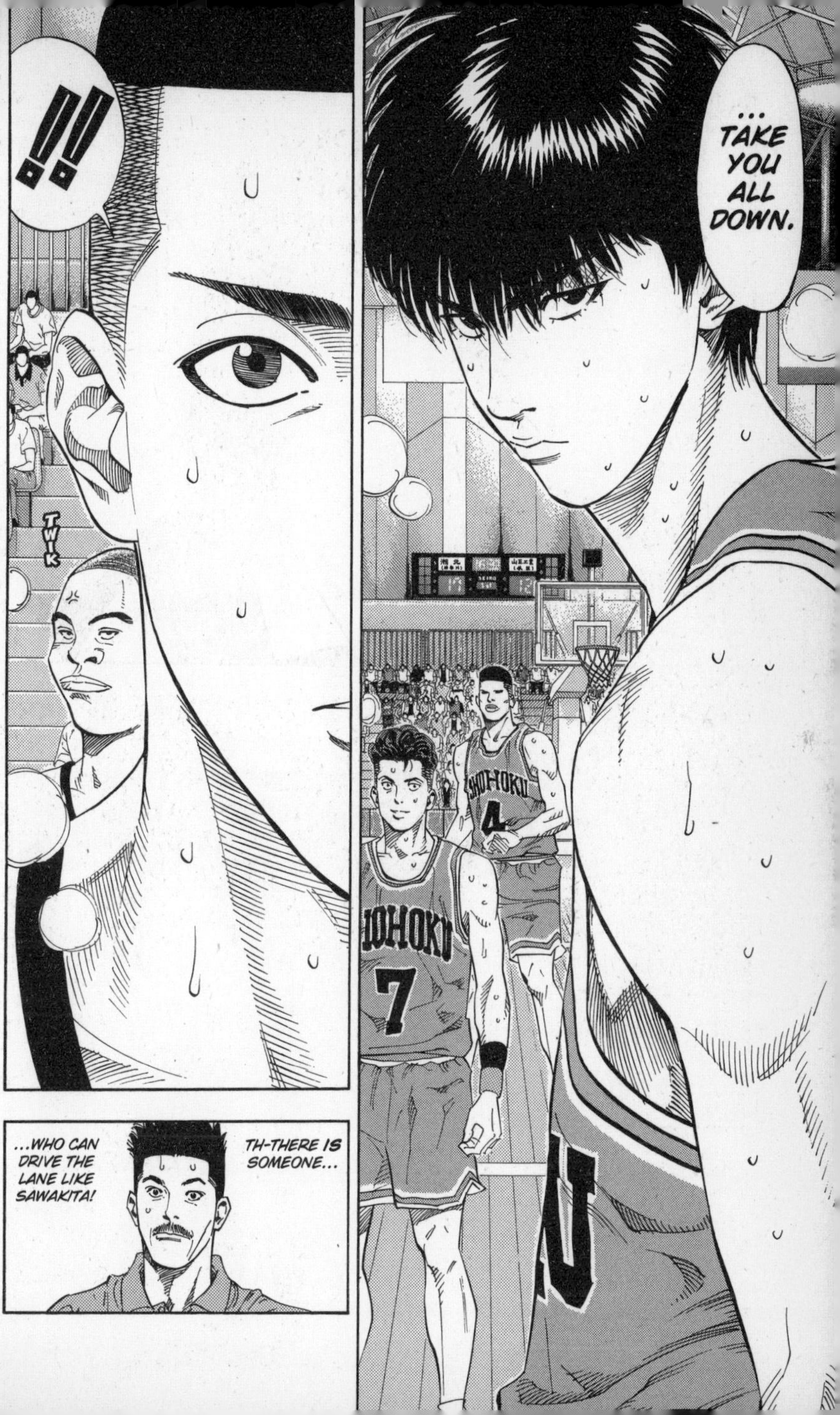
...TAKE YOU ALL DOWN.
!!
TWIK
TH-THERE IS SOMEONE...
...WHO CAN DRIVE THE LANE LIKE SAWAKITA!

READ THIS WAY

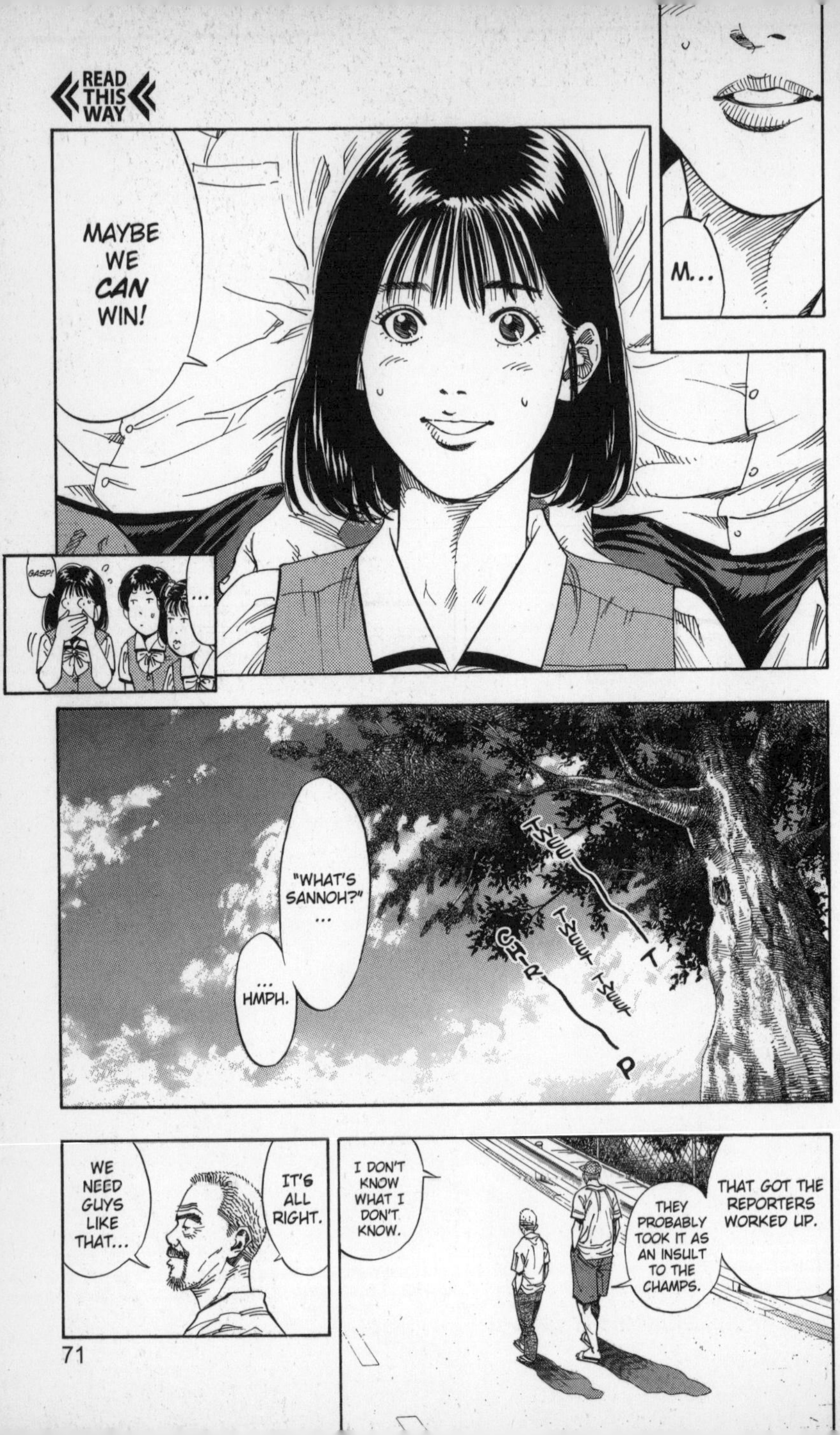
M...
MAYBE WE CAN WIN!
GASP!
...
"WHAT'S SANNOH?" ...
... HMPH.
TSEE-T
TSUUK TSUUK
CHI-R-P
THAT GOT THE REPORTERS WORKED UP.
THEY PROBABLY TOOK IT AS AN INSULT TO THE CHAMPS.
I DON'T KNOW WHAT I DON'T KNOW.
IT'S ALL RIGHT.
WE NEED GUYS LIKE THAT...

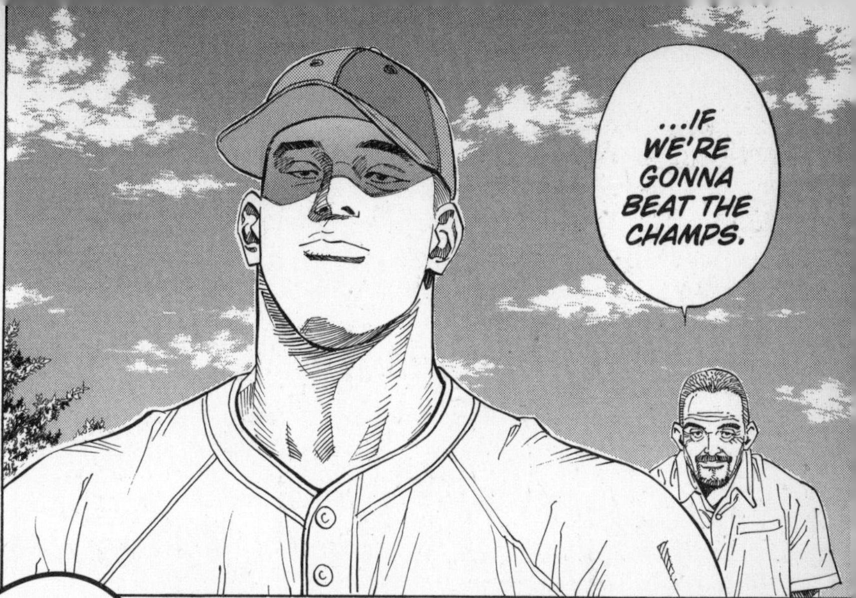
...IF WE'RE GONNA BEAT THE CHAMPS.

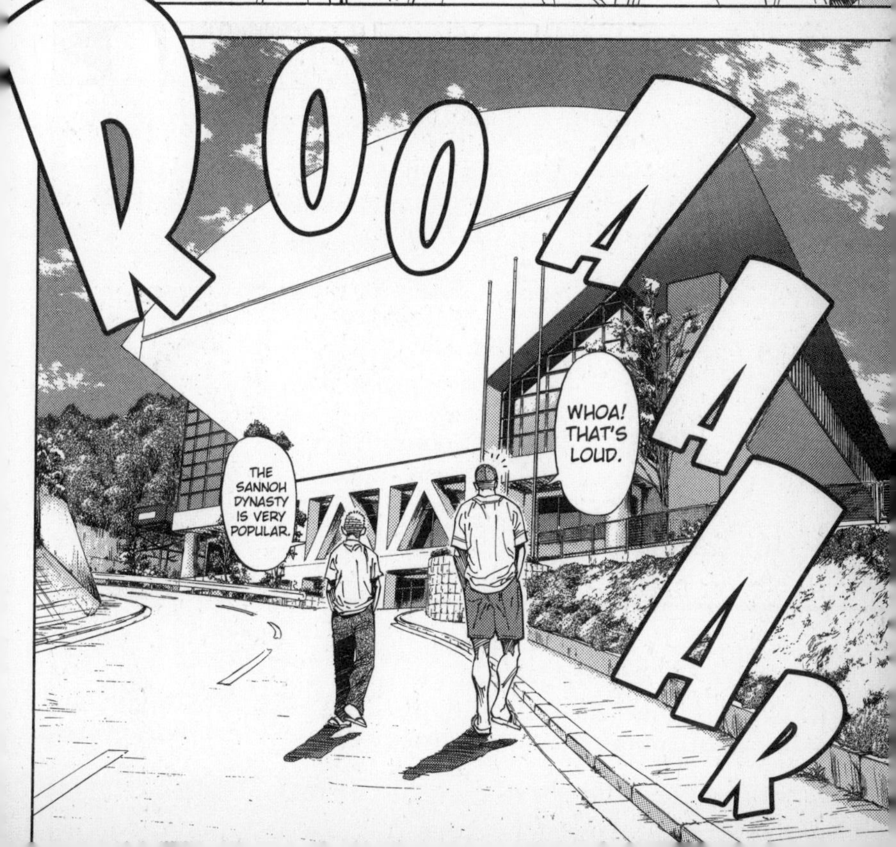
ROOAAAR
WHOA! THAT'S LOUD.
THE SANNOH DYNASTY IS VERY POPULAR.

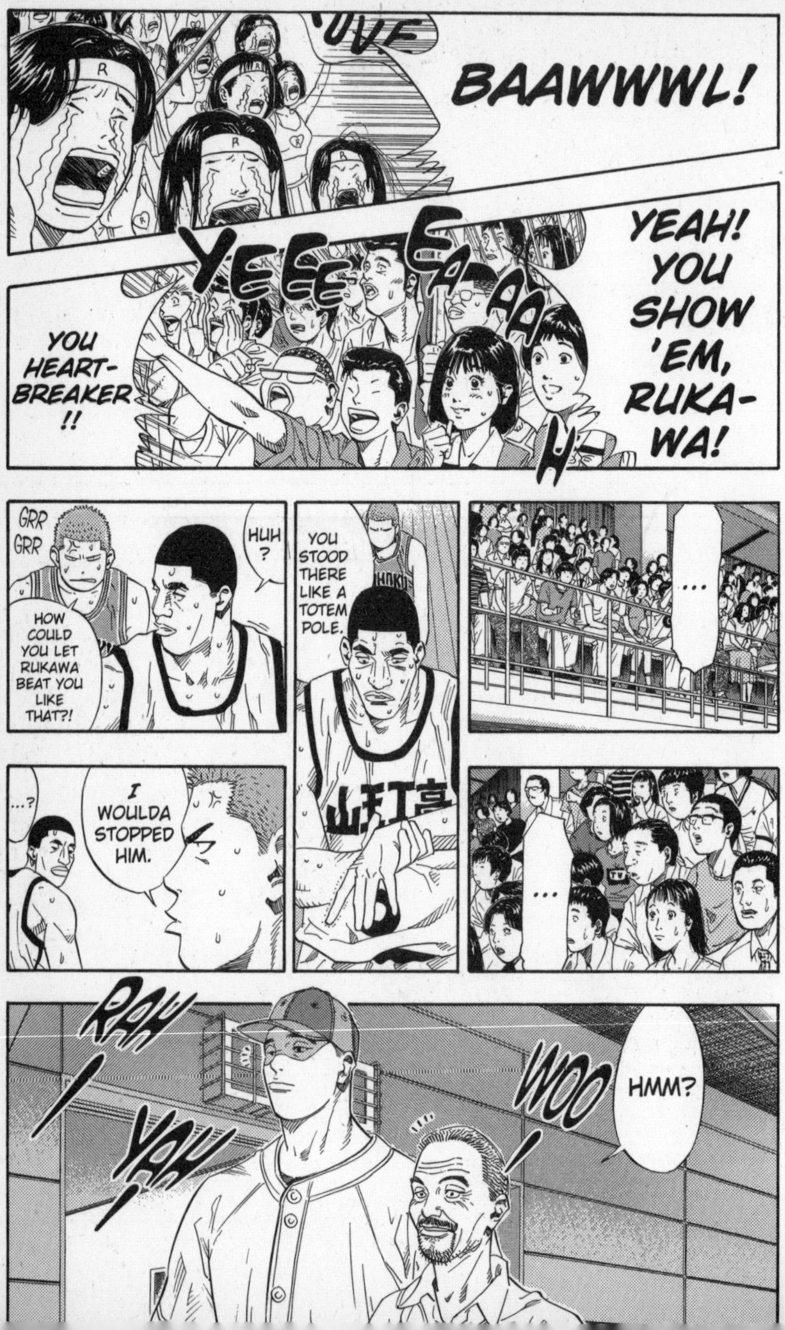
BAAWWWL!
YEAH! YOU SHOW 'EM, RUKAWA!
YEEEEAAAAH-
YOU HEART-BREAKER!!
...
YOU STOOD THERE LIKE A TOTEM POLE.
HUH?
GRR GRR
HOW COULD YOU LET RUKAWA BEAT YOU LIKE THAT?!
...
I WOULDA STOPPED HIM.
...?
HMM?
WOO!
RAH! YAH!

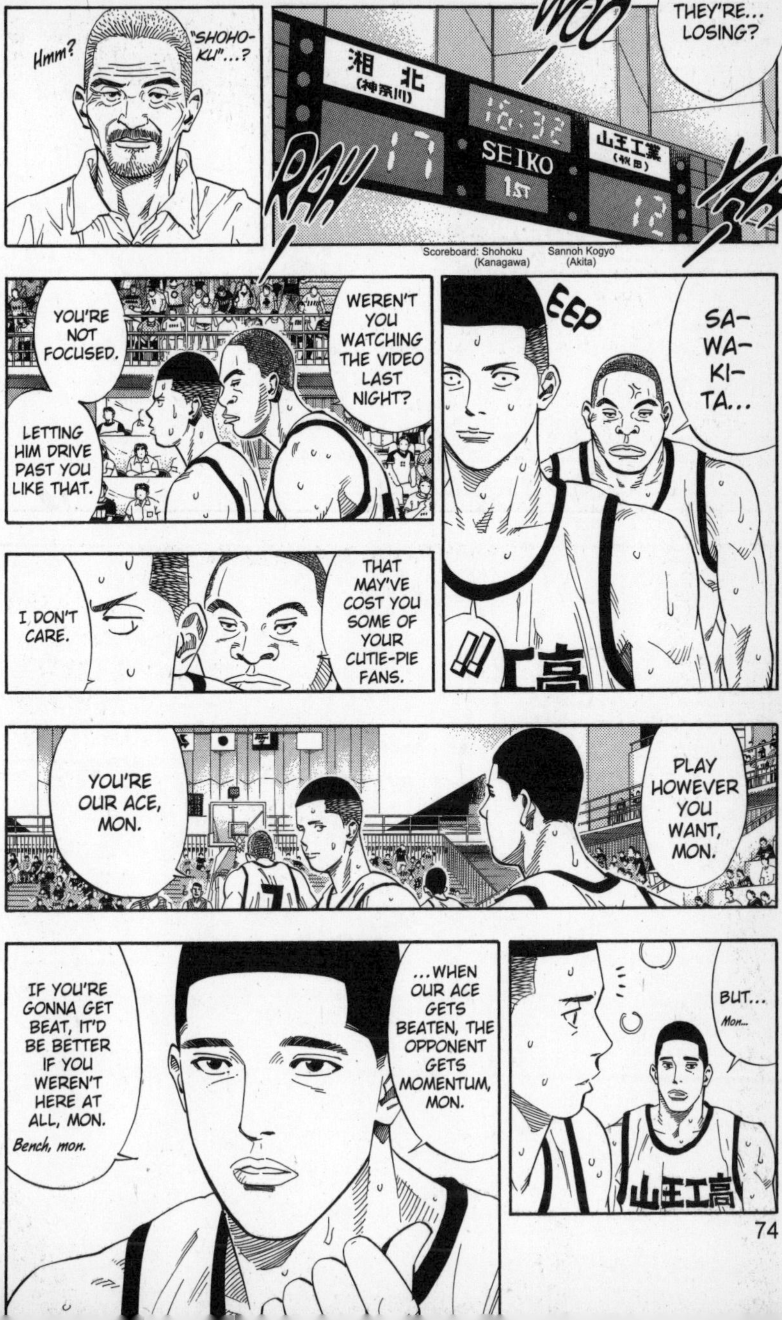
WOO
THEY'RE... LOSING?
YAH
湘北 (神奈川)
16:32
SEIKO
1ST
17
山王工業 (秋田)
12
RAH
Scoreboard: Shohoku (Kanagawa) Sannoh Kogyo (Akita)
"SHOHO-KU"...?
Hmm?
SA-WA-KI-TA...
EEP
!!
WEREN'T YOU WATCHING THE VIDEO LAST NIGHT?
YOU'RE NOT FOCUSED.
LETTING HIM DRIVE PAST YOU LIKE THAT.
THAT MAY'VE COST YOU SOME OF YOUR CUTIE-PIE FANS.
I DON'T CARE.
PLAY HOWEVER YOU WANT, MON.
YOU'RE OUR ACE, MON.
BUT...
Mon...
...WHEN OUR ACE GETS BEATEN, THE OPPONENT GETS MOMENTUM, MON.
IF YOU'RE GONNA GET BEAT, IT'D BE BETTER IF YOU WEREN'T HERE AT ALL, MON.
Bench, mon.

READ THIS WAY

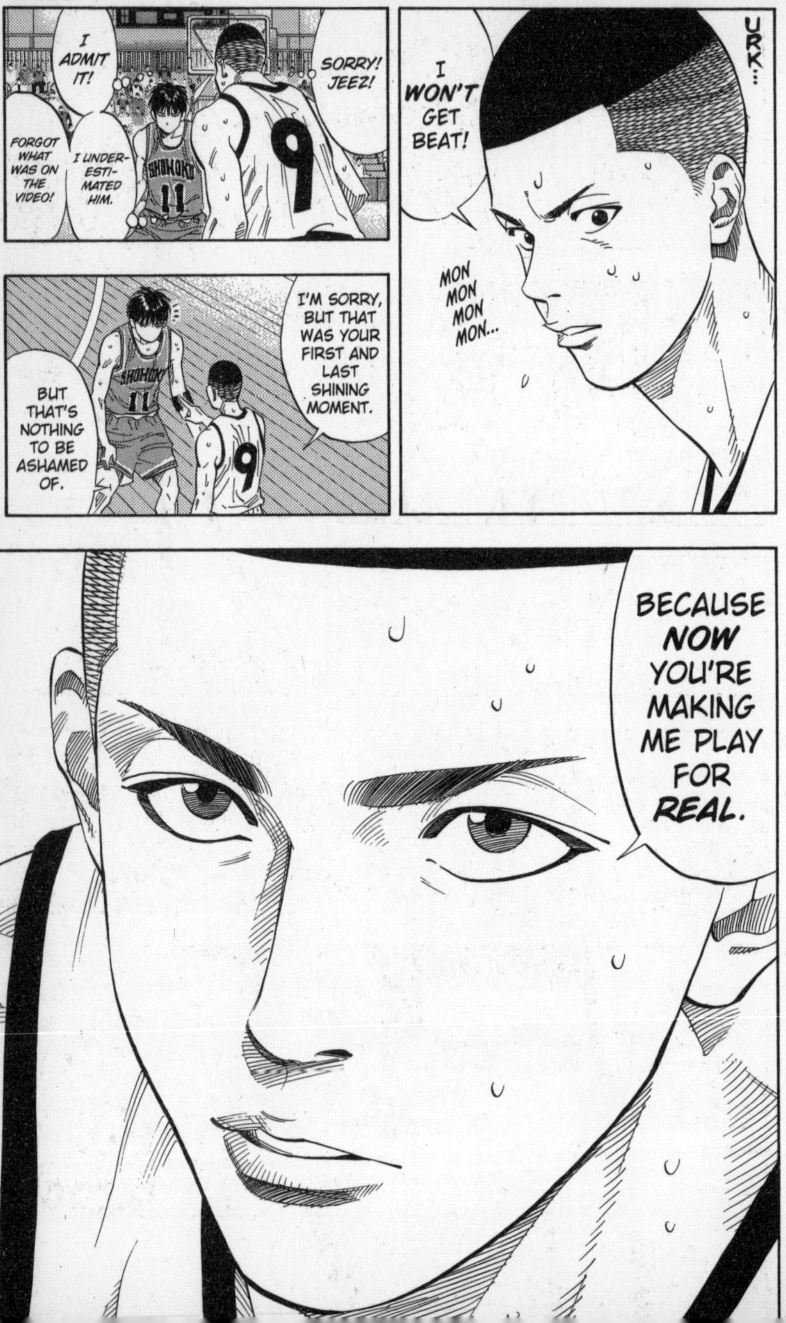
URK...
I WON'T GET BEAT!
MON MON MON MON...
SORRY! JEEZ!
I ADMIT IT!
I UNDER-ESTI-MATED HIM.
FORGOT WHAT WAS ON THE VIDEO!
I'M SORRY, BUT THAT WAS YOUR FIRST AND LAST SHINING MOMENT.
BUT THAT'S NOTHING TO BE ASHAMED OF.
BECAUSE NOW YOU'RE MAKING ME PLAY FOR REAL.

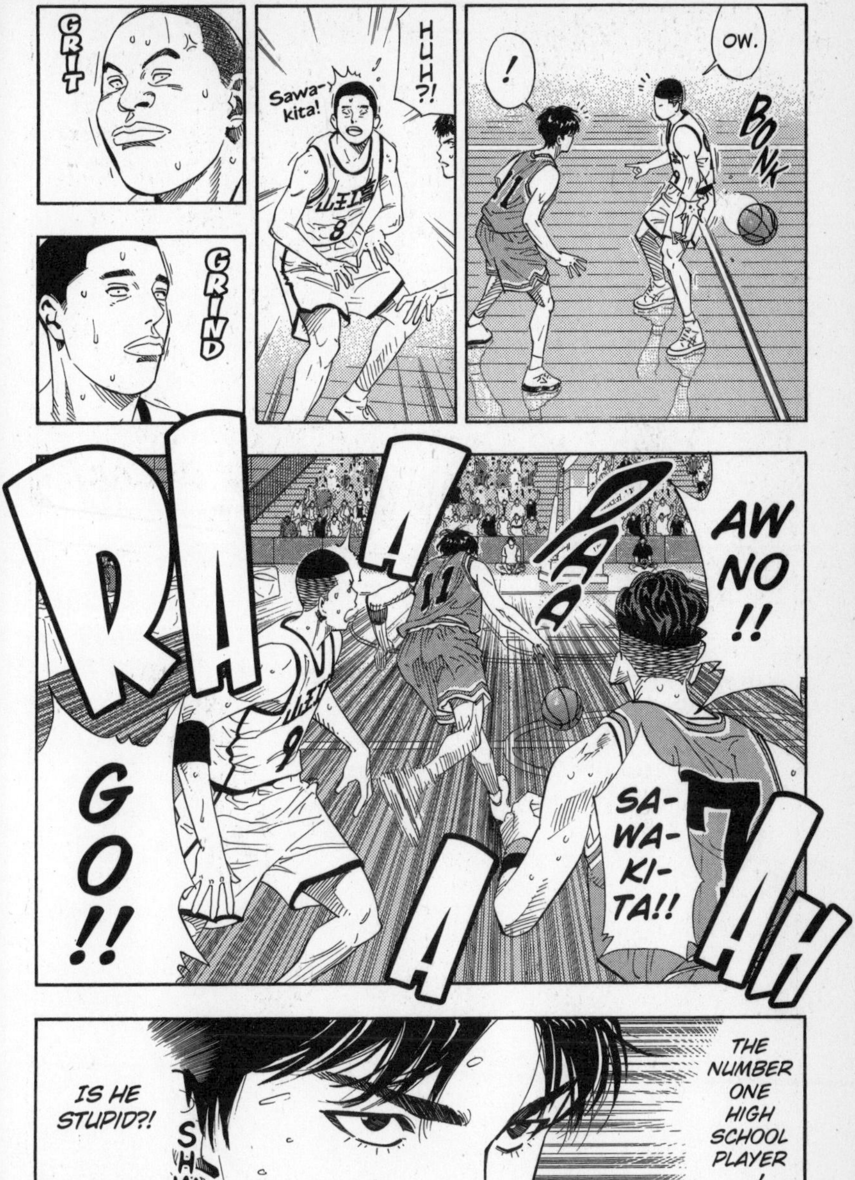
OW.
!
BONK
HUH?!
Sawa-kita!
GRIT
GRIND
AW NO!!
RAA
SA-WA-KI-TA!!
AAAH
A
RA
GO GO!!
THE NUMBER ONE HIGH SCHOOL PLAYER ...!
SHWN
IS HE STUPID?!

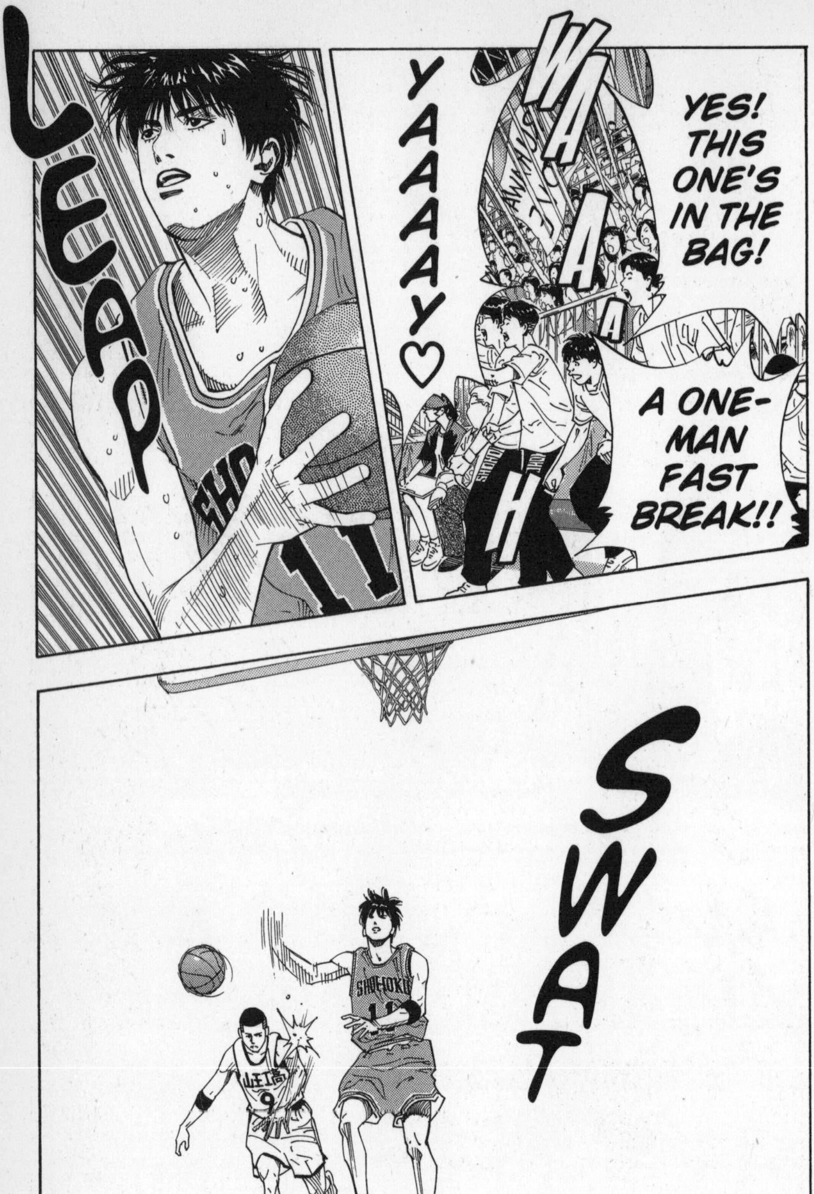
WAAAH
YAAAAAY♡
YES! THIS ONE'S IN THE BAG!
A ONE-MAN FAST BREAK!!
LEAP
SWAT

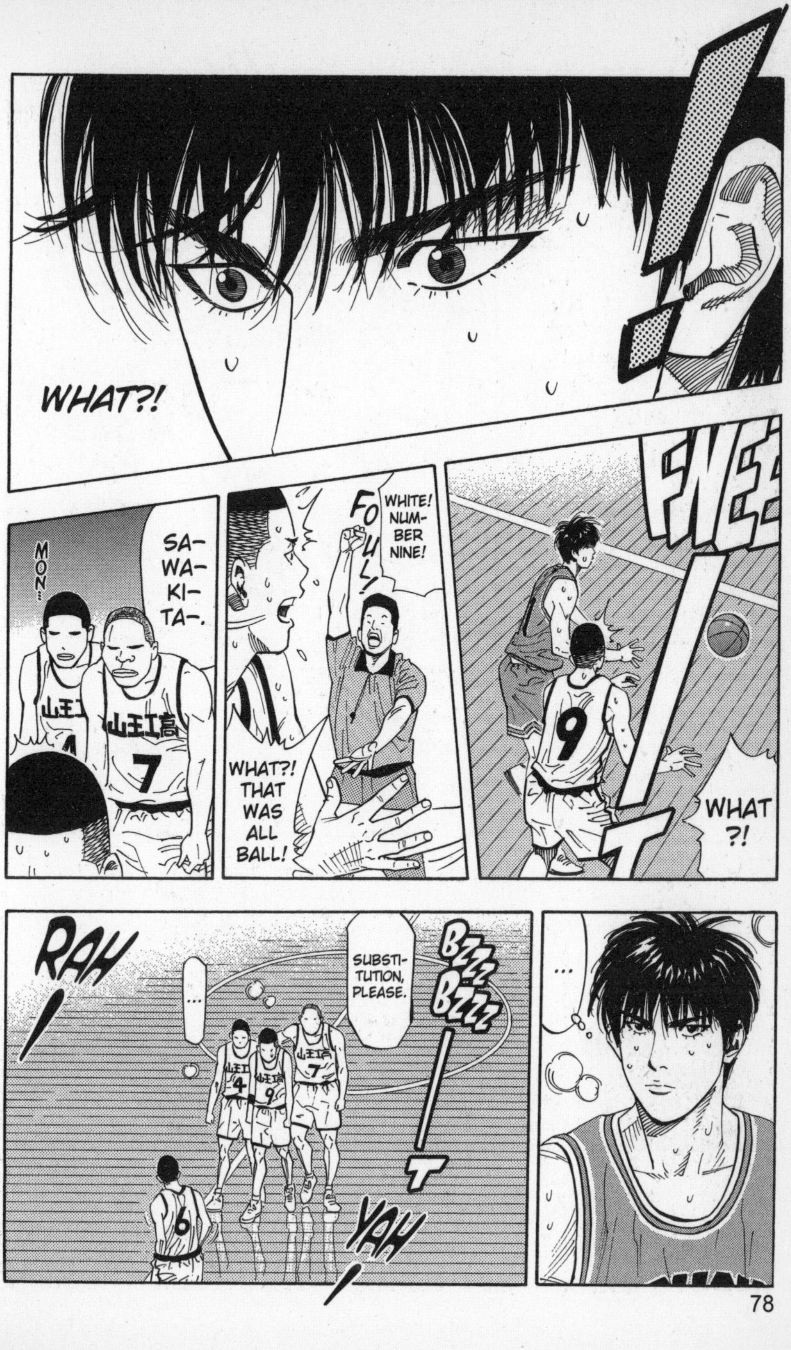
!
WHAT?!
FWEE T
WHAT?!
FOUL!
WHITE! NUMBER NINE!
WHAT?! THAT WAS ALL BALL!
SA-WA-KI-TA-.
MON...
...
BZZZ BZZZ T
SUBSTITUTION, PLEASE.
...
RAH!
YAH!

READ THIS WAY

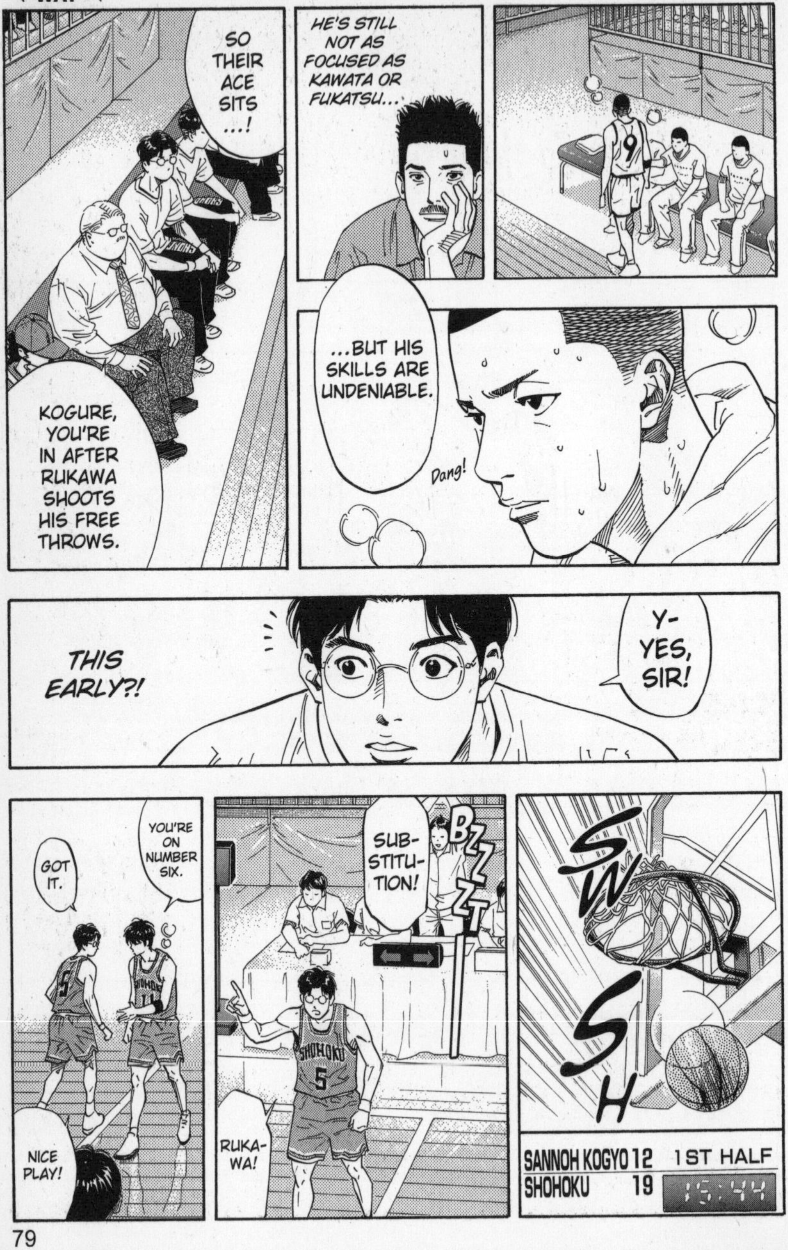
HE'S STILL NOT AS FOCUSED AS KAWATA OR FUKATSU...
...BUT HIS SKILLS ARE UNDENIABLE.
Dang!
SO THEIR ACE SITS ...!
KOGURE, YOU'RE IN AFTER RUKAWA SHOOTS HIS FREE THROWS.
Y- YES, SIR!
THIS EARLY?!
SWISH
SANNOH KOGYO 12
SHOHOKU 19
1ST HALF
15:44
BZZZT
SUB-STITU-TION!
RUKA-WA!
SHOHOKU
YOU'RE ON NUMBER SIX.
GOT IT.
NICE PLAY!

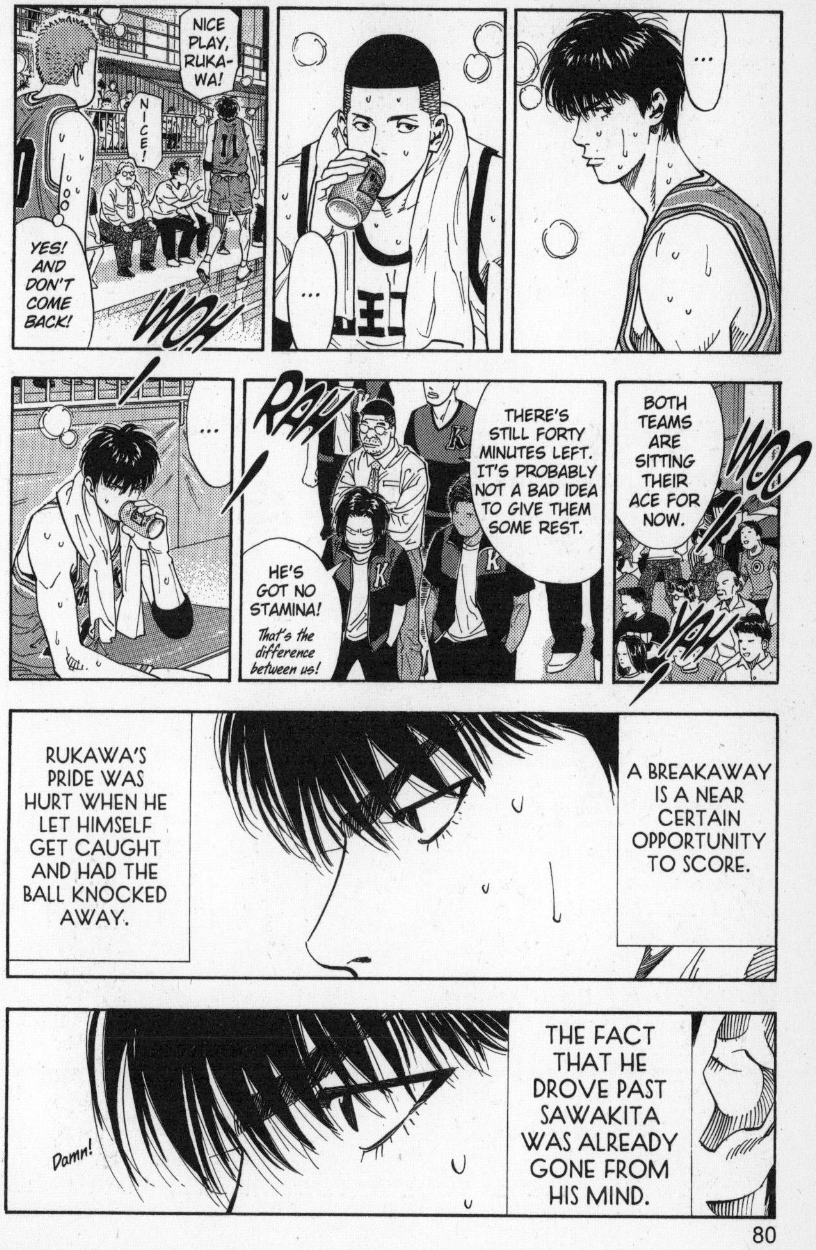
...
...
NICE PLAY, RUKAWA!
NICE!
YES! AND DON'T COME BACK!
WOH!
BOTH TEAMS ARE SITTING THEIR ACE FOR NOW.
WOO!
YAH!
THERE'S STILL FORTY MINUTES LEFT. IT'S PROBABLY NOT A BAD IDEA TO GIVE THEM SOME REST.
RAH!
HE'S GOT NO STAMINA!
That's the difference between us!
...
A BREAKAWAY IS A NEAR CERTAIN OPPORTUNITY TO SCORE.
RUKAWA'S PRIDE WAS HURT WHEN HE LET HIMSELF GET CAUGHT AND HAD THE BALL KNOCKED AWAY.
THE FACT THAT HE DROVE PAST SAWAKITA WAS ALREADY GONE FROM HIS MIND.
Damn!

READ THIS WAY

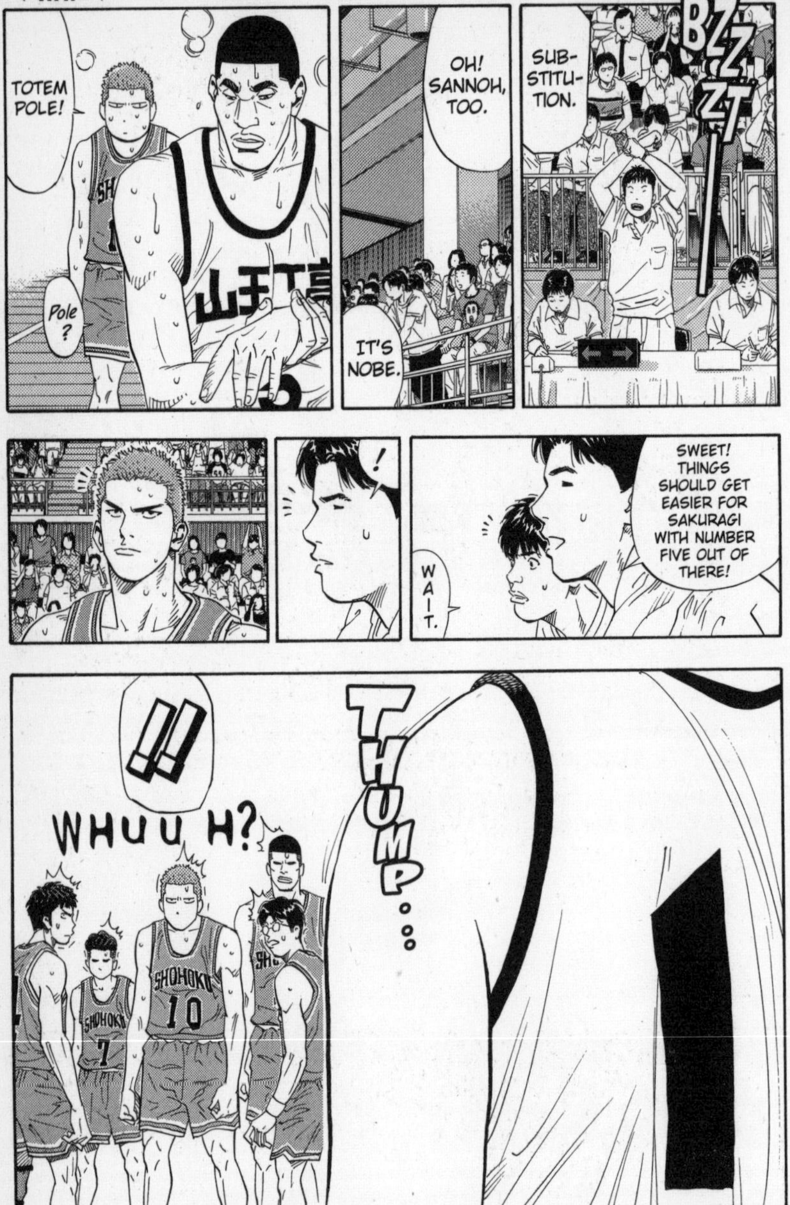
BZZZT
SUB-STITU-TION.
OH! SANNOH, TOO.
IT'S NOBE.
TOTEM POLE!
Pole ?
SWEET! THINGS SHOULD GET EASIER FOR SAKURAGI WITH NUMBER FIVE OUT OF THERE!
WAIT.
!
THUMP...
!!
WHUU H?

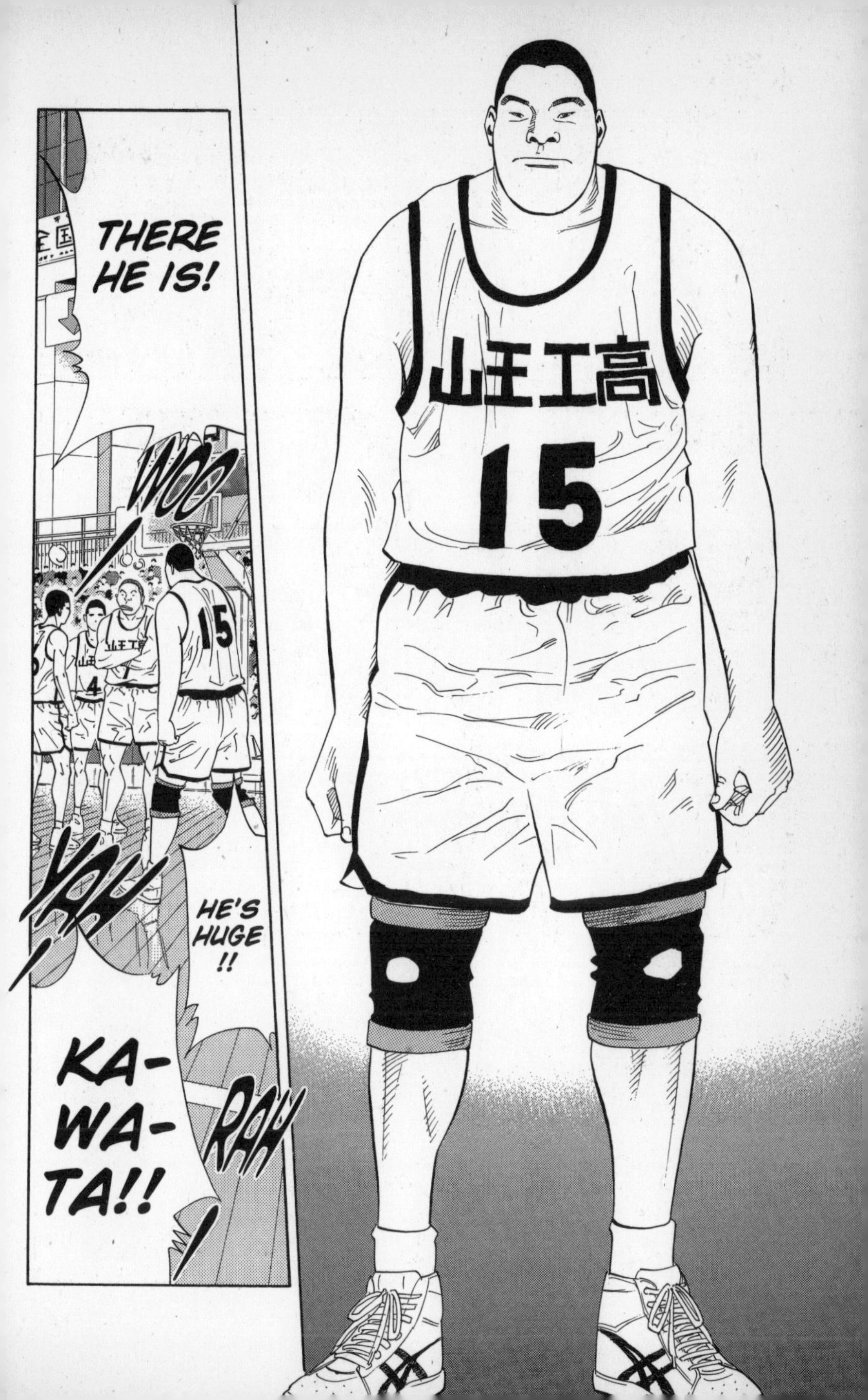
山王工高
15
THERE HE IS!
WOO
YAH
HE'S HUGE!!
KA-WA-TA!!
RAH

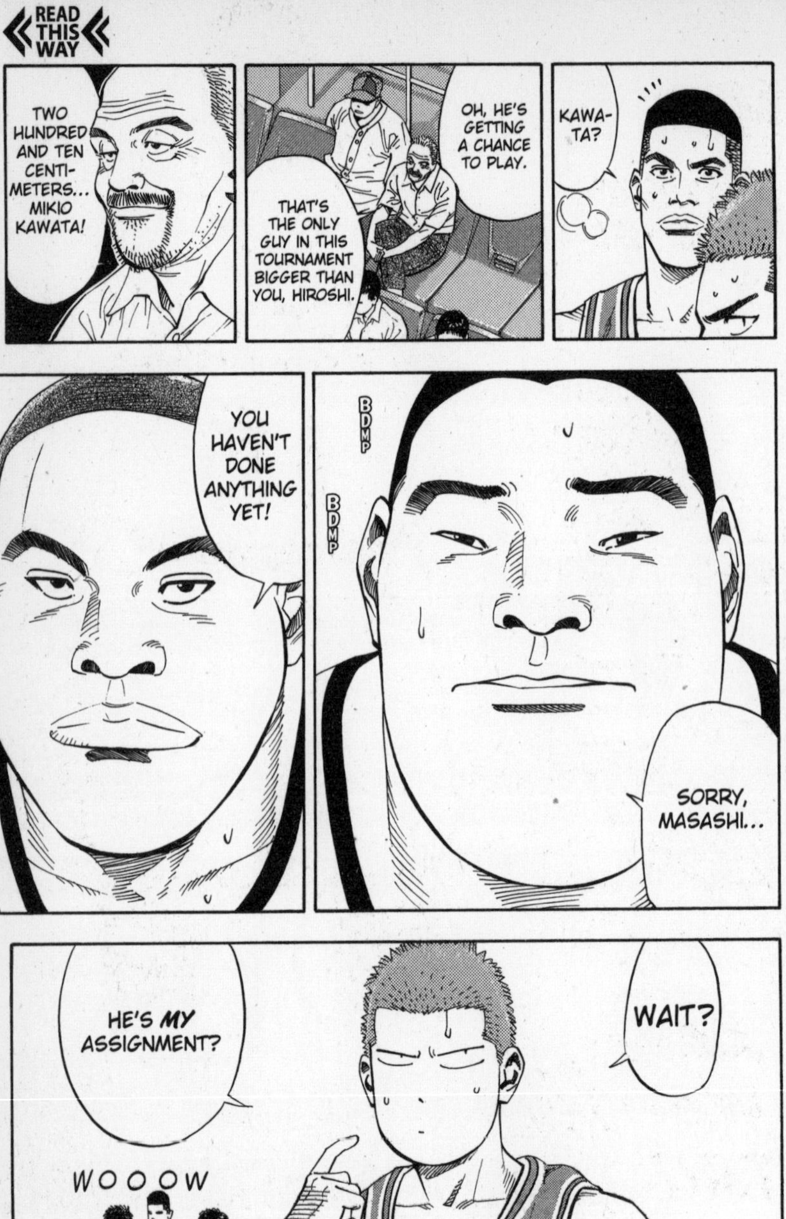
READ THIS WAY
KAWA-TA?
OH, HE'S GETTING A CHANCE TO PLAY.
THAT'S THE ONLY GUY IN THIS TOURNAMENT BIGGER THAN YOU, HIROSHI.
TWO HUNDRED AND TEN CENTI-METERS... MIKIO KAWATA!
BDMP
BDMP
SORRY, MASASHI...
YOU HAVEN'T DONE ANYTHING YET!
WAIT?
HE'S *MY* ASSIGNMENT?
WOOOW

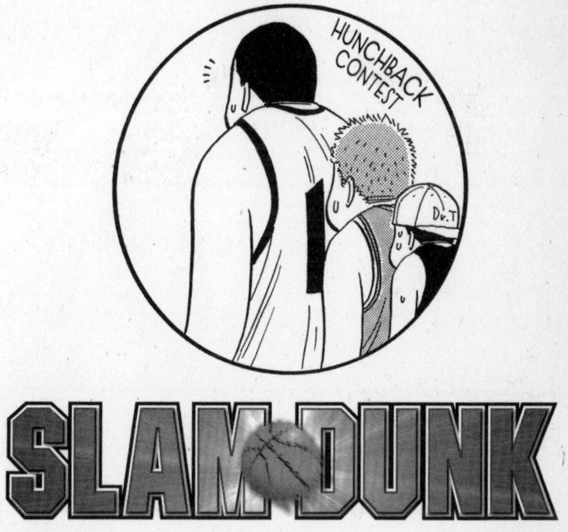
HUNCHBACK CONTEST
Dr.T

SLAM DUNK

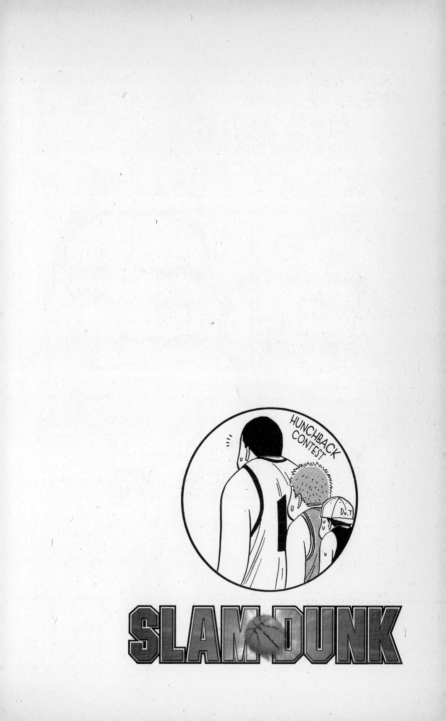

#229
BIG MAN

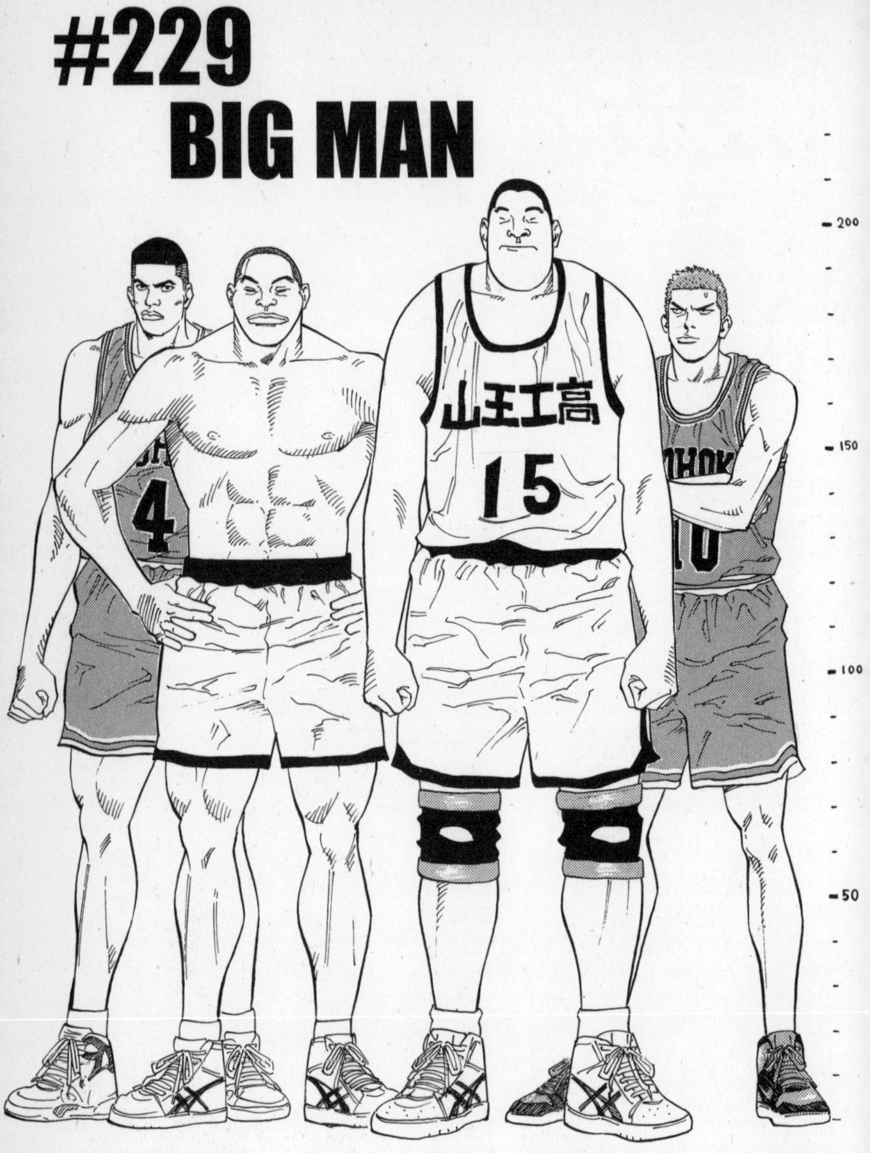

200
150
100
50
山王工高
15
4
10

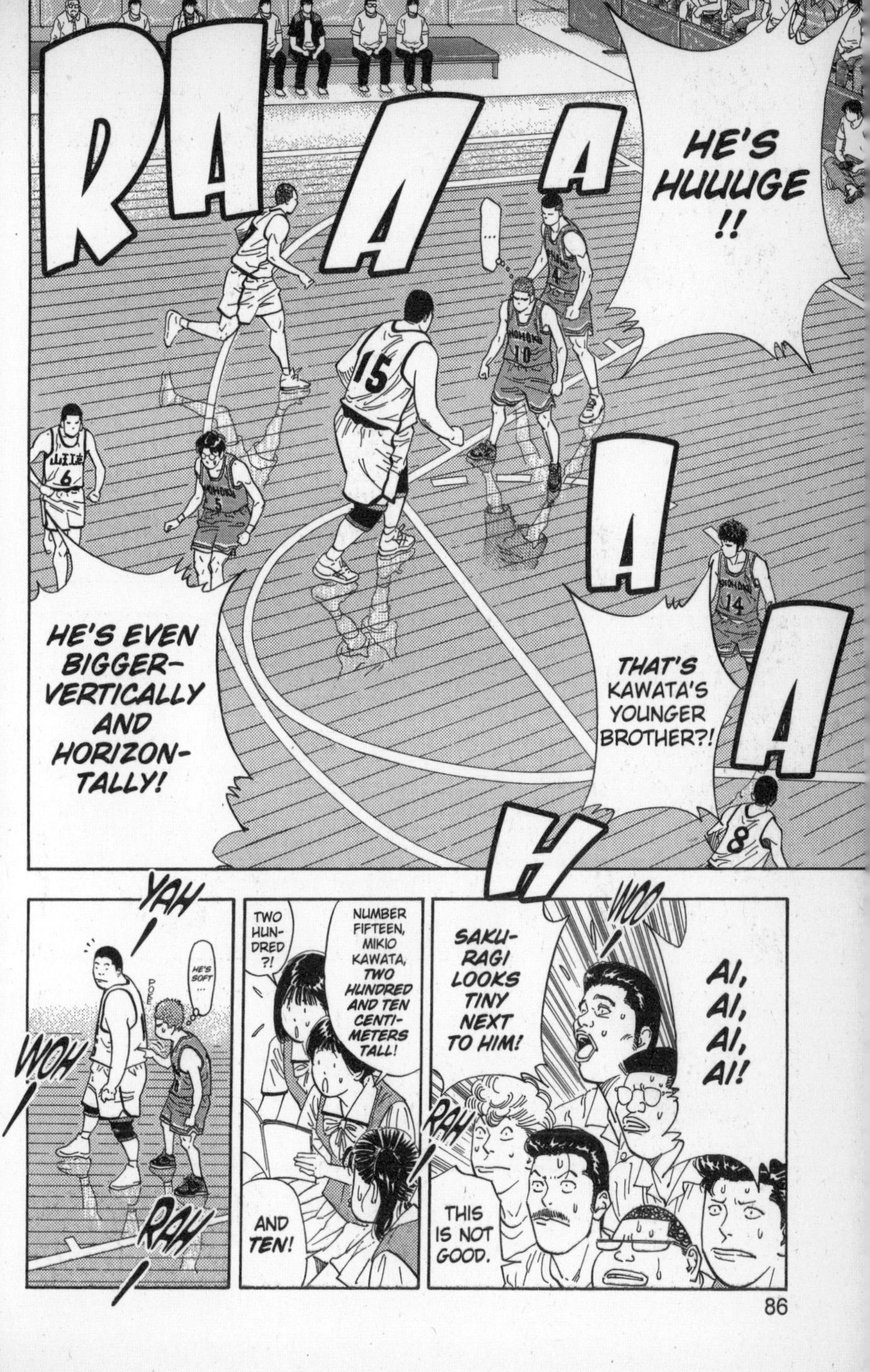
RAAAAAAH
HE'S HUUUGE!!
...
THAT'S KAWATA'S YOUNGER BROTHER?!
HE'S EVEN BIGGER- VERTICALLY AND HORIZON-TALLY!
WOO!
AI, AI, AI, AI!
SAKU-RAGI LOOKS TINY NEXT TO HIM!
RAH!
THIS IS NOT GOOD.
NUMBER FIFTEEN, MIKIO KAWATA, TWO HUNDRED AND TEN CENTI-METERS TALL!
TWO HUN-DRED ?!
AND TEN!
YAH!
HE'S SOFT ...
POKE
WOH!
RAH!

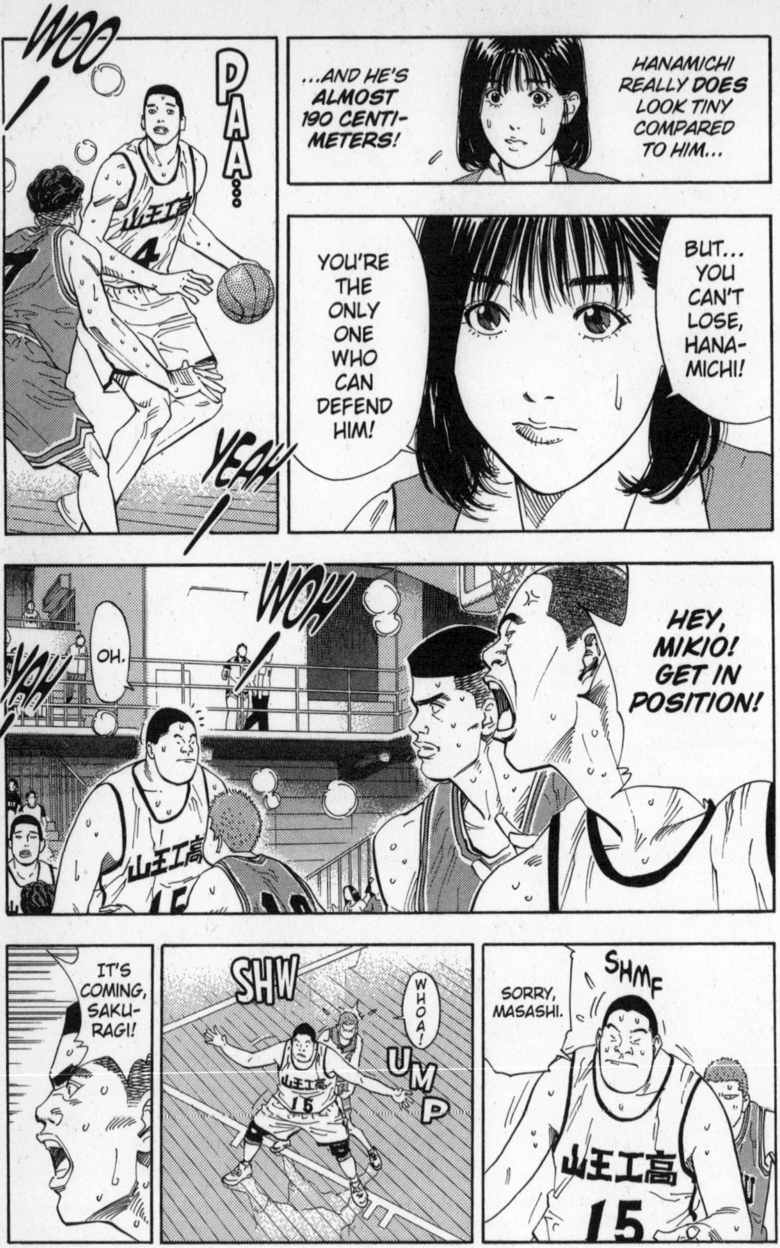
HANAMICHI REALLY DOES LOOK TINY COMPARED TO HIM...
...AND HE'S ALMOST 190 CENTIMETERS!
BUT... YOU CAN'T LOSE, HANAMICHI!
YOU'RE THE ONLY ONE WHO CAN DEFEND HIM!
WOO-!
PAA...
YEAH!
HEY, MIKIO! GET IN POSITION!
WOH!
OH.
YAH!
SHMF
SORRY, MASASHI.
SHW
WHOA!
UMP
IT'S COMING, SAKURAGI!

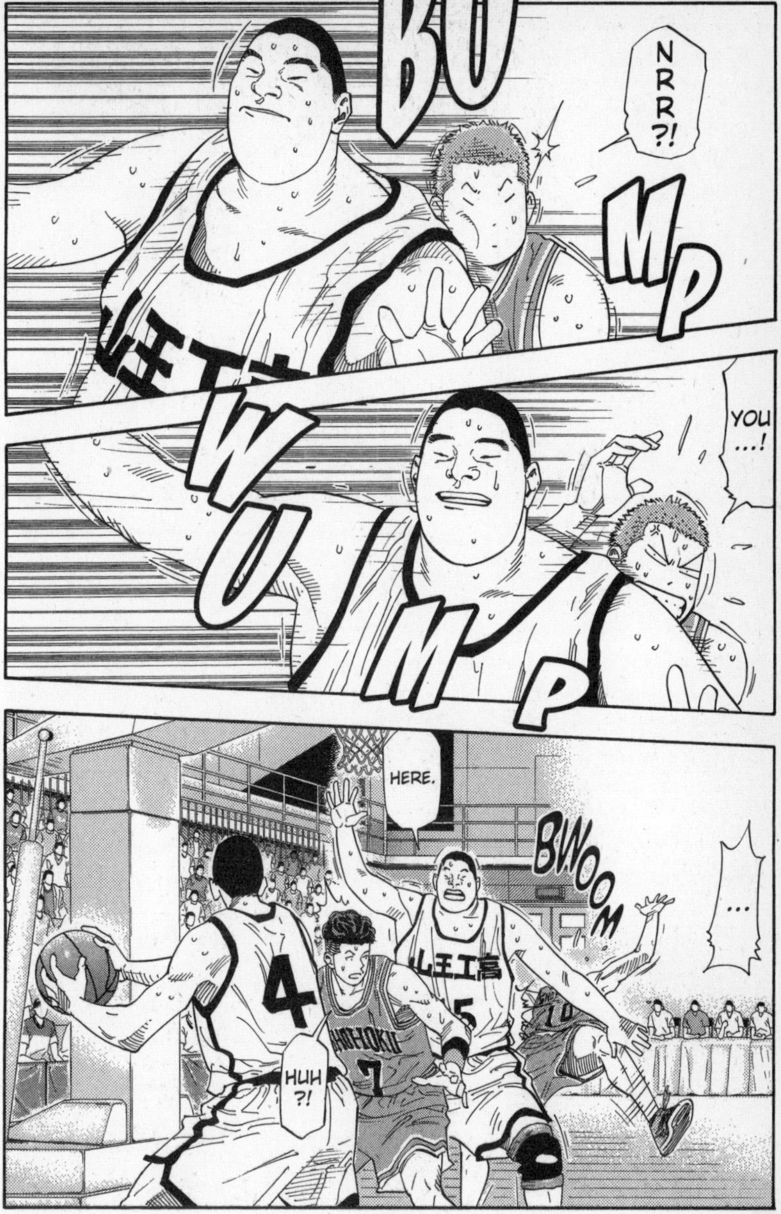
NRR ?!
BUMP
YOU ...!
WUMP
...
BWOOM
HERE.
HUH ?!

READ THIS WAY

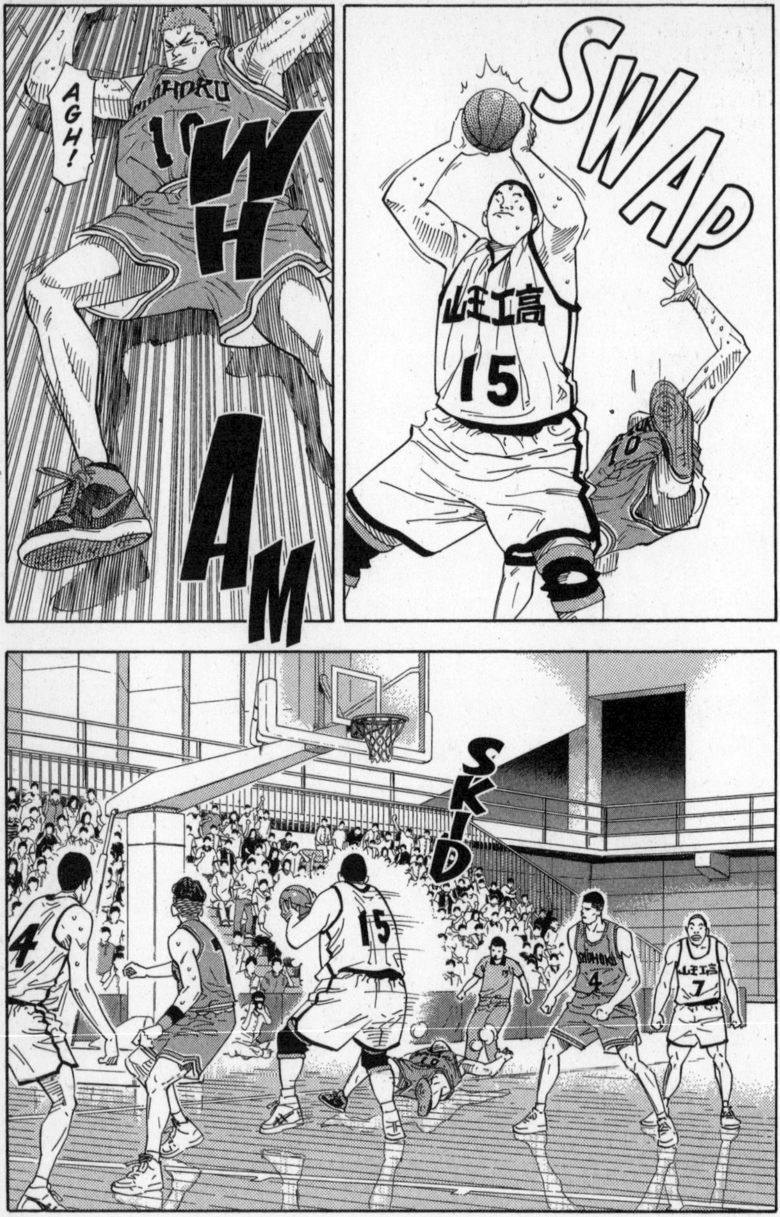
SWAP
AGH!
WHAM
SKID

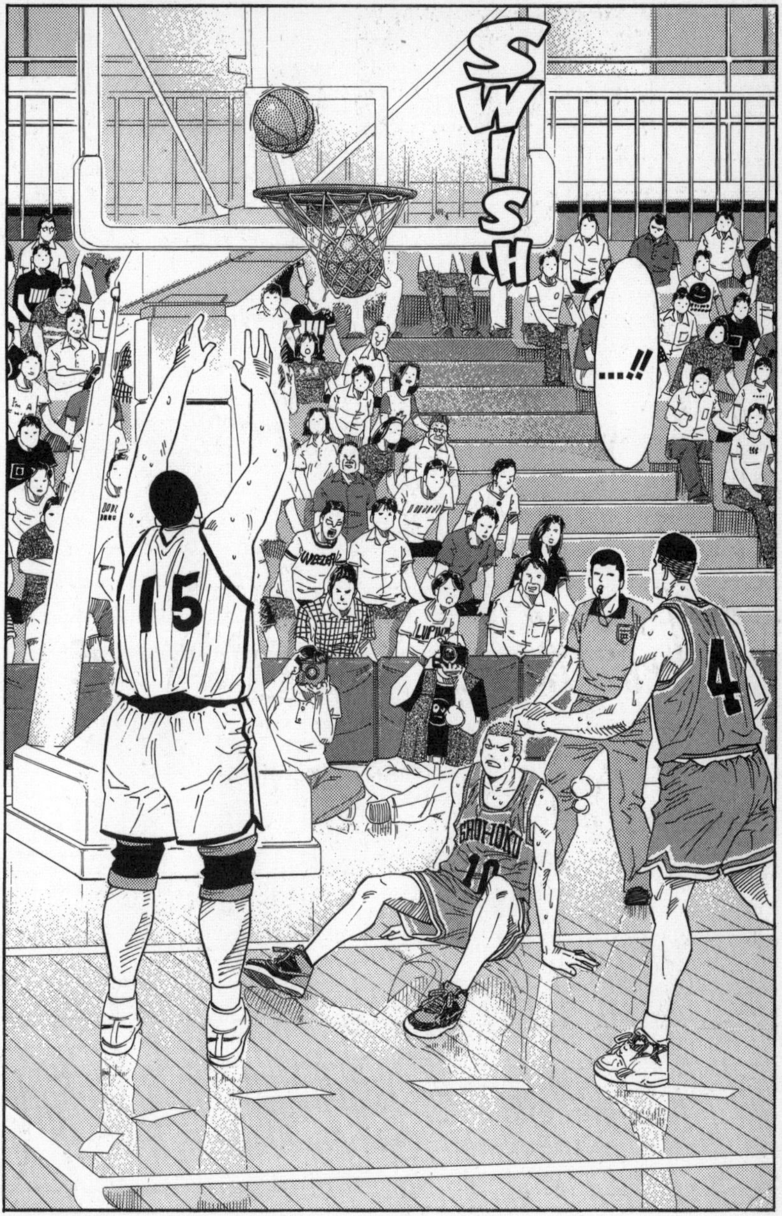
SWISH
...!!

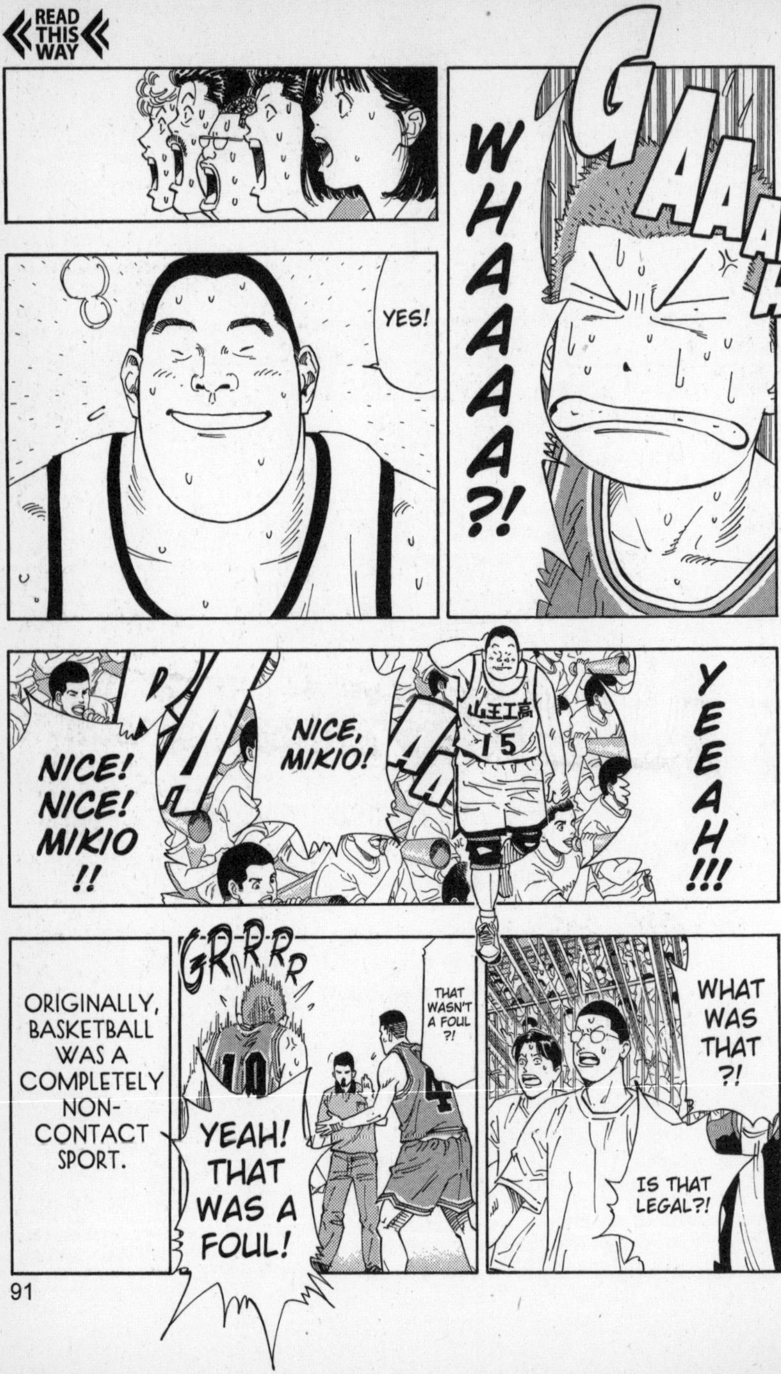
READ THIS WAY
GAAAAH
WHAAAAA?!
YES!
YEEAH!!!
NICE, MIKIO!
NICE! NICE! MIKIO!!
山王工高
15
WHAT WAS THAT?!
IS THAT LEGAL?!
THAT WASN'T A FOUL?!
GRRRR
YEAH! THAT WAS A FOUL!
ORIGINALLY, BASKETBALL WAS A COMPLETELY NON-CONTACT SPORT.

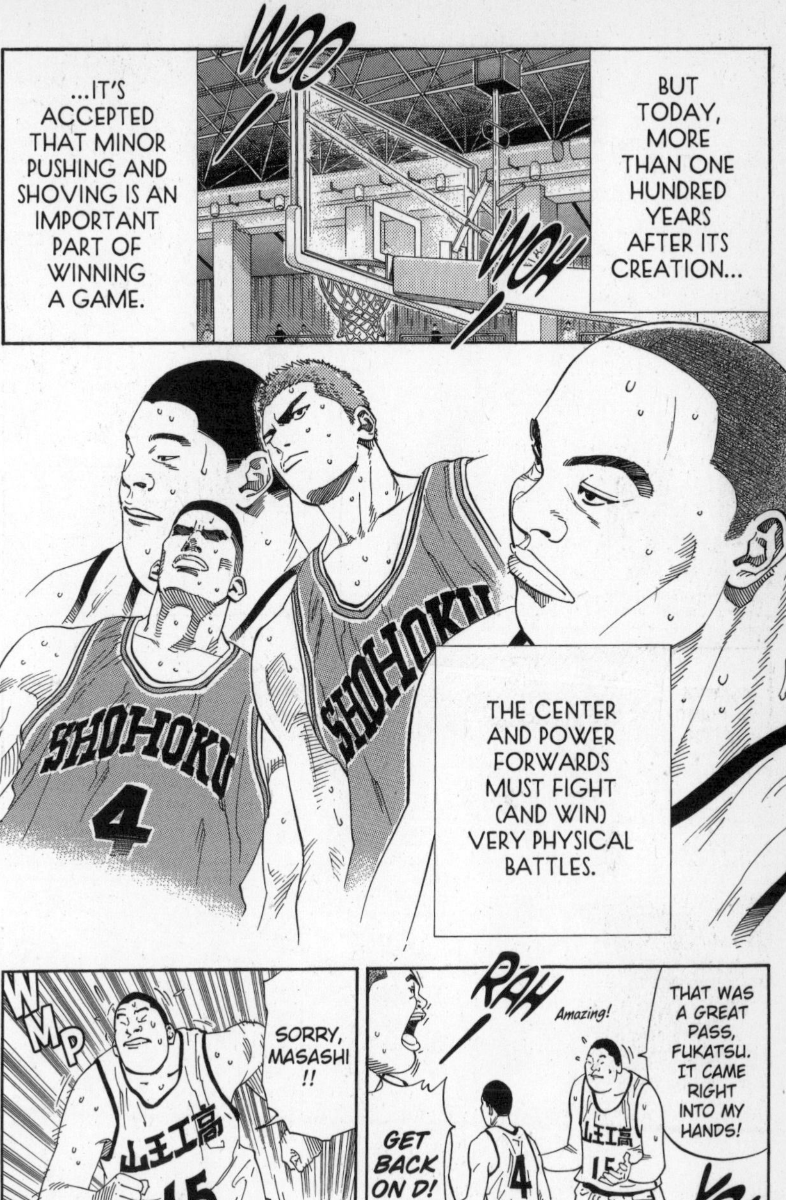

WOO
BUT TODAY, MORE THAN ONE HUNDRED YEARS AFTER ITS CREATION...
...IT'S ACCEPTED THAT MINOR PUSHING AND SHOVING IS AN IMPORTANT PART OF WINNING A GAME.
WOH
THE CENTER AND POWER FORWARDS MUST FIGHT (AND WIN) VERY PHYSICAL BATTLES.
THAT WAS A GREAT PASS, FUKATSU. IT CAME RIGHT INTO MY HANDS!
RAH
Amazing!
GET BACK ON D!
YAH
SORRY, MASASHI !!
WMP

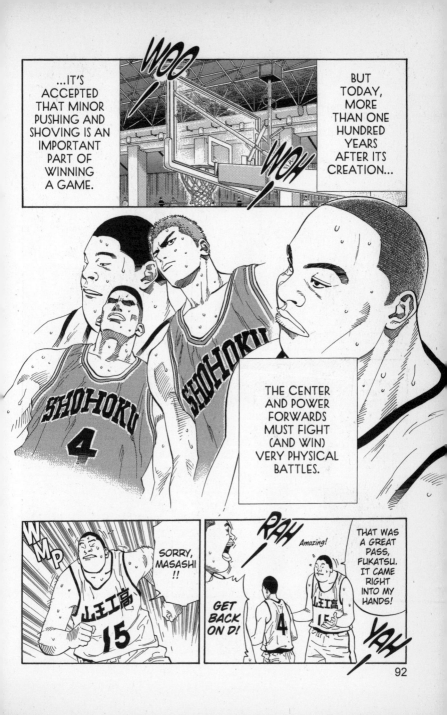

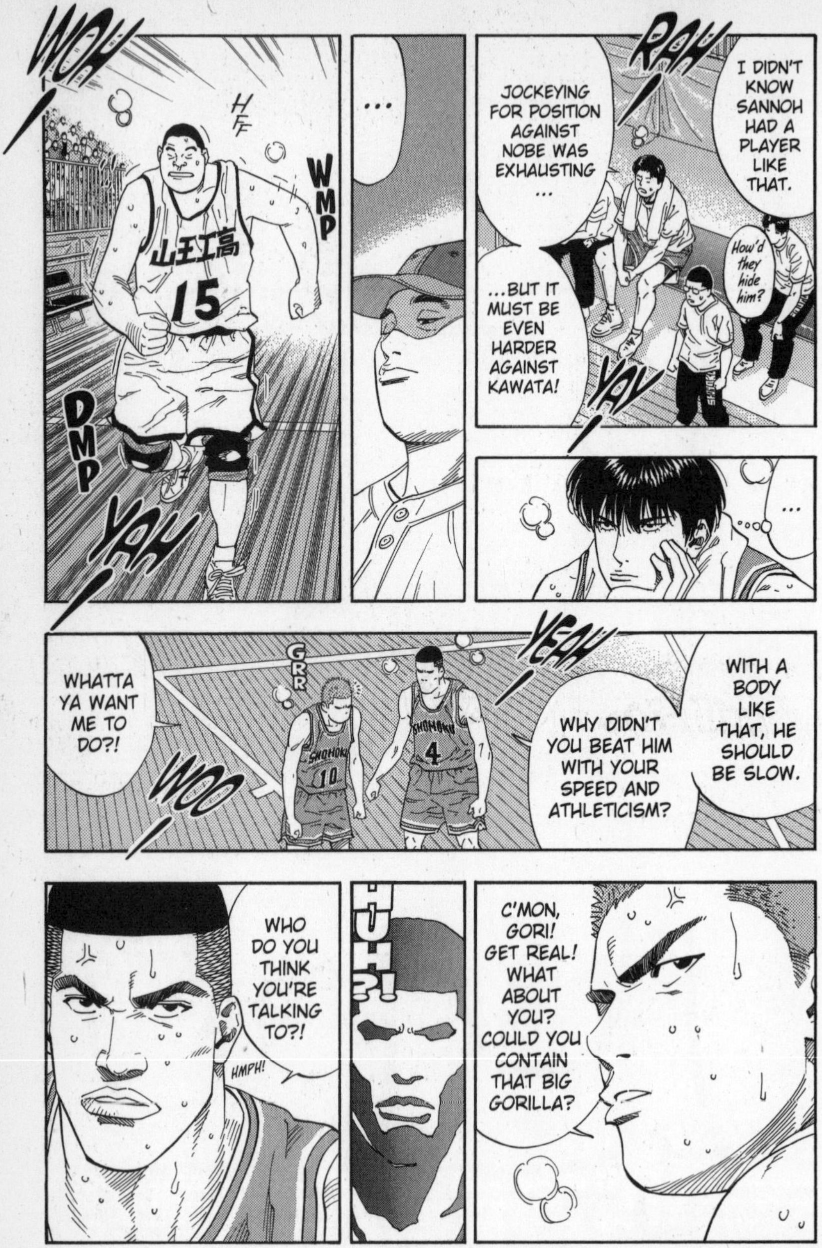
RAH!
I DIDN'T KNOW SANNOH HAD A PLAYER LIKE THAT.
How'd they hide him?
JOCKEYING FOR POSITION AGAINST NOBE WAS EXHAUSTING...
...BUT IT MUST BE EVEN HARDER AGAINST KAWATA!
YAY!
...
...
WOH!
HFF
WMP
DMP
YAH!
YEAH!
WITH A BODY LIKE THAT, HE SHOULD BE SLOW.
WHY DIDN'T YOU BEAT HIM WITH YOUR SPEED AND ATHLETICISM?
GRR
WHATTA YA WANT ME TO DO?!
WOO!
C'MON, GORI! GET REAL! WHAT ABOUT YOU? COULD YOU CONTAIN THAT BIG GORILLA?
HUH?!
WHO DO YOU THINK YOU'RE TALKING TO?!
HMPH!

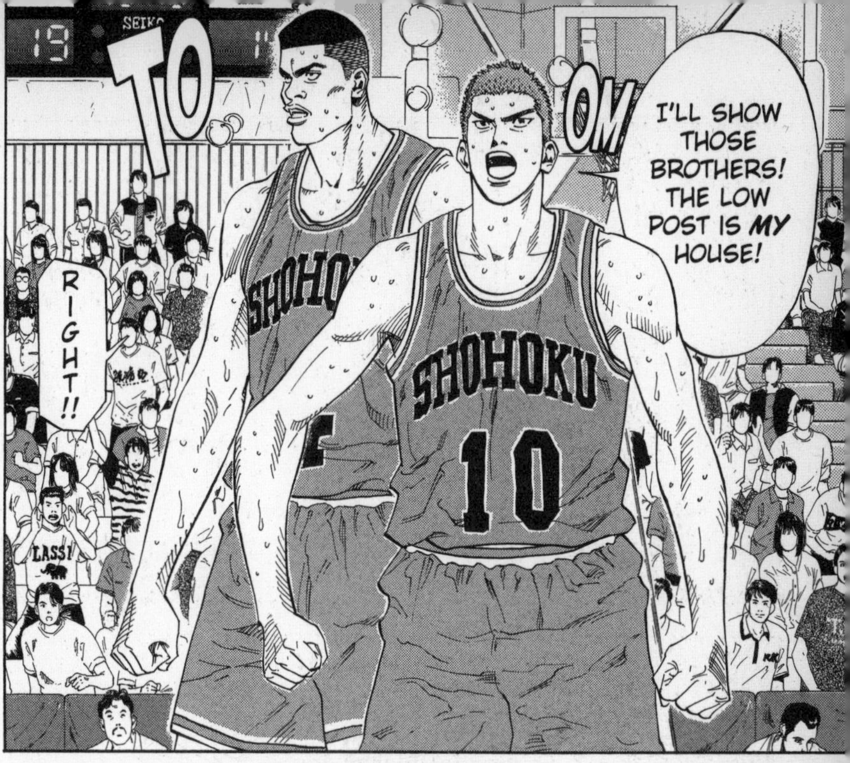
I'LL SHOW THOSE BROTHERS! THE LOW POST IS *MY* HOUSE!
TOOM
RIGHT!!
SHOHOKU
10
SEIKO
19

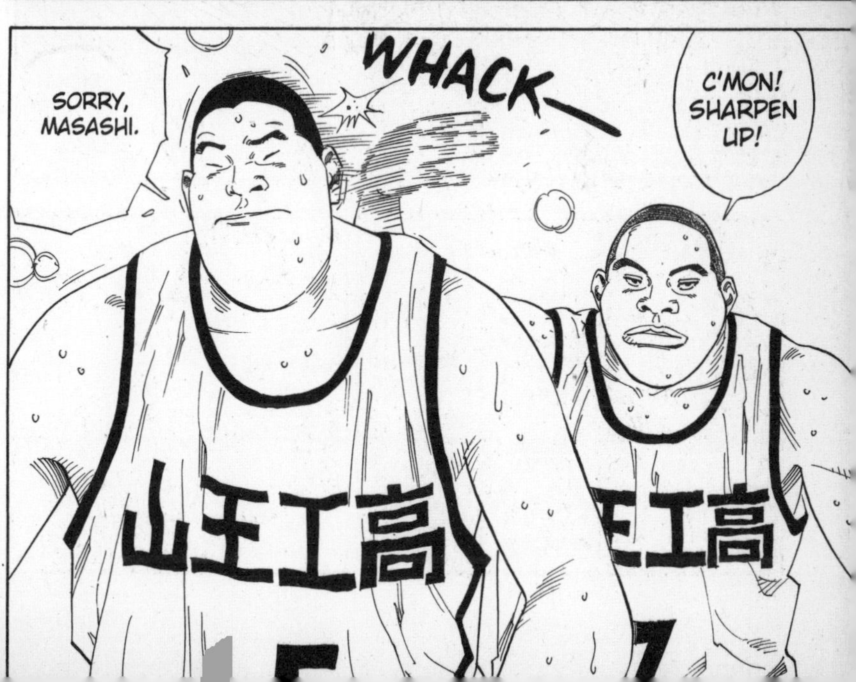
C'MON! SHARPEN UP!
WHACK
SORRY, MASASHI.
山王工高
王工高

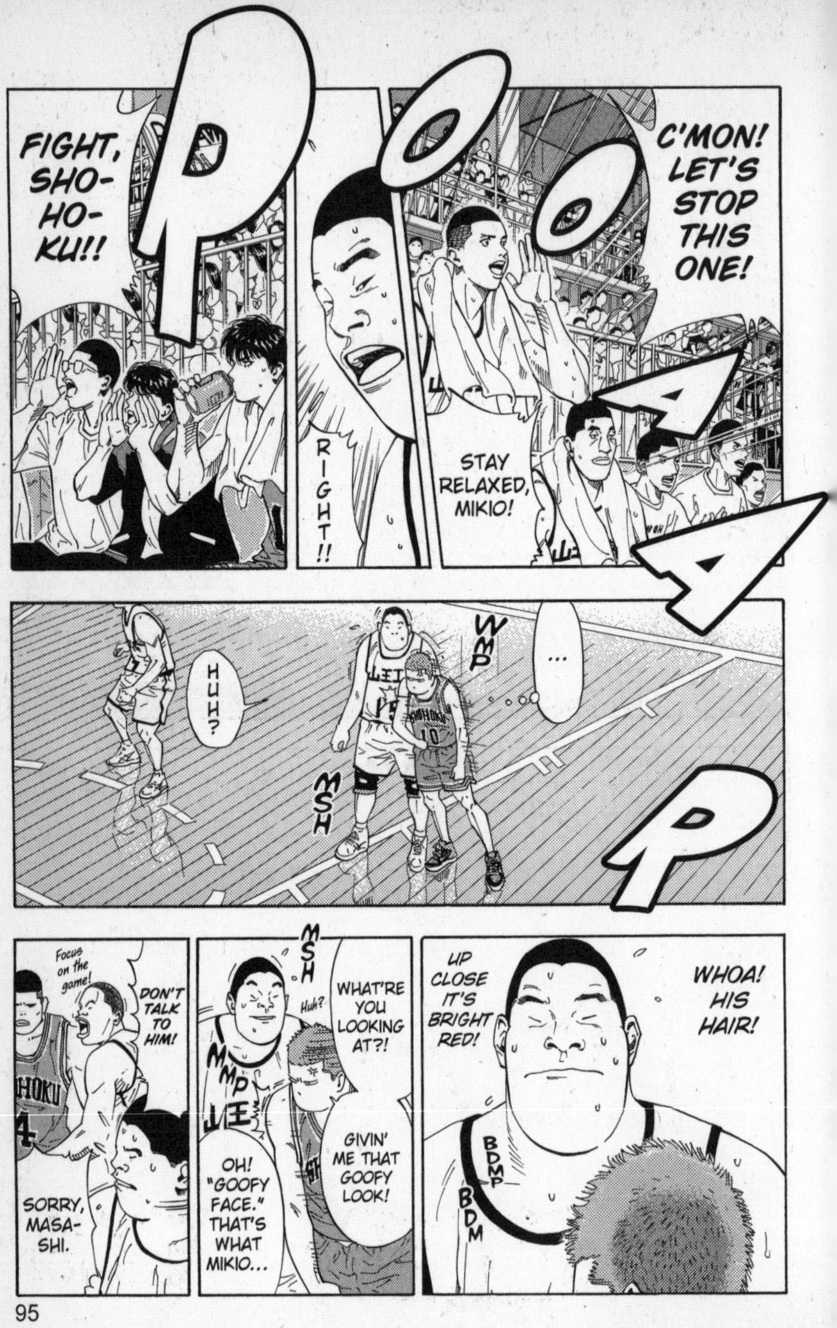
POOOAAAP
C'MON! LET'S STOP THIS ONE!
STAY RELAXED, MIKIO!
RIGHT!!
FIGHT, SHOHOKU!!
...
WMP
HUH?
MSH
WHOA! HIS HAIR!
UP CLOSE IT'S BRIGHT RED!
BDMP
BDM
MSH
WHAT'RE YOU LOOKING AT?!
Huh?
MMP
GIVIN' ME THAT GOOFY LOOK!
OH! "GOOFY FACE." THAT'S WHAT MIKIO...
DON'T TALK TO HIM!
Focus on the game!
SORRY, MASASHI.

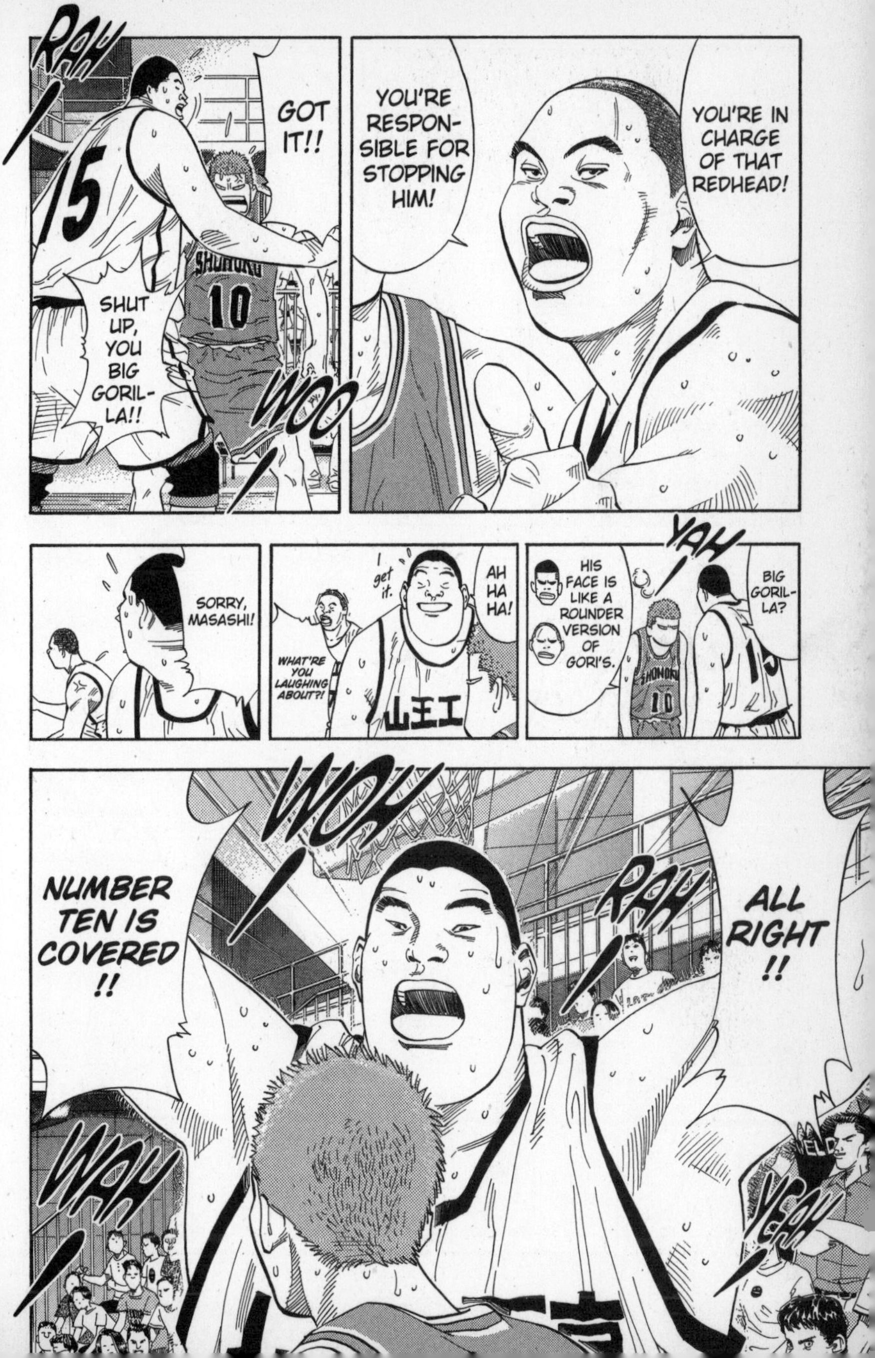
YOU'RE IN CHARGE OF THAT REDHEAD!
YOU'RE RESPONSIBLE FOR STOPPING HIM!
GOT IT!!
RAH
SHUT UP, YOU BIG GORILLA!!
WOO
YAH
BIG GORILLA?
HIS FACE IS LIKE A ROUNDER VERSION OF GORI'S.
AH HA HA!
I get it.
WHAT'RE YOU LAUGHING ABOUT?!
山王工
SORRY, MASASHI!
ALL RIGHT!!
RAH
WOH
NUMBER TEN IS COVERED!!
YEAH
WAH

READ THIS WAY

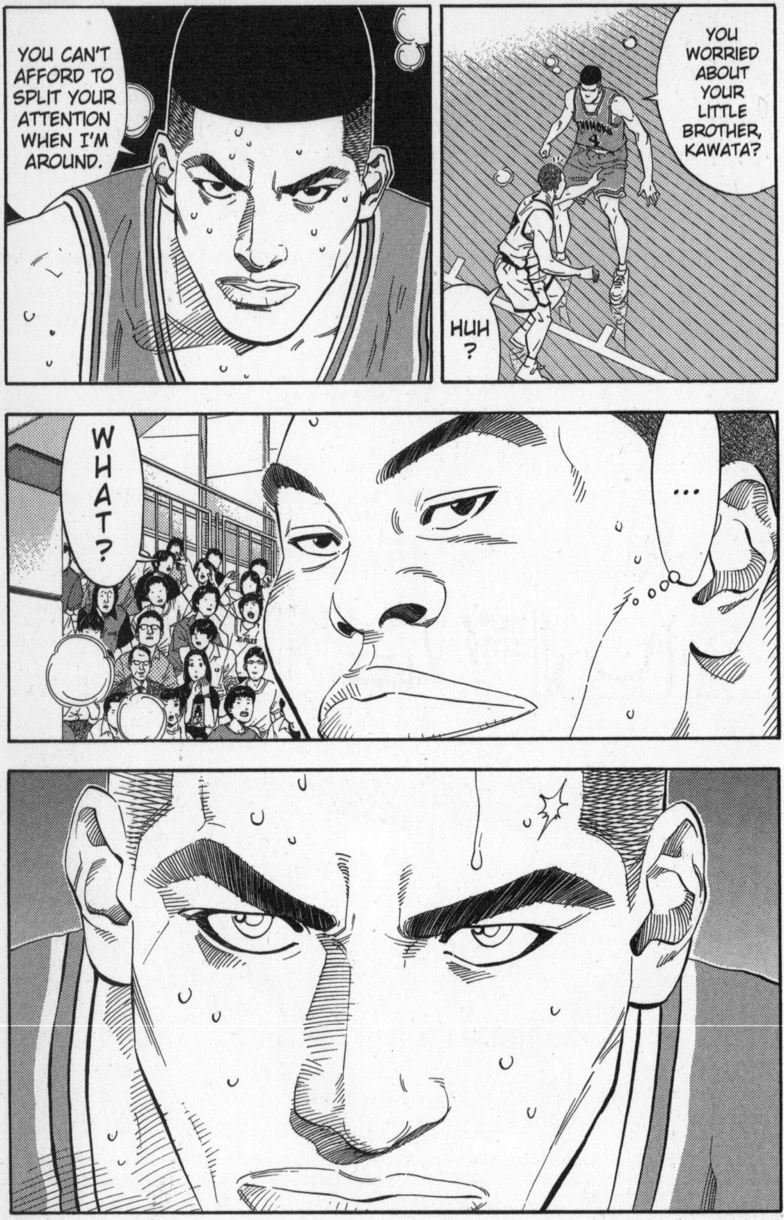
YOU WORRIED ABOUT YOUR LITTLE BROTHER, KAWATA?
HUH ?
YOU CAN'T AFFORD TO SPLIT YOUR ATTENTION WHEN I'M AROUND.
...
WHAT?

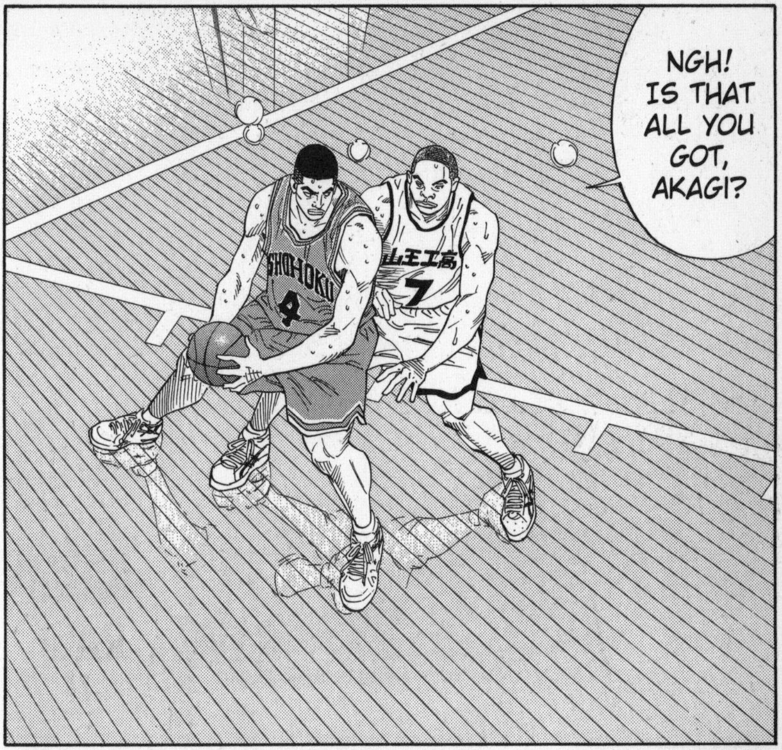
NGH! IS THAT ALL YOU GOT, AKAGI?
SHOHOKU
4
山王工高
7

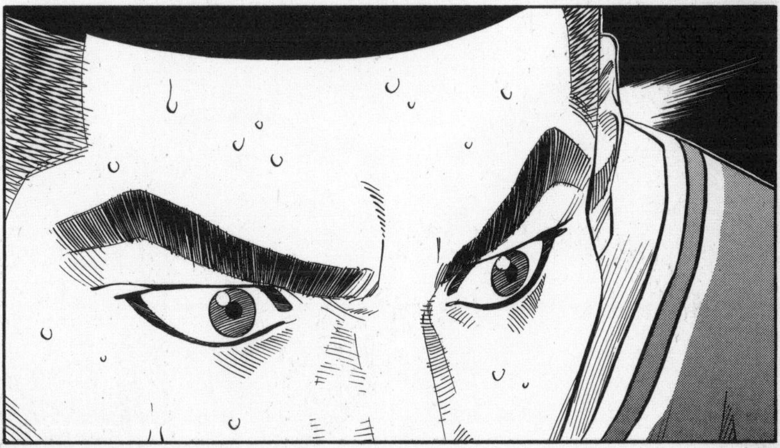

READ THIS WAY

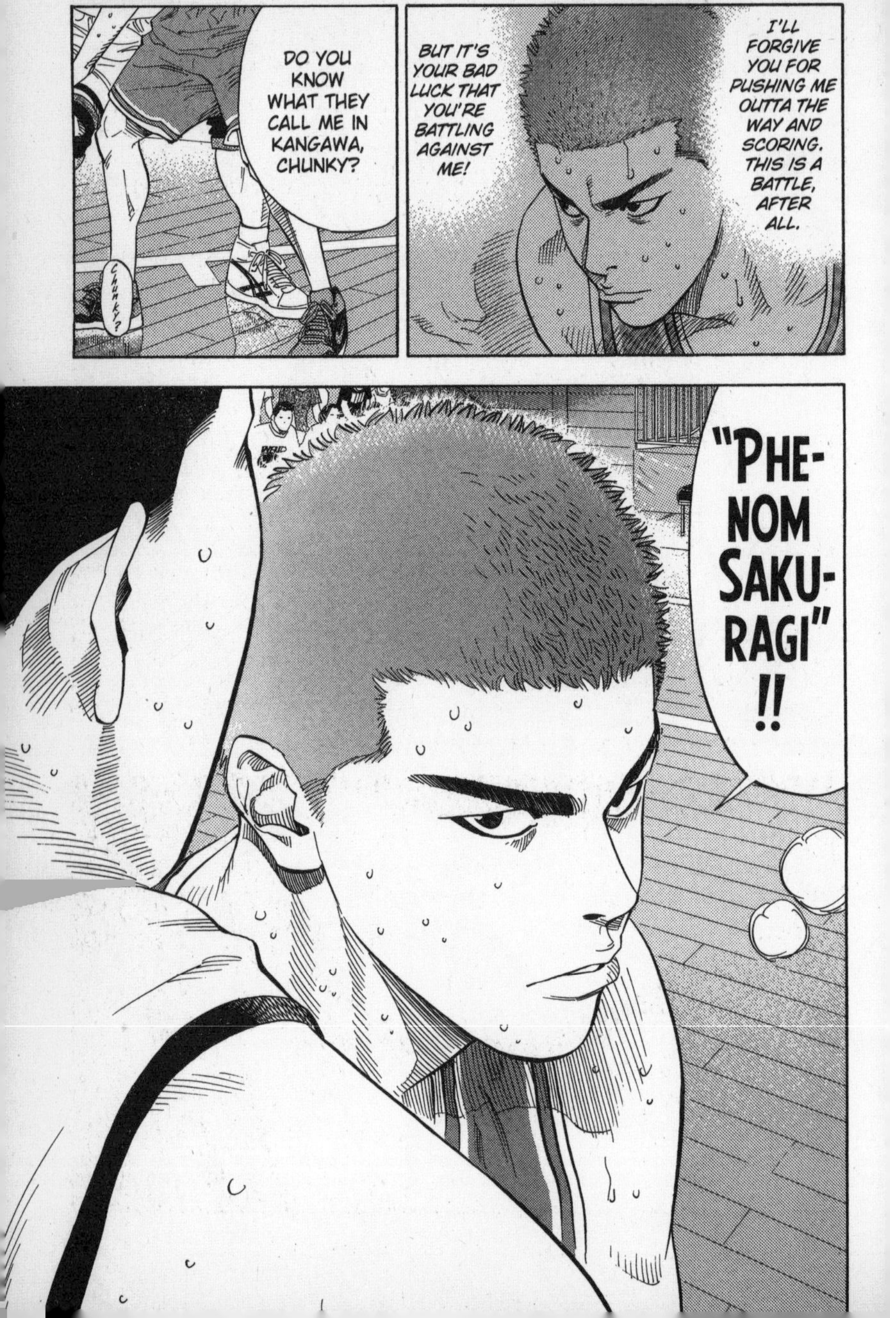
I'LL FORGIVE YOU FOR PUSHING ME OUTTA THE WAY AND SCORING. THIS IS A BATTLE, AFTER ALL.
BUT IT'S YOUR BAD LUCK THAT YOU'RE BATTLING AGAINST ME!
DO YOU KNOW WHAT THEY CALL ME IN KANGAWA, CHUNKY?
Chunky?
"PHE-NOM SAKU-RAGI" !!

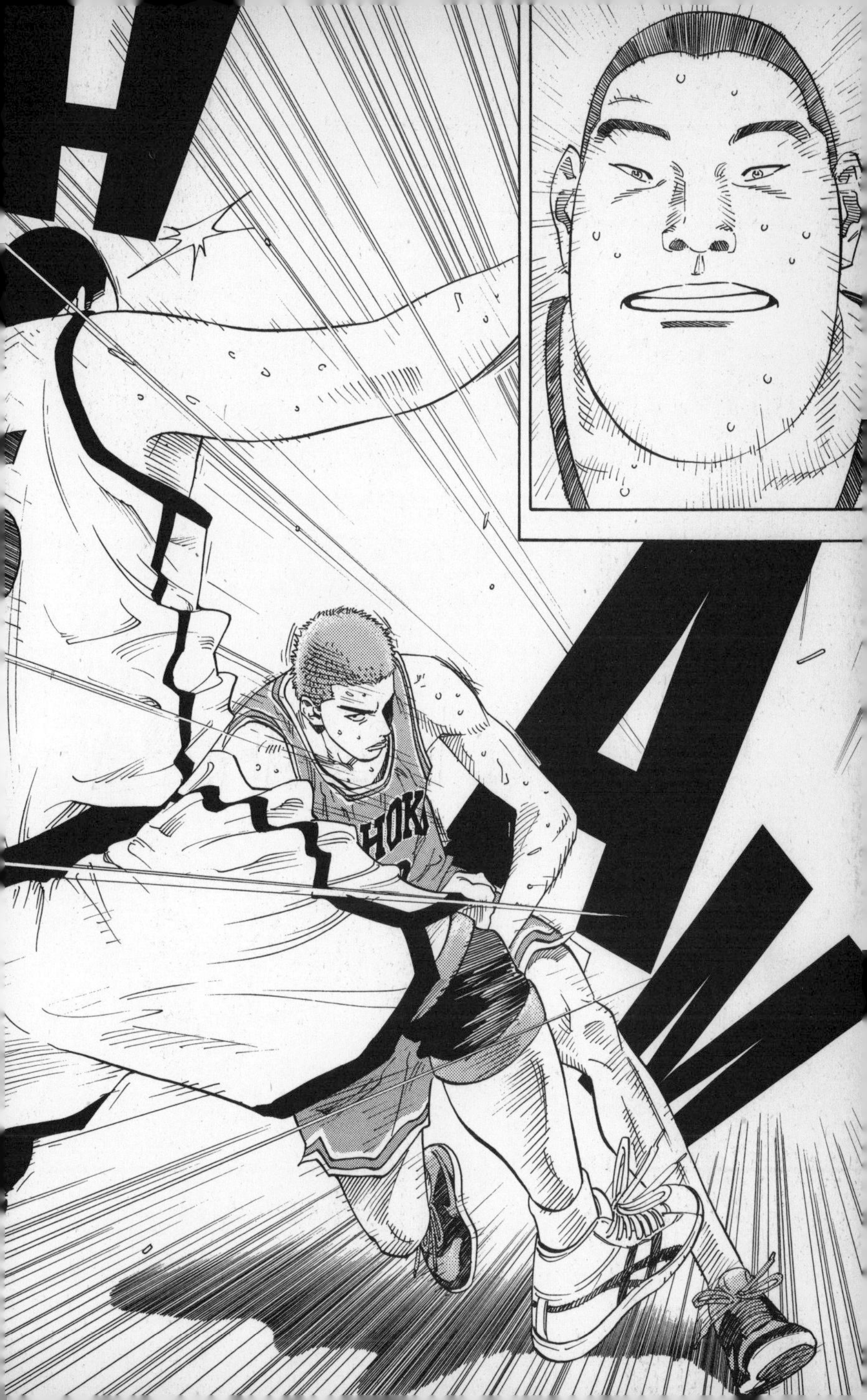

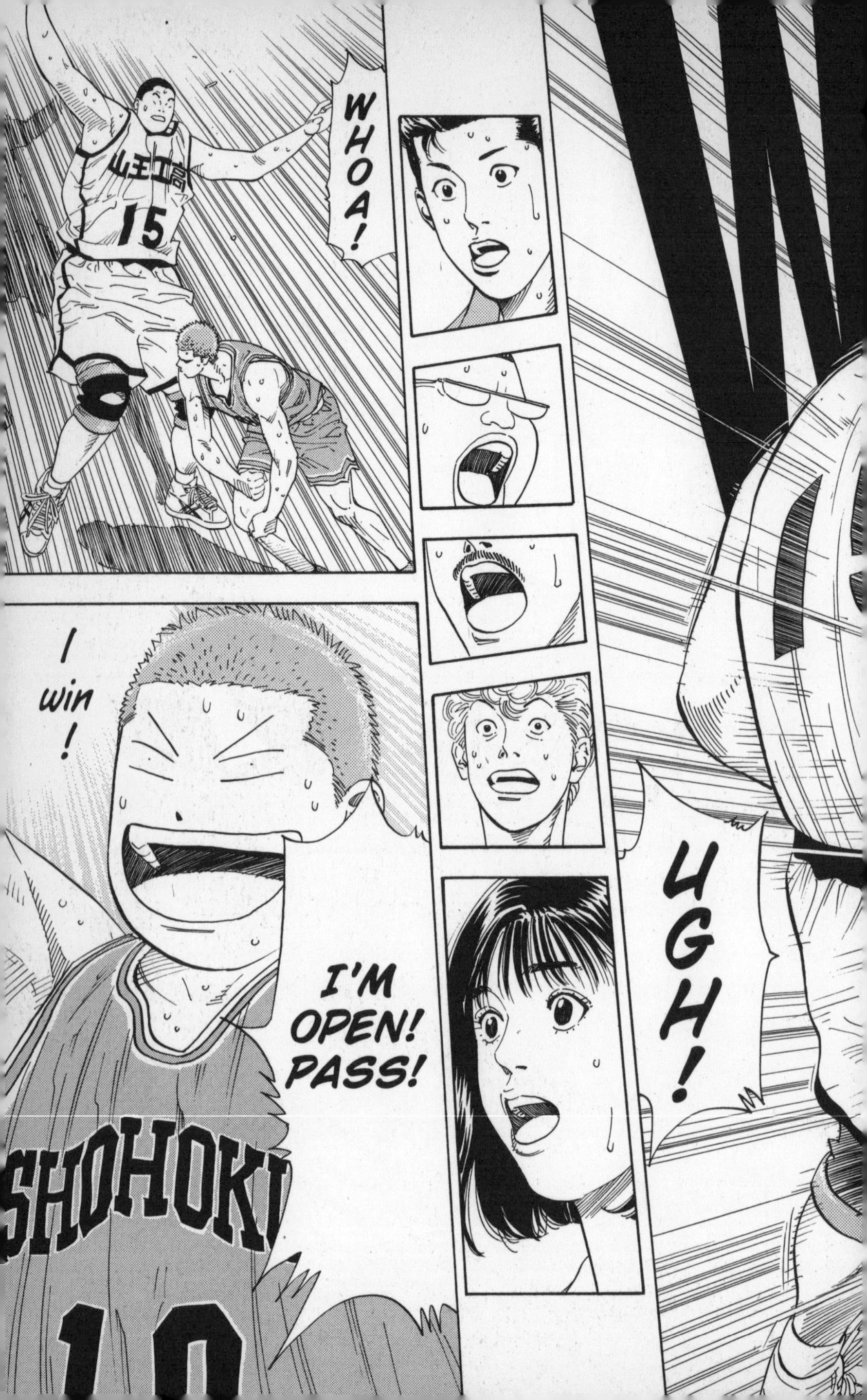
UGH!
WHOA!
I win!
I'M OPEN! PASS!

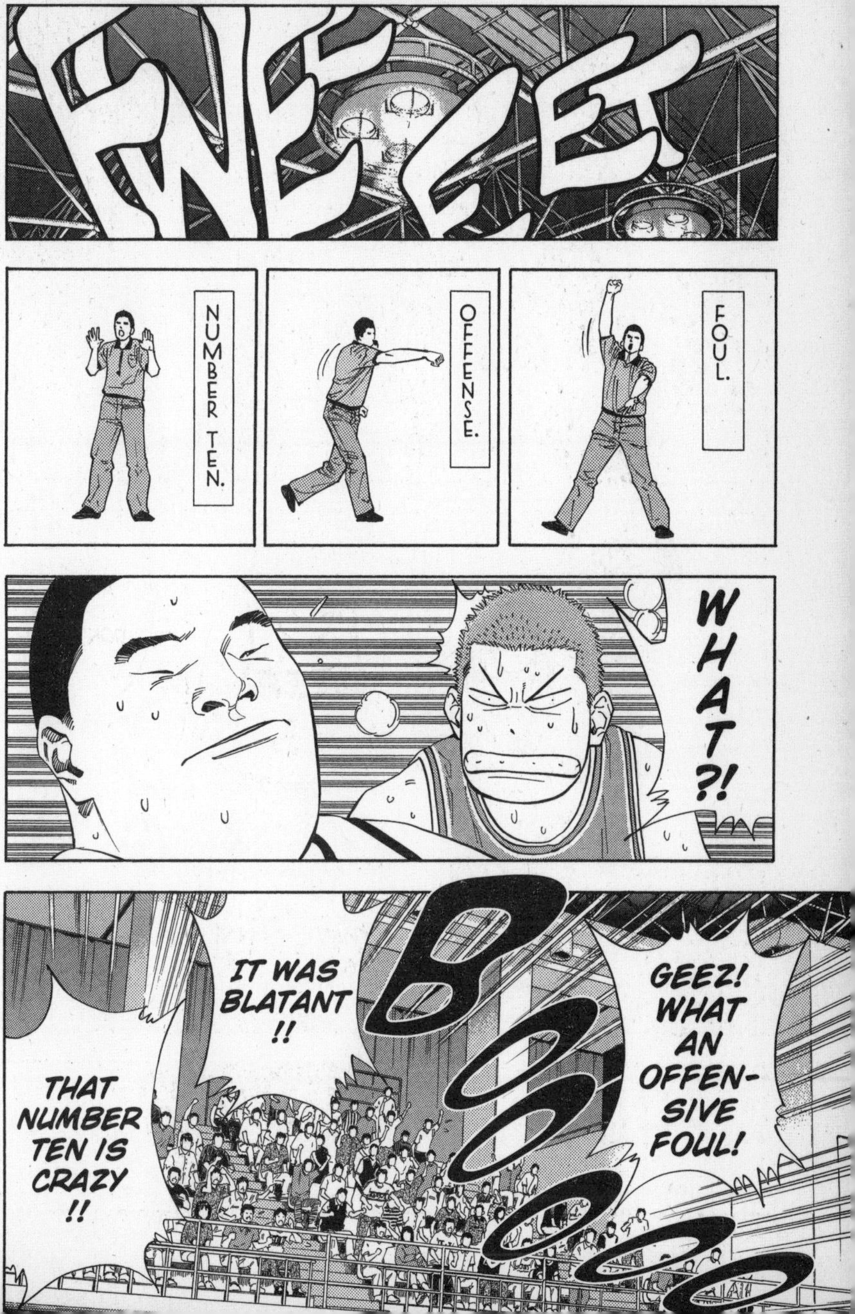
FWEEET
NUMBER TEN.
OFFENSE.
FOUL.
WHAT?!
BOOOOO
THAT NUMBER TEN IS CRAZY !!
IT WAS BLATANT !!
GEEZ! WHAT AN OFFEN-SIVE FOUL!

READ THIS WAY

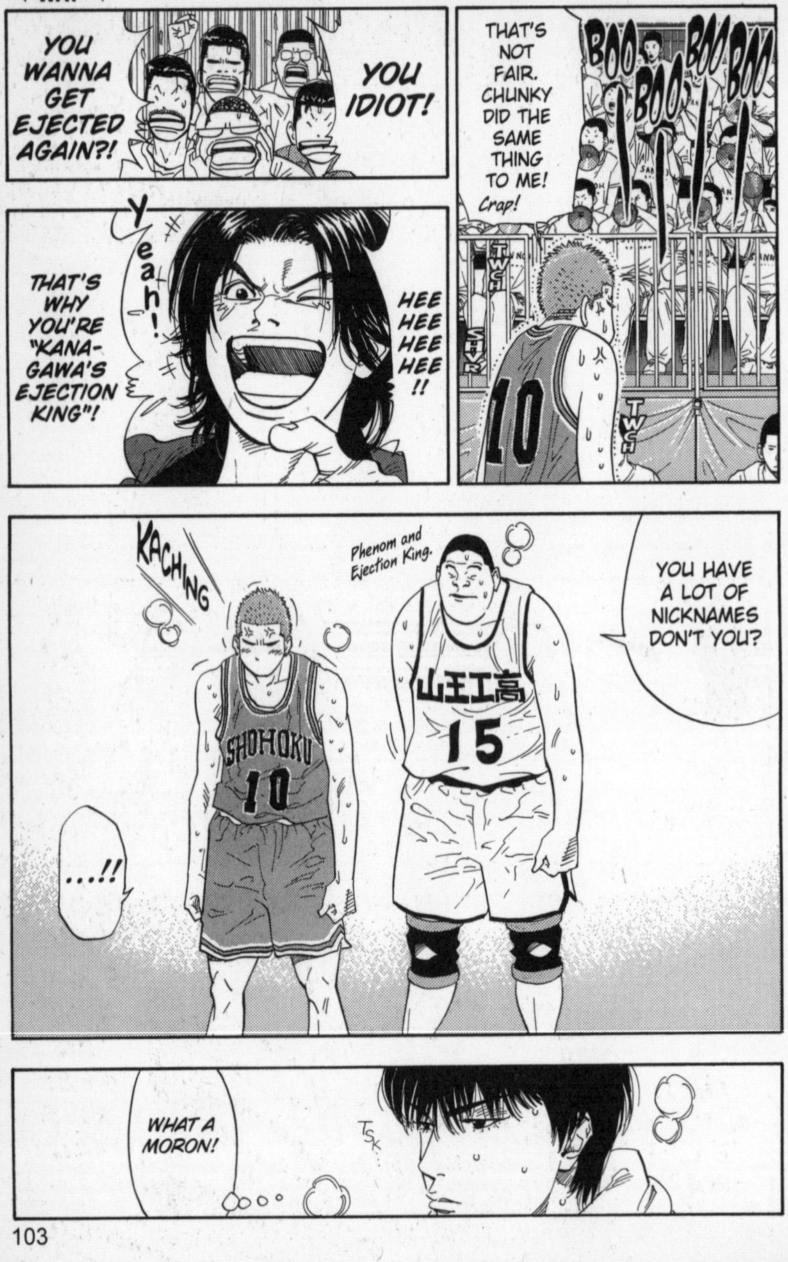
BOO BOO BOO BOO
THAT'S NOT FAIR. CHUNKY DID THE SAME THING TO ME!
Crap!
YOU IDIOT!
YOU WANNA GET EJECTED AGAIN?!
HEE HEE HEE HEE!!
Yeah!
THAT'S WHY YOU'RE "KANAGAWA'S EJECTION KING"!
YOU HAVE A LOT OF NICKNAMES DON'T YOU?
Phenom and Ejection King.
KACHING
...!!
TSK...
WHAT A MORON!

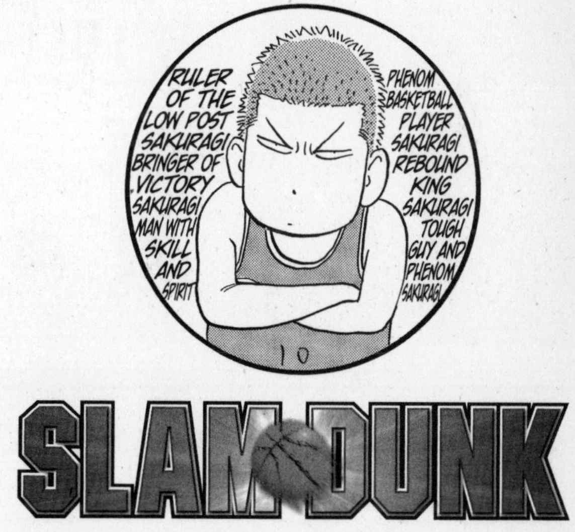
PHENOM BASKETBALL PLAYER SAKURAGI REBOUND KING SAKURAGI TOUGH GUY AND PHENOM SAKURAGI
RULER OF THE LOW POST SAKURAGI BRINGER OF VICTORY SAKURAGI MAN WITH SKILL AND SPIRIT
10

SLAM DUNK

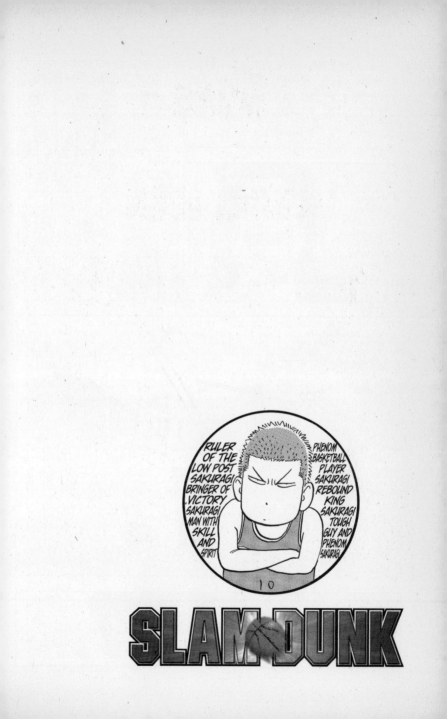

#230

LOCAL WAR

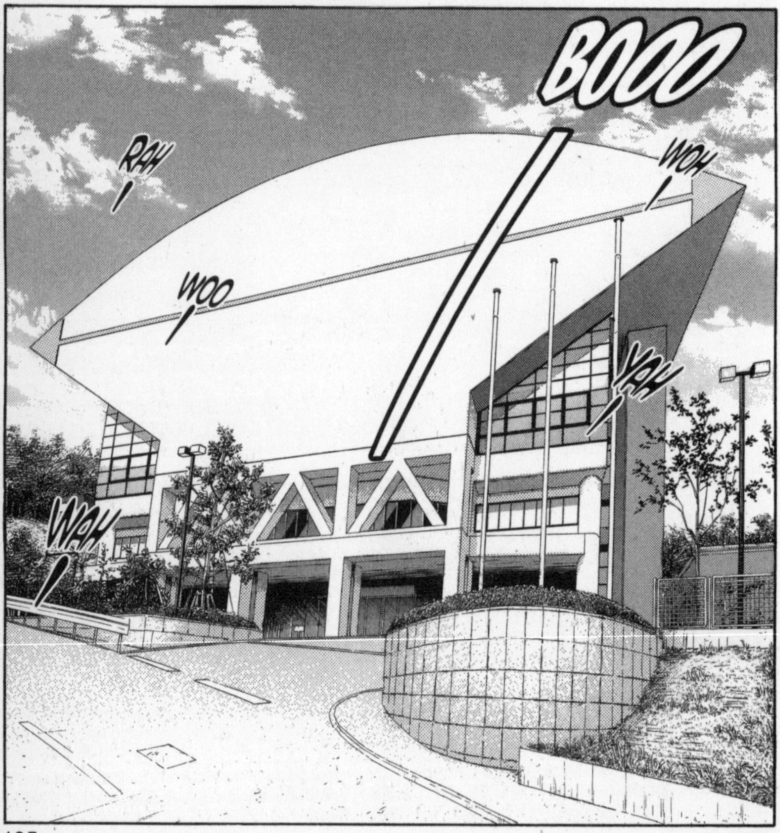
BOOO
WOH!
YAH!
RAH!
WOO!
WAH!

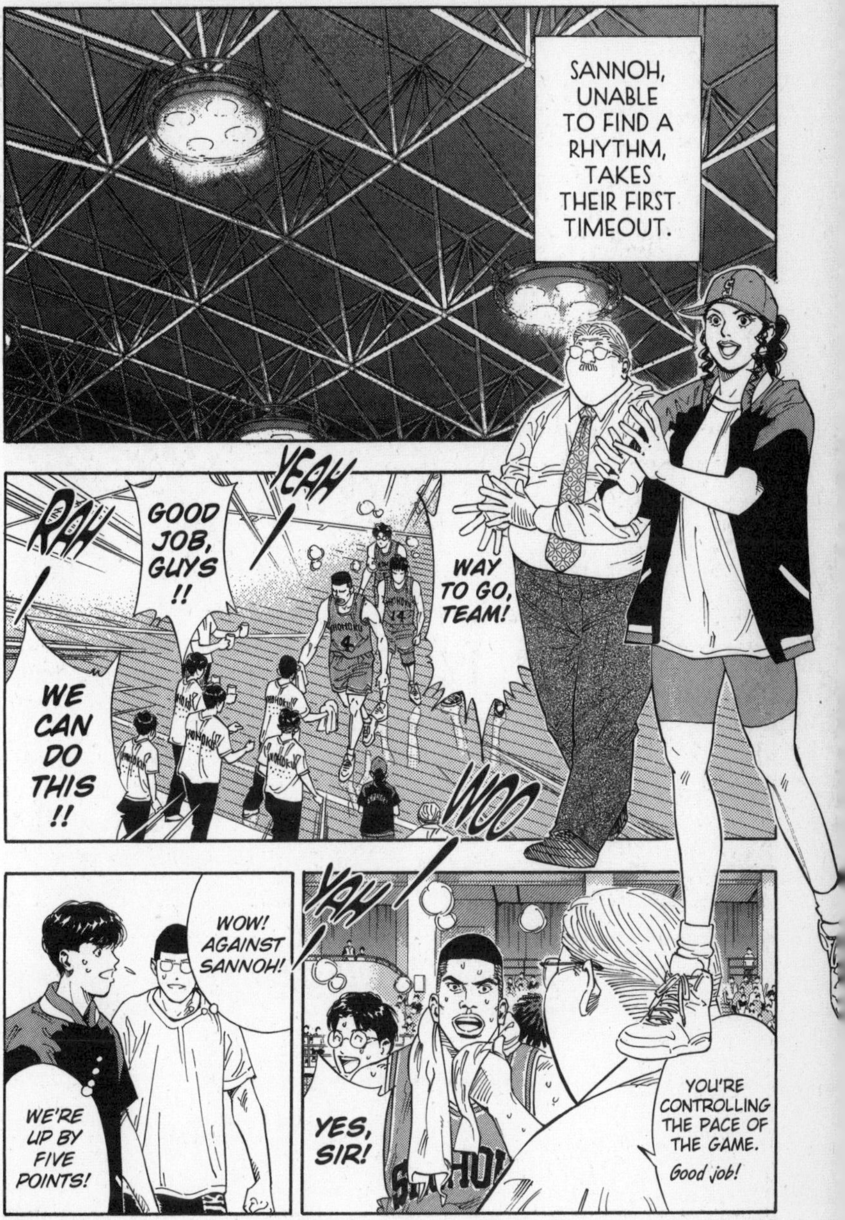
SANNOH, UNABLE TO FIND A RHYTHM, TAKES THEIR FIRST TIMEOUT.
WAY TO GO, TEAM!
YEAH!
GOOD JOB, GUYS!!
RAH!
WE CAN DO THIS!!
WOO!
YAH!
YOU'RE CONTROLLING THE PACE OF THE GAME.
Good job!
YES, SIR!
WOW! AGAINST SANNOH!
WE'RE UP BY FIVE POINTS!

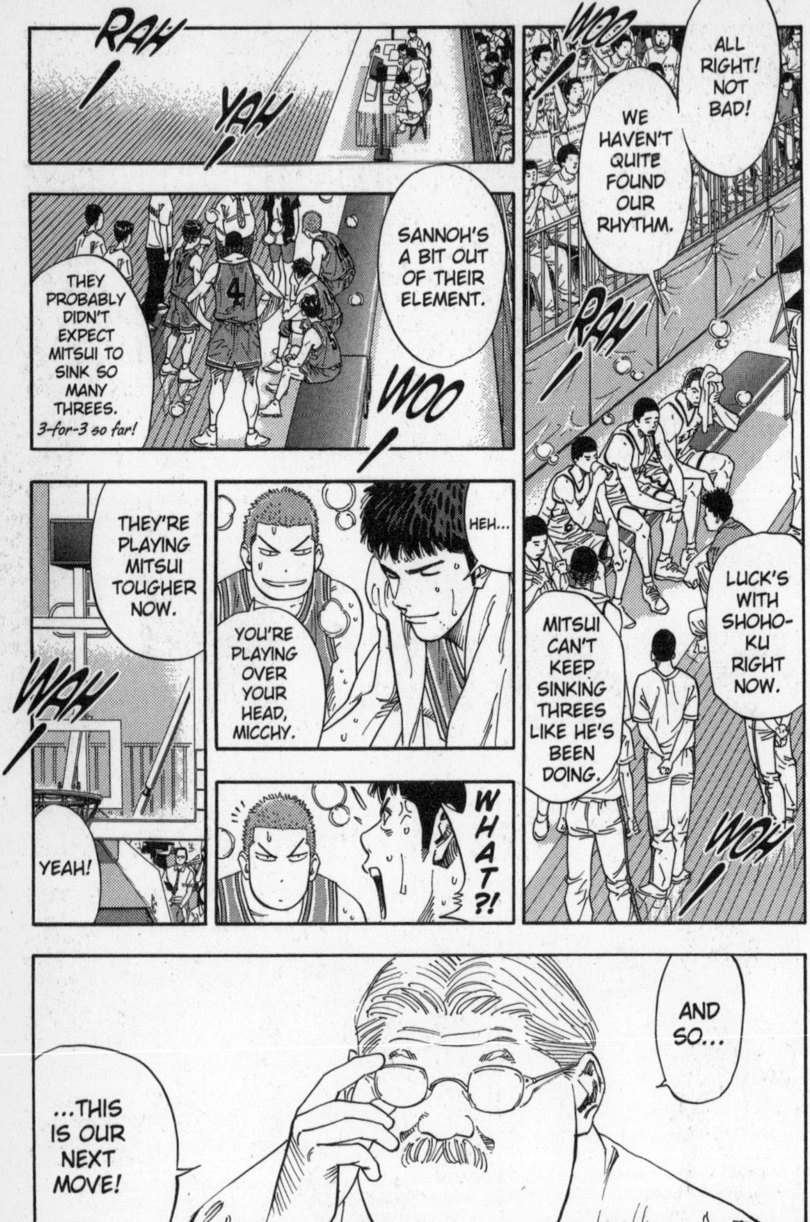
WOO
ALL RIGHT! NOT BAD!
WE HAVEN'T QUITE FOUND OUR RHYTHM.
RAH
LUCK'S WITH SHOHOKU RIGHT NOW.
MITSUI CAN'T KEEP SINKING THREES LIKE HE'S BEEN DOING.
WOH
RAH
YAH
SANNOH'S A BIT OUT OF THEIR ELEMENT.
THEY PROBABLY DIDN'T EXPECT MITSUI TO SINK SO MANY THREES.
3-for-3 so far!
WOO
HEH...
YOU'RE PLAYING OVER YOUR HEAD, MICCHY.
WHAT?!
THEY'RE PLAYING MITSUI TOUGHER NOW.
WAH
YEAH!
AND SO...
...THIS IS OUR NEXT MOVE!

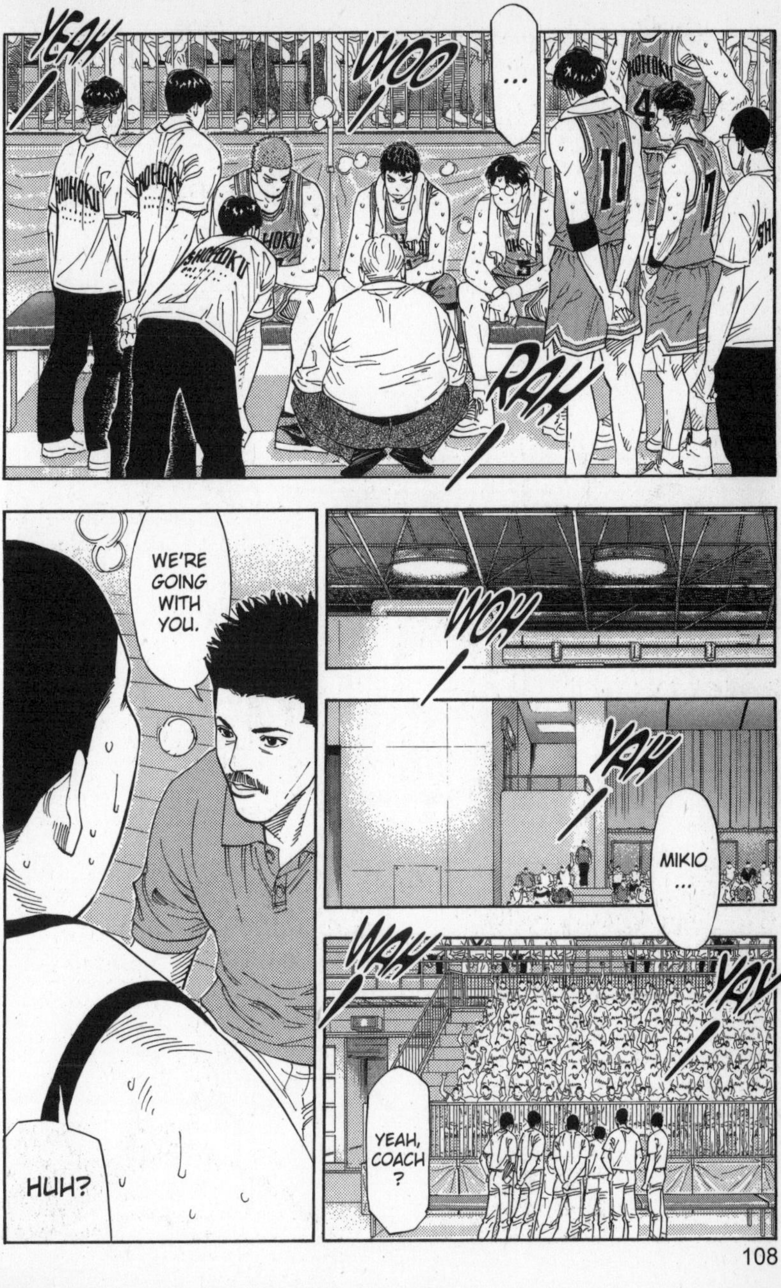
...
WOO
YEAH
RAH
WOH
YAH
MIKIO ...
YAY
WAH
YEAH, COACH?
WE'RE GOING WITH YOU.
HUH?

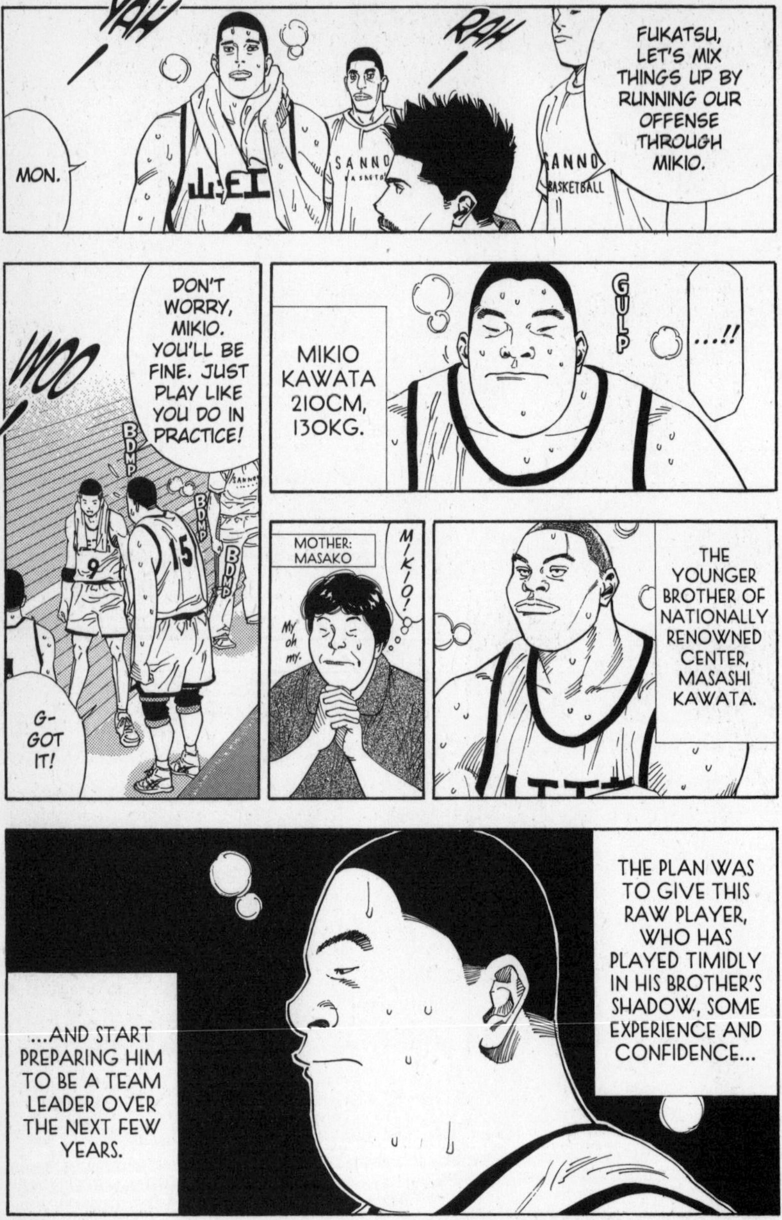
FUKATSU, LET'S MIX THINGS UP BY RUNNING OUR OFFENSE THROUGH MIKIO.
RAH
YAH
MON.
...!!
GULP
MIKIO KAWATA 210CM, 130KG.
THE YOUNGER BROTHER OF NATIONALLY RENOWNED CENTER, MASASHI KAWATA.
MIKIO!
MOTHER: MASAKO
My oh my.
DON'T WORRY, MIKIO. YOU'LL BE FINE. JUST PLAY LIKE YOU DO IN PRACTICE!
WOO
BDMP
BDMP
BDMP
G-GOT IT!
THE PLAN WAS TO GIVE THIS RAW PLAYER, WHO HAS PLAYED TIMIDLY IN HIS BROTHER'S SHADOW, SOME EXPERIENCE AND CONFIDENCE...
...AND START PREPARING HIM TO BE A TEAM LEADER OVER THE NEXT FEW YEARS.

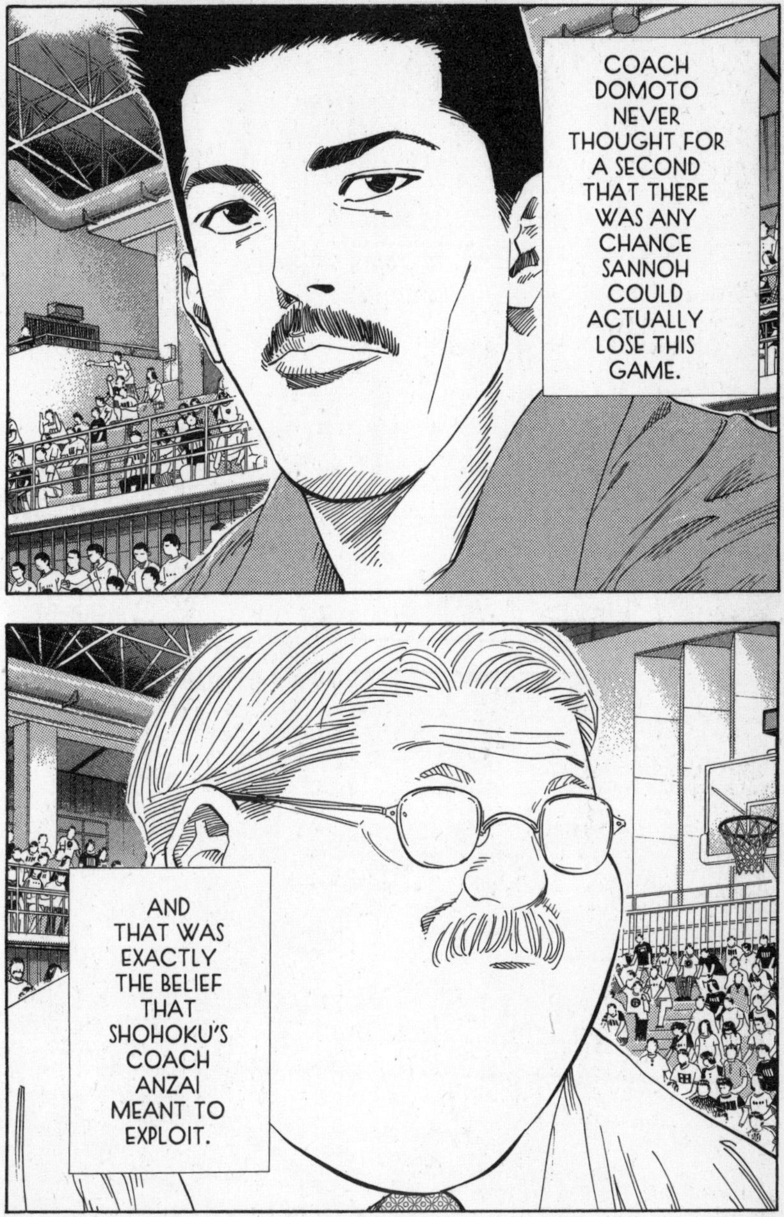
COACH DOMOTO NEVER THOUGHT FOR A SECOND THAT THERE WAS ANY CHANCE SANNOH COULD ACTUALLY LOSE THIS GAME.
AND THAT WAS EXACTLY THE BELIEF THAT SHOHOKU'S COACH ANZAI MEANT TO EXPLOIT.

READ THIS WAY

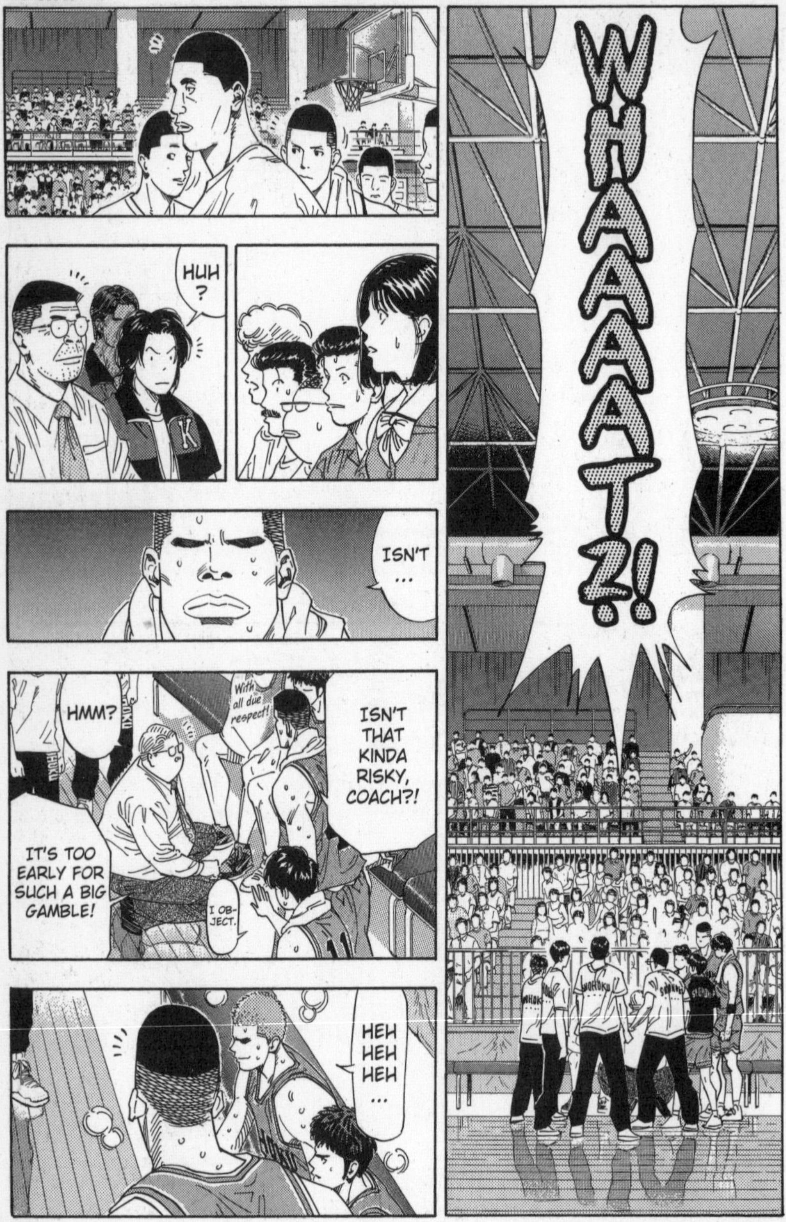
WHAAAATZ!
HUH ?
ISN'T ...
ISN'T THAT KINDA RISKY, COACH?!
With all due respect!
HMM?
I OB-JECT.
IT'S TOO EARLY FOR SUCH A BIG GAMBLE!
HEH HEH HEH ...

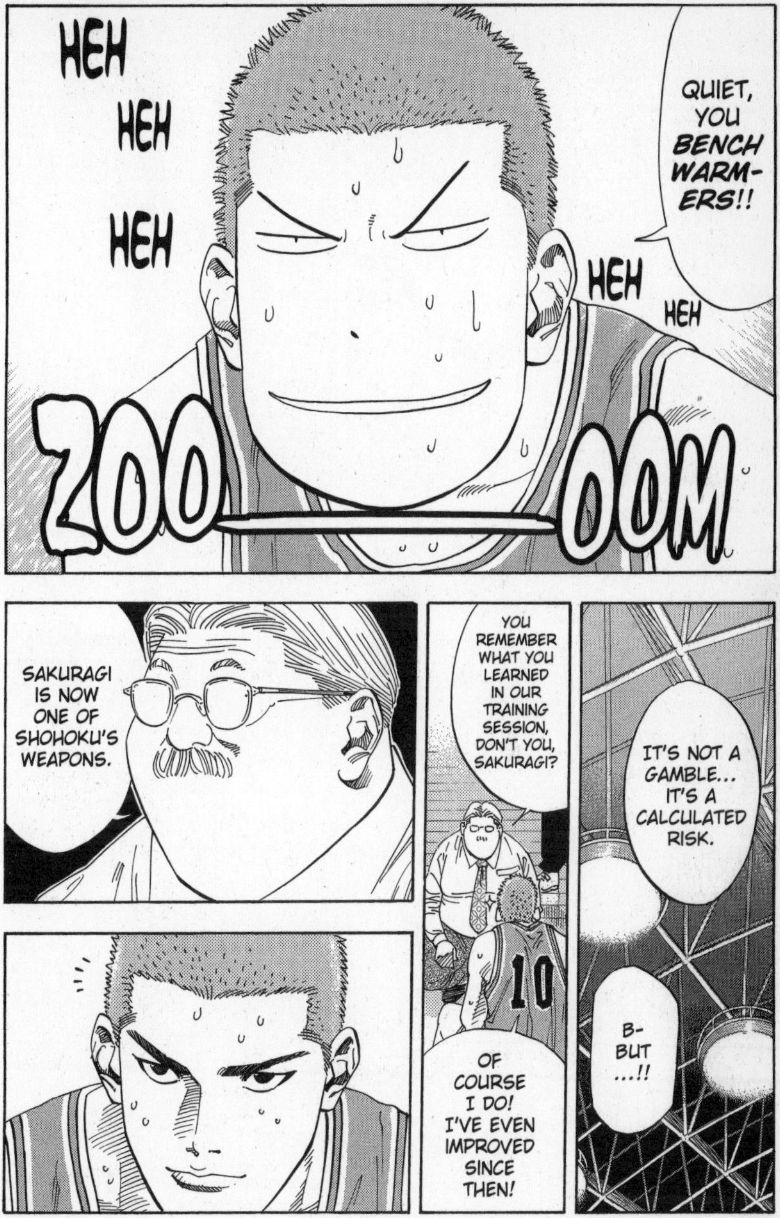
QUIET, YOU BENCH WARMERS!!
HEH
HEH
HEH
HEH
HEH
ZOOOOM
IT'S NOT A GAMBLE... IT'S A CALCULATED RISK.
B-BUT ...!!
YOU REMEMBER WHAT YOU LEARNED IN OUR TRAINING SESSION, DON'T YOU, SAKURAGI?
OF COURSE I DO! I'VE EVEN IMPROVED SINCE THEN!
SAKURAGI IS NOW ONE OF SHOHOKU'S WEAPONS.

READ THIS WAY

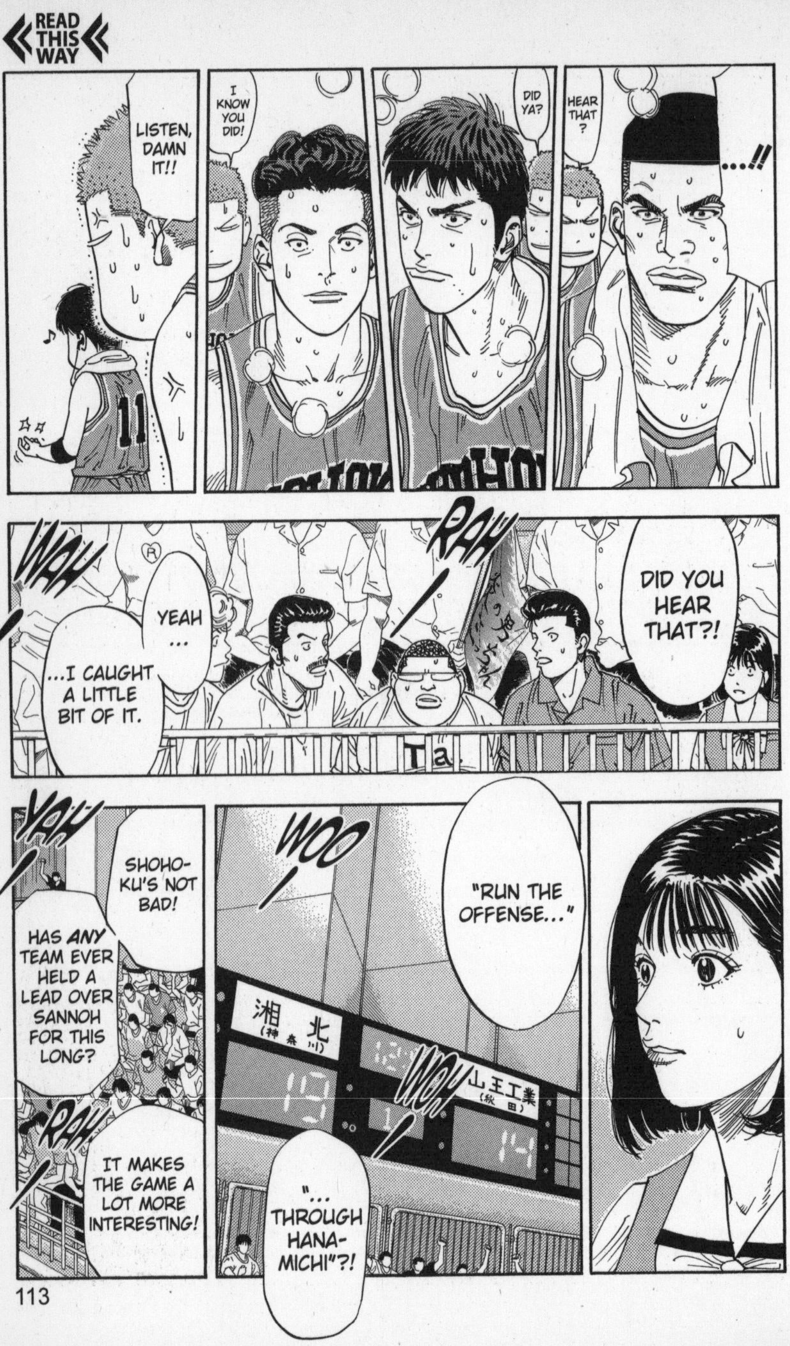

...!!
HEAR THAT?
DID YA?
I KNOW YOU DID!
LISTEN, DAMN IT!!
DID YOU HEAR THAT?!
RAH
YEAH ...
...I CAUGHT A LITTLE BIT OF IT.
WAH
"RUN THE OFFENSE..."
WOO
湘北 (神奈川)
山王工業 (秋田)
WOH
"... THROUGH HANA-MICHI"?!
YAH
SHOHOKU'S NOT BAD!
HAS ***ANY*** TEAM EVER HELD A LEAD OVER SANNOH FOR THIS LONG?
RAH
IT MAKES THE GAME A LOT MORE INTERESTING!

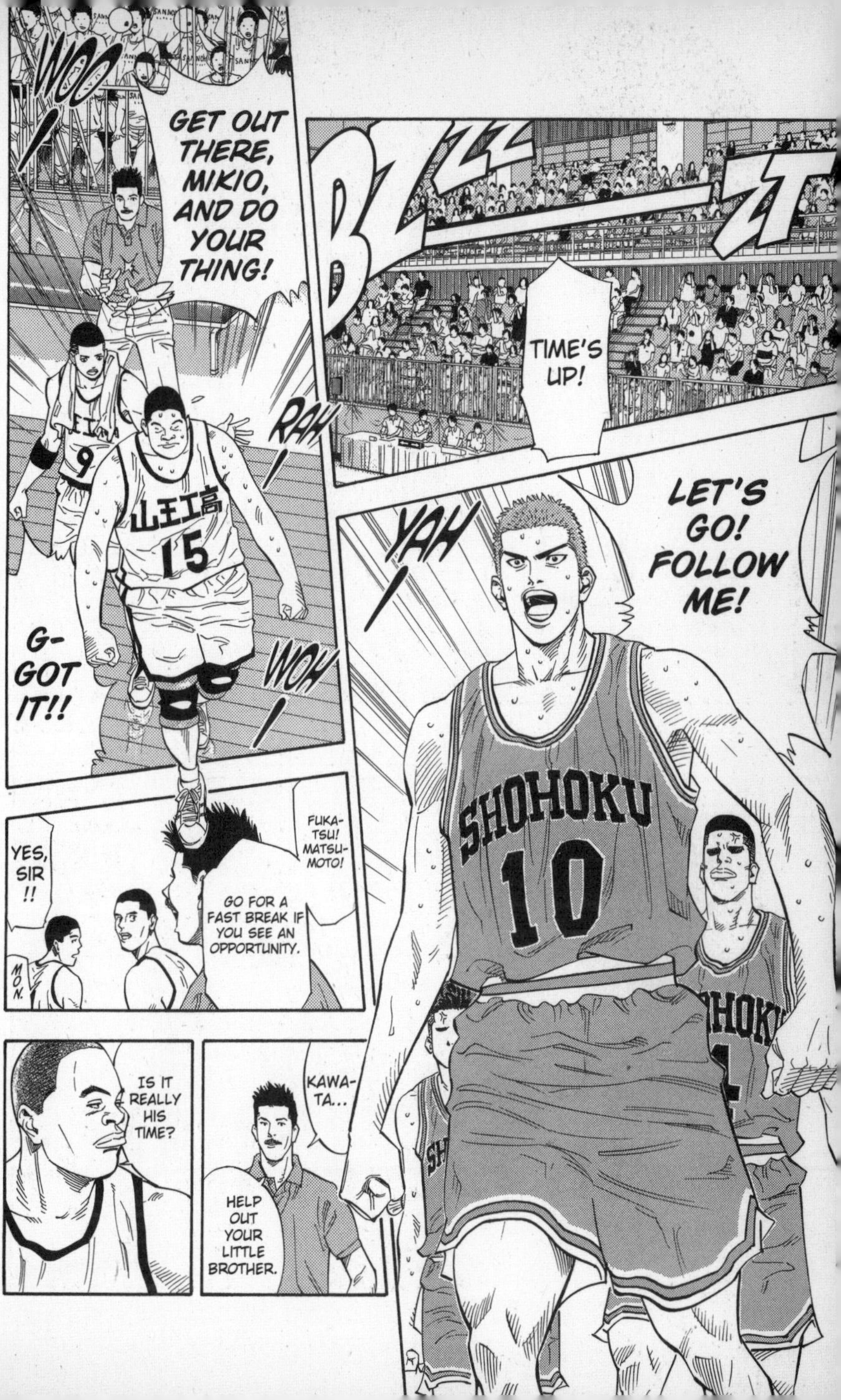
BZZZ—ZT
TIME'S UP!
WOO!
GET OUT THERE, MIKIO, AND DO YOUR THING!
RAH!
WOH!
G-GOT IT!!
YAH!
LET'S GO! FOLLOW ME!
FUKATSU! MATSUMOTO!
GO FOR A FAST BREAK IF YOU SEE AN OPPORTUNITY.
YES, SIR!!
MON.
KAWATA...
HELP OUT YOUR LITTLE BROTHER.
IS IT REALLY HIS TIME?

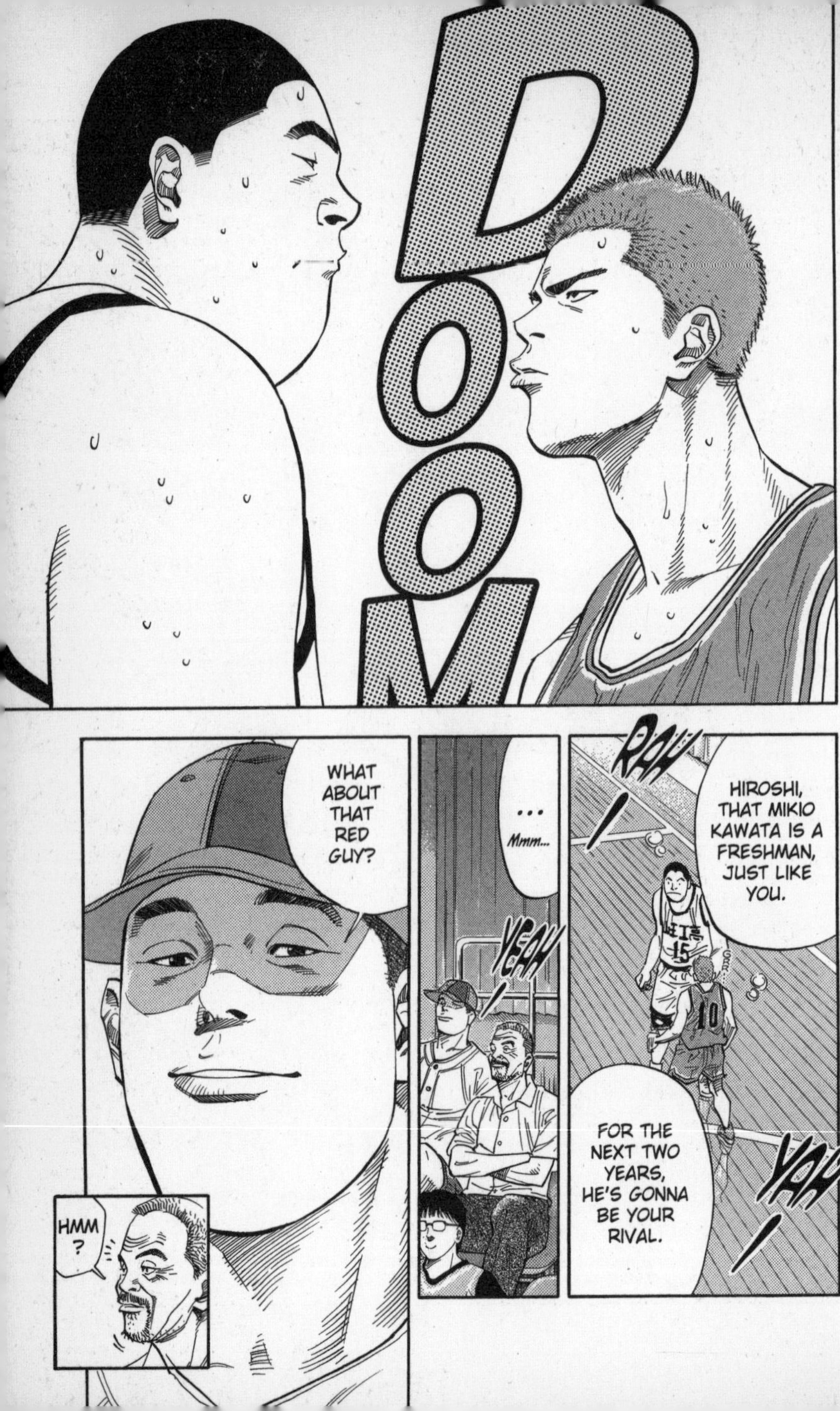
DOOM
RAH!
HIROSHI, THAT MIKIO KAWATA IS A FRESHMAN, JUST LIKE YOU.
GRR...
FOR THE NEXT TWO YEARS, HE'S GONNA BE YOUR RIVAL.
YAH!
...
Mmm...
YEAH!
WHAT ABOUT THAT RED GUY?
HMM ?

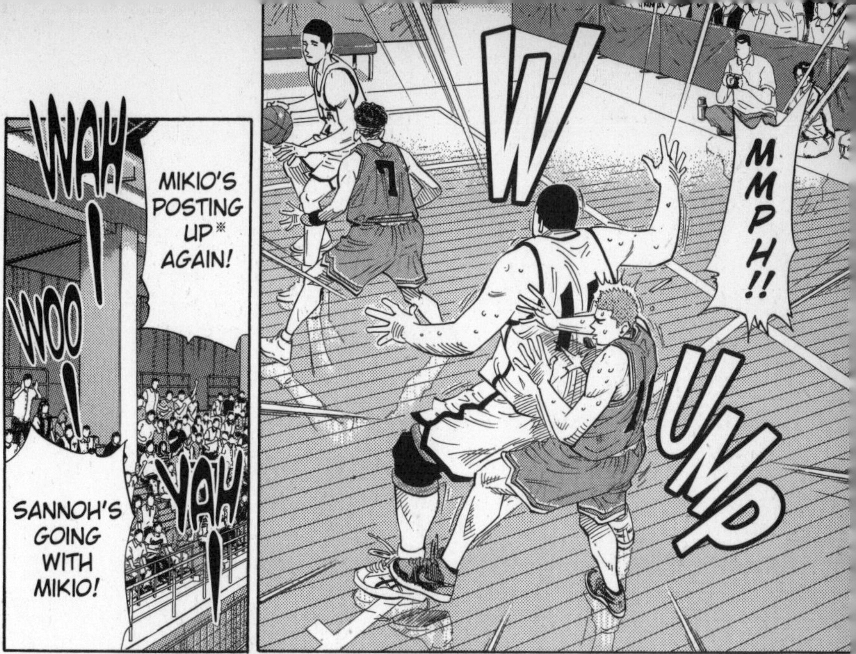
W
UMP
MMPH!!
WAH!
MIKIO'S POSTING UP※ AGAIN!
WOO!
YAH!
SANNOH'S GOING WITH MIKIO!

※POST-UP — STANDING NEAR THE BASKET AND POSITIONING YOURSELF TO RECEIVE A PASS.

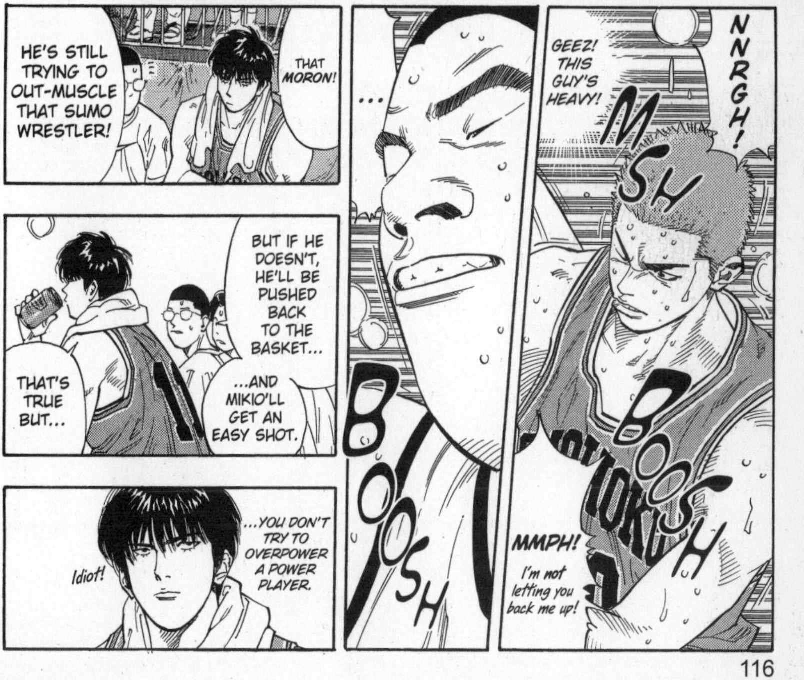
NNRGH!
GEEZ! THIS GUY'S HEAVY!
MSH
BOOSH
MMPH!
I'm not letting you back me up!
...
BOOSH
THAT MORON!
HE'S STILL TRYING TO OUT-MUSCLE THAT SUMO WRESTLER!
BUT IF HE DOESN'T, HE'LL BE PUSHED BACK TO THE BASKET...
...AND MIKIO'LL GET AN EASY SHOT.
THAT'S TRUE BUT...
...YOU DON'T TRY TO OVERPOWER A POWER PLAYER.
Idiot!

READ THIS WAY

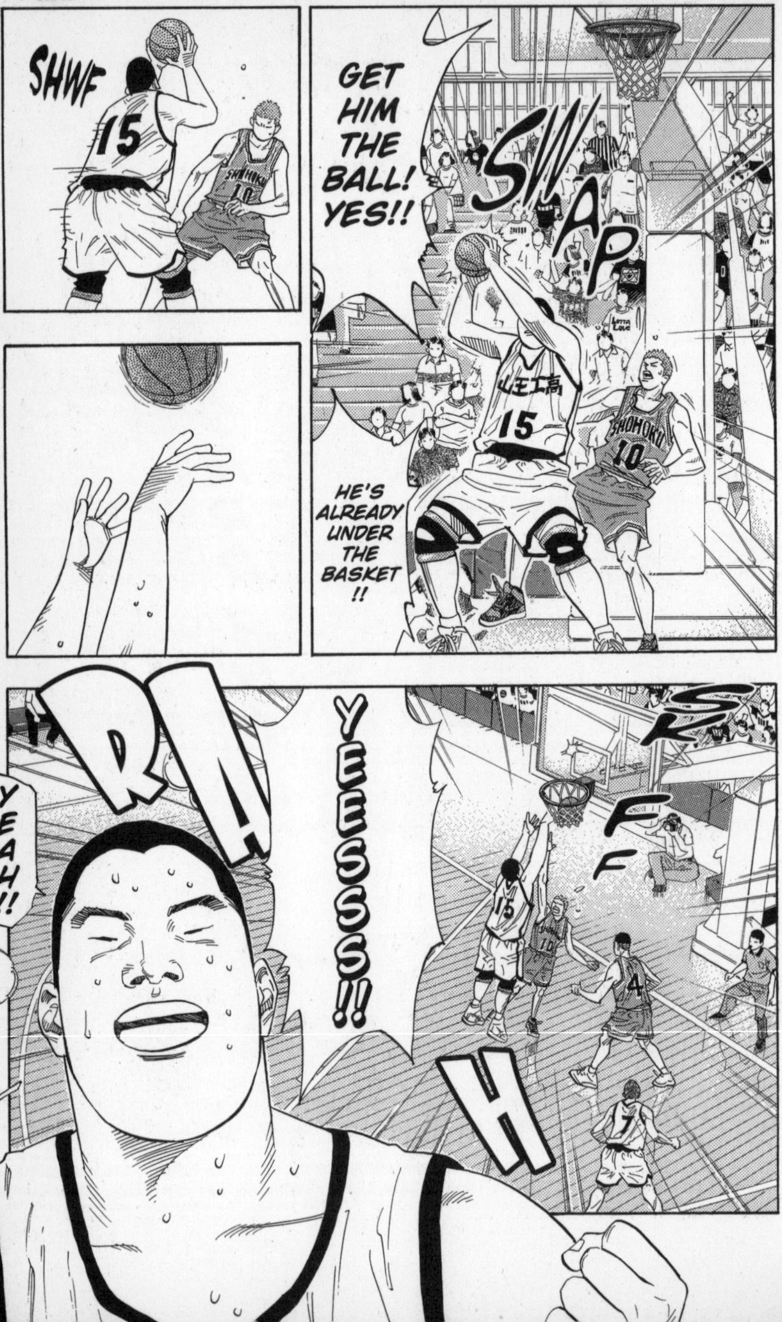
GET HIM THE BALL! YES!!
SWAP
HE'S ALREADY UNDER THE BASKET!!
SHWF
SKFF
YEESSSS!!
RAH
YEAH!!

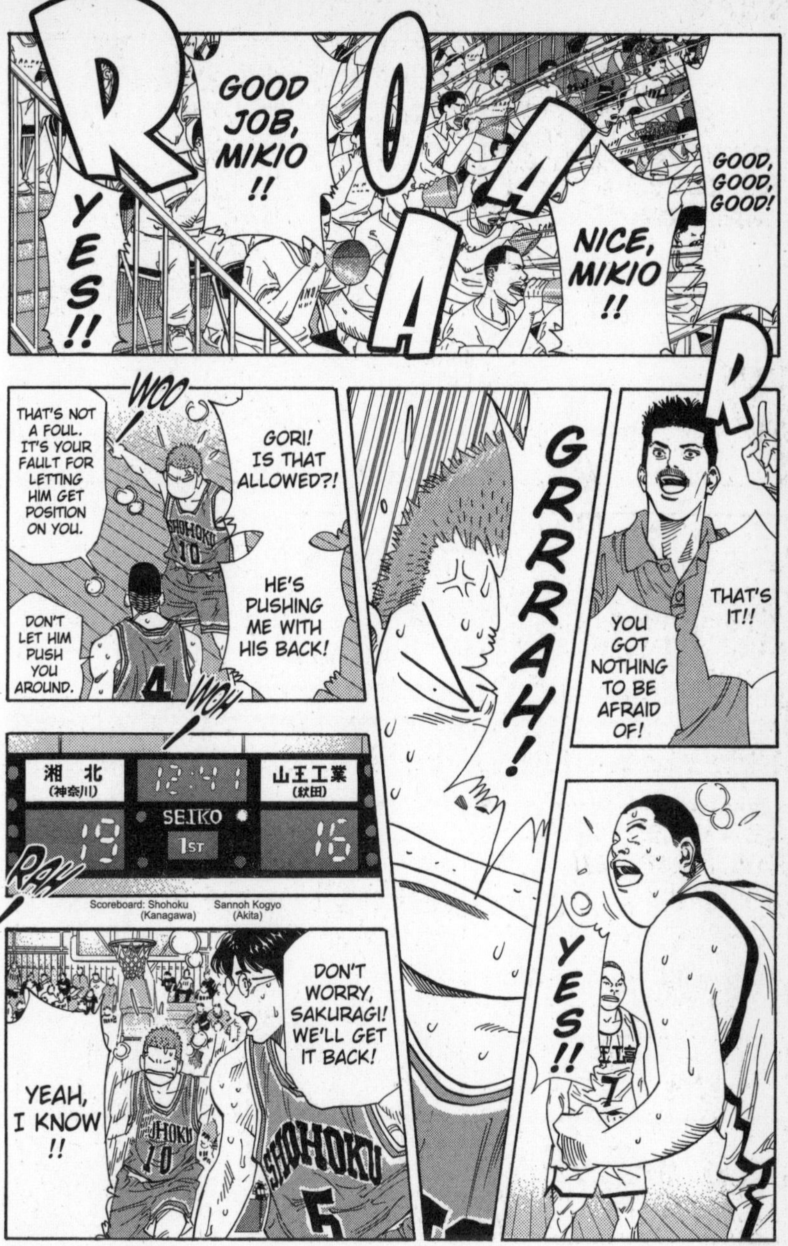
ROAAR
GOOD, GOOD, GOOD!
NICE, MIKIO!!
GOOD JOB, MIKIO!!
YES!!
THAT'S IT!!
YOU GOT NOTHING TO BE AFRAID OF!
YES!!
GRRRAH!
WOO
GORI! IS THAT ALLOWED?!
HE'S PUSHING ME WITH HIS BACK!
THAT'S NOT A FOUL. IT'S YOUR FAULT FOR LETTING HIM GET POSITION ON YOU.
DON'T LET HIM PUSH YOU AROUND.
WOH
湘北 (神奈川)
12:41
山王工業 (秋田)
SEIKO
1ST
19
16
RAH
DON'T WORRY, SAKURAGI! WE'LL GET IT BACK!
YEAH, I KNOW!!
Scoreboard: Shohoku (Kanagawa) Sannoh Kogyo (Akita)

READ THIS WAY

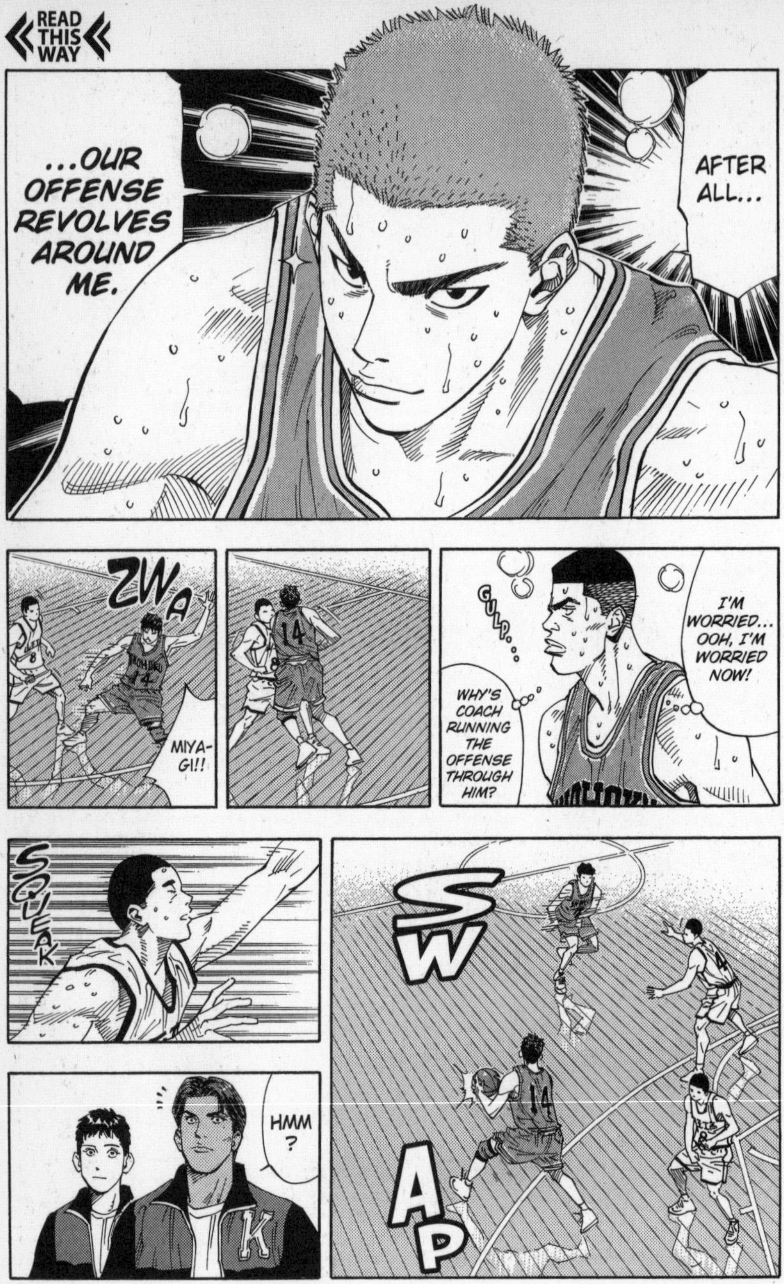

AFTER ALL...
...OUR OFFENSE REVOLVES AROUND ME.
I'M WORRIED... OOH, I'M WORRIED NOW!
GULP...
WHY'S COACH RUNNING THE OFFENSE THROUGH HIM?
ZWA
MIYAGI!!
SWAP
SQUEAK
HMM?

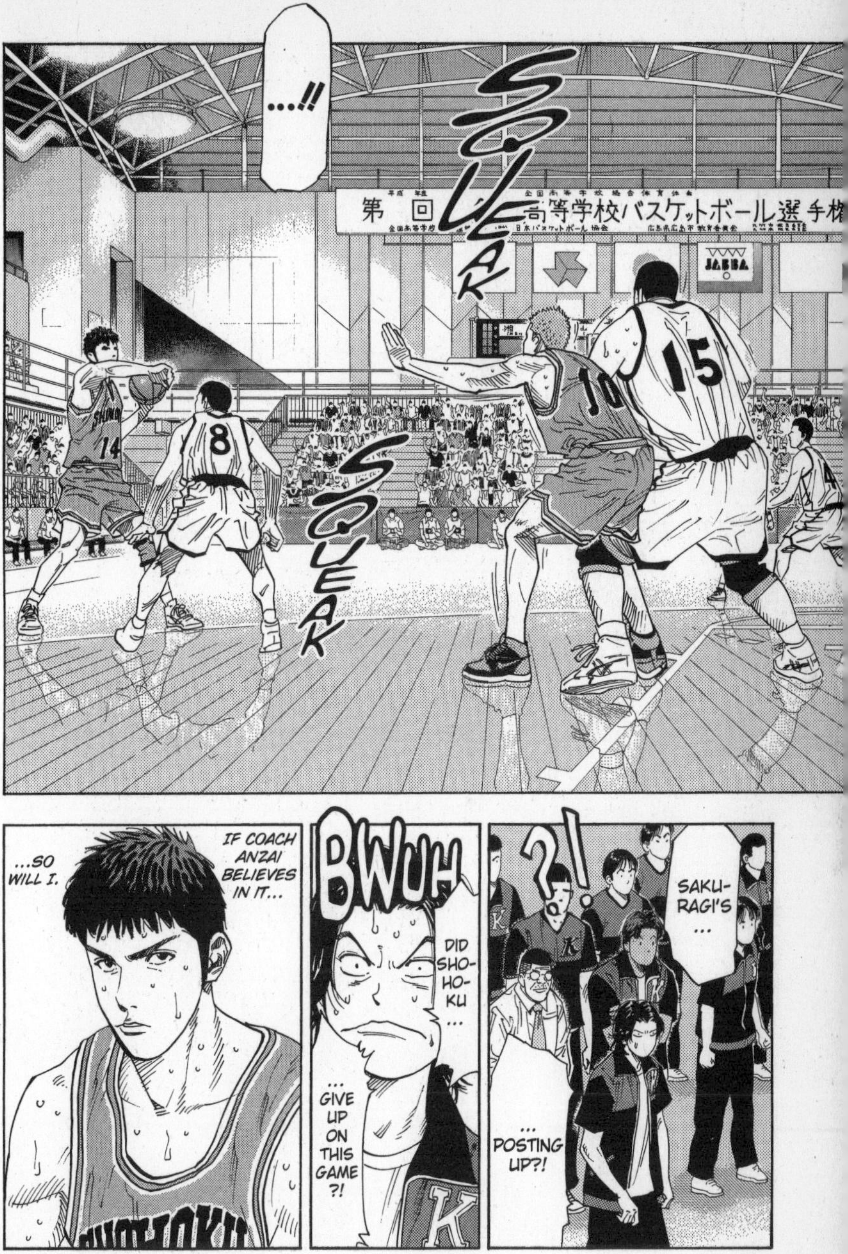
...!!
SQUEAK
SQUEAK
?!
SAKU-RAGI'S ...
... POSTING UP?!
BWUH
DID SHO-HO-KU ...
... GIVE UP ON THIS GAME ?!
IF COACH ANZAI BELIEVES IN IT...
...SO WILL I.

READ THIS WAY

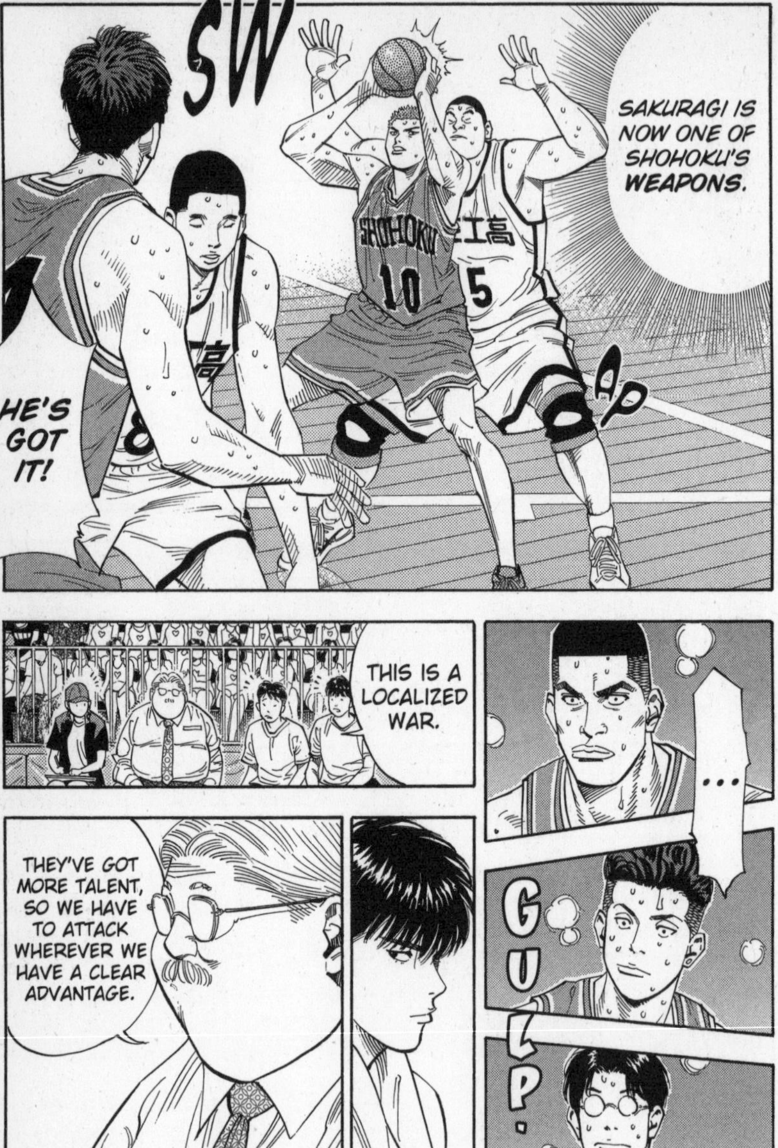
SAKURAGI IS NOW ONE OF SHOHOKU'S WEAPONS.
SW
AP
HE'S GOT IT!
...
THIS IS A LOCALIZED WAR.
GULP..
THEY'VE GOT MORE TALENT, SO WE HAVE TO ATTACK WHEREVER WE HAVE A CLEAR ADVANTAGE.

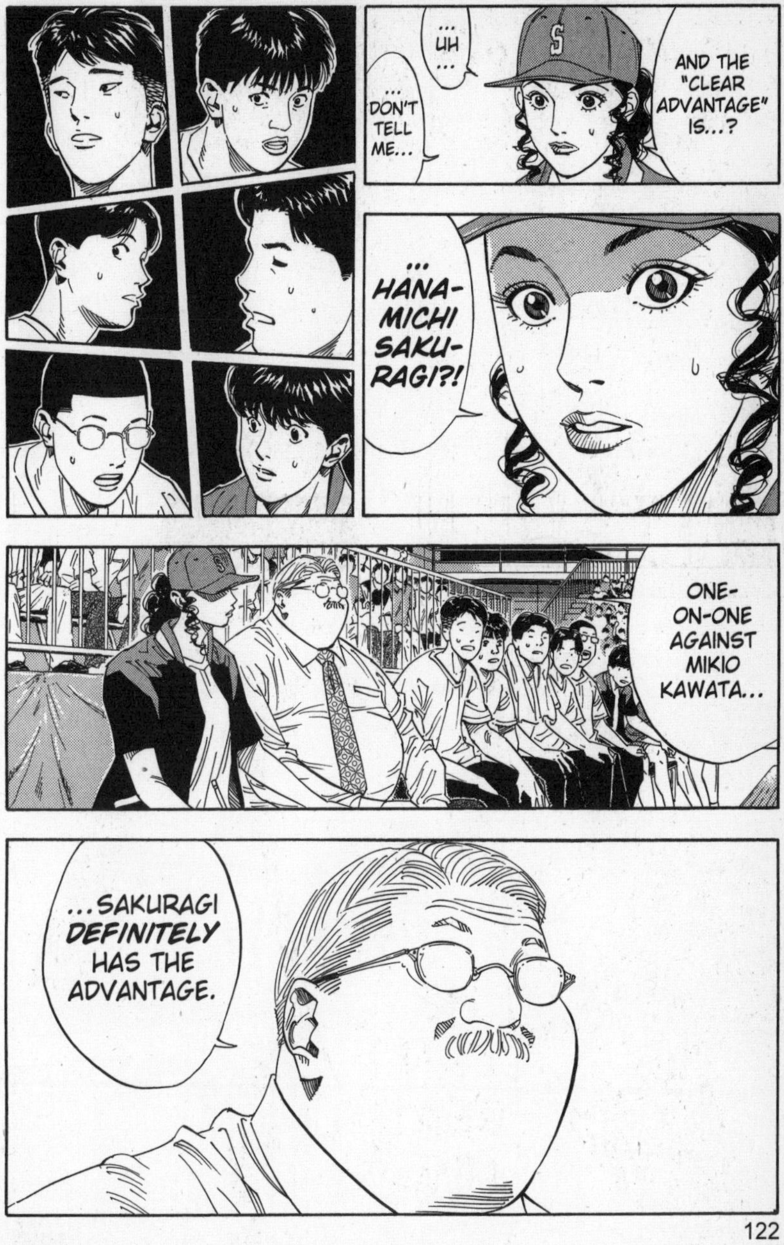
AND THE "CLEAR ADVANTAGE" IS...?
...UH...
...DON'T TELL ME...
...HANAMICHI SAKURAGI?!
ONE-ON-ONE AGAINST MIKIO KAWATA...
...SAKURAGI DEFINITELY HAS THE ADVANTAGE.

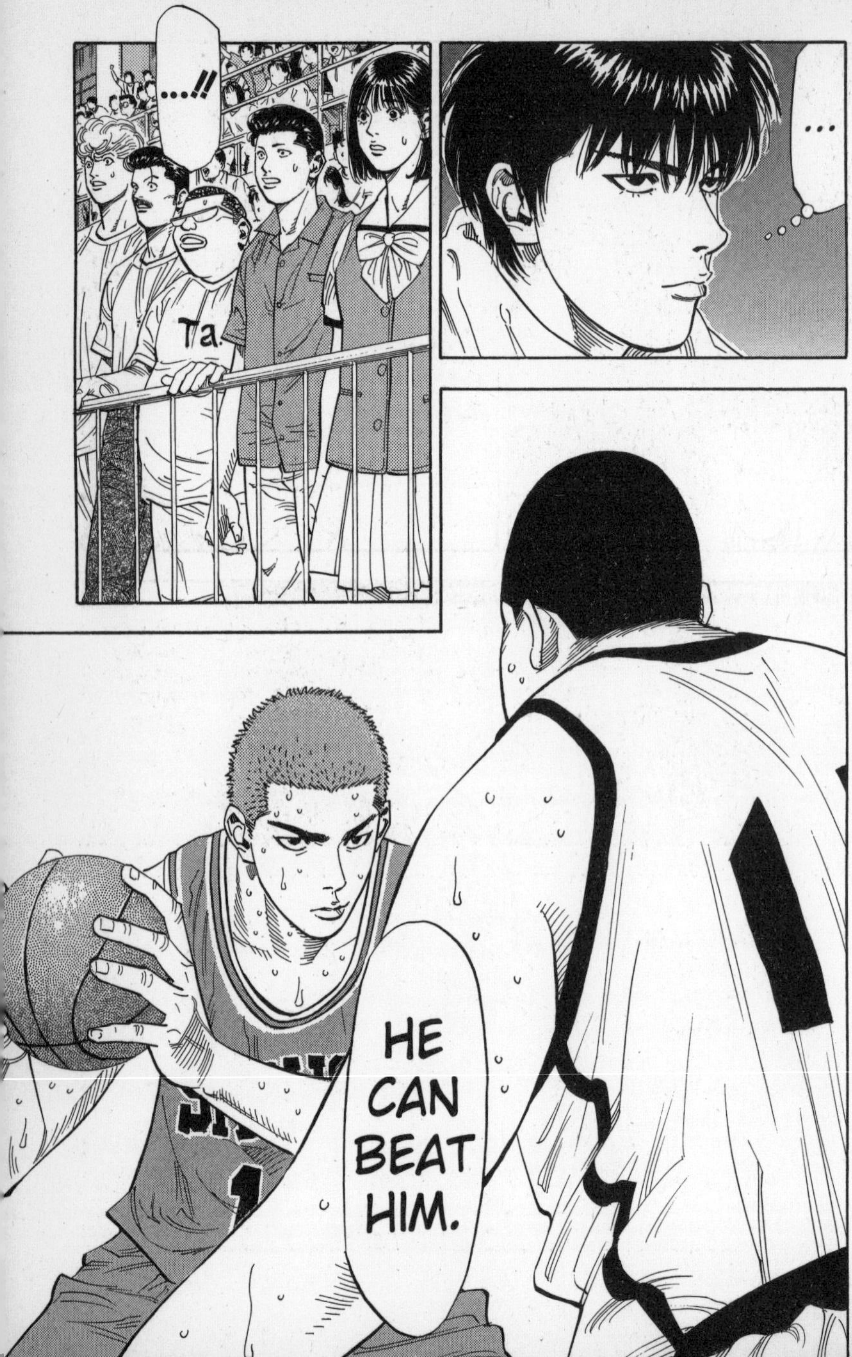
...
...!!
Ta.
HE CAN BEAT HIM.

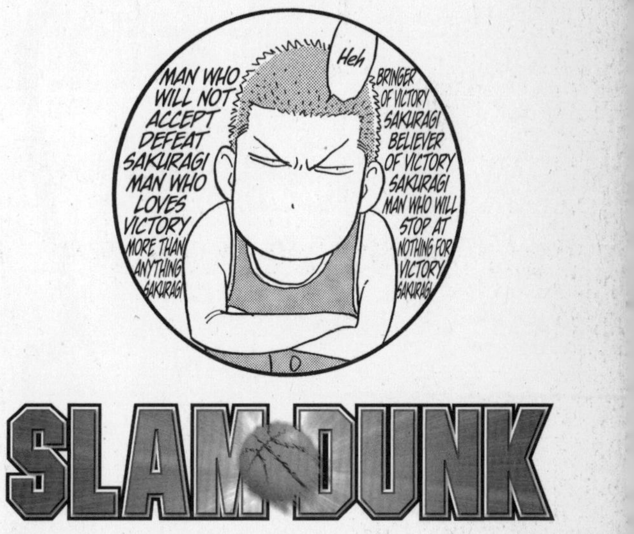
Heh
BRINGER OF VICTORY SAKURAGI BELIEVER OF VICTORY SAKURAGI MAN WHO WILL STOP AT NOTHING FOR VICTORY SAKURAGI
MAN WHO WILL NOT ACCEPT DEFEAT SAKURAGI MAN WHO LOVES VICTORY MORE THAN ANYTHING SAKURAGI

SLAM DUNK

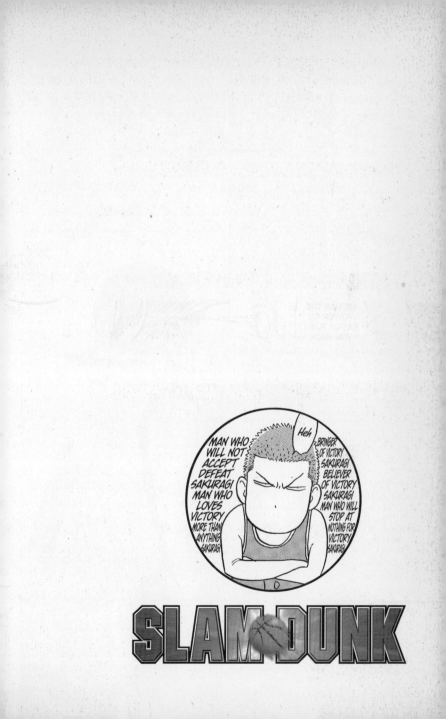

POWER MATCH

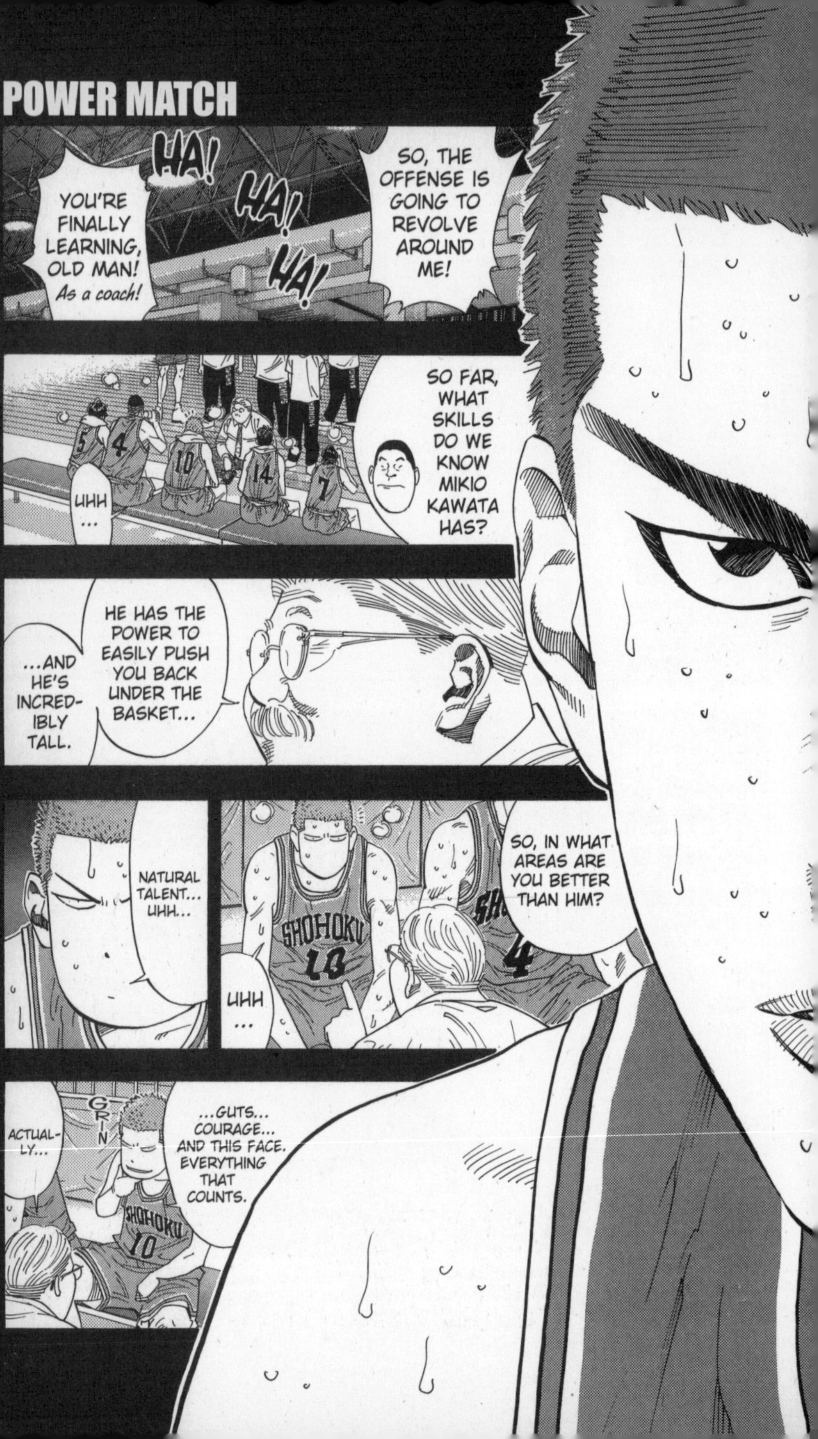
SO, THE OFFENSE IS GOING TO REVOLVE AROUND ME!
HA! HA! HA!
YOU'RE FINALLY LEARNING, OLD MAN! As a coach!
SO FAR, WHAT SKILLS DO WE KNOW MIKIO KAWATA HAS?
UHH ...
HE HAS THE POWER TO EASILY PUSH YOU BACK UNDER THE BASKET...
...AND HE'S INCREDIBLY TALL.
SO, IN WHAT AREAS ARE YOU BETTER THAN HIM?
UHH ...
NATURAL TALENT... UHH...
...GUTS... COURAGE... AND THIS FACE. EVERYTHING THAT COUNTS.
GRIN
ACTUALLY...

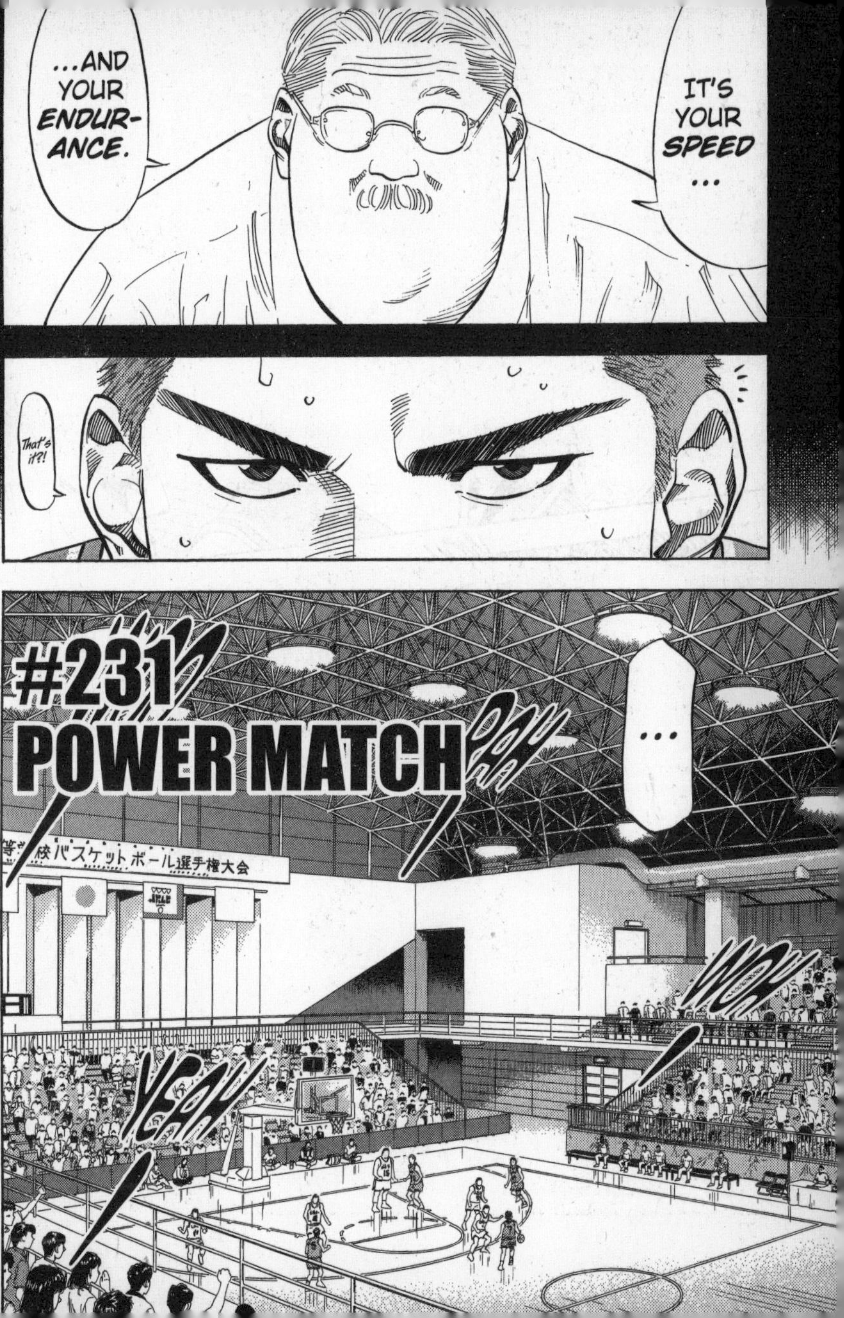

IT'S YOUR SPEED ...
...AND YOUR ENDURANCE.
That's it?!
#231 POWER MATCH
...
校バスケットボール選手権大会
WOW
YEAH

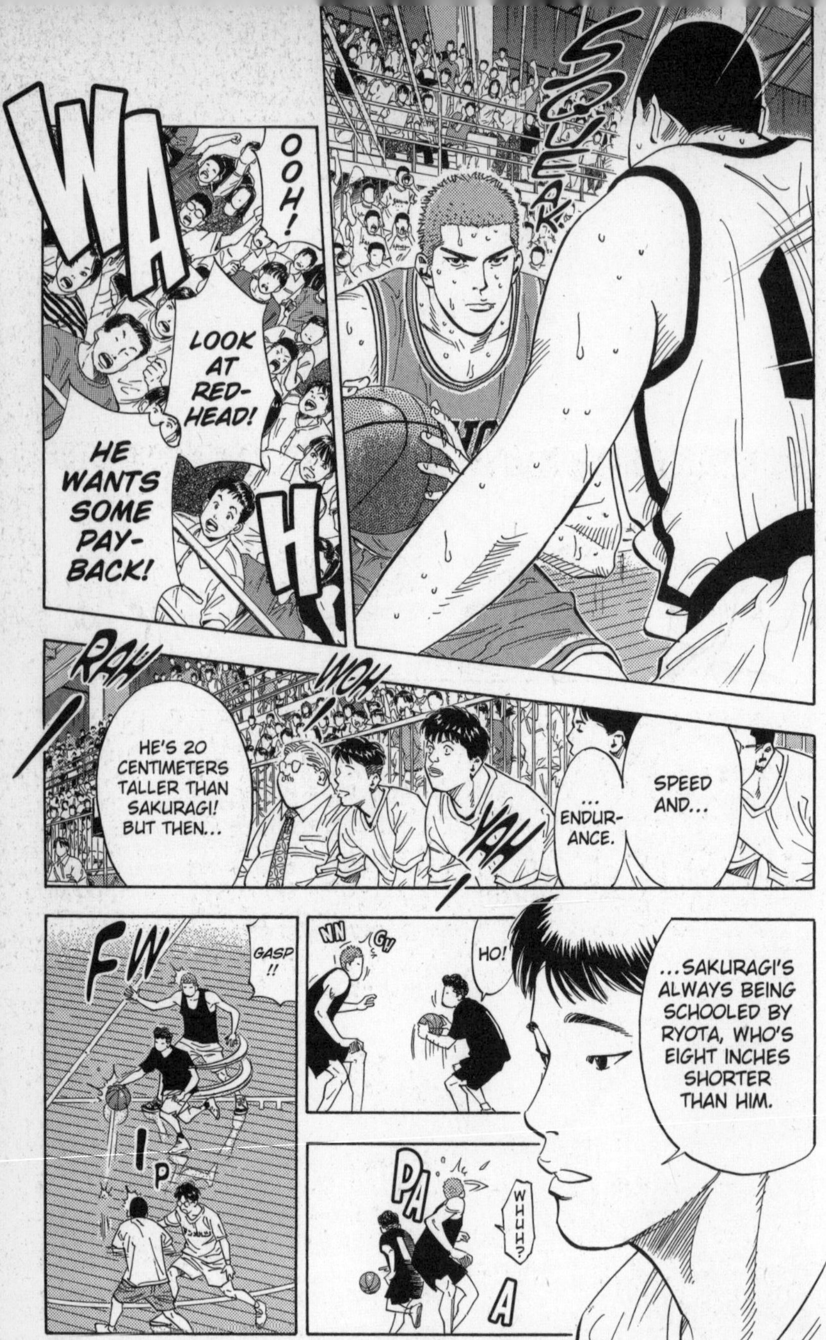
SQUEAK
WA
OOH!
LOOK AT RED-HEAD!
HE WANTS SOME PAY-BACK!
H
SPEED AND...
...ENDURANCE.
YAH
WOH
HE'S 20 CENTIMETERS TALLER THAN SAKURAGI! BUT THEN...
RAH
...SAKURAGI'S ALWAYS BEING SCHOOLED BY RYOTA, WHO'S EIGHT INCHES SHORTER THAN HIM.
NN
GH
HO!
PA
WHUH?
A
FW
GASP!!
I
P

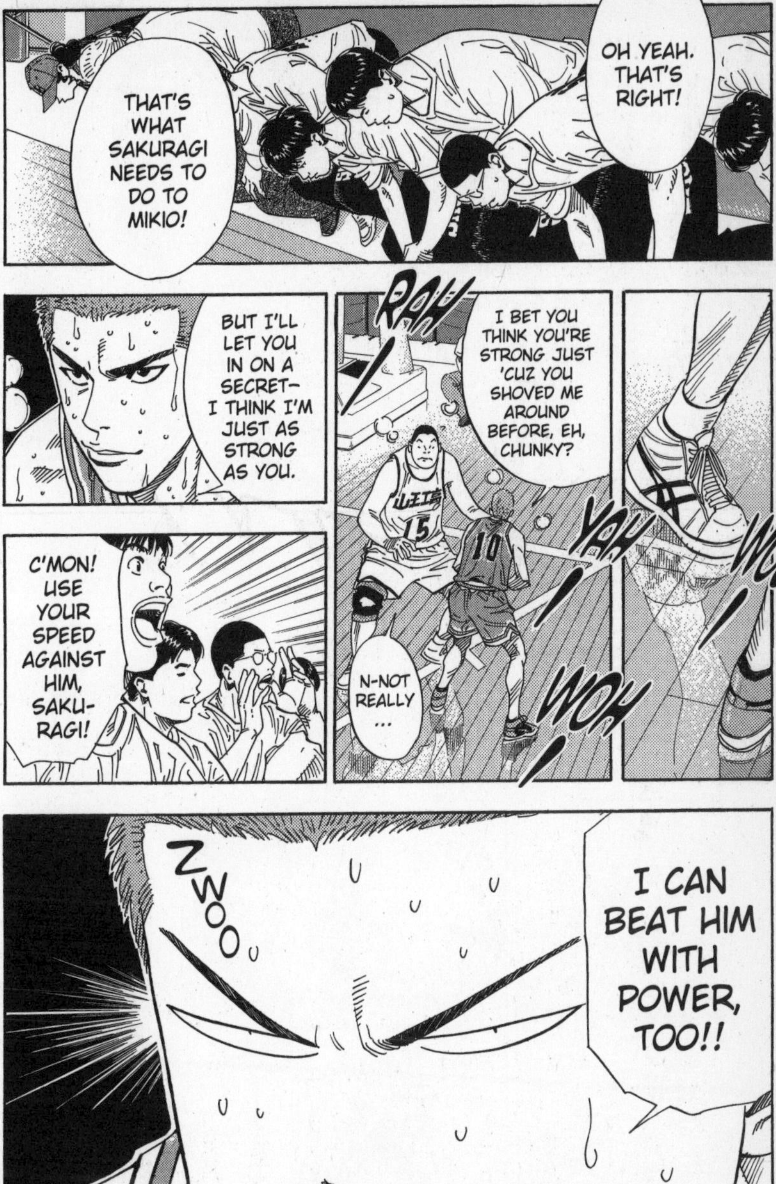

OH YEAH. THAT'S RIGHT!
THAT'S WHAT SAKURAGI NEEDS TO DO TO MIKIO!
WOO!
YAH!
WOH!
RAH!
I BET YOU THINK YOU'RE STRONG JUST 'CUZ YOU SHOVED ME AROUND BEFORE, EH, CHUNKY?
N-NOT REALLY ...
BUT I'LL LET YOU IN ON A SECRET— I THINK I'M JUST AS STRONG AS YOU.
C'MON! USE YOUR SPEED AGAINST HIM, SAKURAGI!
I CAN BEAT HIM WITH POWER, TOO!!
ZWOO

READ THIS WAY

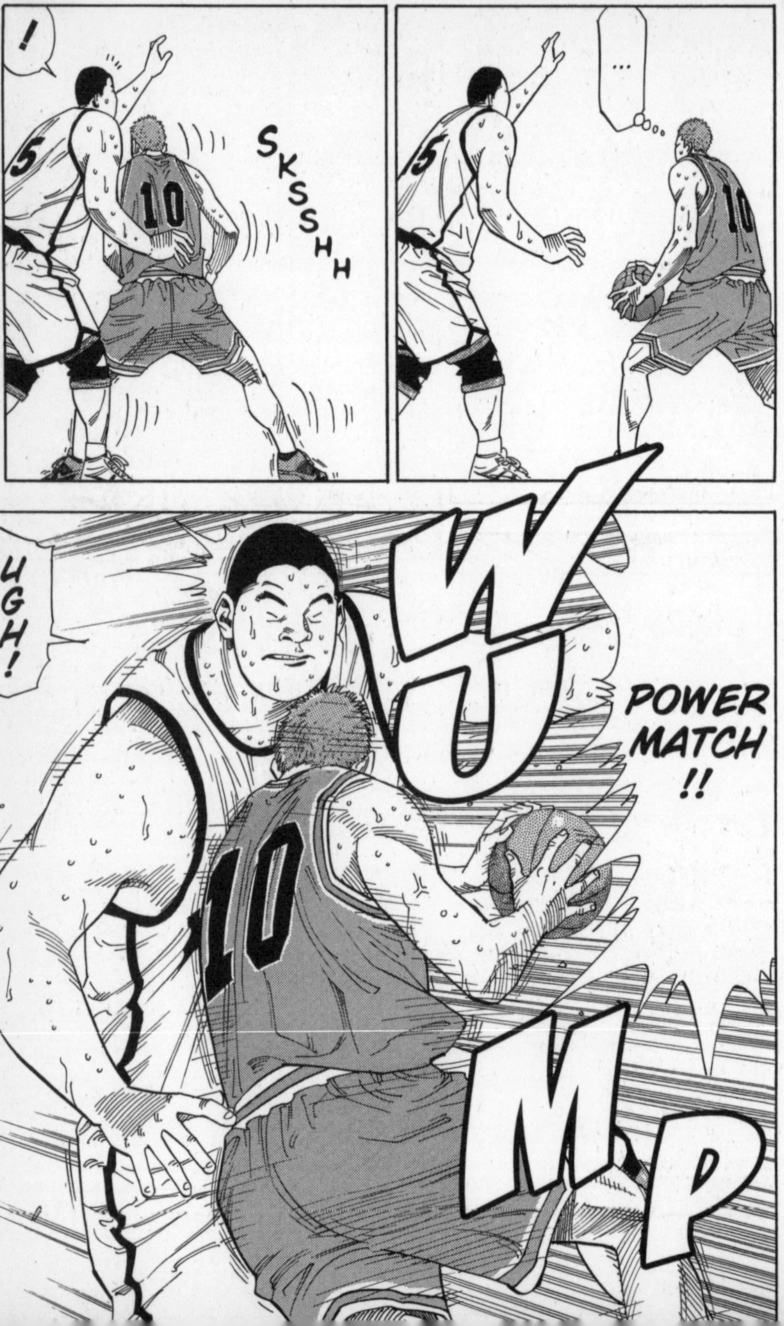
...
!
SKSSHH
WUMP
POWER MATCH !!
UGH!

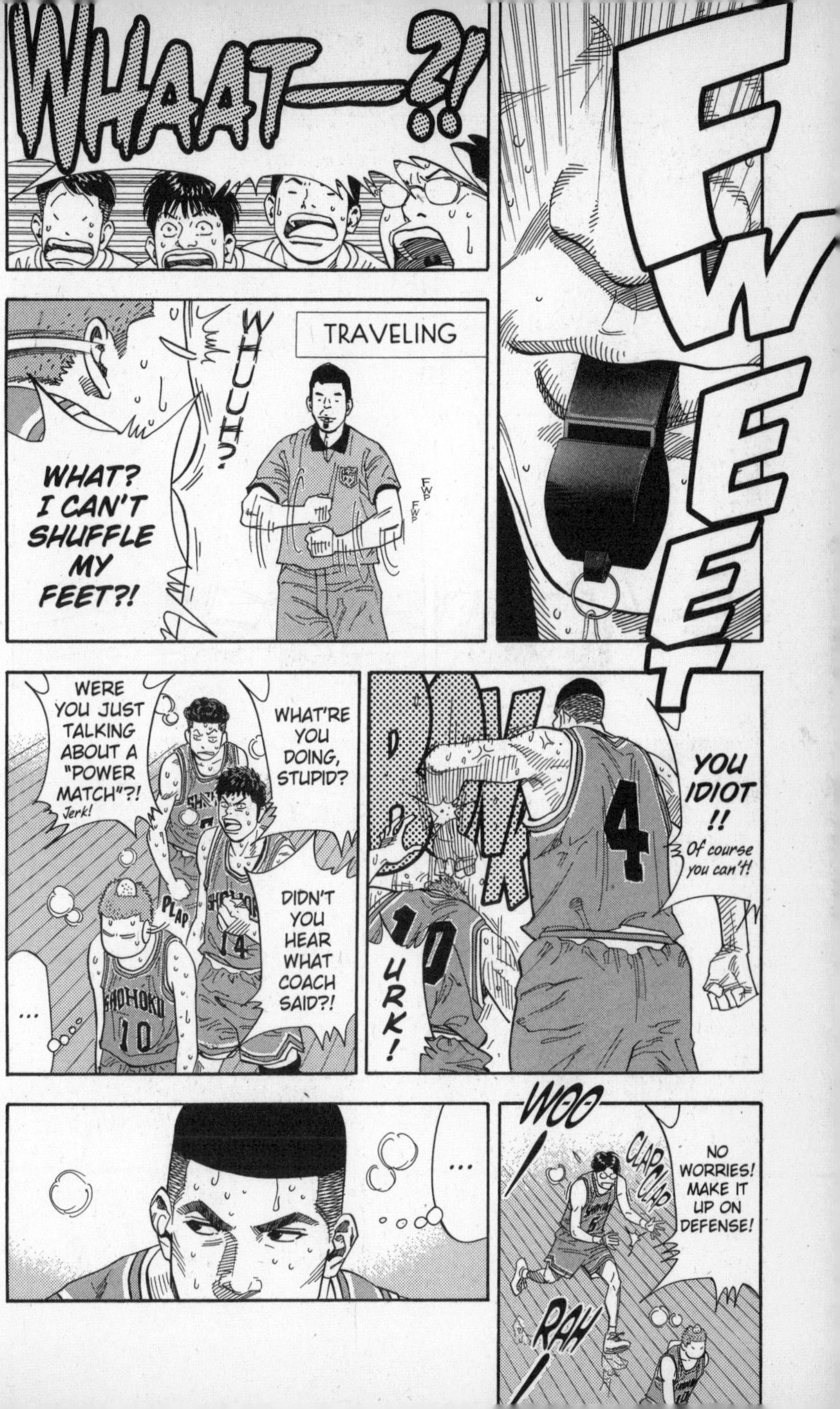
FWEEET
WHAAT—?!
TRAVELING
WHUUH?
WHAT? I CAN'T SHUFFLE MY FEET?!
FWP FWP
YOU IDIOT!!
Of course you can't!
URK!
WHAT'RE YOU DOING, STUPID?
WERE YOU JUST TALKING ABOUT A "POWER MATCH"?!
Jerk!
PLAP
DIDN'T YOU HEAR WHAT COACH SAID?!
...
WOO-!
CLAP CLAP
NO WORRIES! MAKE IT UP ON DEFENSE!
RAH-!
...

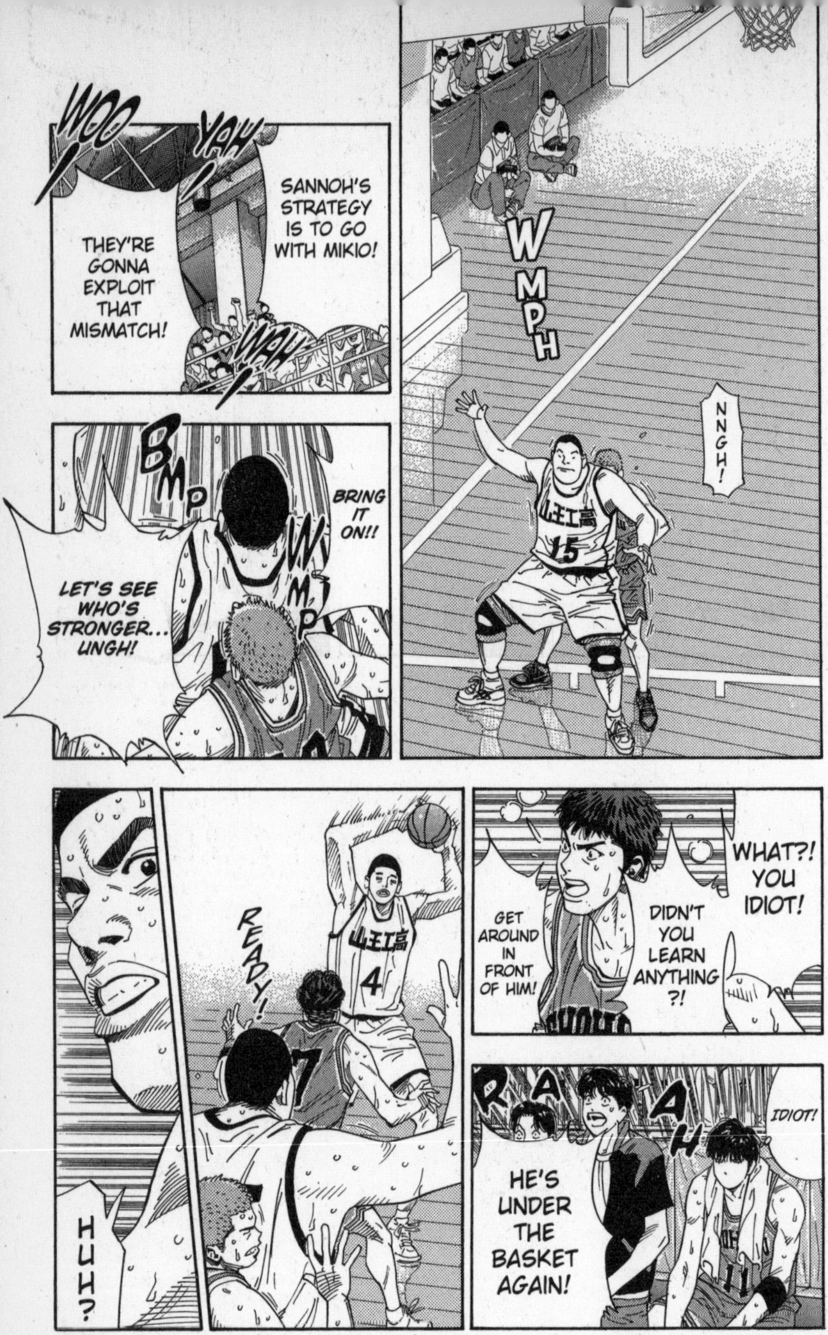

WMPH
NNGH!
WOO
YAH
SANNOH'S STRATEGY IS TO GO WITH MIKIO!
THEY'RE GONNA EXPLOIT THAT MISMATCH!
WAH
BMP
BRING IT ON!!
WMP
LET'S SEE WHO'S STRONGER... UNGH!
WHAT?! YOU IDIOT!
DIDN'T YOU LEARN ANYTHING ?!
GET AROUND IN FRONT OF HIM!
RAAAH
IDIOT!
HE'S UNDER THE BASKET AGAIN!
READY!
HUH?

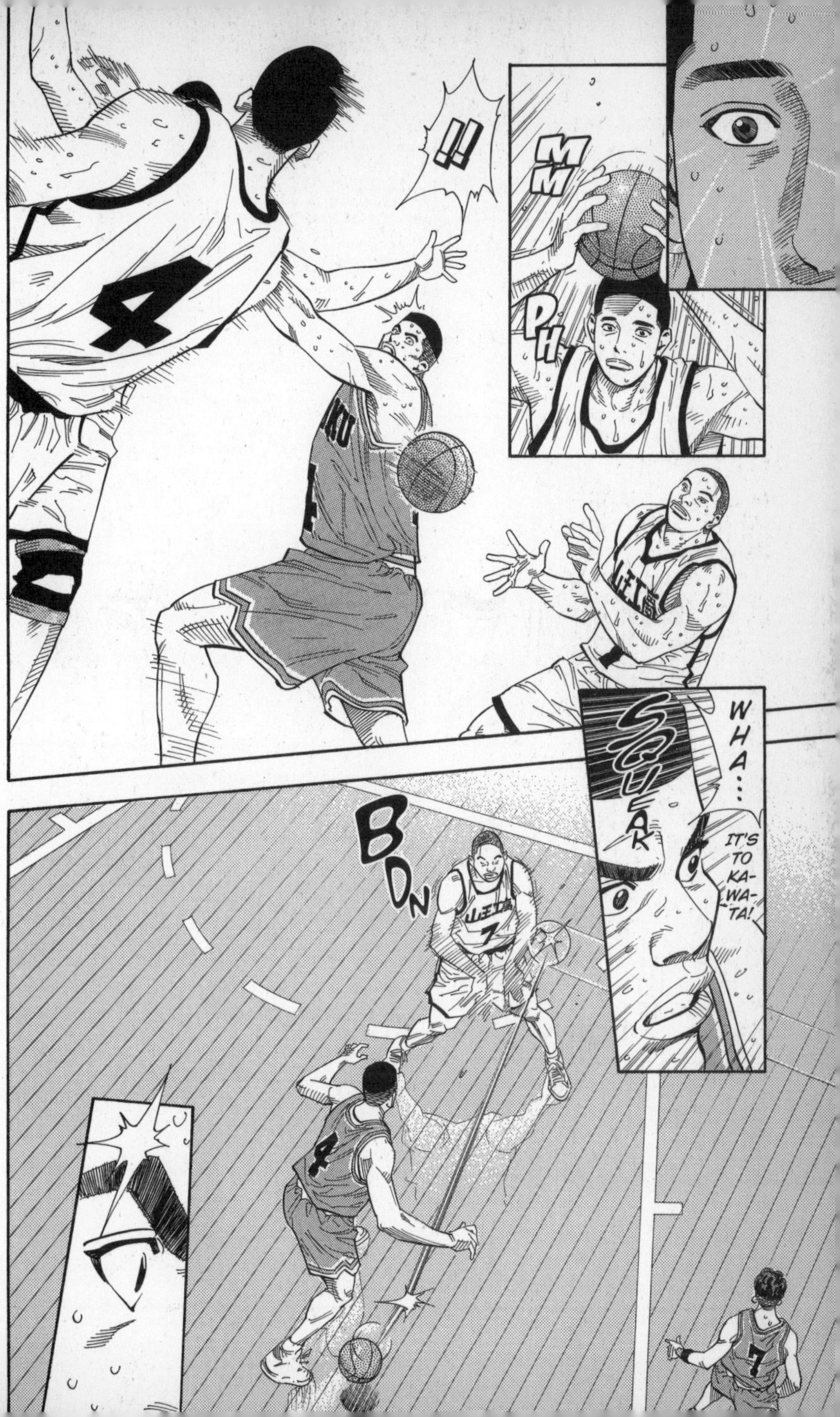
MM
PH
!!
SQUEAK
WHA...
IT'S TO KA-WA-TA!
BDN

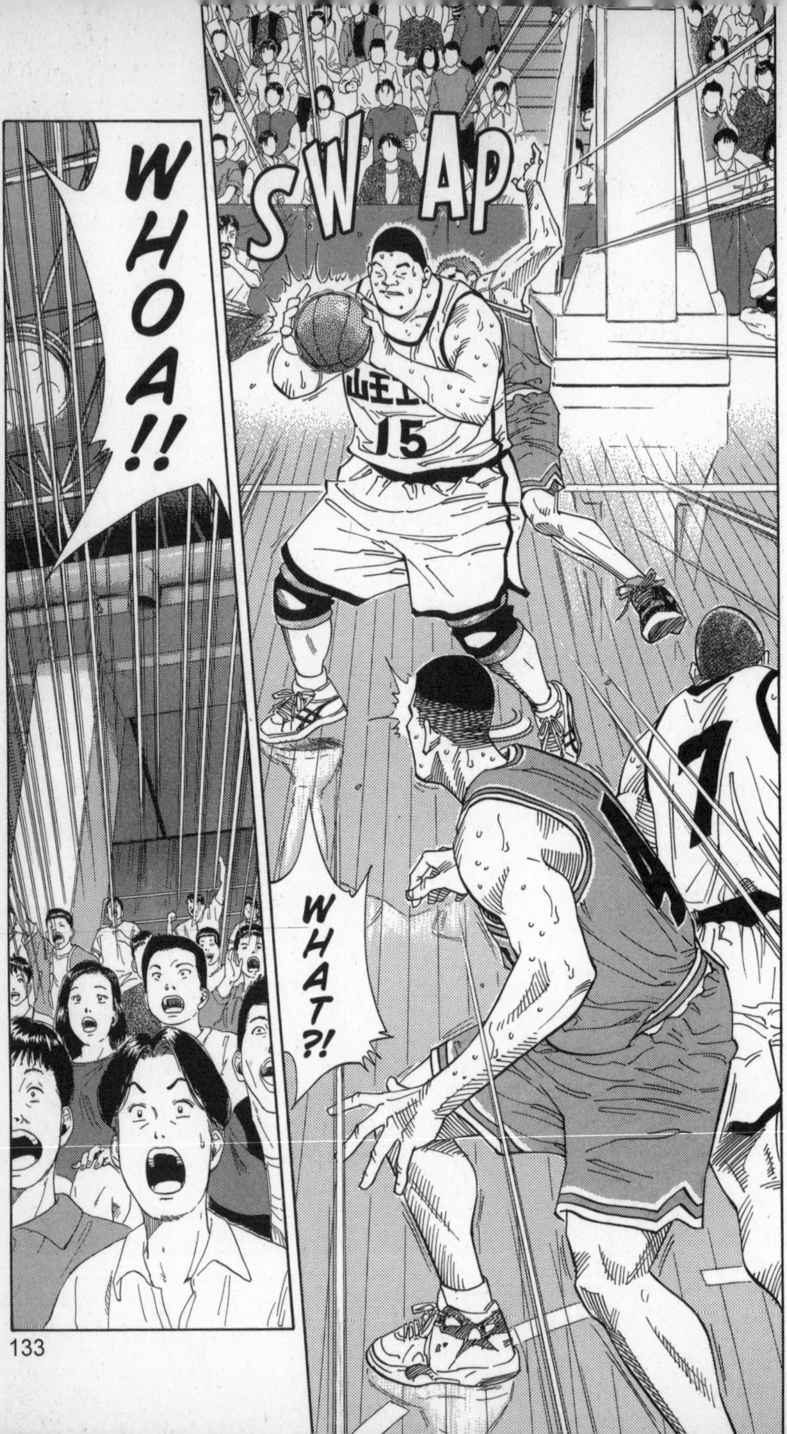
SWAP
WHAT?!
WHOA!!

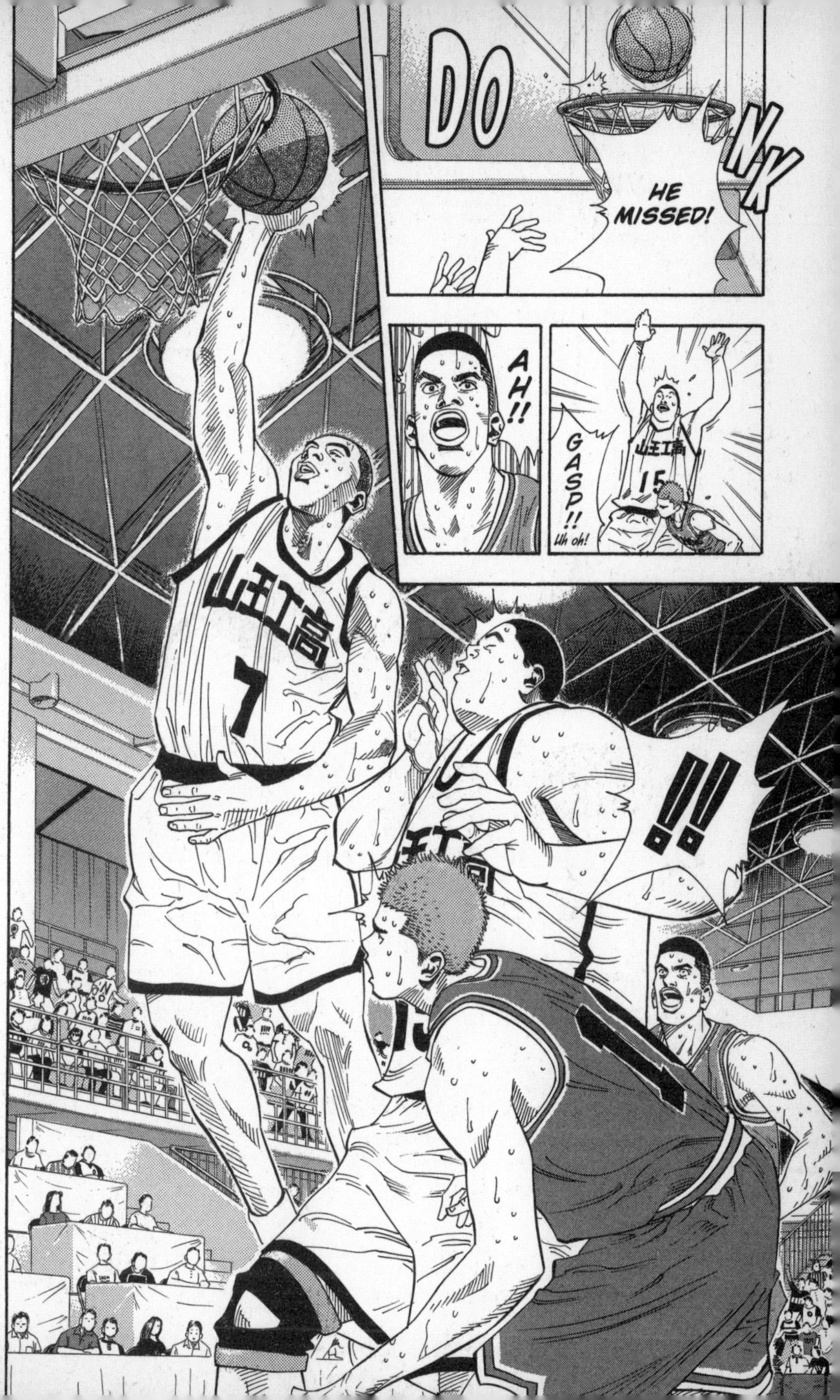
DONK
HE MISSED!
GASP!!
Uh oh!
AH!!
!!

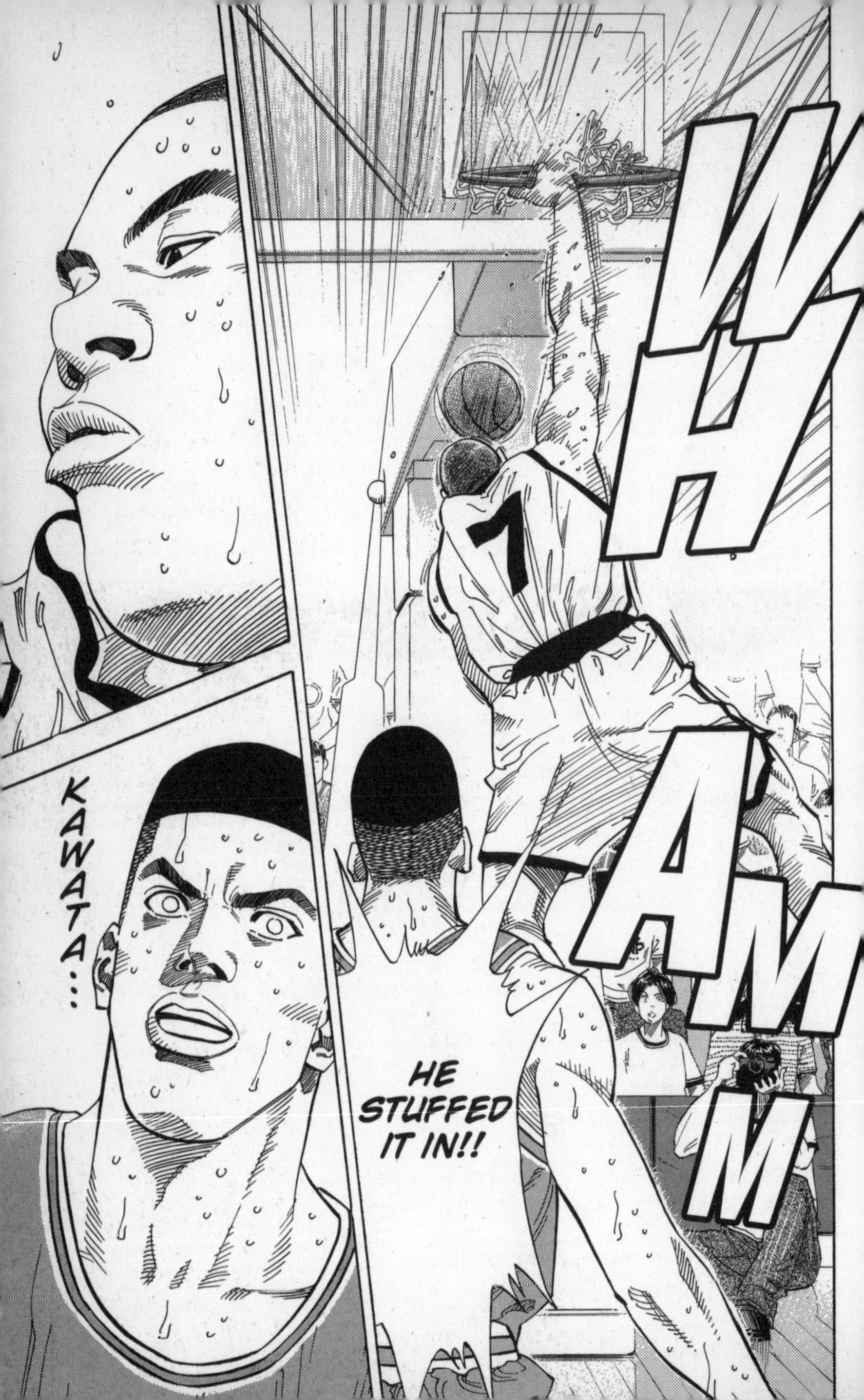
WHAMM
HE STUFFED IT IN!!
KAWATA...

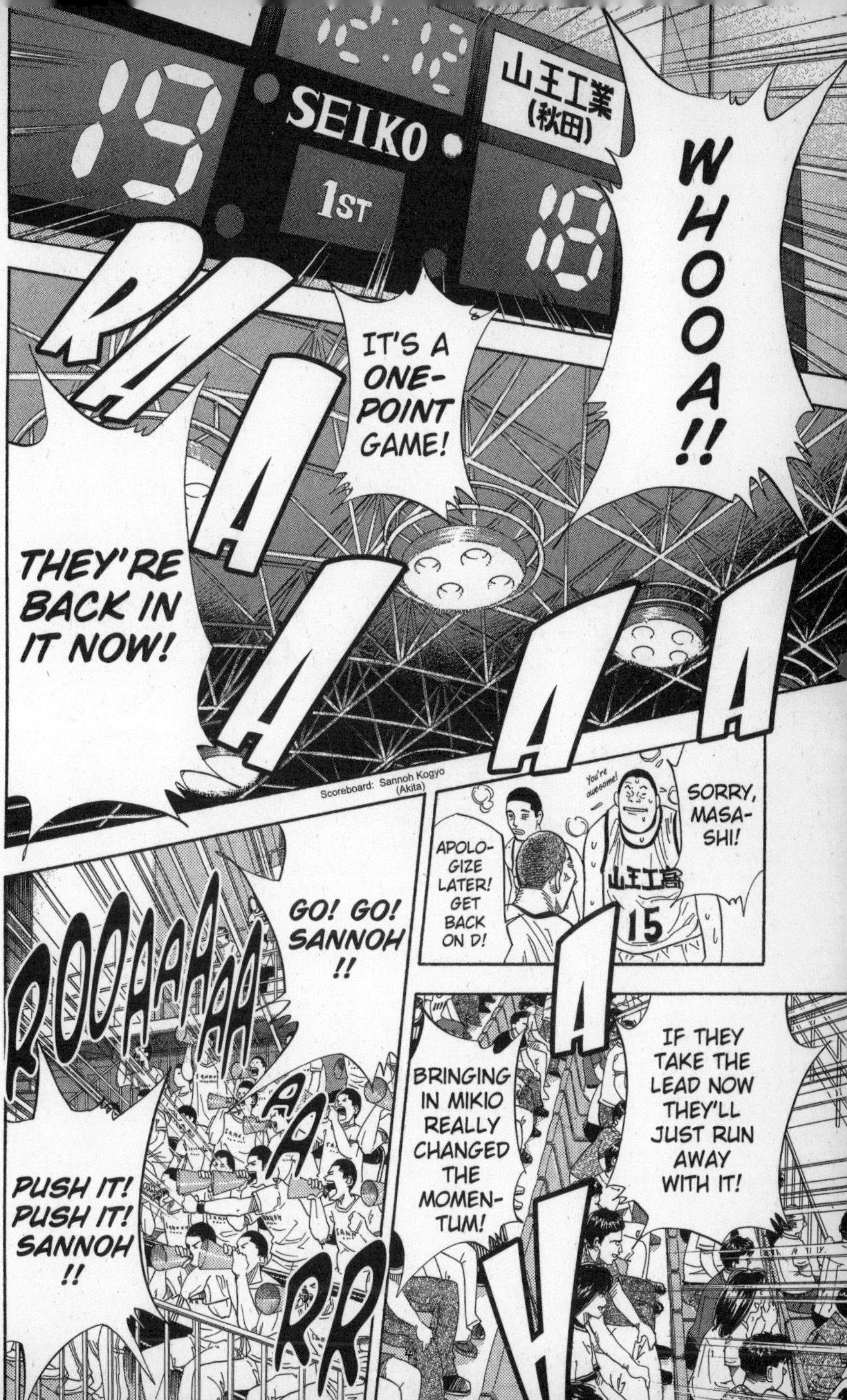

12:12
19
SEIKO
1ST
山王工業
(秋田)
18
WHOOA!!
IT'S A ONE-POINT GAME!
RAAAAA
THEY'RE BACK IN IT NOW!
Scoreboard: Sannoh Kogyo (Akita)
SORRY, MASASHI!
You're awesome!
APOLOGIZE LATER! GET BACK ON D!
山王工高
15
IF THEY TAKE THE LEAD NOW THEY'LL JUST RUN AWAY WITH IT!
BRINGING IN MIKIO REALLY CHANGED THE MOMENTUM!
ROOAAAAAAAAARRH
GO! GO! SANNOH!!
PUSH IT! PUSH IT! SANNOH!!

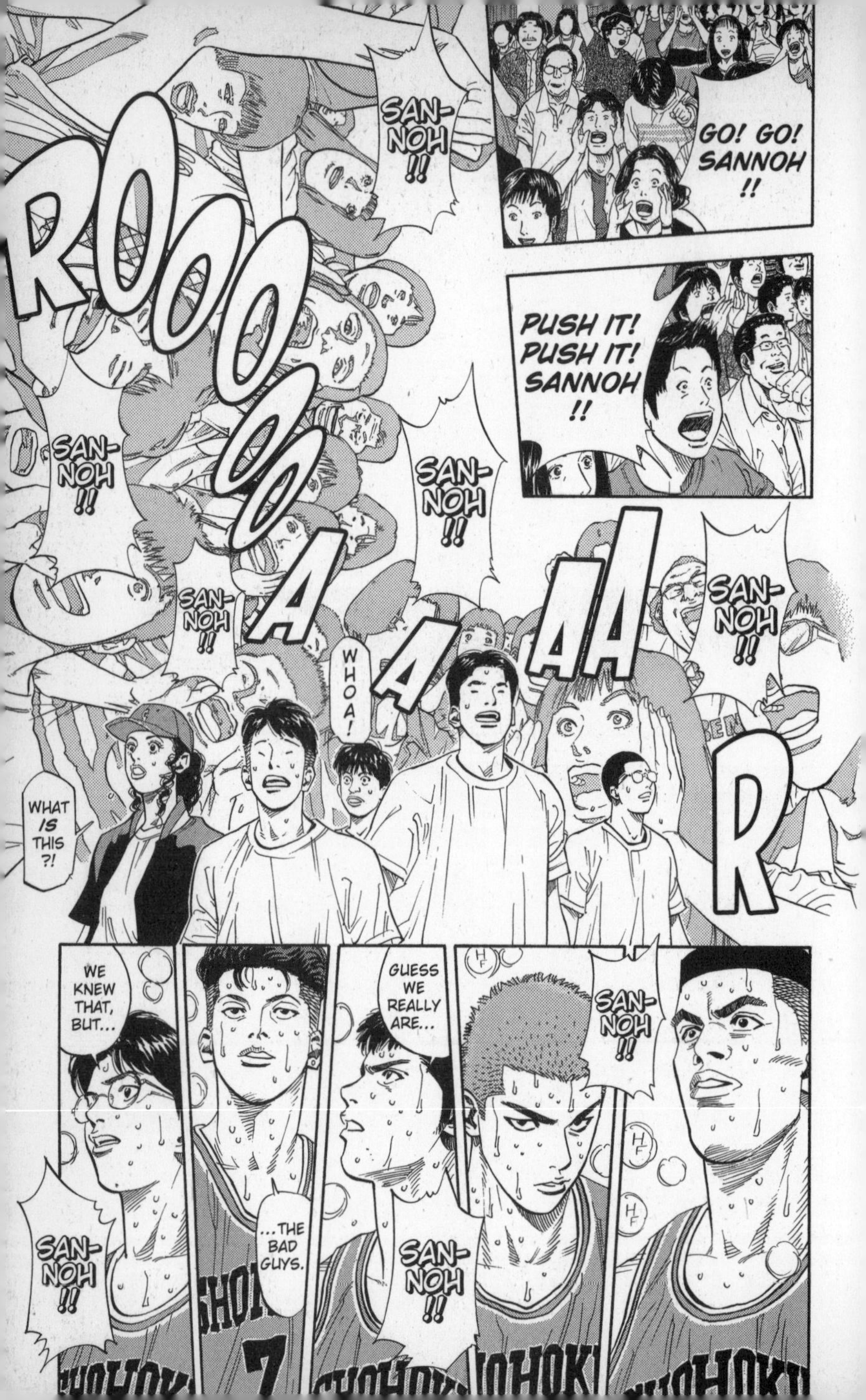
GO! GO! SANNOH!!
PUSH IT! PUSH IT! SANNOH!!
SAN-NOH!!
SAN-NOH!!
SAN-NOH!!
ROOOOOOOAAAAAR
SAN-NOH!!
SAN-NOH!!
WHOA!
WHAT IS THIS?!
SAN-NOH!!
GUESS WE REALLY ARE...
SAN-NOH!!
...THE BAD GUYS.
WE KNEW THAT, BUT...
SAN-NOH!!

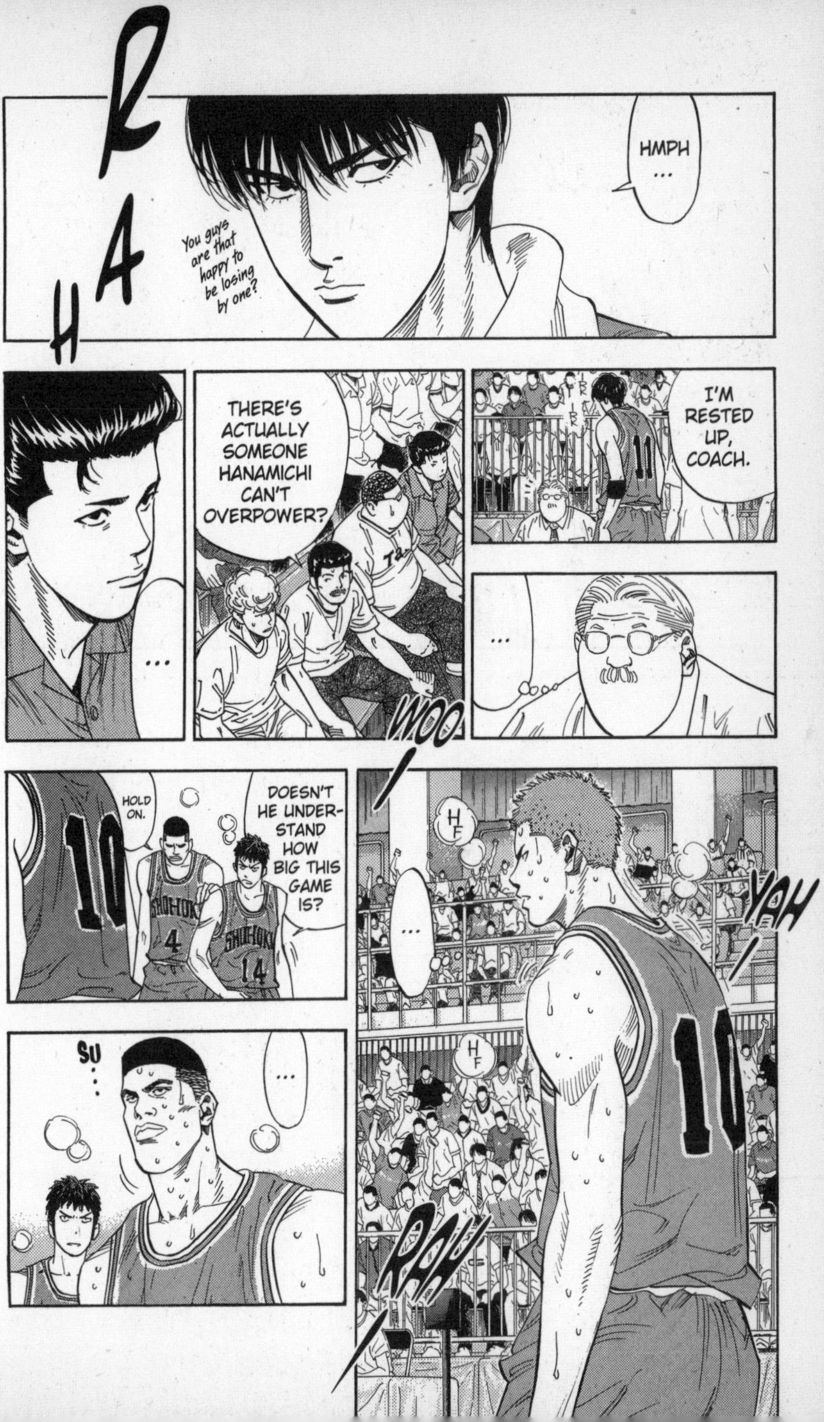
HMPH ...
You guys are that happy to be losing by one?
RAH
I'M RESTED UP, COACH.
...
THERE'S ACTUALLY SOMEONE HANAMICHI CAN'T OVERPOWER?
...
WOO
...
HF
YAH
HF
RAH
DOESN'T HE UNDERSTAND HOW BIG THIS GAME IS?
HOLD ON.
...
SU...

READ THIS WAY

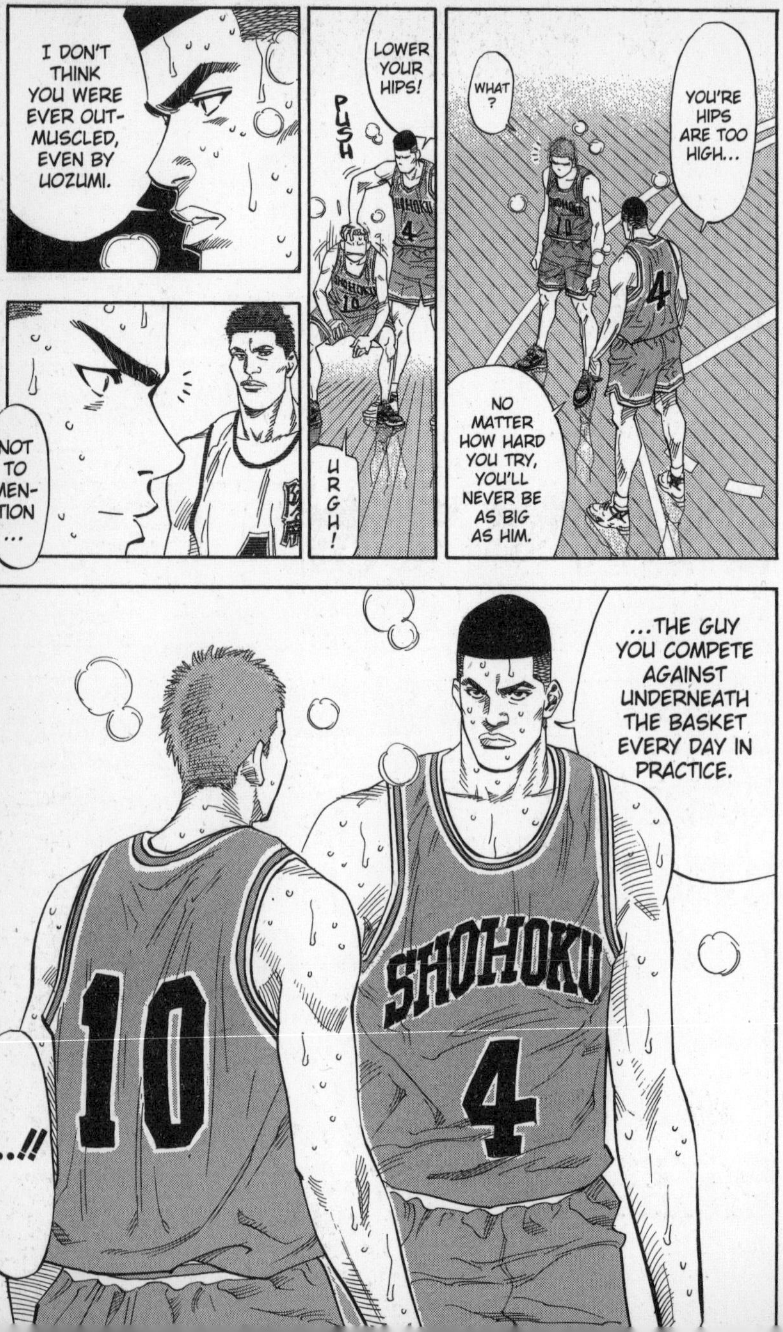
YOU'RE HIPS ARE TOO HIGH...
WHAT?
NO MATTER HOW HARD YOU TRY, YOU'LL NEVER BE AS BIG AS HIM.
LOWER YOUR HIPS!
PUSH
URGH!
I DON'T THINK YOU WERE EVER OUT-MUSCLED, EVEN BY UOZUMI.
NOT TO MEN-TION...
...THE GUY YOU COMPETE AGAINST UNDERNEATH THE BASKET EVERY DAY IN PRACTICE.
...!!

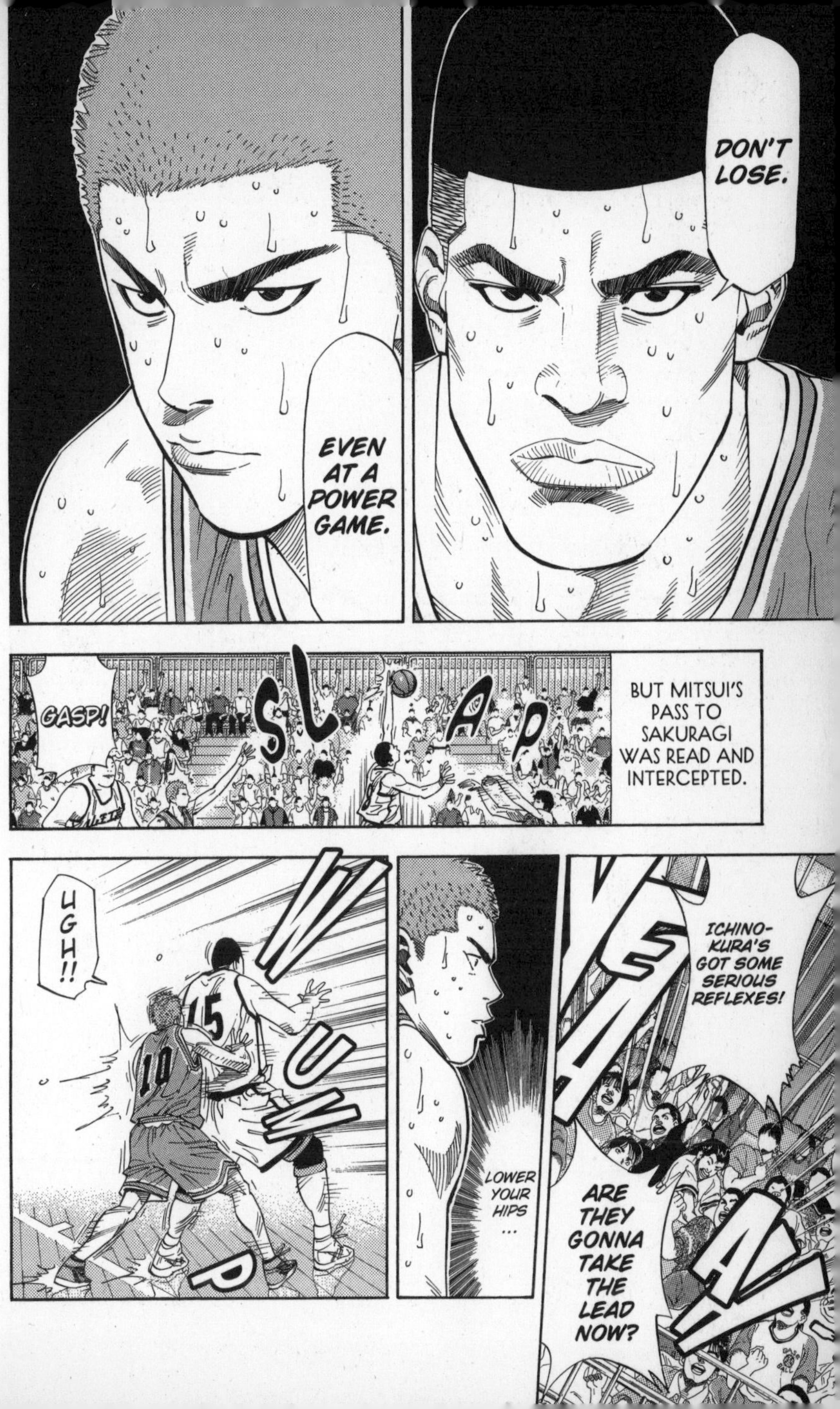
DON'T LOSE.
EVEN AT A POWER GAME.
BUT MITSUI'S PASS TO SAKURAGI WAS READ AND INTERCEPTED.
SLAP
GASP!
ICHINO-KURA'S GOT SOME SERIOUS REFLEXES!
ARE THEY GONNA TAKE THE LEAD NOW?
LOWER YOUR HIPS ...
WUMP
UGH!!

READ THIS WAY

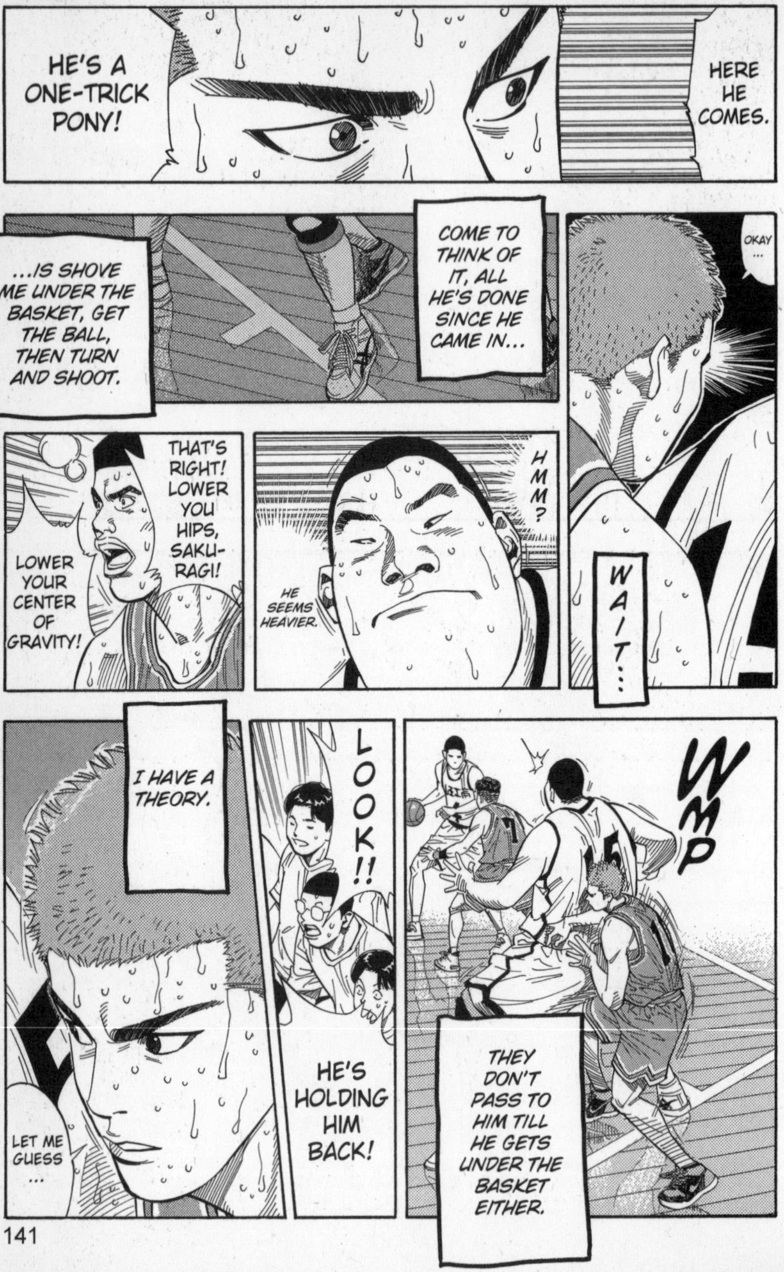
HERE HE COMES.
HE'S A ONE-TRICK PONY!
OKAY...
WAIT...
COME TO THINK OF IT, ALL HE'S DONE SINCE HE CAME IN...
...IS SHOVE ME UNDER THE BASKET, GET THE BALL, THEN TURN AND SHOOT.
HMM?
HE SEEMS HEAVIER.
THAT'S RIGHT! LOWER YOU HIPS, SAKURAGI!
LOWER YOUR CENTER OF GRAVITY!
WMP
THEY DON'T PASS TO HIM TILL HE GETS UNDER THE BASKET EITHER.
LOOK!!
HE'S HOLDING HIM BACK!
I HAVE A THEORY.
LET ME GUESS...

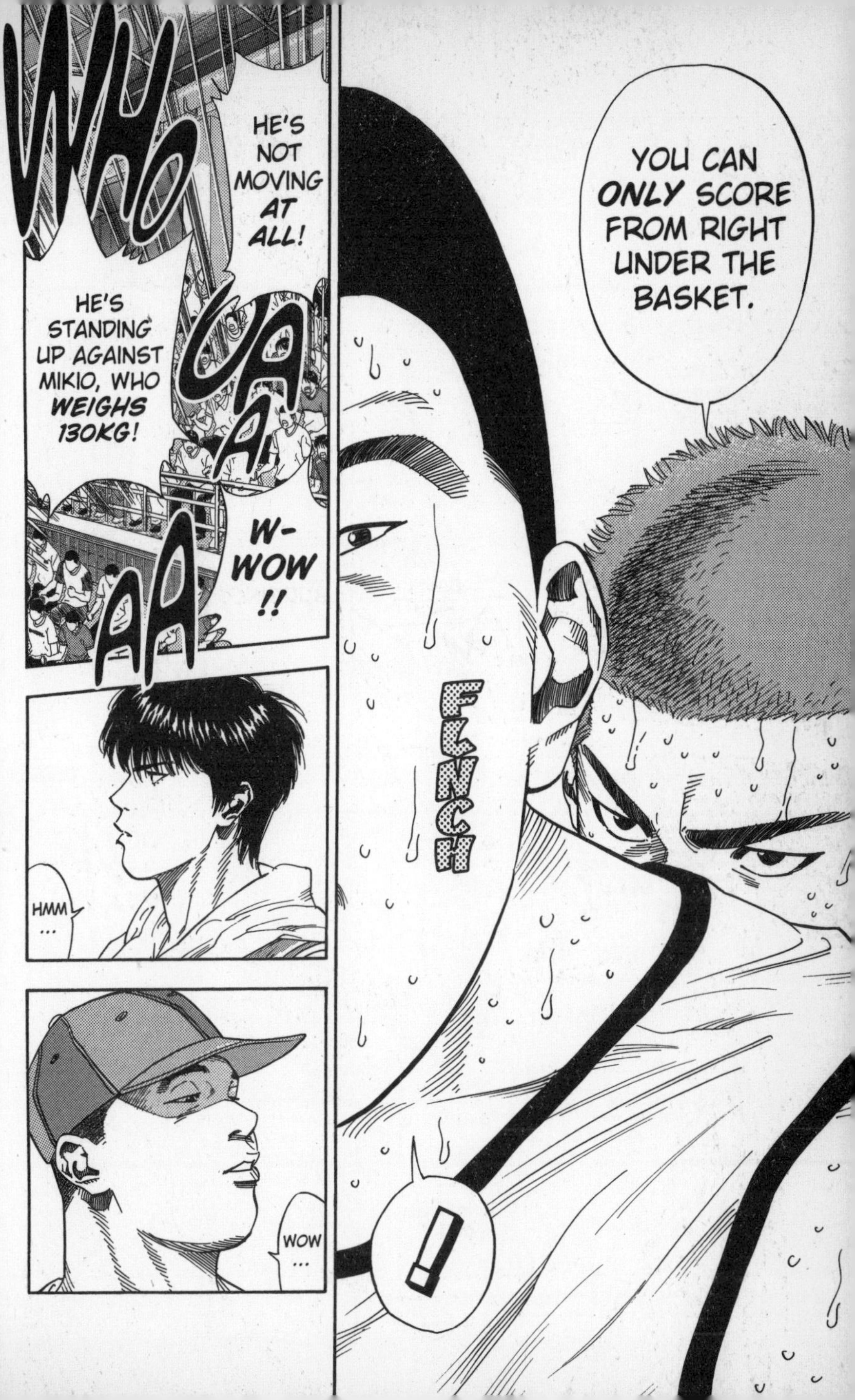
YOU CAN ONLY SCORE FROM RIGHT UNDER THE BASKET.
FLINCH
!
WHOAAAA
HE'S NOT MOVING AT ALL!
HE'S STANDING UP AGAINST MIKIO, WHO WEIGHS 130KG!
W-WOW!!
HMM...
WOW...

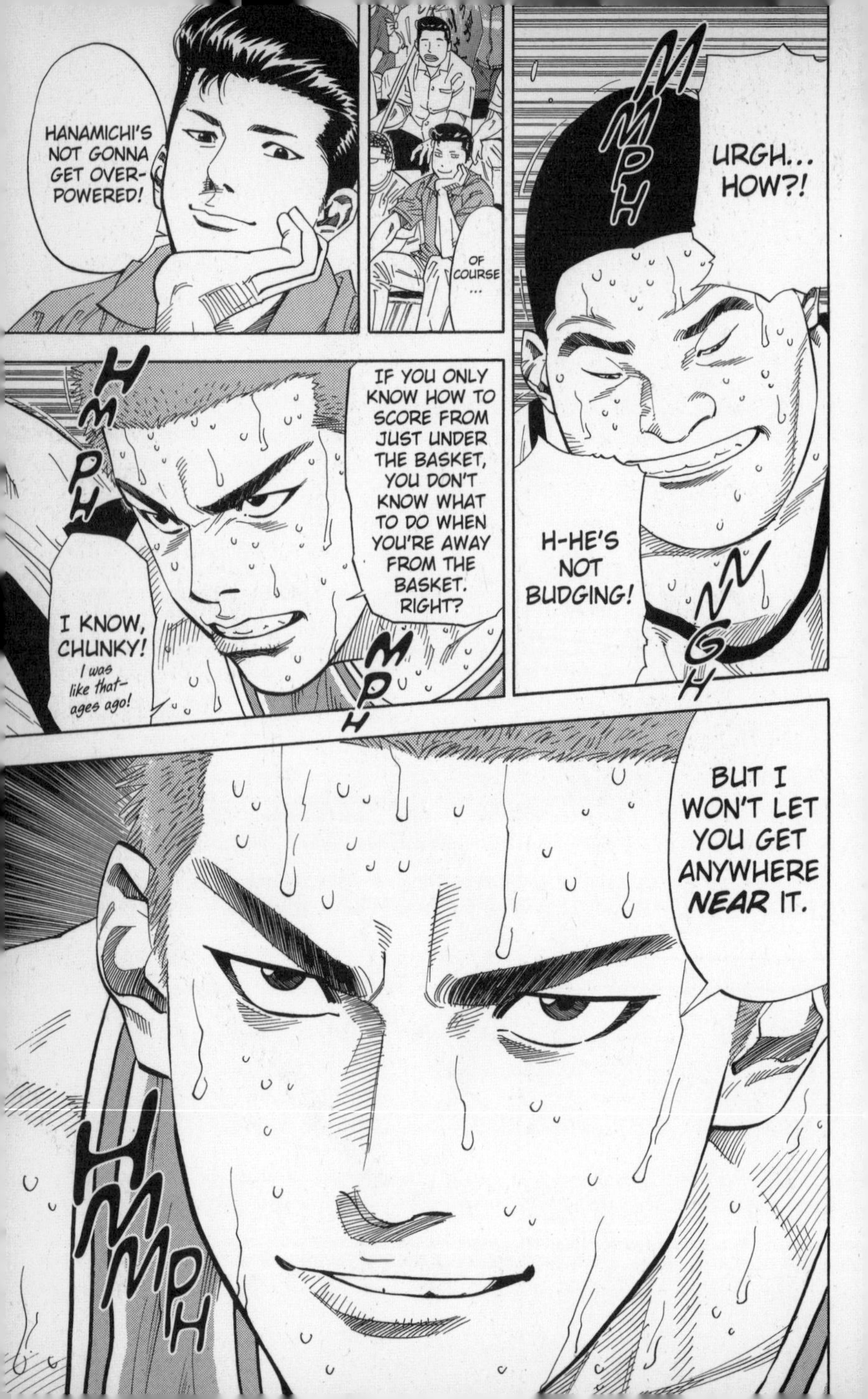
MMMPH
URGH... HOW?!
H-HE'S NOT BUDGING!
NNNGH
OF COURSE...
HANAMICHI'S NOT GONNA GET OVER-POWERED!
IF YOU ONLY KNOW HOW TO SCORE FROM JUST UNDER THE BASKET, YOU DON'T KNOW WHAT TO DO WHEN YOU'RE AWAY FROM THE BASKET. RIGHT?
HMMPH
I KNOW, CHUNKY!
I was like that-ages ago!
MMPH
BUT I WON'T LET YOU GET ANYWHERE NEAR IT.
HMMMPH

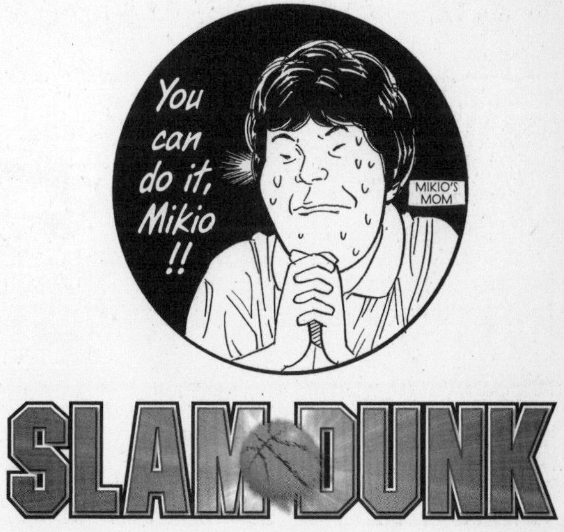
You can do it, Mikio !!
MIKIO'S MOM

SLAM DUNK

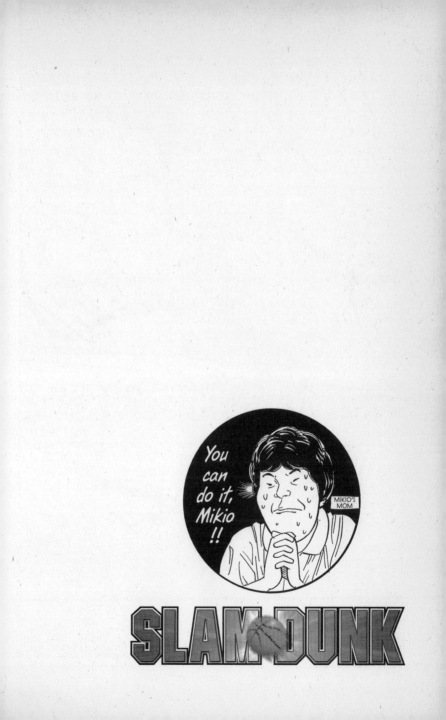

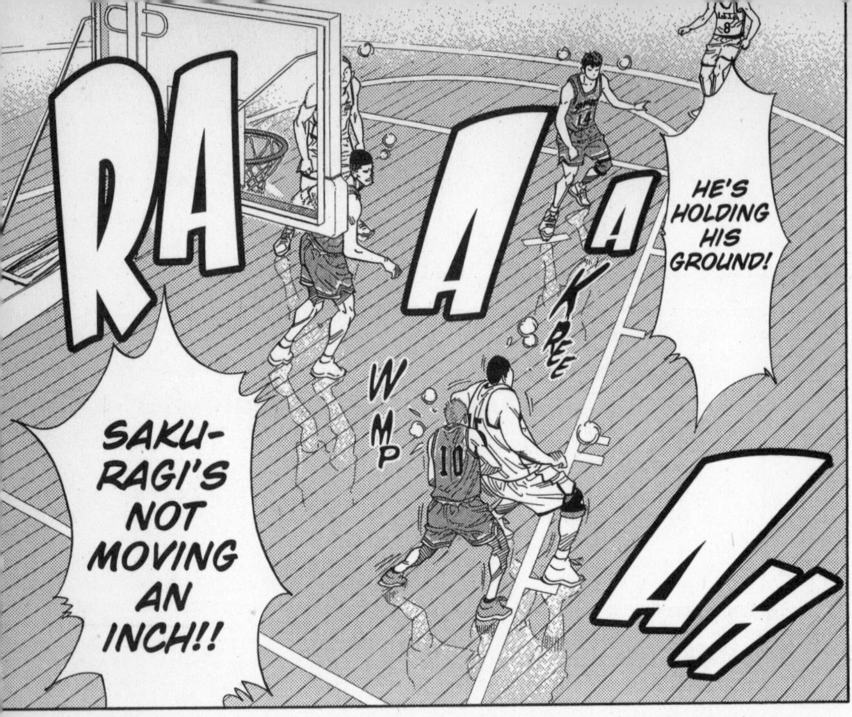
RAAAAH
KREE
WMP
HE'S HOLDING HIS GROUND!
SAKURAGI'S NOT MOVING AN INCH!!

#232 SAYONARA, CHUNKY

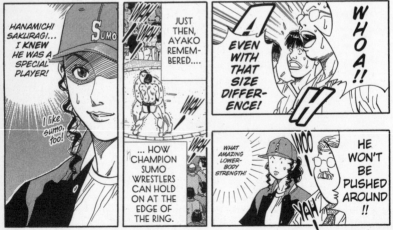

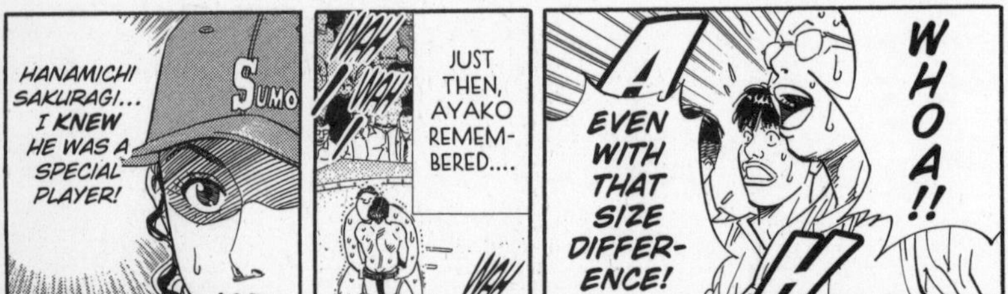
WHOA!!
AH
EVEN WITH THAT SIZE DIFFERENCE!
HE WON'T BE PUSHED AROUND!!
WOO
YAH
WHAT AMAZING LOWER-BODY STRENGTH!
WAH
WAH
JUST THEN, AYAKO REMEMBERED....
WAH
WAH
... HOW CHAMPION SUMO WRESTLERS CAN HOLD ON AT THE EDGE OF THE RING.
SUMO
HANAMICHI SAKURAGI... I KNEW HE WAS A SPECIAL PLAYER!
I like sumo, too!

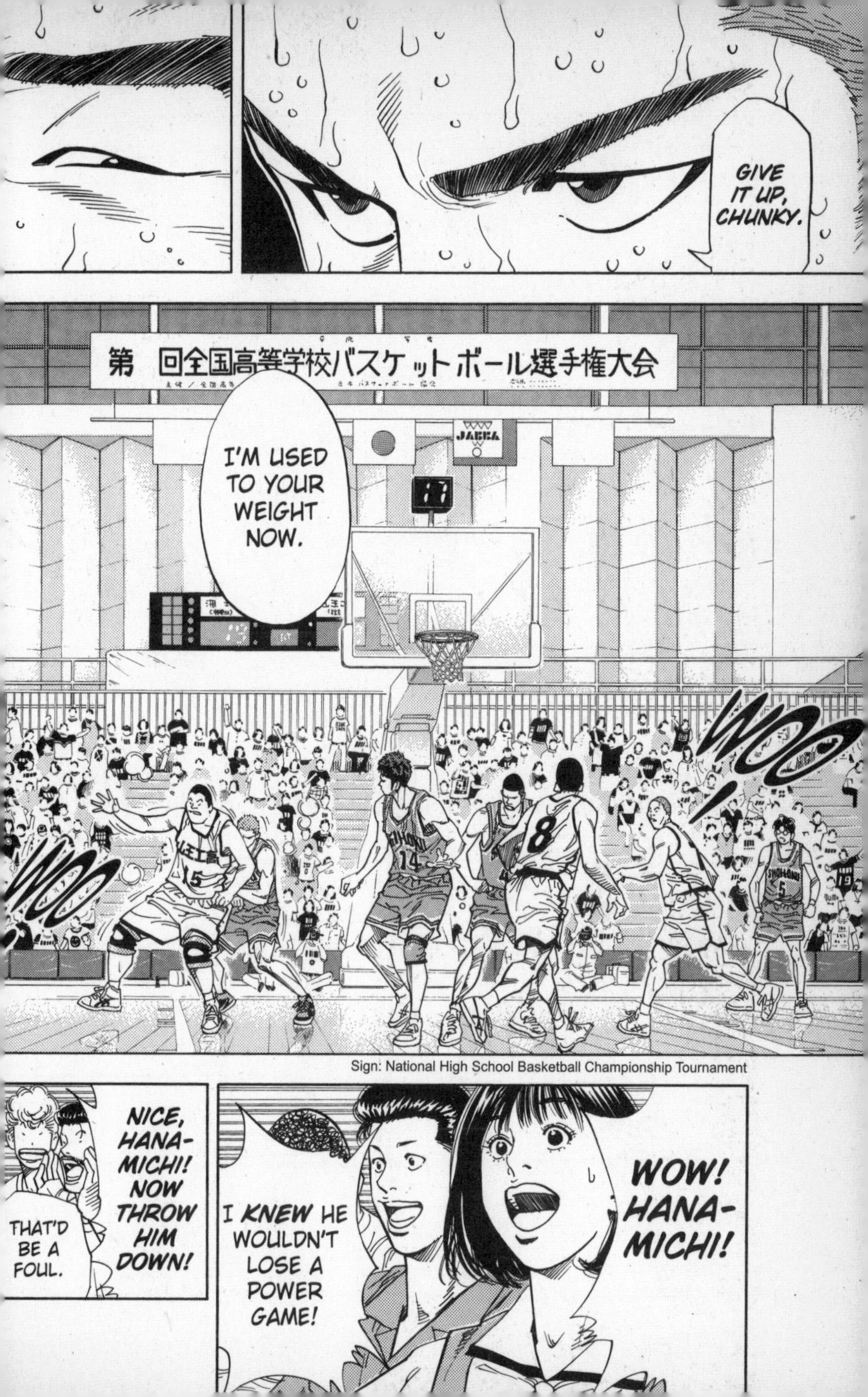
GIVE IT UP, CHUNKY.
第 回全国高等学校バスケットボール選手権大会
I'M USED TO YOUR WEIGHT NOW.
WOO
WOO
Sign: National High School Basketball Championship Tournament
WOW! HANAMICHI!
I KNEW HE WOULDN'T LOSE A POWER GAME!
NICE, HANAMICHI! NOW THROW HIM DOWN!
THAT'D BE A FOUL.

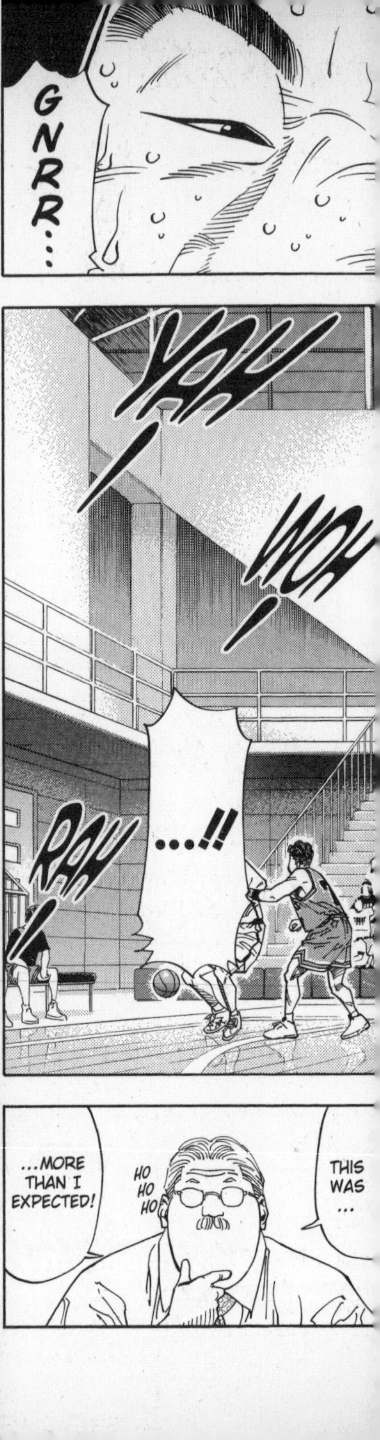
GNRR...
YAH!
WOH!
...!!
RAH!!
THIS WAS...
HO HO HO
...MORE THAN I EXPECTED!
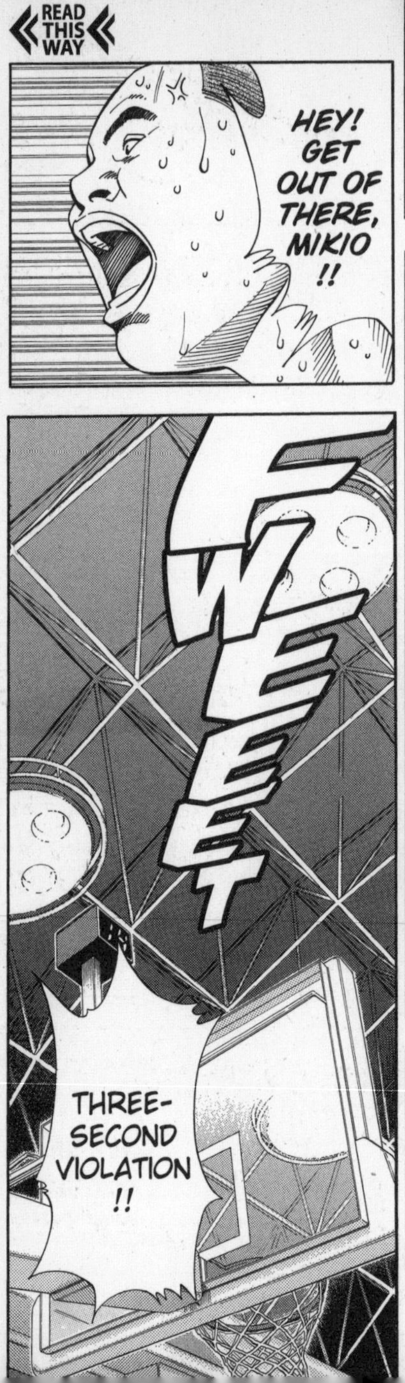
READ THIS WAY
HEY! GET OUT OF THERE, MIKIO!!
SWEEET
THREE-SECOND VIOLATION!!

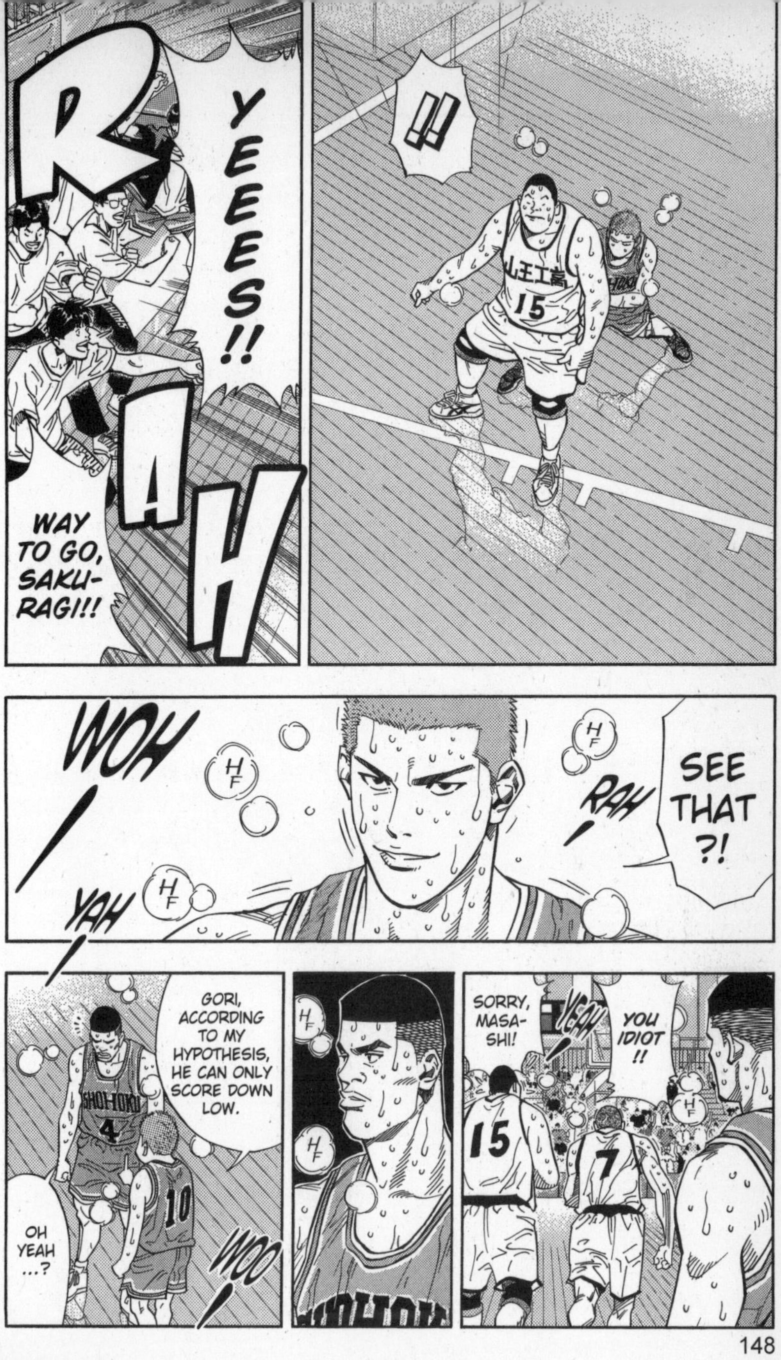
!!
RAH
YEEEES!!
WAY TO GO, SAKU-RAGI!!
SEE THAT?!
RAH
WOH
YAH
HF
YOU IDIOT!!
YEAH
SORRY, MASA-SHI!
GORI, ACCORDING TO MY HYPOTHESIS, HE CAN ONLY SCORE DOWN LOW.
OH YEAH ...?
WOO

READ THIS WAY

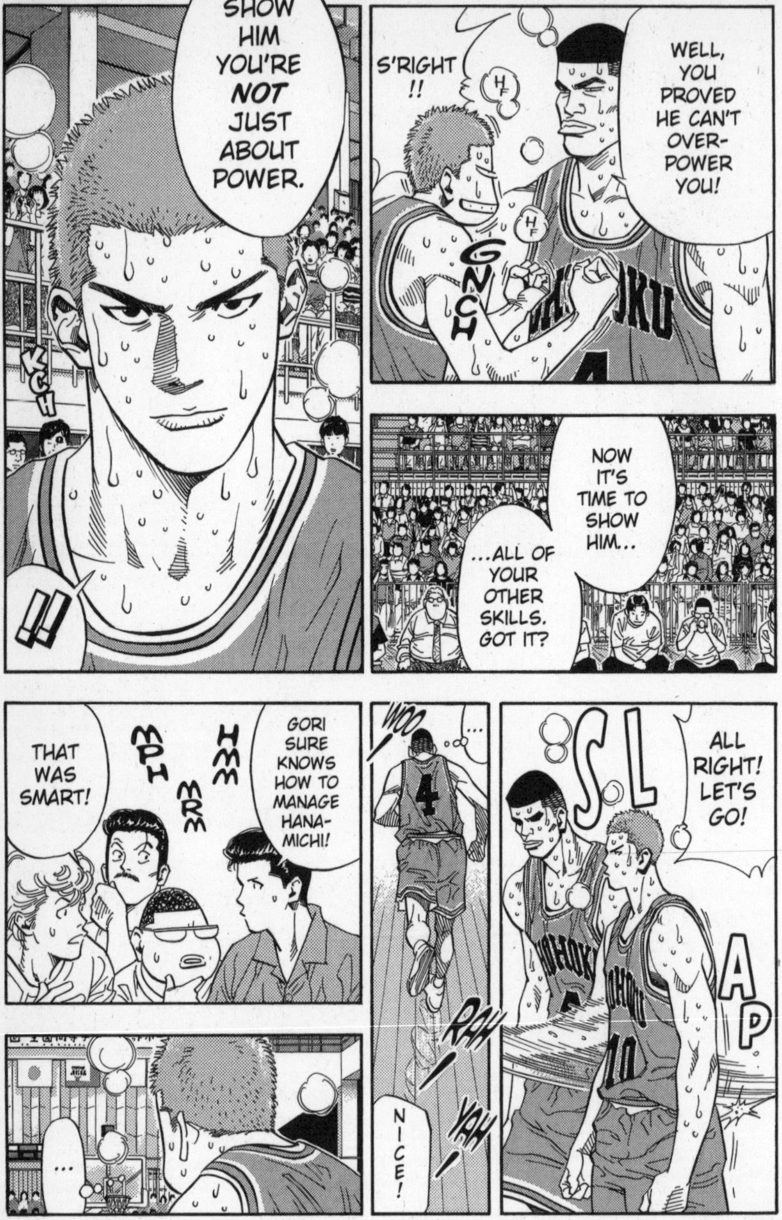
WELL, YOU PROVED HE CAN'T OVER-POWER YOU!
S'RIGHT!!
HF
HF
GNCH
NOW IT'S TIME TO SHOW HIM...
...ALL OF YOUR OTHER SKILLS. GOT IT?
SHOW HIM YOU'RE NOT JUST ABOUT POWER.
KCH
!!
ALL RIGHT! LET'S GO!
SL
AP
...
WOO
RAH
YAH
NICE!
GORI SURE KNOWS HOW TO MANAGE HANA-MICHI!
HMM
MRM
MPH
THAT WAS SMART!
...

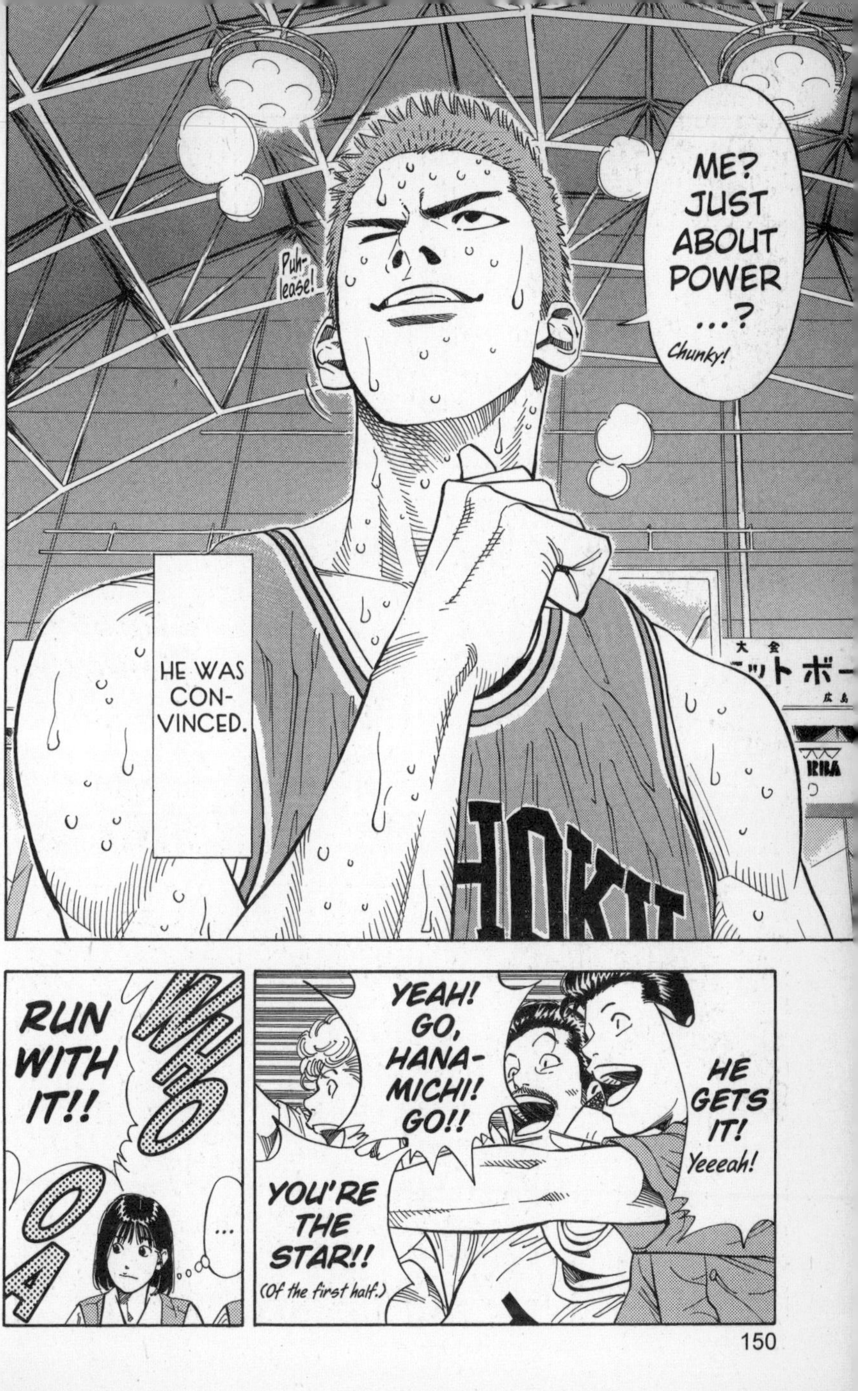
ME? JUST ABOUT POWER ...?
Chunky!
Puh-lease!
HE WAS CONVINCED.
HE GETS IT!
Yeeeah!
YEAH! GO, HANAMICHI! GO!!
YOU'RE THE STAR!!
(Of the first half.)
WHOA
RUN WITH IT!!
...

READ THIS WAY

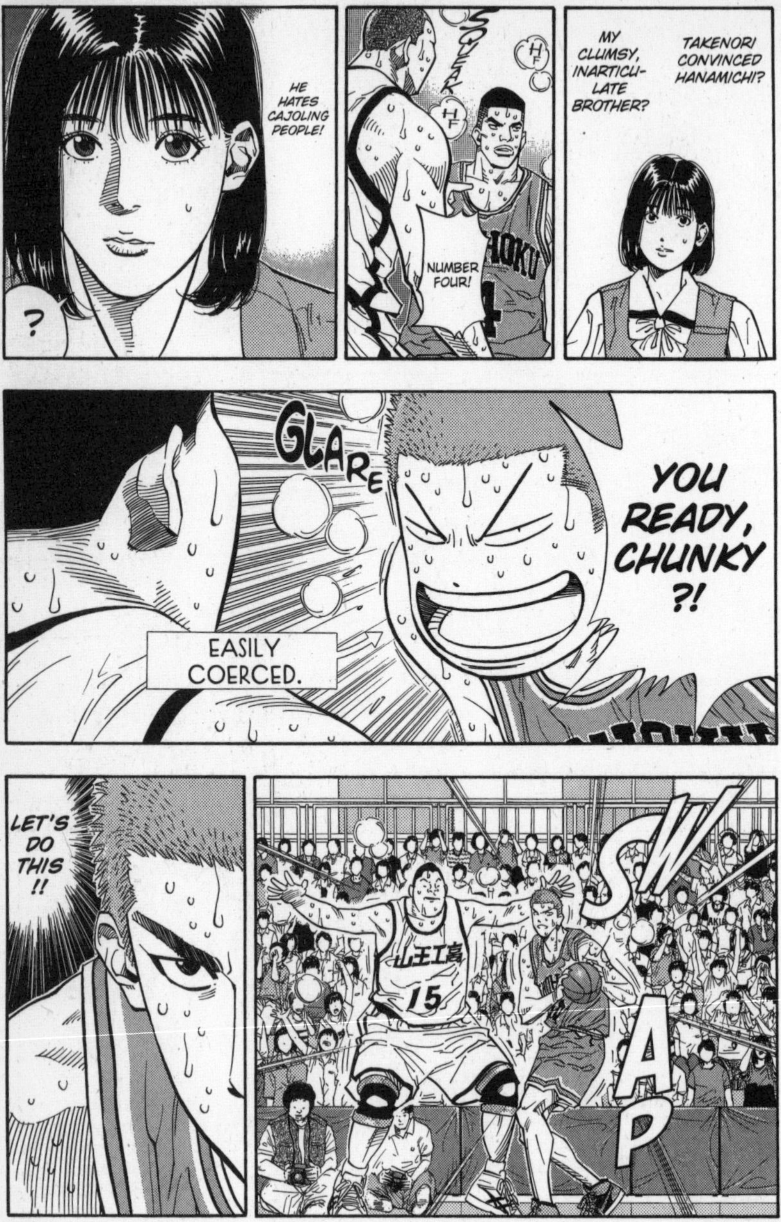
TAKENORI CONVINCED HANAMICHI?
MY CLUMSY, INARTICULATE BROTHER?
SQUEAK
HF
HF
NUMBER FOUR!
HE HATES CAJOLING PEOPLE!
?
YOU READY, CHUNKY?!
GLARE
EASILY COERCED.
SWAP
LET'S DO THIS!!

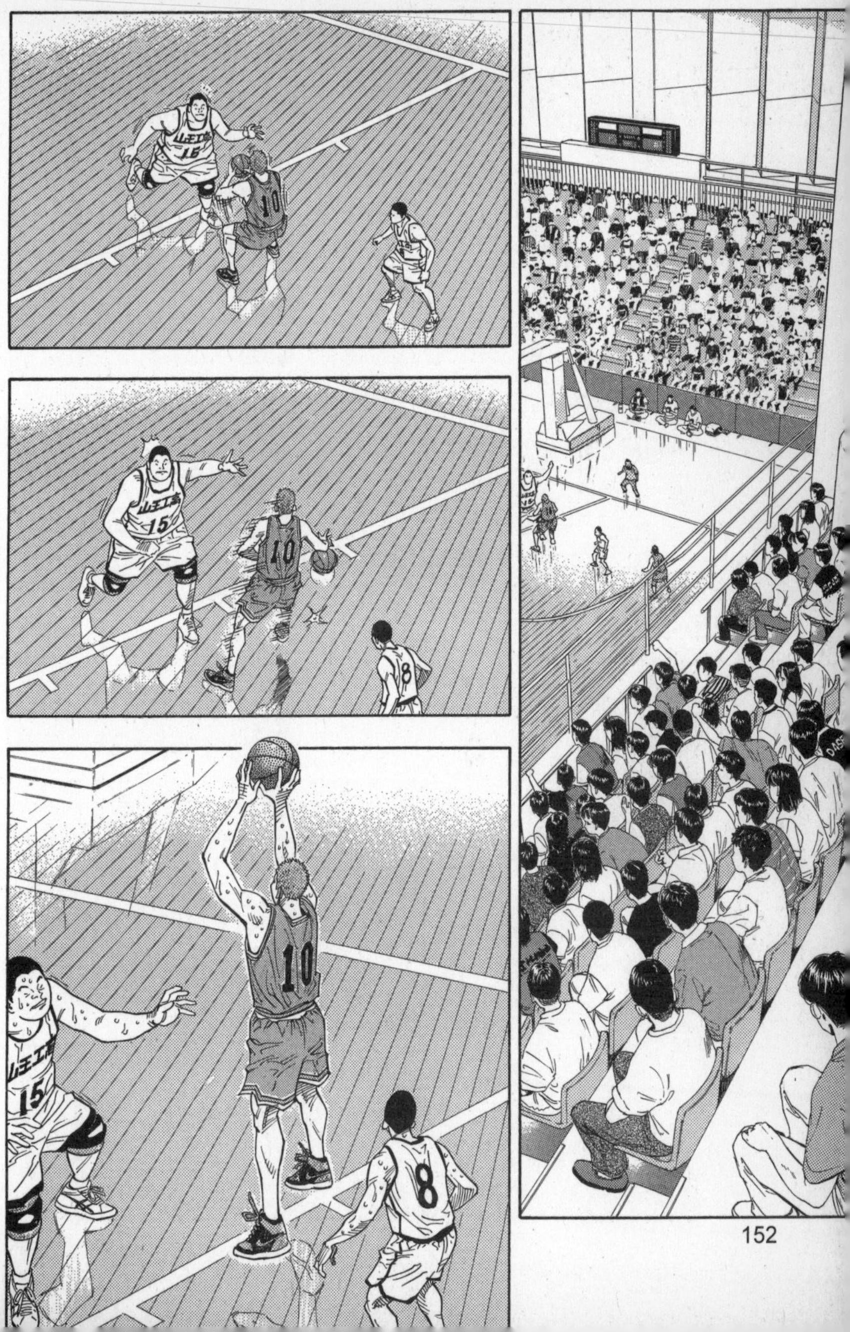

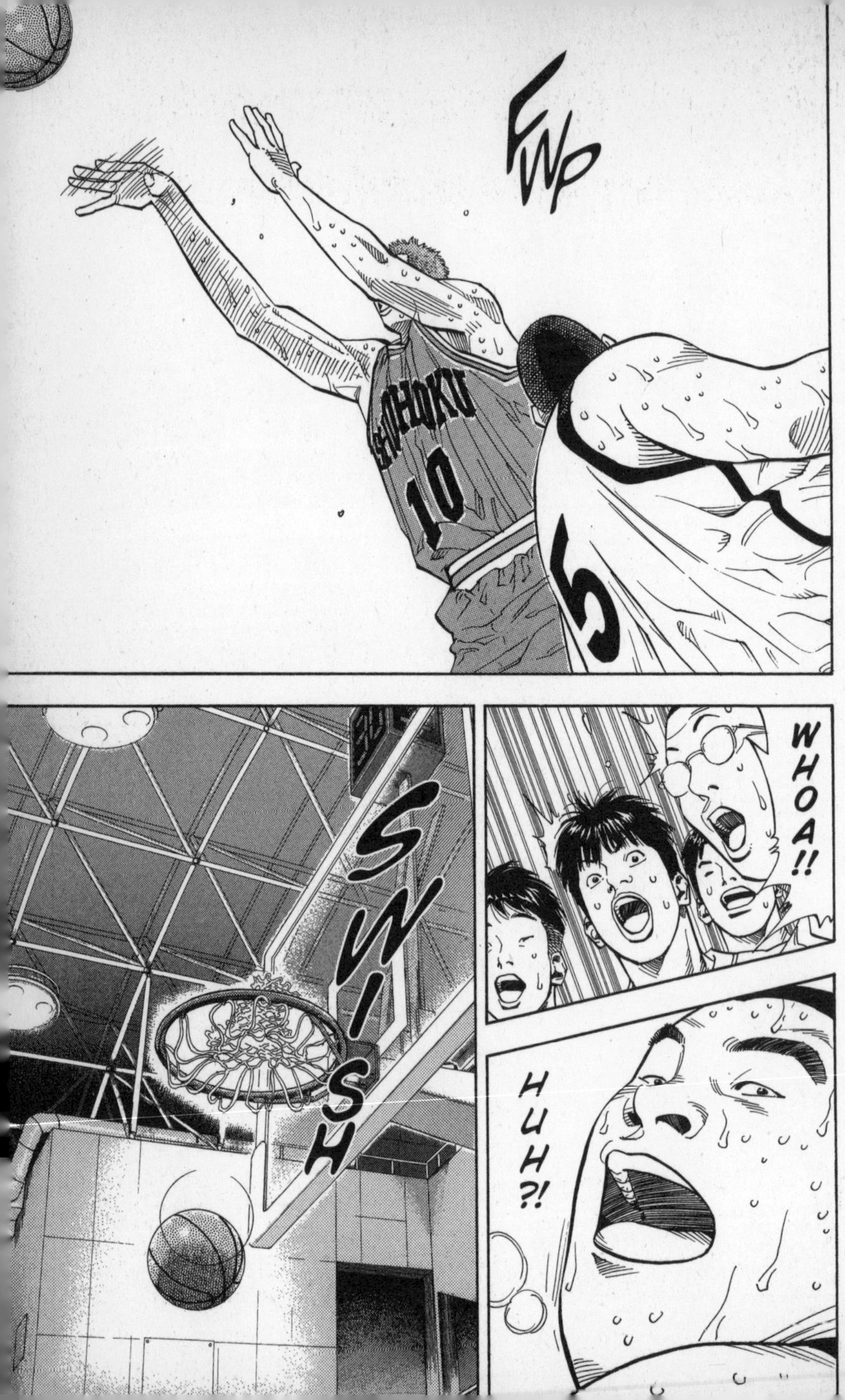
FWP
WHOA!!
HUH?!
SWISH

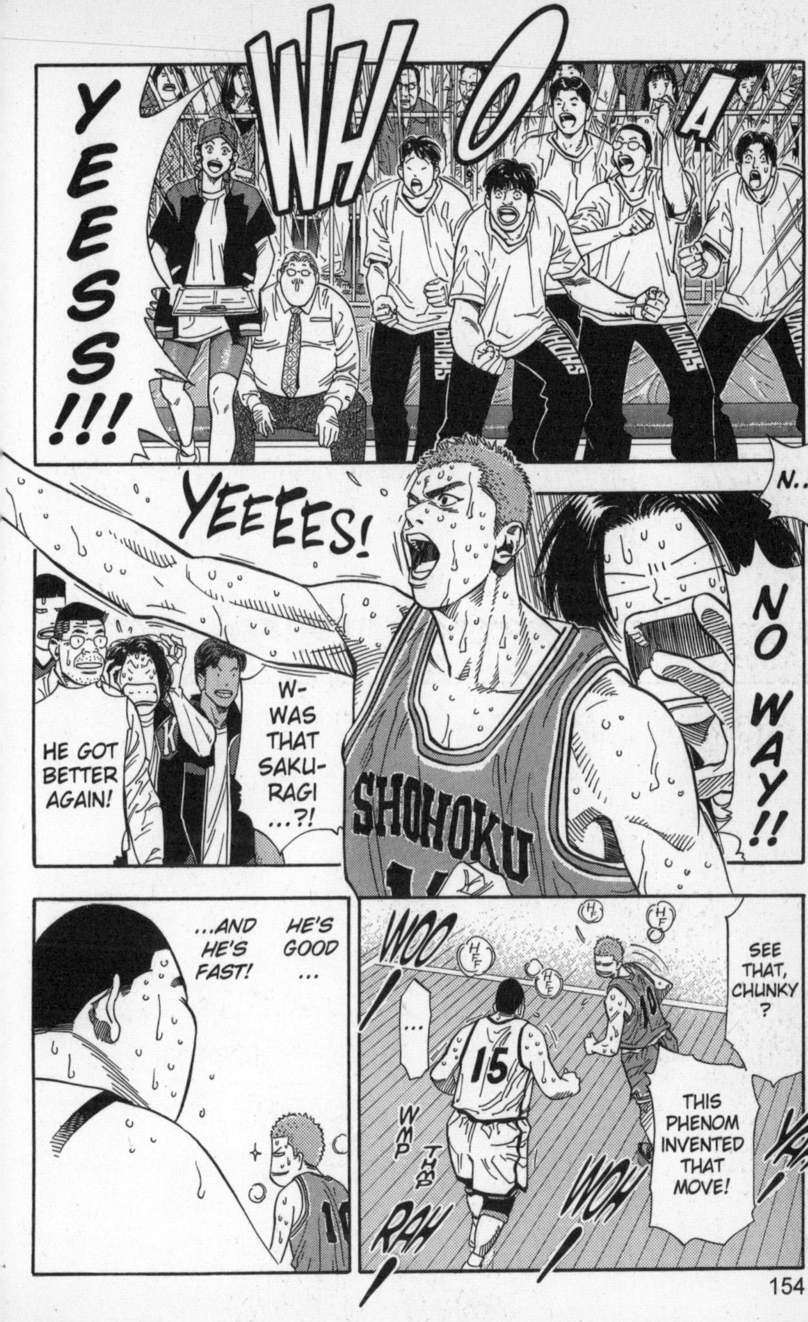
WHOA
YEESS!!!
N...
NO WAY!!
YEEEES!
W-WAS THAT SAKURAGI...?!
HE GOT BETTER AGAIN!
SEE THAT, CHUNKY?
THIS PHENOM INVENTED THAT MOVE!
YAH!
WOO!
...
HEF
HEF
HEF
HEF
WMP
THMP
WOH!
RAH!
HE'S GOOD...
...AND HE'S FAST!

READ THIS WAY

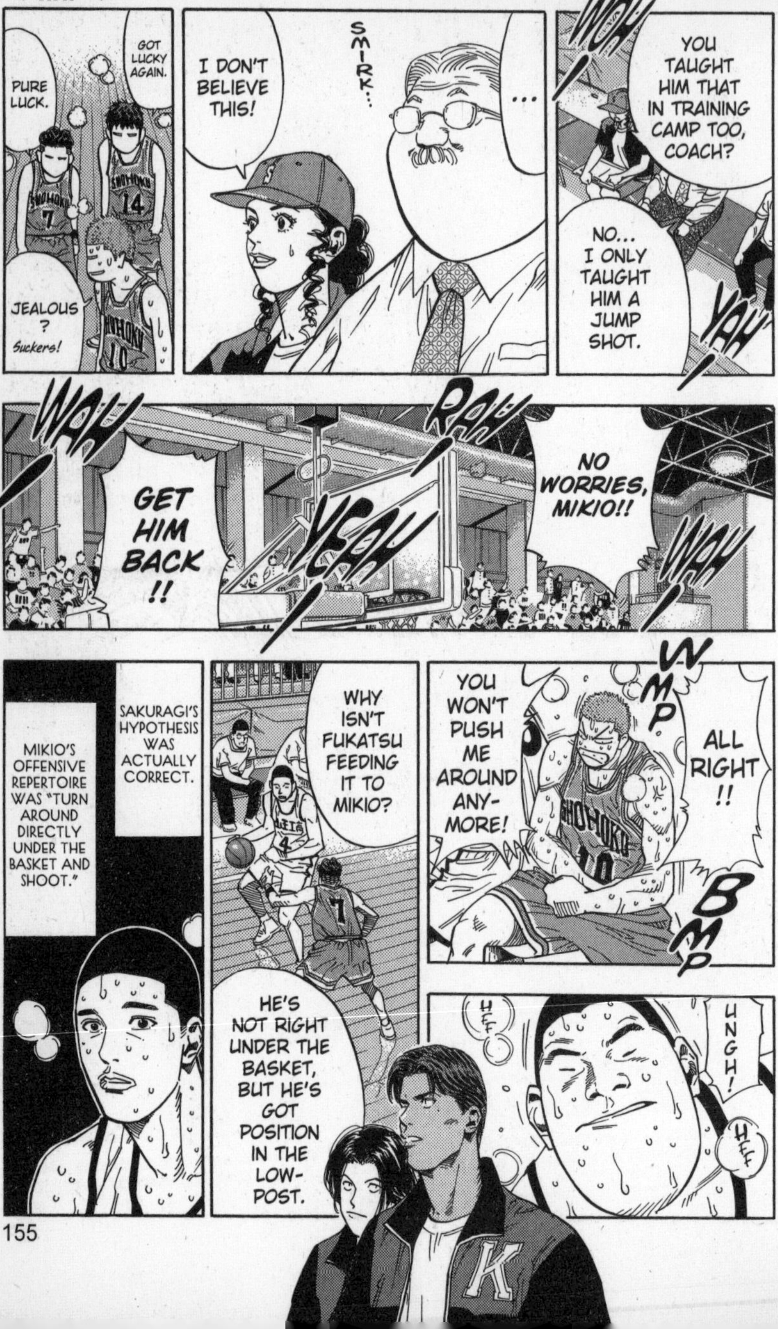
WAH!
YOU TAUGHT HIM THAT IN TRAINING CAMP TOO, COACH?
NO... I ONLY TAUGHT HIM A JUMP SHOT.
YAH!
...
SMIRK...
I DON'T BELIEVE THIS!
GOT LUCKY AGAIN.
PURE LUCK.
JEALOUS? Suckers!
WAH!
NO WORRIES, MIKIO!!
RAH!
YEAH!
GET HIM BACK!!
WAH!
WMP.
ALL RIGHT!!
YOU WON'T PUSH ME AROUND ANY-MORE!
BMP
UNGH!
HEF
HEF
WHY ISN'T FUKATSU FEEDING IT TO MIKIO?
HE'S NOT RIGHT UNDER THE BASKET, BUT HE'S GOT POSITION IN THE LOW-POST.
SAKURAGI'S HYPOTHESIS WAS ACTUALLY CORRECT.
MIKIO'S OFFENSIVE REPERTOIRE WAS "TURN AROUND DIRECTLY UNDER THE BASKET AND SHOOT."

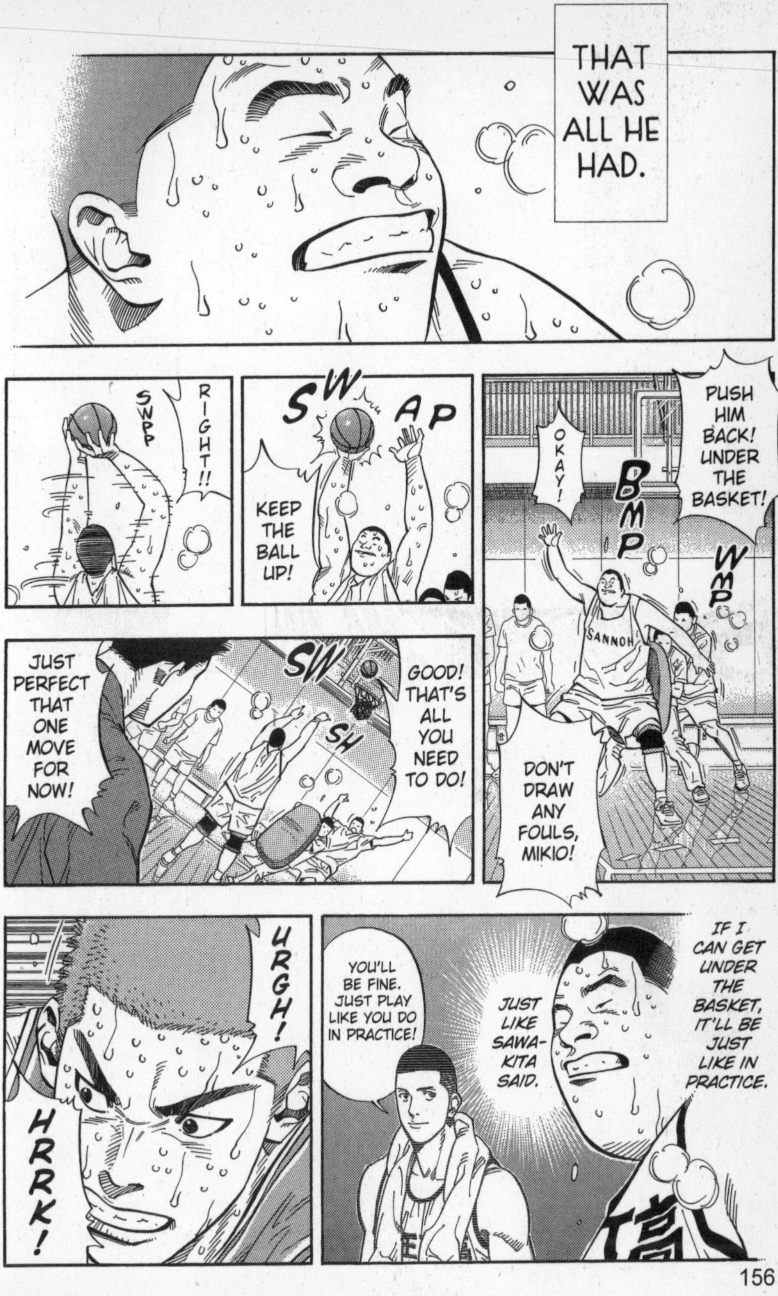
THAT WAS ALL HE HAD.
PUSH HIM BACK! UNDER THE BASKET!
OKAY!
BMP
WMP
DON'T DRAW ANY FOULS, MIKIO!
SWAP
KEEP THE BALL UP!
RIGHT!!
SWPP
GOOD! THAT'S ALL YOU NEED TO DO!
SW
SH
JUST PERFECT THAT ONE MOVE FOR NOW!
IF I CAN GET UNDER THE BASKET, IT'LL BE JUST LIKE IN PRACTICE.
JUST LIKE SAWAKITA SAID.
YOU'LL BE FINE. JUST PLAY LIKE YOU DO IN PRACTICE!
URGH!
HRRK!

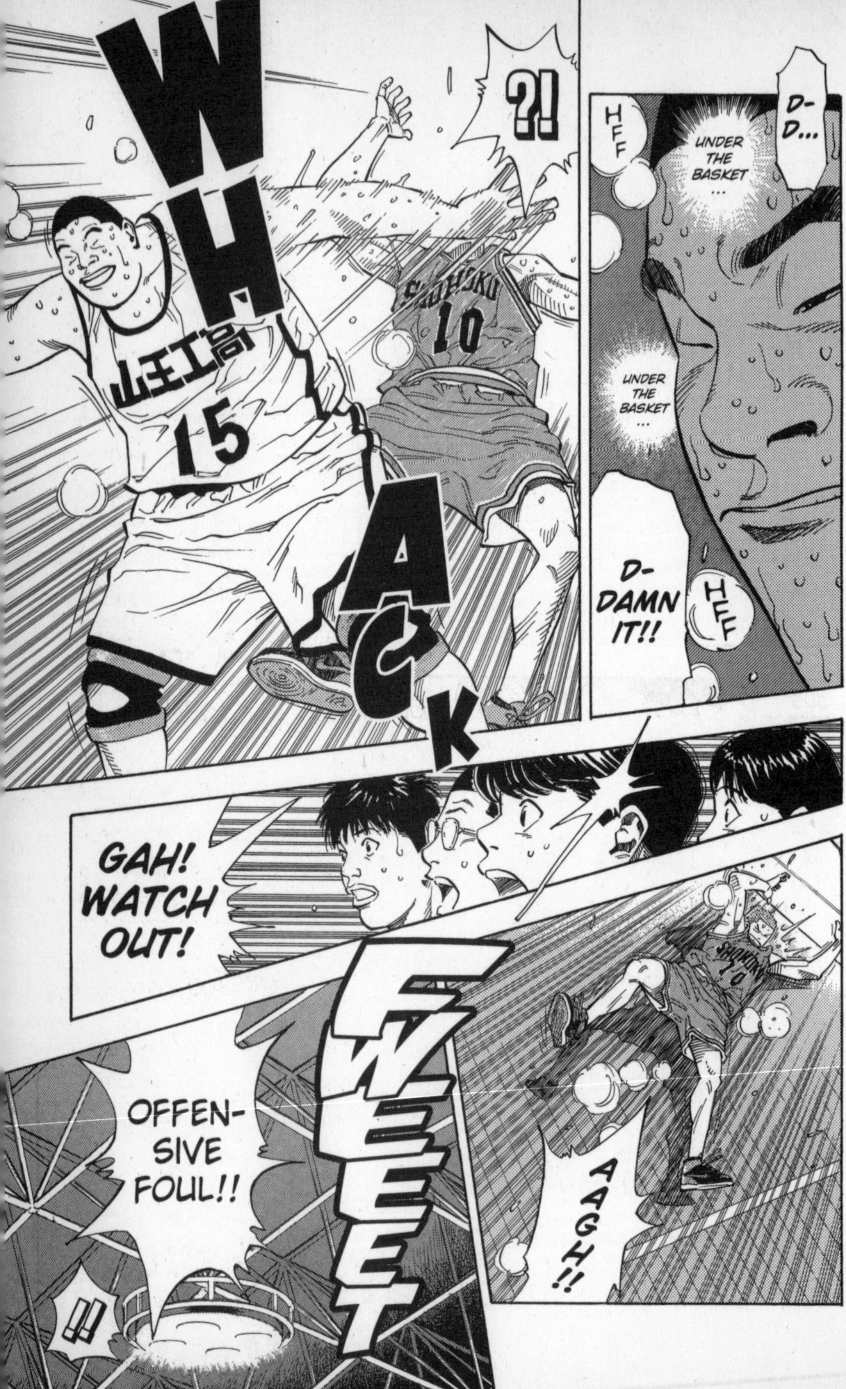
D-D...
HFF
UNDER THE BASKET ...
UNDER THE BASKET ...
HFF
D-DAMN IT!!
?!
WHACK
GAH! WATCH OUT!
AAGH!!
FWEEEET
OFFEN-SIVE FOUL!!
!!

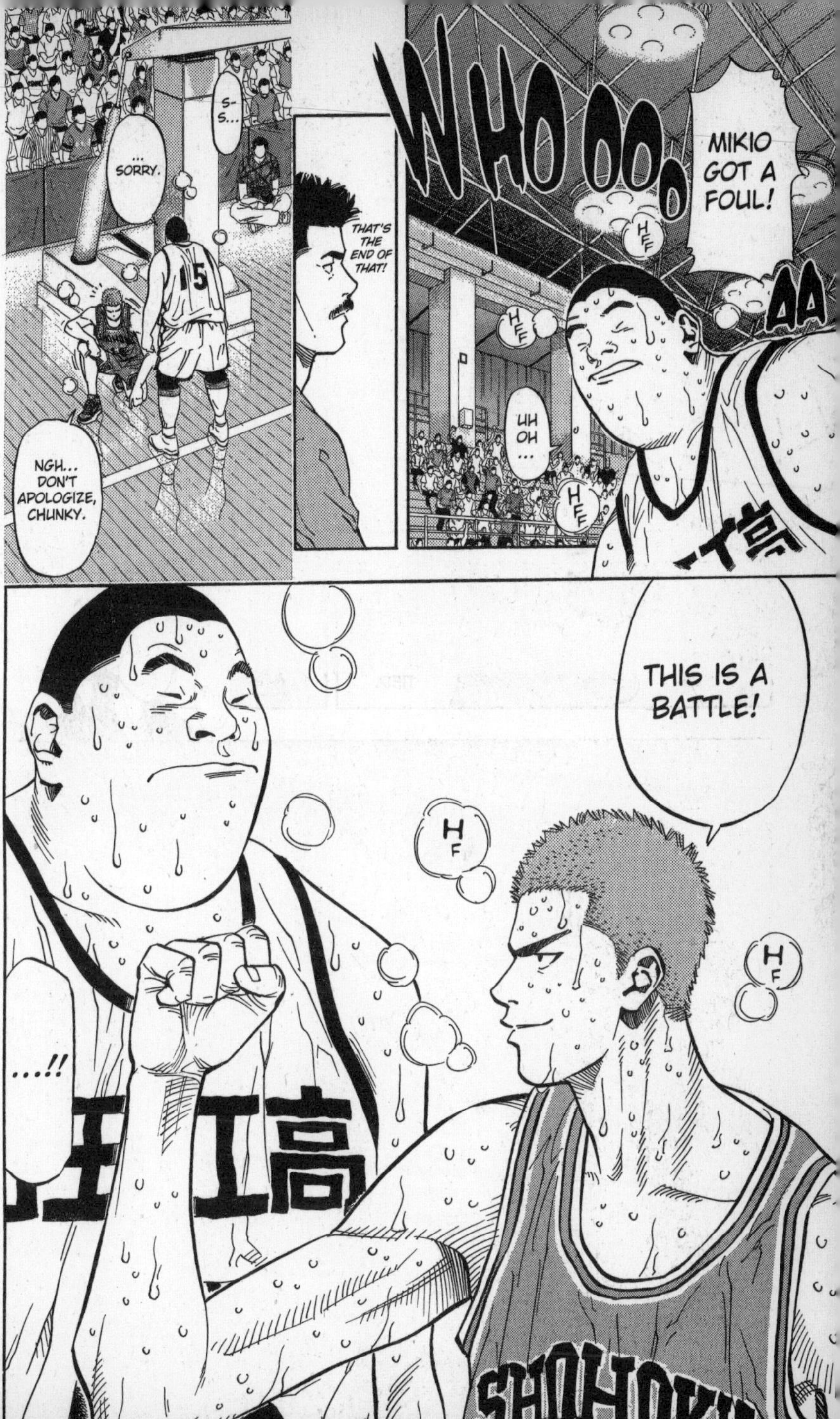
MIKIO GOT A FOUL!
WHOOOOOAA
HFF
HFF
UH OH...
HFF
THAT'S THE END OF THAT!
S-S...
...SORRY.
NGH... DON'T APOLOGIZE, CHUNKY.
THIS IS A BATTLE!
HF
HF
...!!

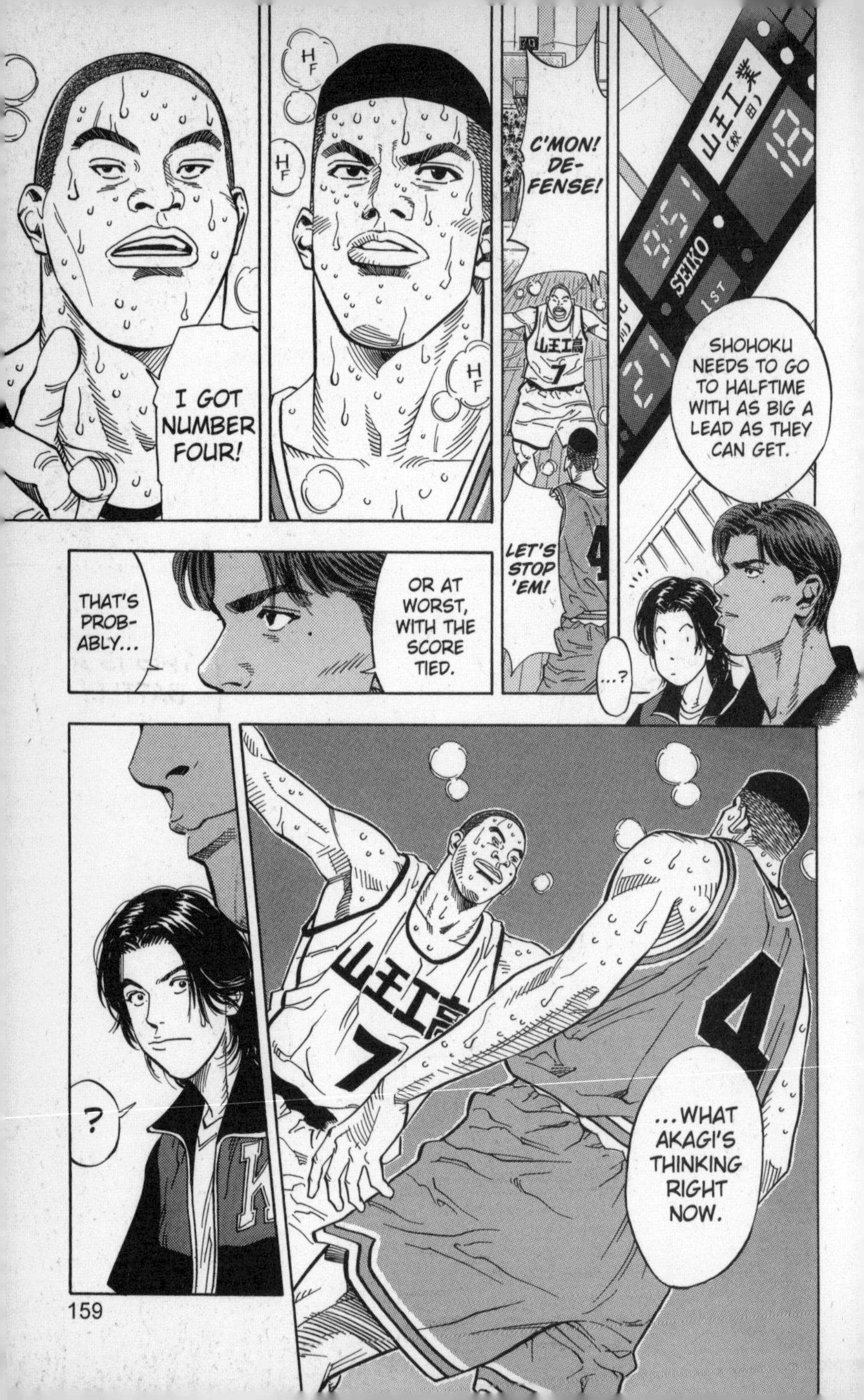
SHOHOKU NEEDS TO GO TO HALFTIME WITH AS BIG A LEAD AS THEY CAN GET.
...?
C'MON! DE-FENSE!
LET'S STOP 'EM!
H F
H F
H F
I GOT NUMBER FOUR!
OR AT WORST, WITH THE SCORE TIED.
THAT'S PROB-ABLY...
...WHAT AKAGI'S THINKING RIGHT NOW.
?

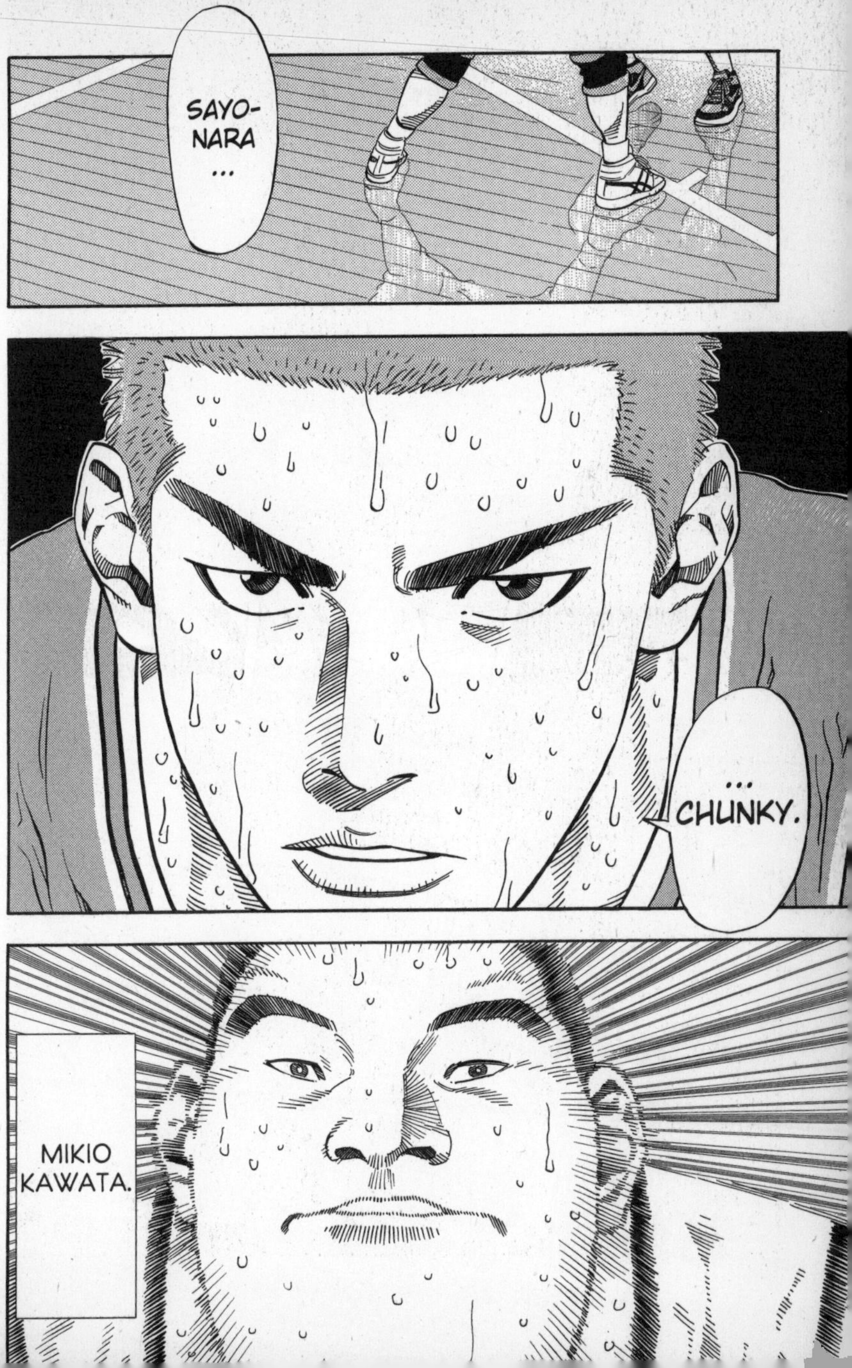
SAYO-
NARA
...
... CHUNKY.
MIKIO
KAWATA.

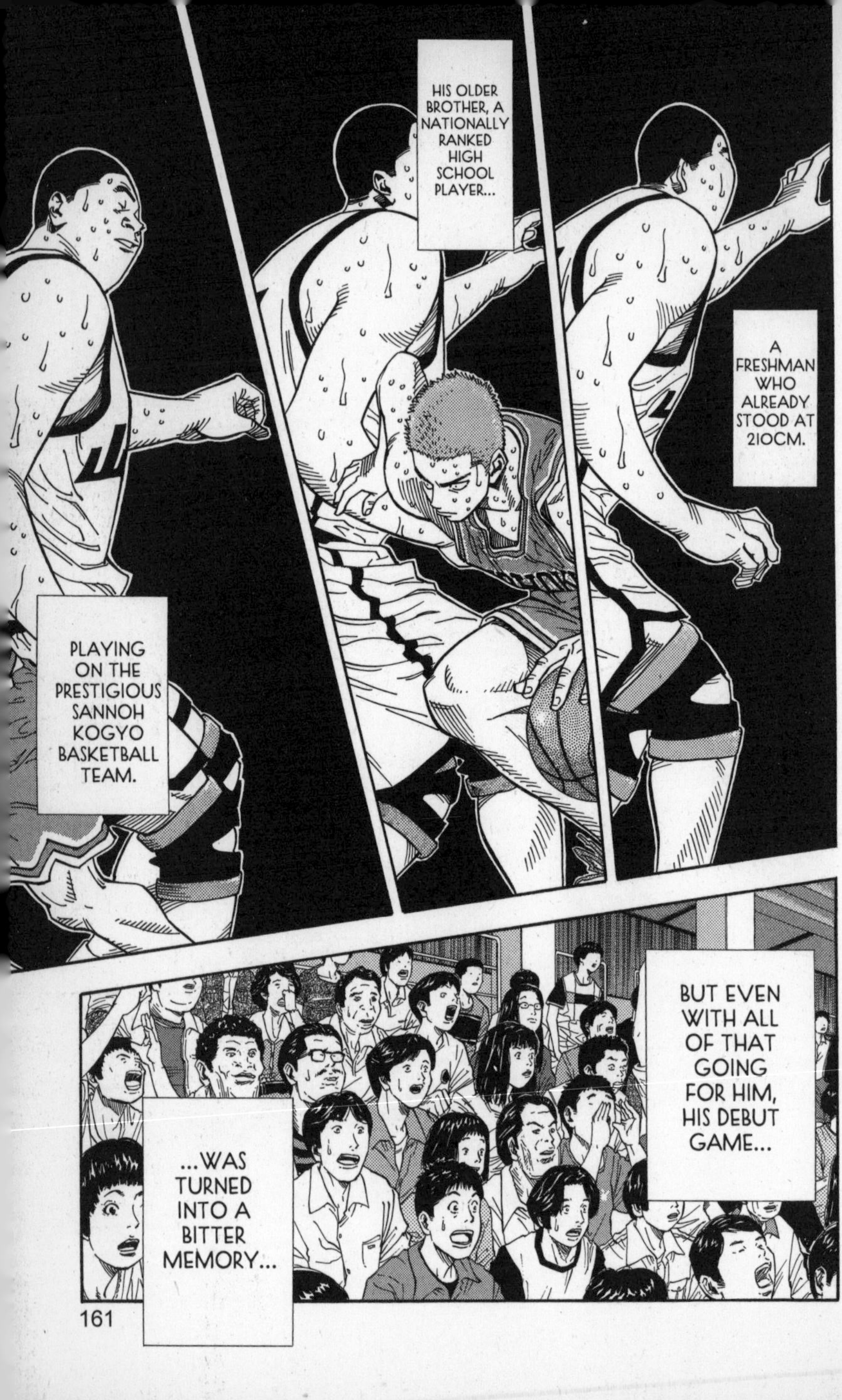
A FRESHMAN WHO ALREADY STOOD AT 210CM.
HIS OLDER BROTHER, A NATIONALLY RANKED HIGH SCHOOL PLAYER...
PLAYING ON THE PRESTIGIOUS SANNOH KOGYO BASKETBALL TEAM.
BUT EVEN WITH ALL OF THAT GOING FOR HIM, HIS DEBUT GAME...
...WAS TURNED INTO A BITTER MEMORY...

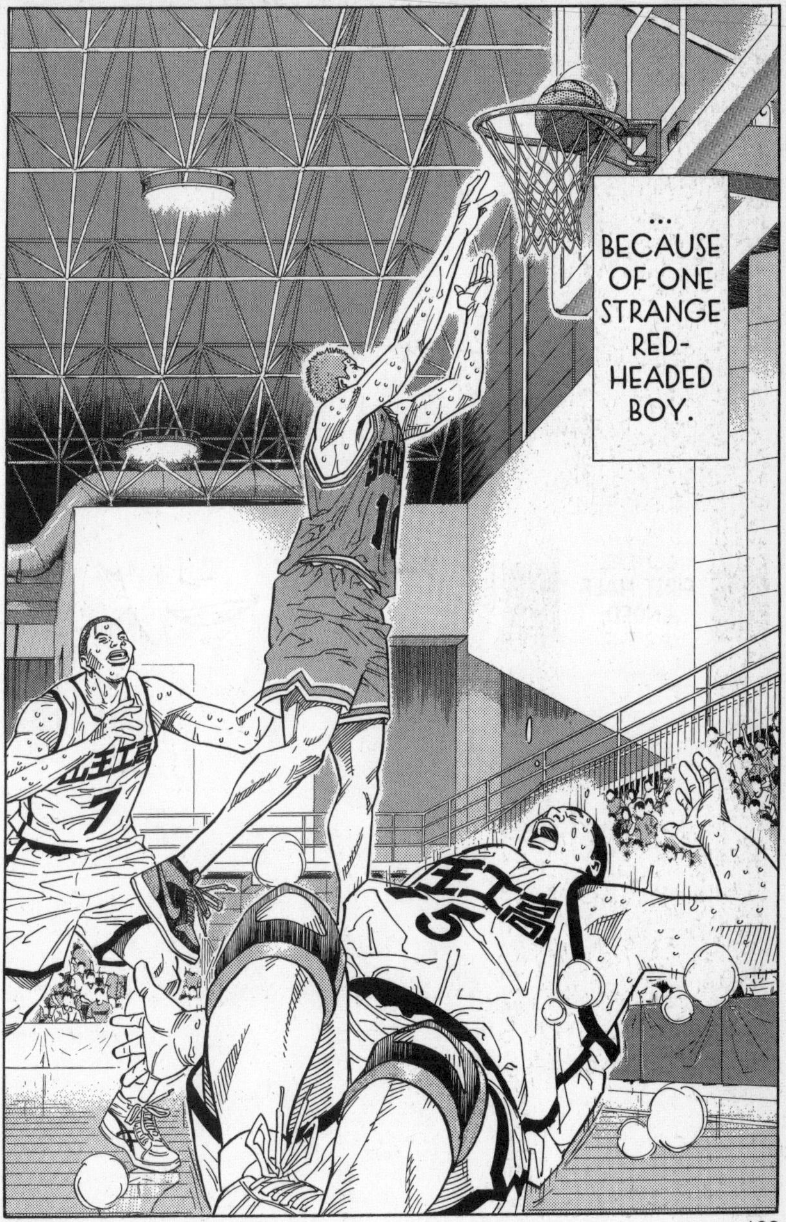
... BECAUSE OF ONE STRANGE RED-HEADED BOY.

READ THIS WAY

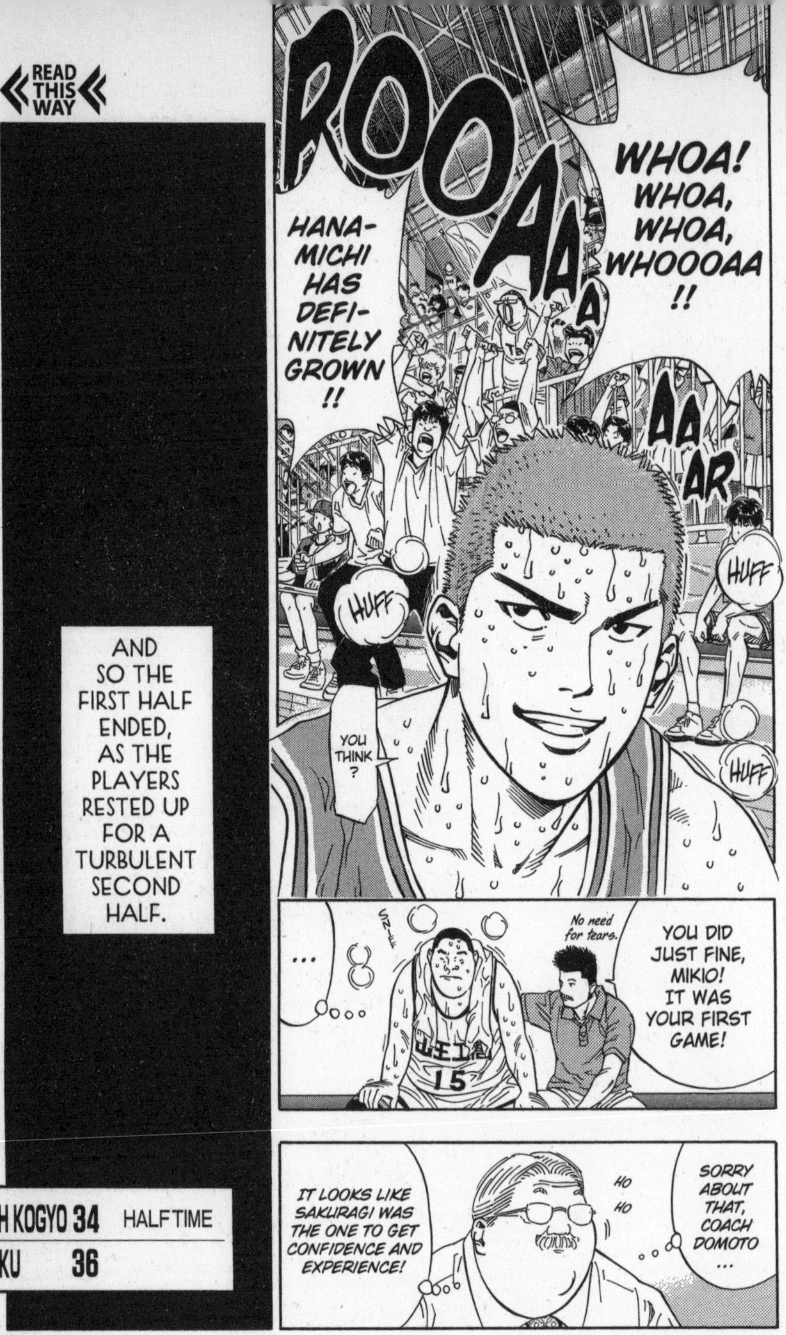
ROOOAAAA
WHOA! WHOA, WHOA, WHOOOAA!!
HANA-MICHI HAS DEFI-NITELY GROWN!!
AAAR
HUFF
HUFF
YOU THINK?
HUFF
YOU DID JUST FINE, MIKIO! IT WAS YOUR FIRST GAME!
No need for tears.
SNIF
...
SORRY ABOUT THAT, COACH DOMOTO...
HO HO
IT LOOKS LIKE SAKURAGI WAS THE ONE TO GET CONFIDENCE AND EXPERIENCE!
AND SO THE FIRST HALF ENDED, AS THE PLAYERS RESTED UP FOR A TURBULENT SECOND HALF.
SANNOH KOGYO 34 HALFTIME
SHOHOKU 36

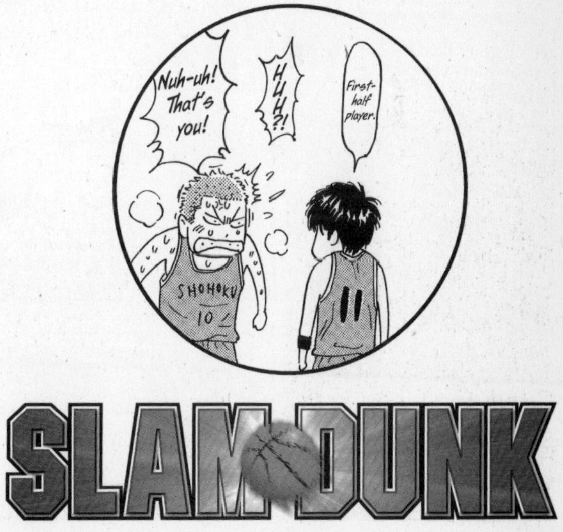
First-half player.
HUUH?!
Nuh-uh! That's you!
SHOHOKU
10

SLAM DUNK

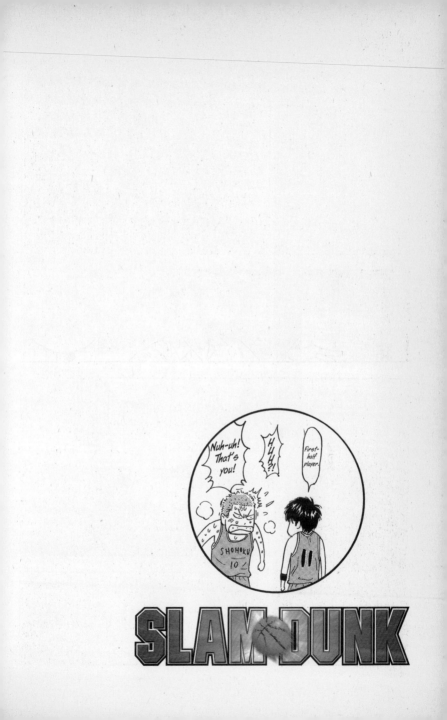

READ THIS WAY

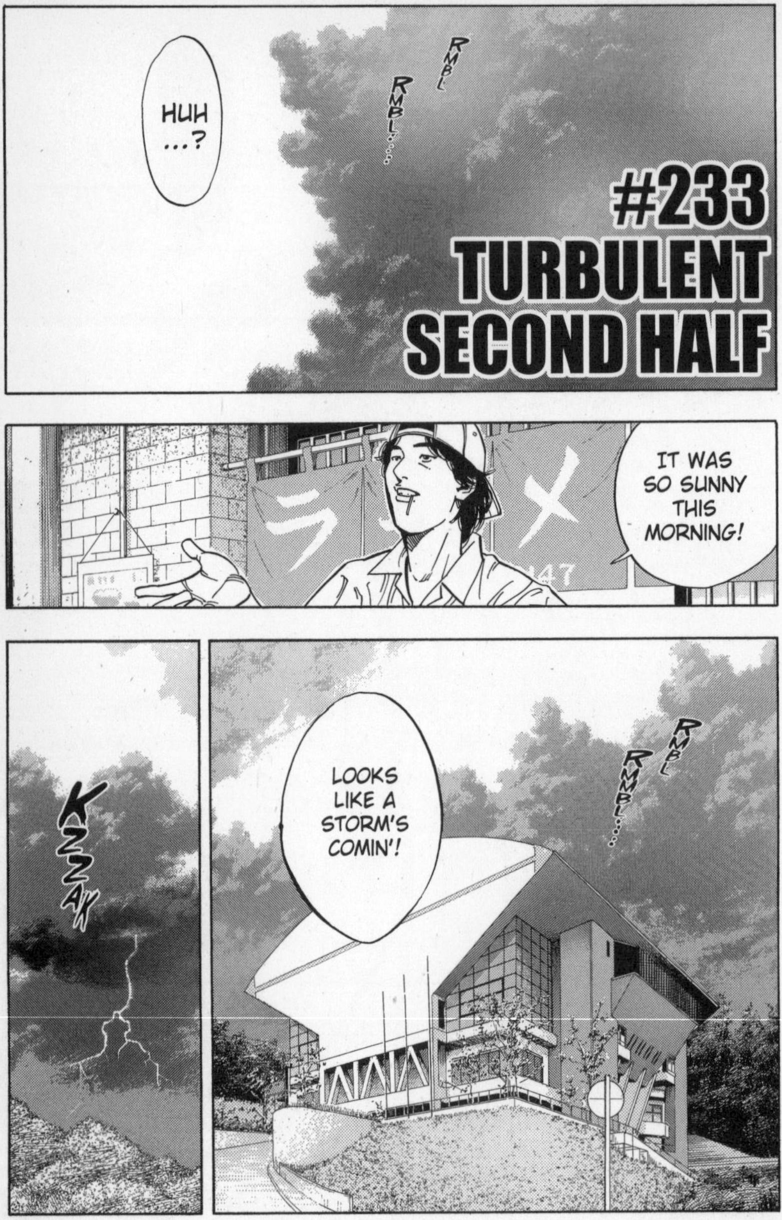
RMBL
RMBL...
#233 TURBULENT SECOND HALF
HUH ...?
IT WAS SO SUNNY THIS MORNING!
RMBL
RMMBL...
LOOKS LIKE A STORM'S COMIN'!
KZZAK

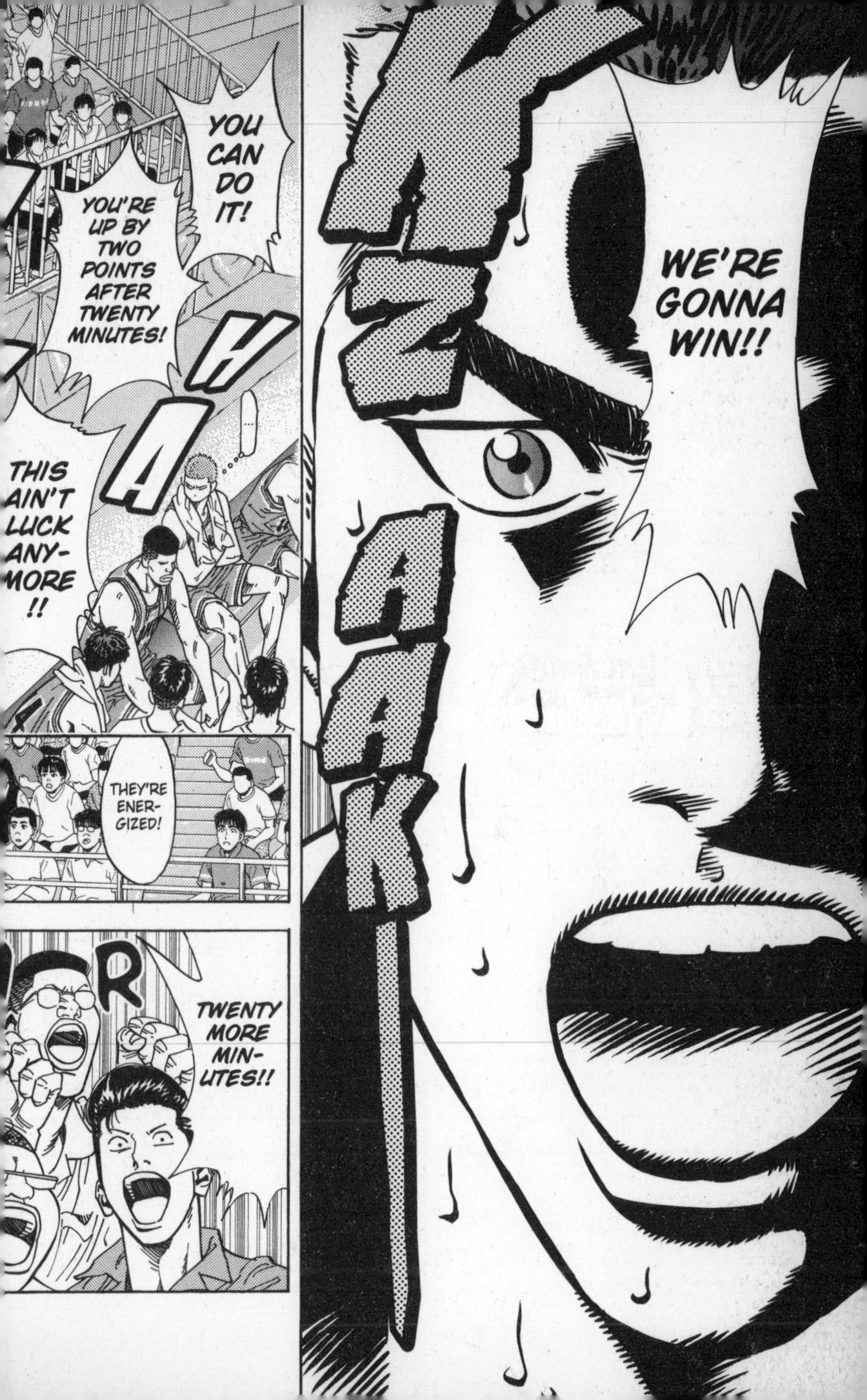
WE'RE GONNA WIN!!
YOU CAN DO IT!
YOU'RE UP BY TWO POINTS AFTER TWENTY MINUTES!
HA
...
THIS AIN'T LUCK ANY-MORE!!
THEY'RE ENER-GIZED!
R
TWENTY MORE MIN-UTES!!

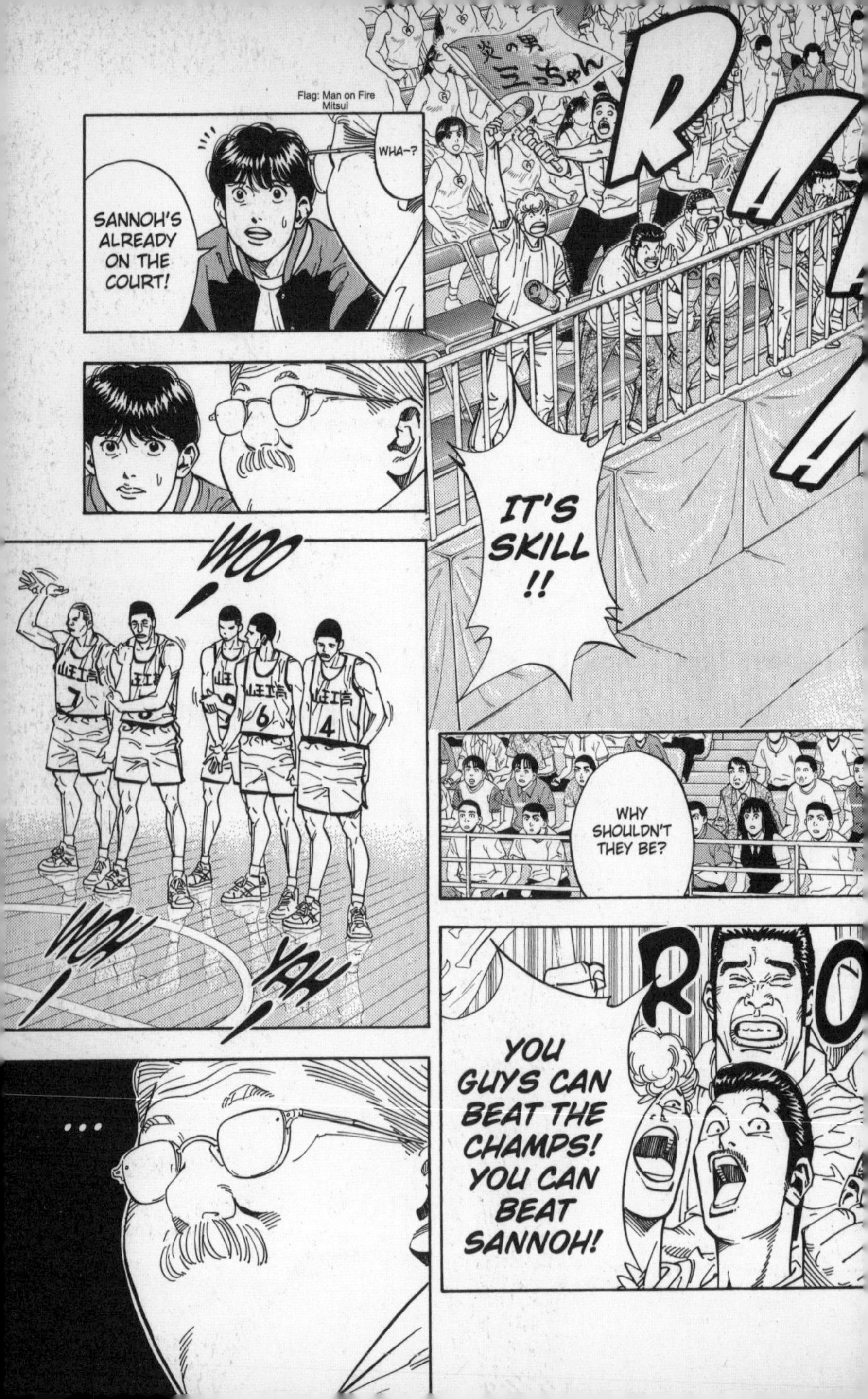
RA
炎の男 三っちゃん
Flag: Man on Fire Mitsui
IT'S SKILL !!
WHA-?
SANNOH'S ALREADY ON THE COURT!
WHY SHOULDN'T THEY BE?
RO
YOU GUYS CAN BEAT THE CHAMPS! YOU CAN BEAT SANNOH!
WOO
WOH
YAH
...

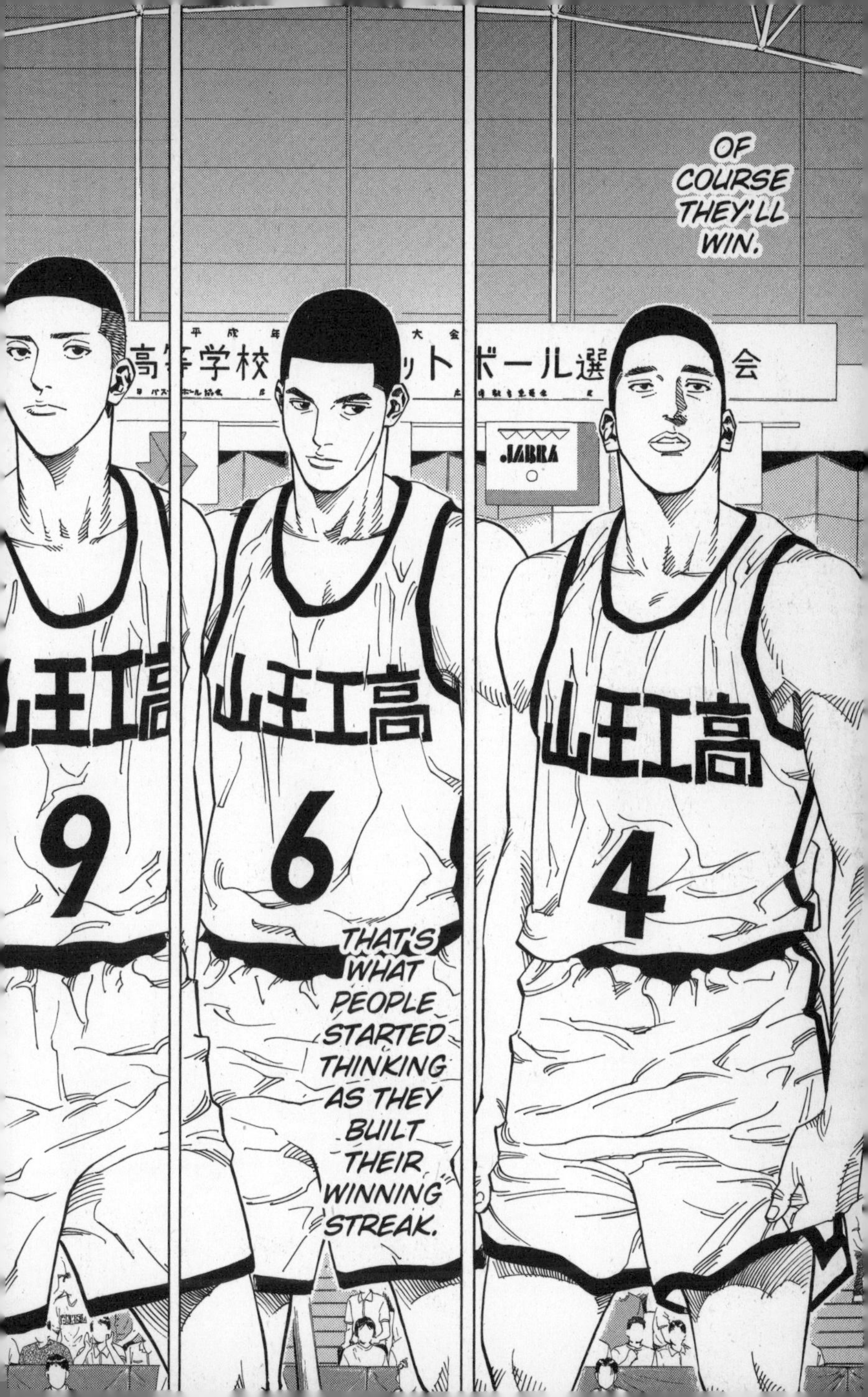
OF COURSE THEY'LL WIN.
THAT'S WHAT PEOPLE STARTED THINKING AS THEY BUILT THEIR WINNING STREAK.

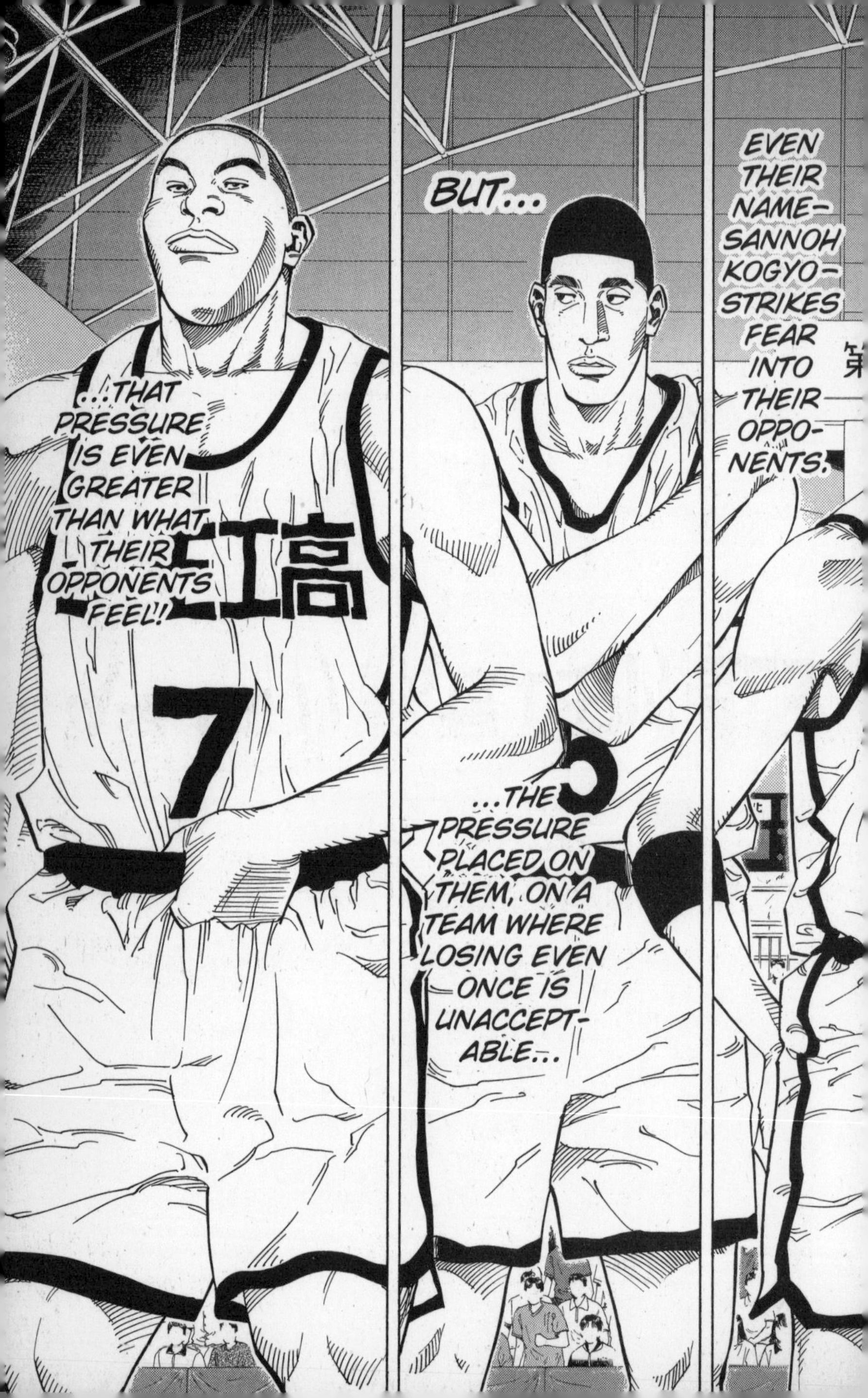
EVEN THEIR NAME—SANNOH KOGYO—STRIKES FEAR INTO THEIR OPPONENTS.
BUT...
...THE PRESSURE PLACED ON THEM, ON A TEAM WHERE LOSING EVEN ONCE IS UNACCEPTABLE...
...THAT PRESSURE IS EVEN GREATER THAN WHAT THEIR OPPONENTS FEEL!!

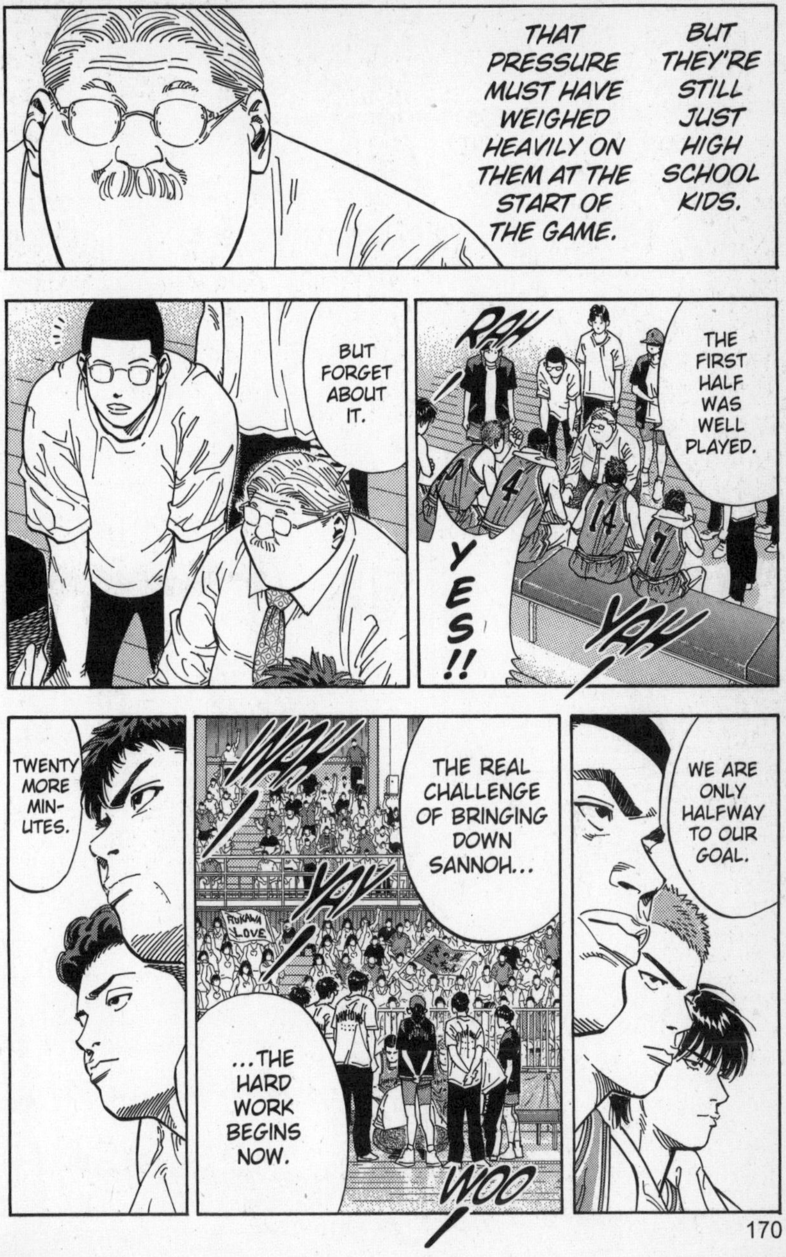
BUT THEY'RE STILL JUST HIGH SCHOOL KIDS.
THAT PRESSURE MUST HAVE WEIGHED HEAVILY ON THEM AT THE START OF THE GAME.
RAH
THE FIRST HALF WAS WELL PLAYED.
YES!!
YAH
BUT FORGET ABOUT IT.
WE ARE ONLY HALFWAY TO OUR GOAL.
WAH
THE REAL CHALLENGE OF BRINGING DOWN SANNOH...
YAY
RUKAWA LOVE
...THE HARD WORK BEGINS NOW.
WOO
TWENTY MORE MIN-UTES.

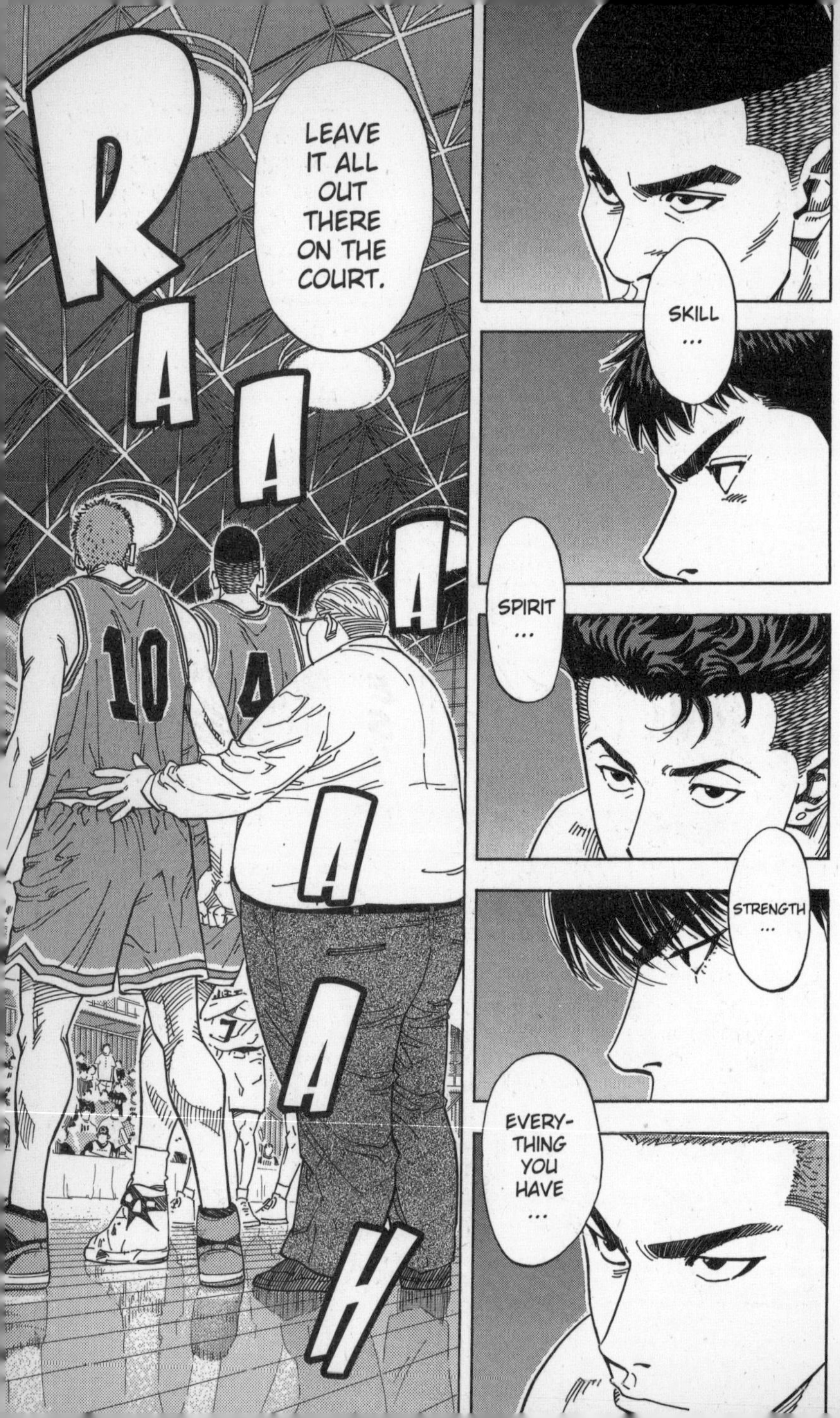
SKILL ...
SPIRIT ...
STRENGTH ...
EVERY-THING YOU HAVE ...
LEAVE IT ALL OUT THERE ON THE COURT.
RAAAAAH

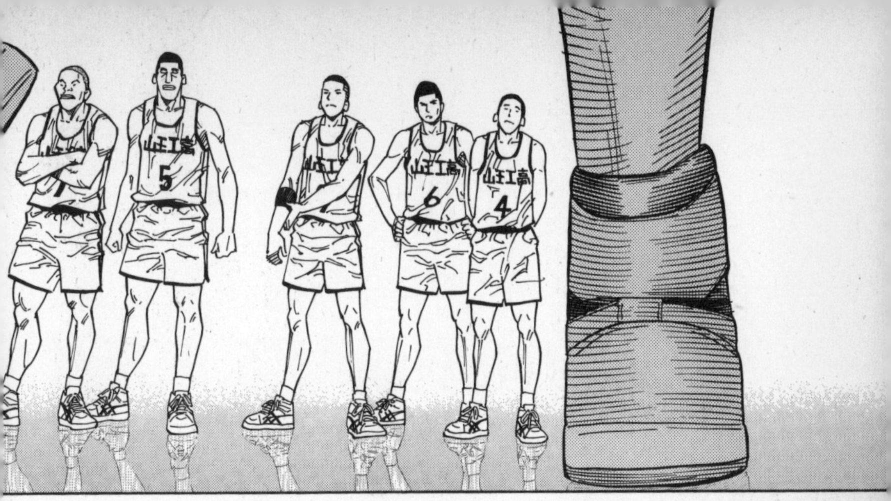
山王工高

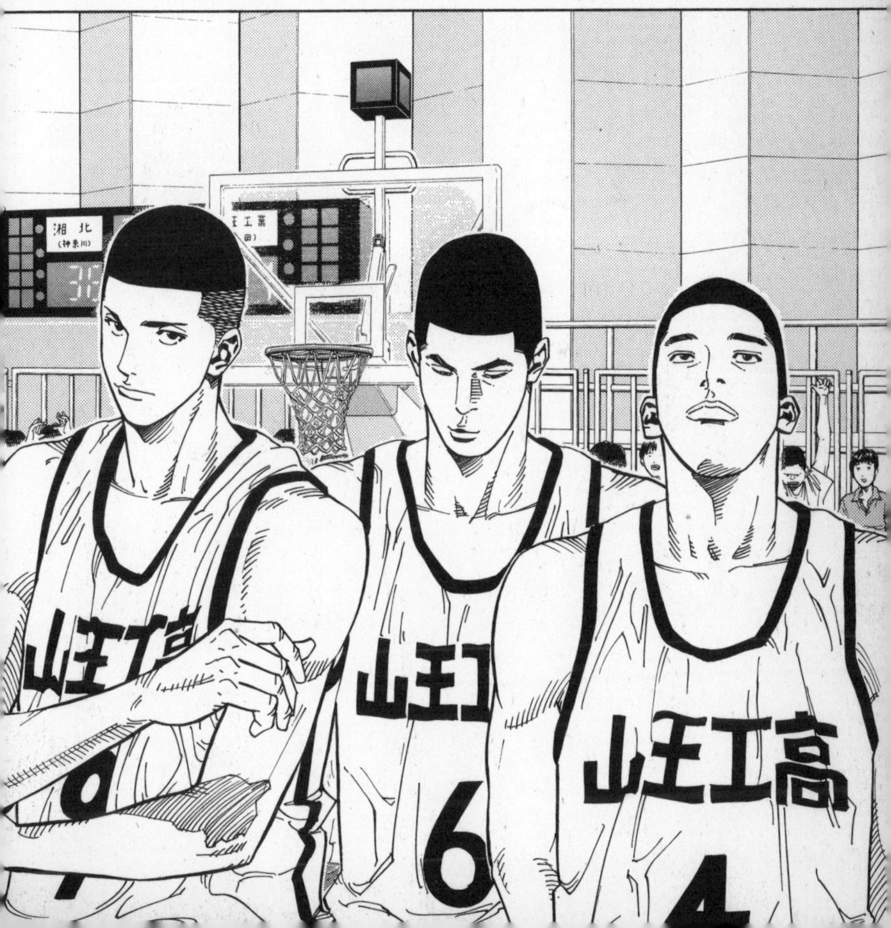
湘北
(神奈川)
山王工高

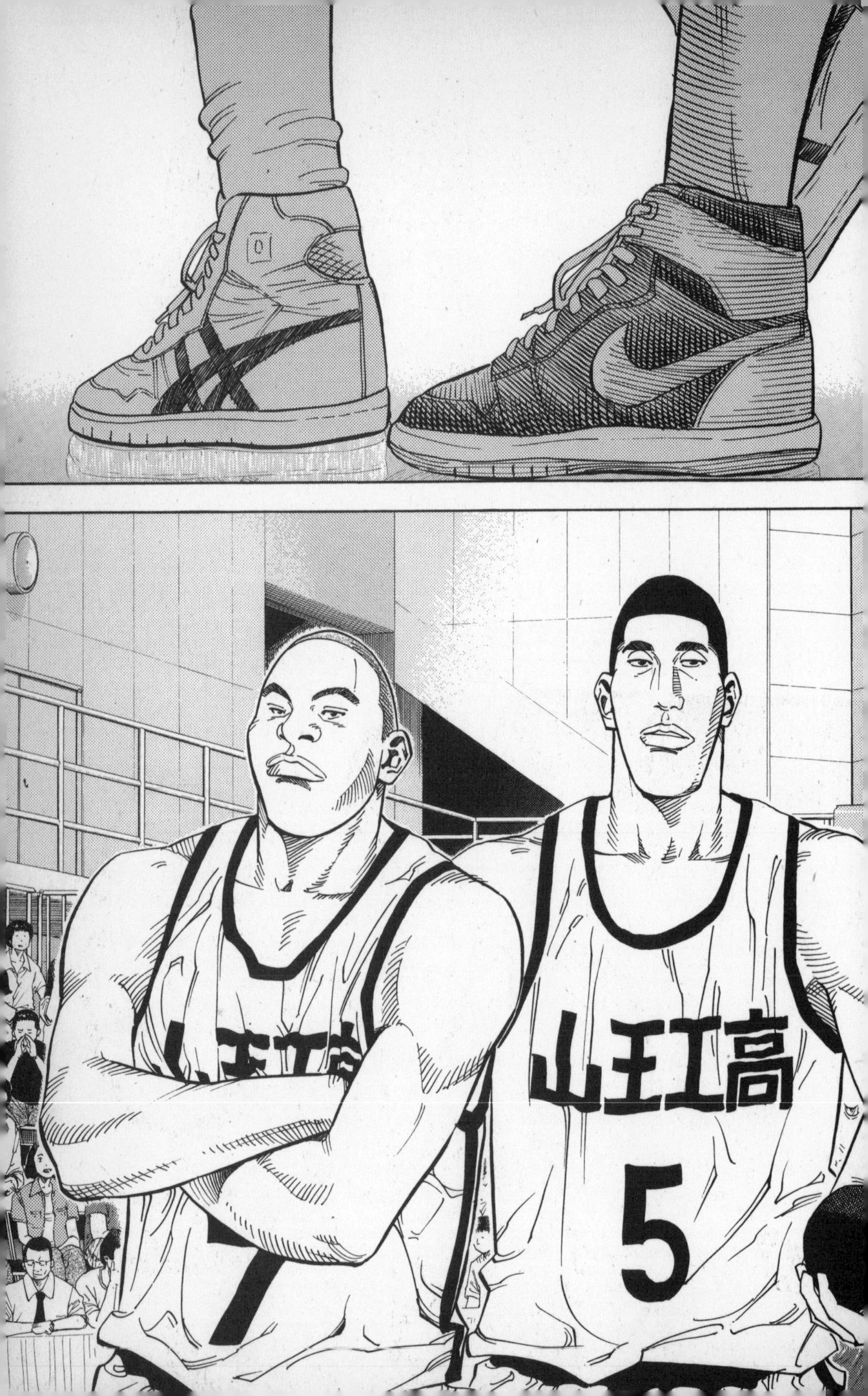
山王工高
5

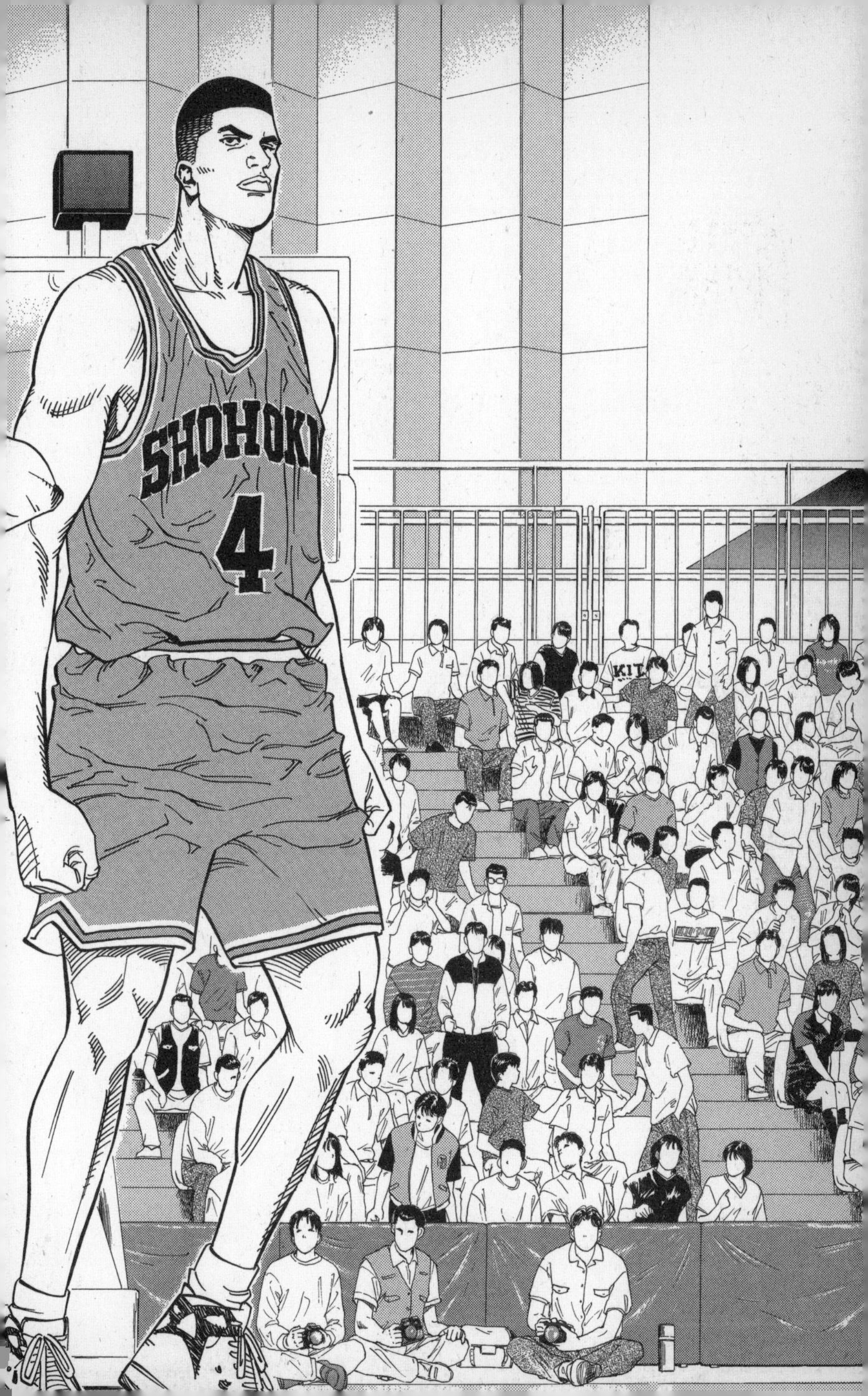
SHOHOKU
4
KIT

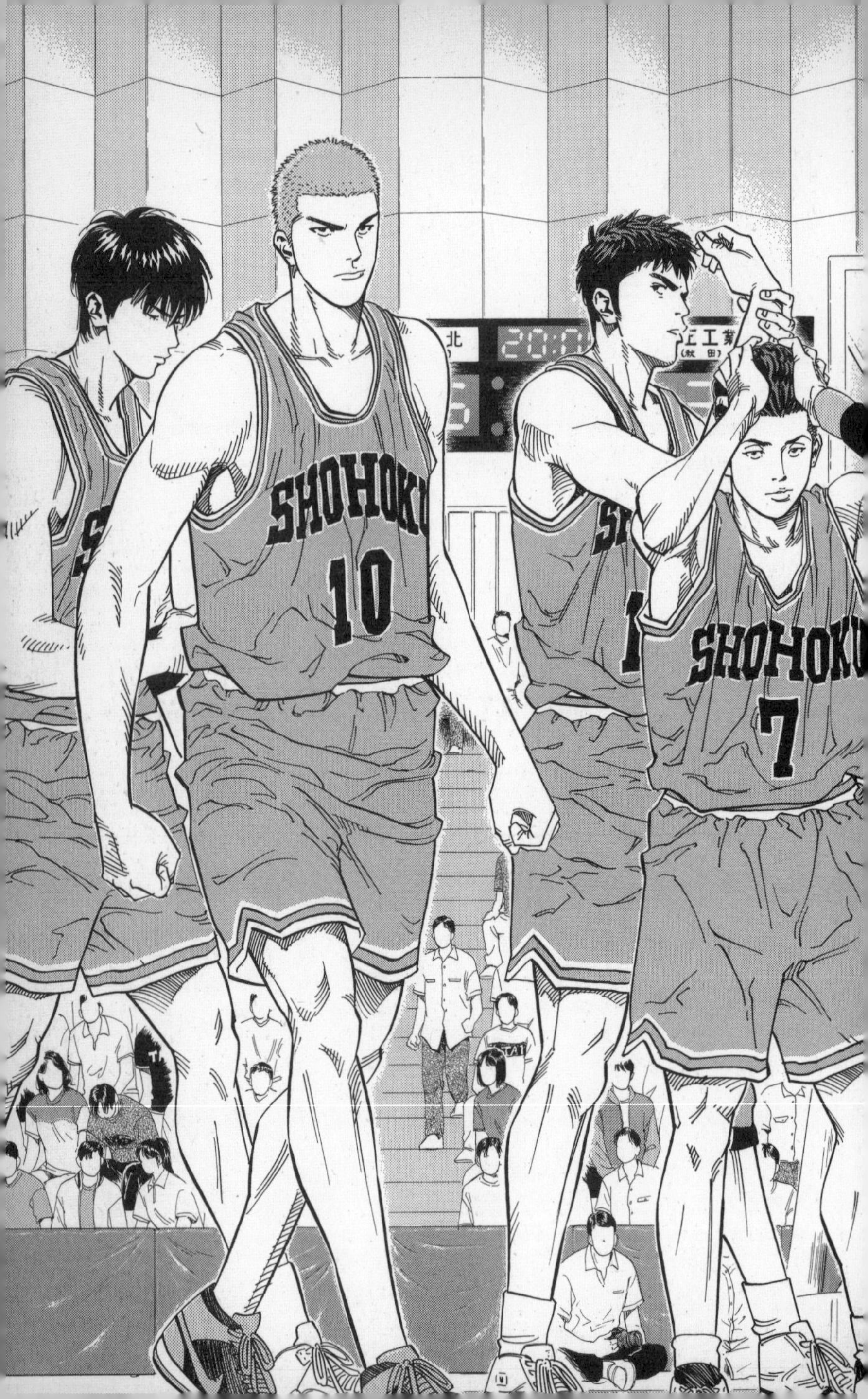
SHOHOKU
10
SHOHOKU
7

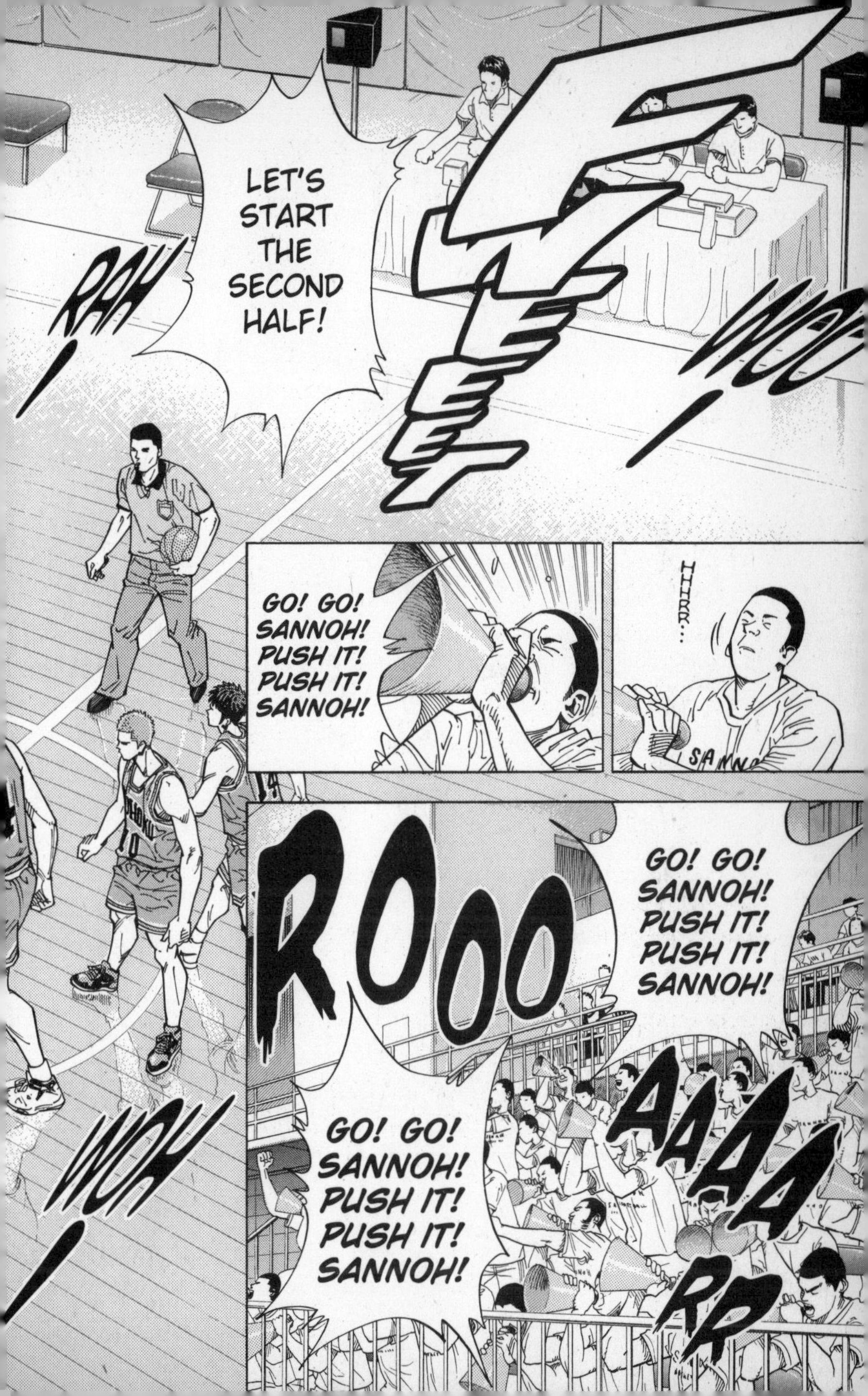
WOO!
LET'S START THE SECOND HALF!
RAH!
WOH!
HHHRR...
GO! GO! SANNOH! PUSH IT! PUSH IT! SANNOH!
GO! GO! SANNOH! PUSH IT! PUSH IT! SANNOH!
ROOOAAAARP
GO! GO! SANNOH! PUSH IT! PUSH IT! SANNOH!

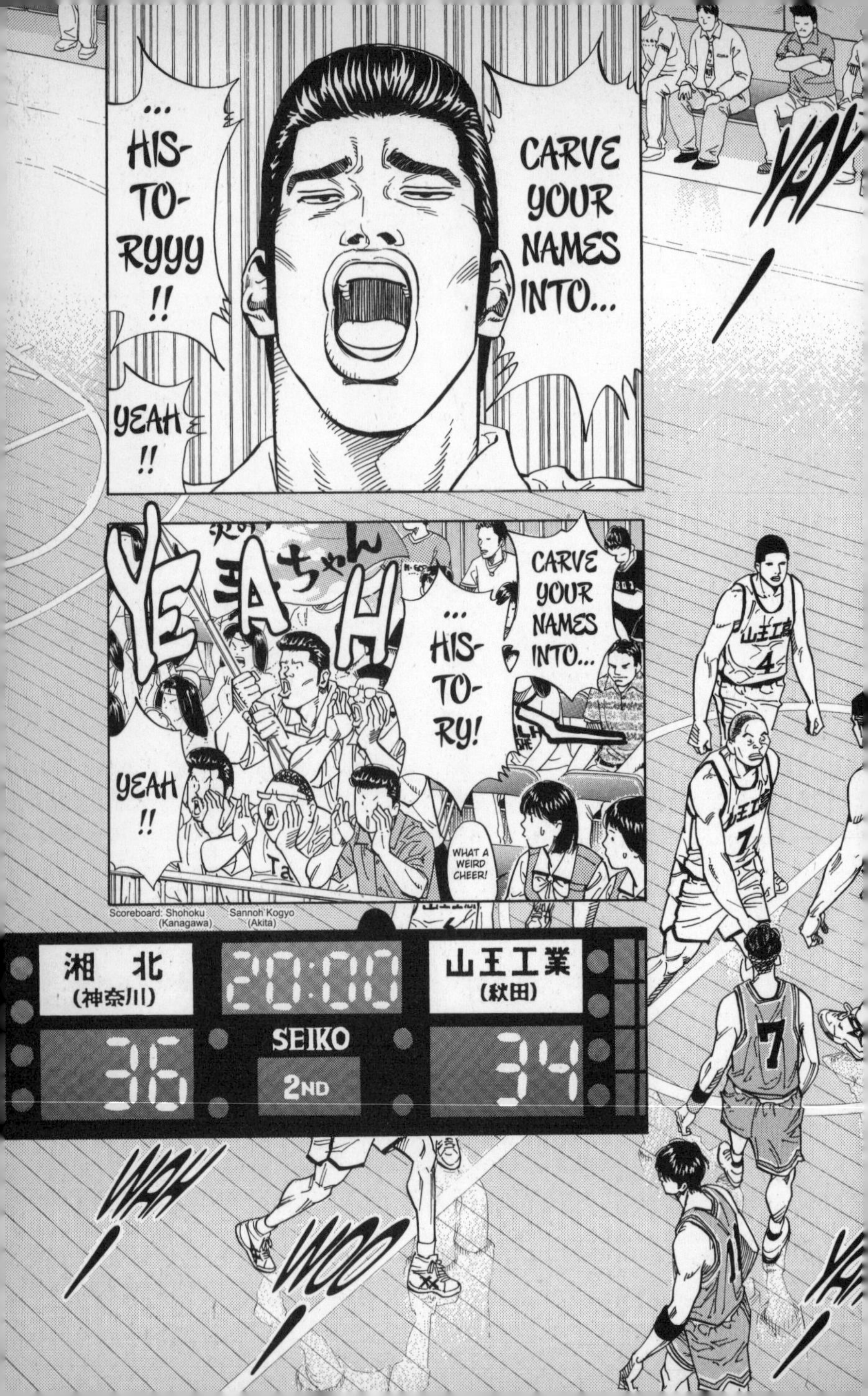
CARVE YOUR NAMES INTO...
... HIS-TO-RYYY!!
YEAH!!
YAY!
CARVE YOUR NAMES INTO...
... HIS-TO-RY!
YEAH
YEAH!!
WHAT A WEIRD CHEER!
Scoreboard: Shohoku (Kanagawa) Sannoh Kogyo (Akita)
湘北 (神奈川)
20:00
山王工業 (秋田)
SEIKO
36
2ND
34
WAH!
WOO!

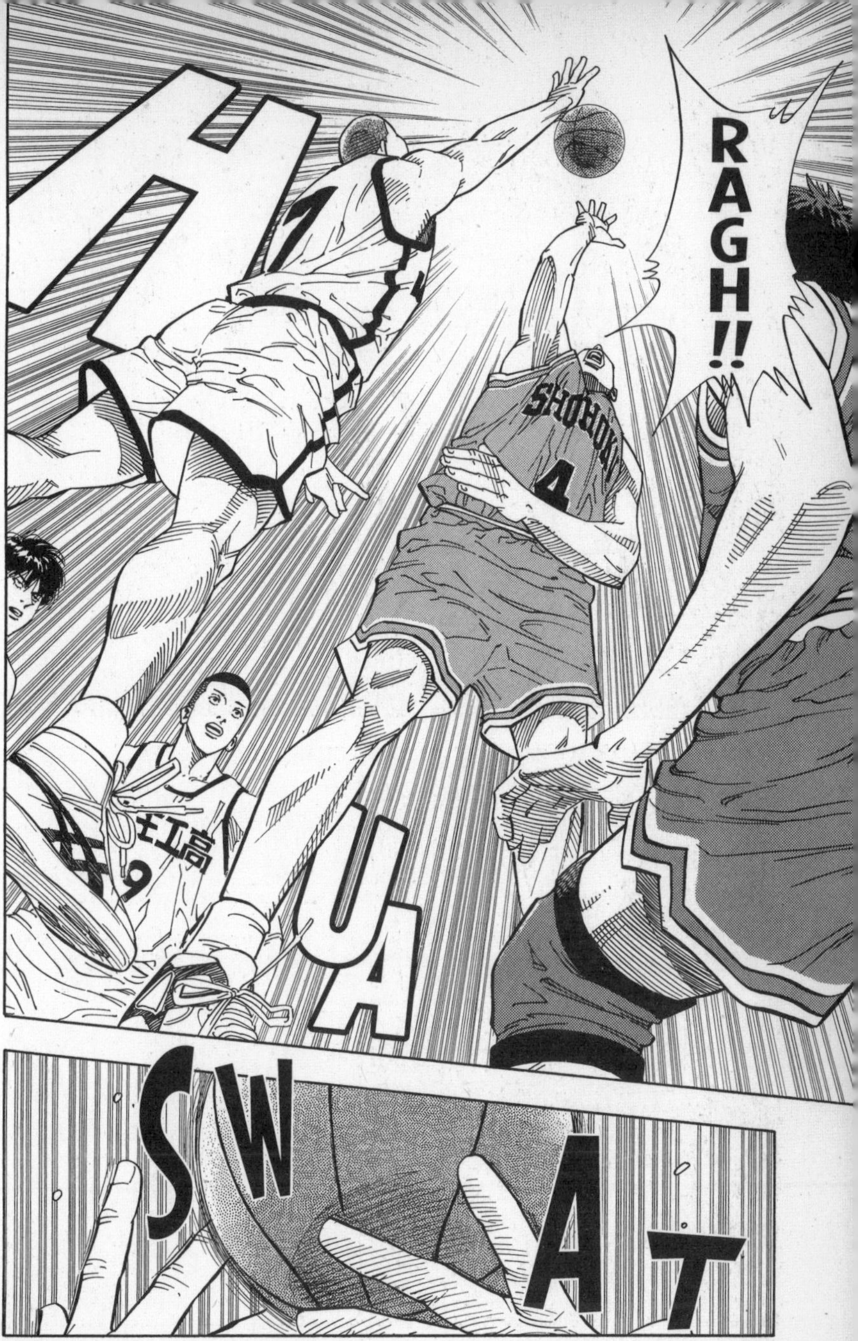
RAGH!!
UA
SWAT

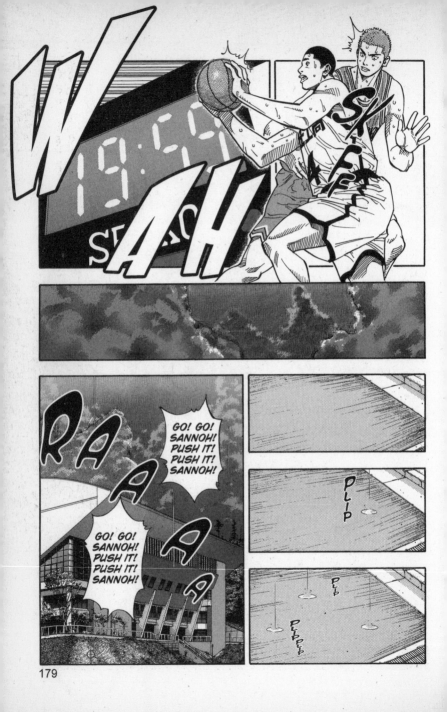

179

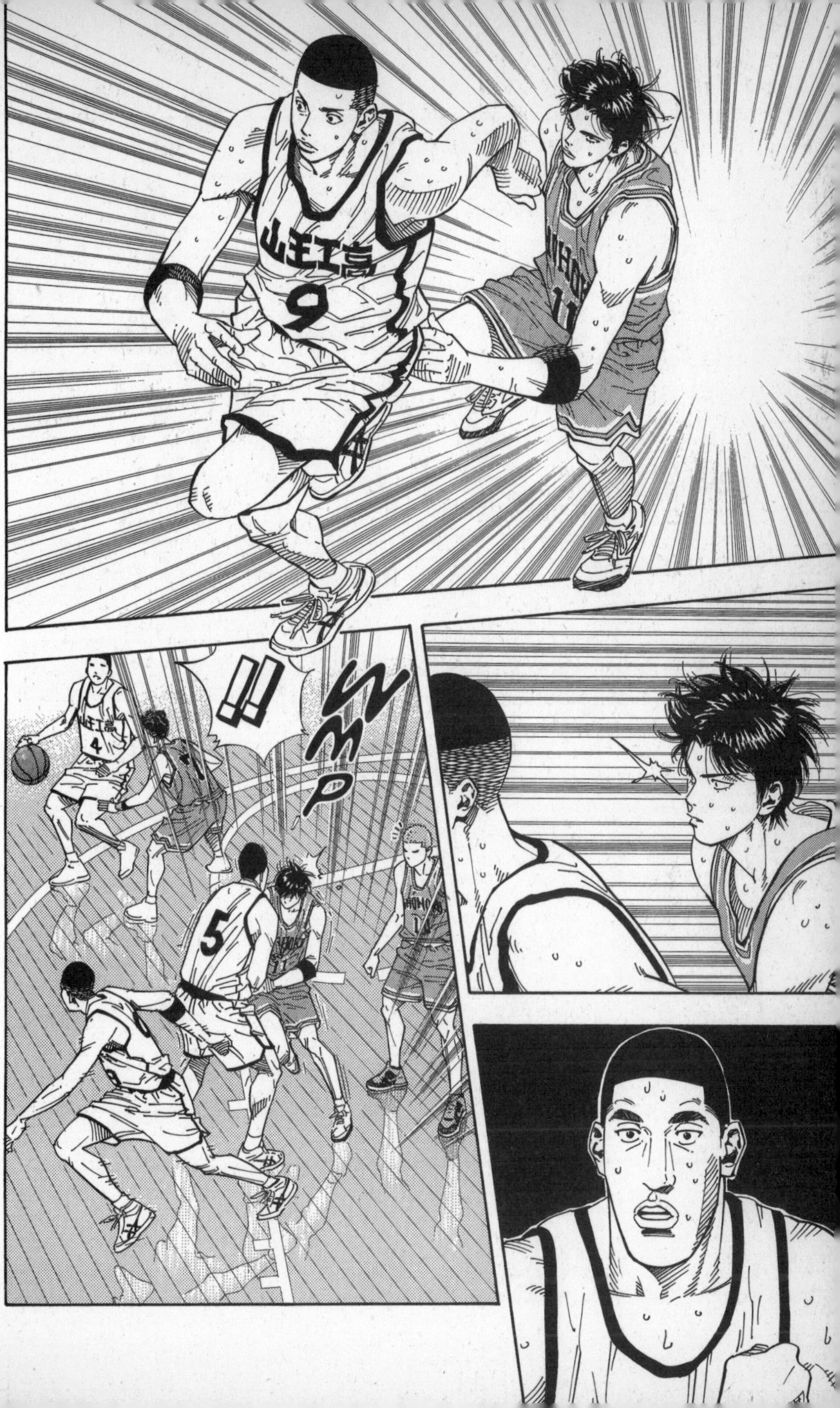
!!

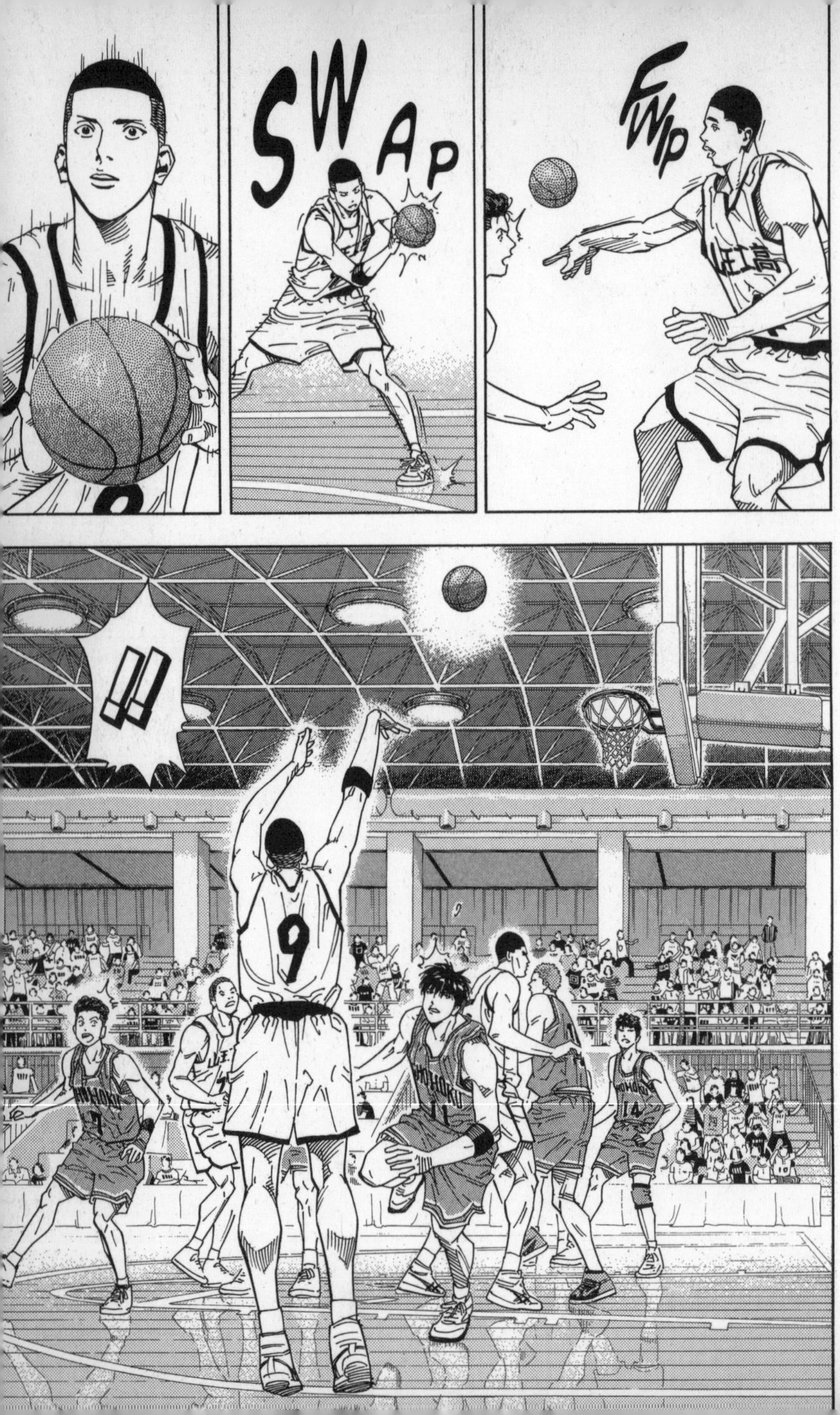
FWIP
SWAP
!!

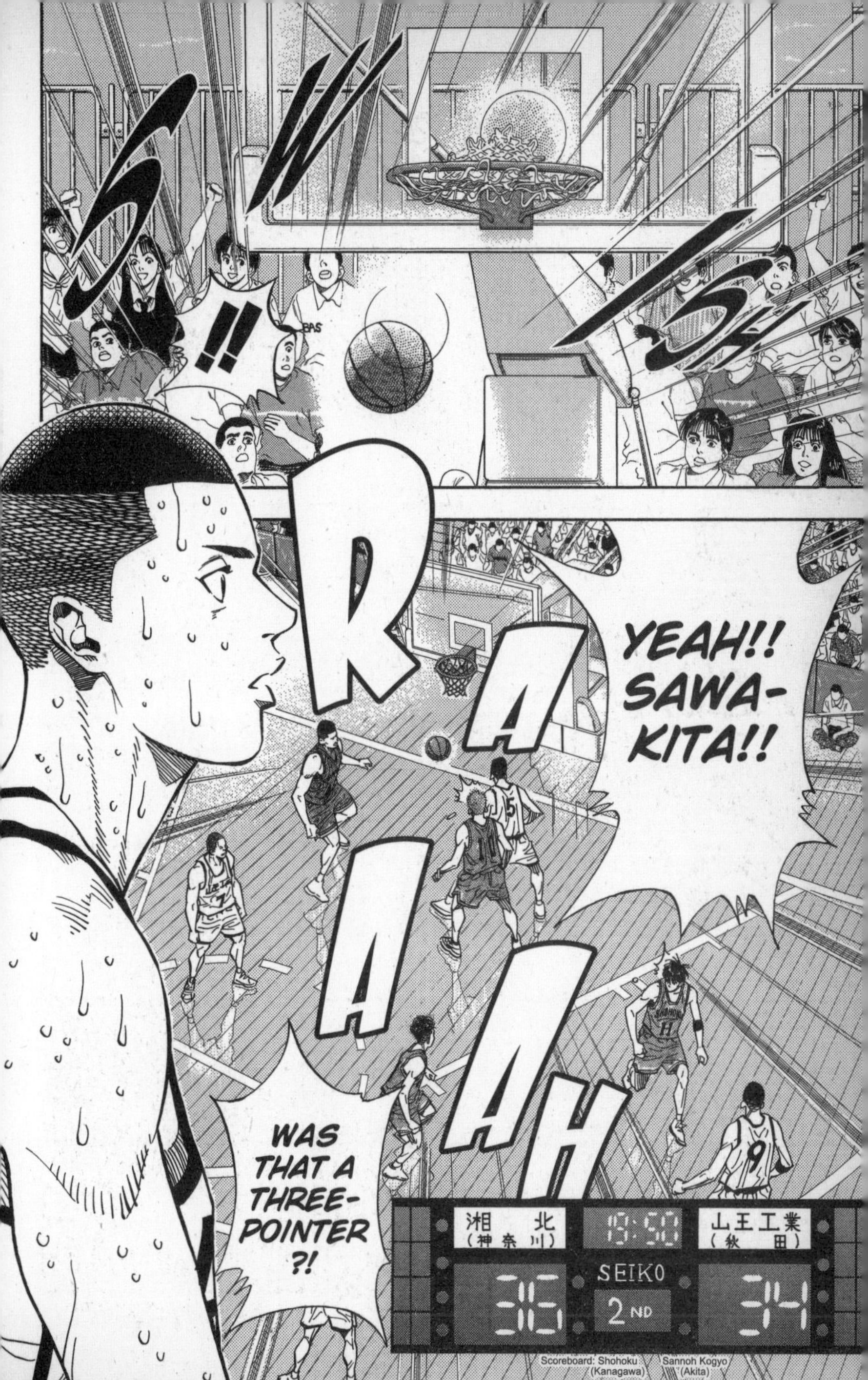
SWISH
!!
RAAAH
YEAH!! SAWA-KITA!!
WAS THAT A THREE-POINTER?!
湘北 (神奈川)
19:50
山王工業 (秋田)
SEIKO
35
2ND
34
Scoreboard: Shohoku (Kanagawa) Sannoh Kogyo (Akita)

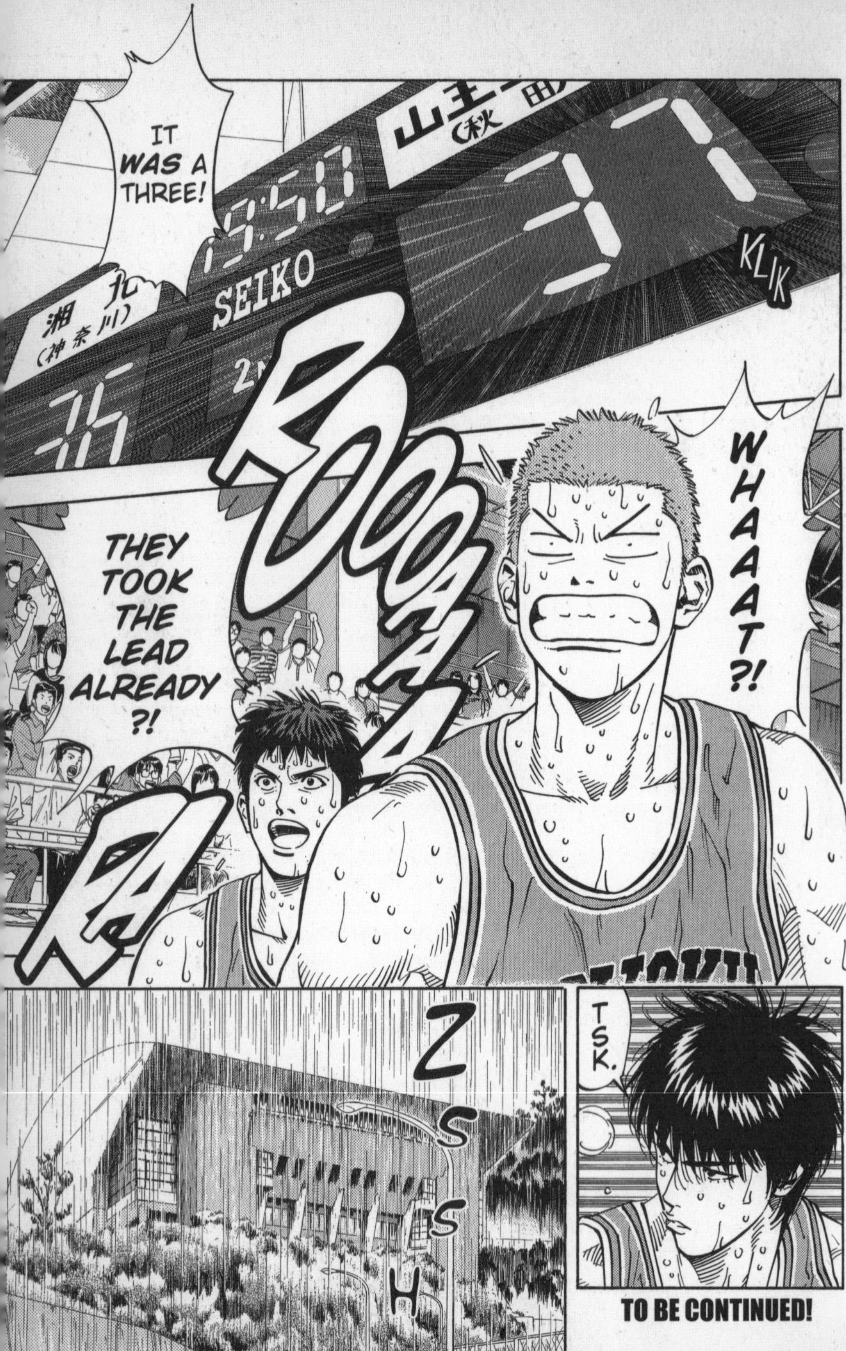
KLIK
山王
(秋 田
IT WAS A THREE!
SEIKO
湘北
(神奈川)
WHAAAAT?!
THEY TOOK THE LEAD ALREADY?!
TSK.
ZSSH
TO BE CONTINUED!

Coming Next Volume

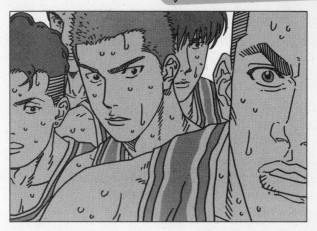

P9-DNB-107

As the game against Sannoh heads into the second half, Shohoku struggles to keep up. Sannoh's coach Domoto isn't about to let Shohoku think they can stage an upset and lets loose his team's explosive offense. With Shohoku on the ropes and Sakuragi upset by a substitution, the players start feeling completely outmatched, and even Akagi begins having doubts. But Coach Anzai hasn't given up yet and begins priming Sakuragi on the sidelines for a comeback!

ON SALE APRIL 2013